Congressional Publications
and Proceedings

Congressional Publications and Proceedings
Research on Legislation, Budgets, and Treaties

Second Edition

JERROLD ZWIRN

1988
Libraries Unlimited, Inc.
Englewood, Colorado

LIBRARIES UNLIMITED, INC.
P.O. Box 3988
Englewood, Colorado 80155-3988

Library of Congress Cataloging-in-Publication Data

Zwirn, Jerrold.
    Congressional publications and proceedings.

    Rev. ed. of: Congressional publications. 1983.
    Includes bibliographies and index.
    1. United States.   Congress--Information services.
2. United States.   Congress--Bibliography.   I. Zwirn,
Jerrold.   Congressional publications.   II. Title.
JK1067.Z85 1988   027.6'5   88-12395
ISBN 0-87287-642-X

Libraries Unlimited books are bound with Type II nonwoven material that meets
and exceeds National Association of State Textbook Administrators' Type II
nonwoven material specifications Class A through E.

To the Miller clan of Schenectady

Contents

List of Figures

Preface

This volume focuses on the vast amount of information consumed, weighed, and issued by the contemporary U.S. Congress. How information in general, and printed information in particular, is transmitted to, within, and by Congress forms the framework of discussion. Emphasis is given to the influence of the institution on information and vice versa. The overall purpose is to explore the relationship between the information environment and the legislative process so as to smooth the path between researchers who pursue and resources that provide certain information.

Three distinct but related means are employed to reach this goal. One route is to offer a guide to the role and use of congressional publications. If one grants the importance of public policies, then the volume and variety of documents that accompany their formulation, consideration, and enactment must be accorded equal status. Though this material is probably most widely known and used to illuminate and interpret legislative history, it can be profitably consulted for at least as many reasons as there are subjects that receive legislative attention.

Another approach is the preparation of a handbook on the options and patterns of legislative decisionmaking. To describe and analyze the internal dynamics of the legislative process requires a close look at the factors and features that influence the logic of congressional choice. By isolating elements and elucidating relationships a picture is presented of how favorable conditions are fostered or exploited. Decisions are viewed as group responses that combine rational calculations and political considerations in the effort to cope with the problems of complexity and uncertainty.

One other avenue is the identification and description of useful sources on policy, procedure, participants, and progress. This listing serves to cover two reservoirs of information. One type is so integrated into the legislative process that its significance may be overlooked in an arena of continuous competition. Another type, though not an integral part of the legislative process, provides salient background information that enables observers to understand the congressional environment better. Both shed further light on the relationship between information sources and institutional courses.

An examination of the perceptions and purposes of legislative authors is meant to orient interested individuals to view congressional publications as parts of an organic whole rather than as unrelated works. Though this perspective may not be necessary for all research needs, it can render their nature more intelligible and their use less arduous. Regardless of research viewpoint, one cannot escape the fact that the legislative process definitely conditions the manner in which information is presented. To encourage and facilitate the use of such information, its sources and purposes are related to its role in the legislative process, while its content and format are related to its sources and purposes.

One may desire information contained in congressional publications either because of or irrespective of its relationship to the legislative process. To focus on the first possibility, there is no conclusive answer to the question of what pertinent information Congress should acquire or convey to establish effective controls over policy formulation. Thus, one who is generally familiar with the legislative process and methods of locating desired information may still find that many matters regarding its production and functions remain unclear. From this standpoint, the major questions addressed in the following pages are: What types of information are emphasized in each type of publication? How can one identify and fill information gaps? Which entities exercise the most control over which publications? How do chronological factors, legislative procedures, and political relationships affect content?

Where subject matter is the only or most significant factor, two major barriers to the use of congressional publications seem to be their relationship to other members of the same family and difficulty in gaining access to particular portions of a text. A study of the links among official publications and between them and formal proceedings is designed to suggest methods for more expeditiously retrieving essential information. Librarians familiar with the documents discussed may find that the legislative process perspective reveals additional ways to service them. Researchers acquainted with the legislative process may find that the publications perspective discloses additional ways to enhance their product. Students or professionals seeking information about a subject are provided with the means to choose or devise a search strategy that best meets their needs.

For those mainly interested in particular documents, whether substantive or bibliographic in nature, four means of access are available. The chapter references cite those sources that form the foundation on which the discussion is based. The documentation sections of chapters 2, 10, and 11 amplify the nature and clarify the status of the principal government publications. Appendix B highlights the value of sources whose merits are not covered elsewhere in this volume. The Document Index lists all publications mentioned in the text, omitting those that appear in the chapter bibliographies and introduced in Appendix B.

The legislative, budget, and treaty processes are the three major vehicles that Congress may use to establish or influence public policy. It is not necessary that a given means be pursued to a conclusion to assure that legislative preferences are taken into account. The mandates that emerge from each carry comparable weight and are subject to similar constraints. However, the key participants and types of decisions vary significantly. These differences demand a detailed and separate treatment of their purview and practice. The purpose of a parallel structure for chapters 2, 10, and 11 is to enable readers to determine which would yield desired information and to facilitate comparison of the products.

Though budgetmaking and treatymaking produce decisions and publications that are outside the formal legislative process, all three activities are interdependent. Presidential initiative and participation are more institutionalized in regard to budgets and treaties. The budget and treaty processes also proceed on schedules separate from that which applies to legislation. Congressional publications derived from the two former activities differ in content and format, though not in name, from their purely legislative counterparts. Budget and treaty proceedings also generate several types of publications unique to their purposes.

In comparison with the legislative and treaty processes, budget process requirements and documents remain in a state of flux. One reason is longevity. The former have existed since the inception of the Constitution and have been thoroughly adapted to their environments. While the presidential budget was initiated in 1921, the congressional budget was introduced as recently as 1974. Another reason is the seemingly intractable nature of economic and financial problems and their increasing impact on all aspects of public policy. Because the economy can neither be accurately predicted nor readily controlled, approaches to prosperity and budgeting are more experimental than traditional.

A survey of the relationship between congressional publications and the legislative process poses the question of logical order. Difficulties are inherent in the dual nature of bicameral proceedings and discretion about whether and when to print. Most publications may be issued at various points in the process, while different ones may appear at nearly the same time. The unique nature of issues and uncertain chronology of decisions preclude any explanatory scheme from being applicable in all cases. The arrangement corresponds with the legislative agenda as described in chapter 1 and the legislative process as detailed in chapter 2. However, it should be understood that the correspondence between issuance and activity can only be approximate rather than exact.

The current work is based on the author's 1983 edition *Congressional Publications: A Research Guide to Legislation, Budgets, and Treaties*, but has had extensive revisions and updating plus the addition of reference information sources in Appendix B. The latter was added to help the reader keep up to date with the changing nature of government organization.

A legislature is an elective assembly whose collective behavior usually inverts the presumed commitments of its individual members.

—Anonymous

1

The Congressional Agenda

In its most basic usage, an agenda denotes a plan. Though its content may be of great interest, the manner of its formation is at least of equal importance. The congressional agenda has two unique features that distinguish it from most other types. First, it is never final, always being subject to modification as legislators continuously review and react to conditions and developments. Second, it is not embodied in a formal document, but exists as a web of informal agreements. An analysis of how this agenda is formulated and structured serves as a starting point from which to investigate what might be described as the information function of Congress.

An in-depth exploration of the relationship between congressional communications and public policy involves a somewhat different approach to the legislative process. Congress is presented as an agency responsible for collecting, producing, organizing, evaluating, maintaining, and distributing information. The availability of information is not, of itself, sufficient for effective legislative action. The consideration of issues requires interest to activate the agenda-setting process and expertise to refine it. While the interrelation of information, interest, and expertise covers much more ground than the subject of publications, it determines the quantity and quality of what appears in print.

LEGISLATIVE AUTHORSHIP

Congressional publications are not printed primarily for the convenience of legislators or for the information of citizens, though they serve both purposes. Neither are they merely a useful by-product of parliamentary proceedings. They are constituent elements of the legislative process whose value stems from the perceived significance of those political decisions that shape their content and engender their appearance. An examination of the environmental origins of congressional publications clearly reveals them to be strategic vehicles in the effort to forge public policy.

Congress serves as a public forum for continual national debate. Its ability to perform this function only partially depends on its role as a national lawmaking body. More importantly, it is a system of relationships that continually adapt to meet the needs of the polity and its own status. This orientation provides a firmer foundation for understanding how Congress keeps itself and interested publics informed of legislative activities and public affairs. For this purpose, it is necessary to reach behind the content of congressional publications to the motives and viewpoints of their authors. The issuance of a publication involves more than the fact that it is a formal obligation or an established custom at a certain stage of legislative proceedings.

Congress is the most accessible and active arbiter of political disputes having national policy implications. Its extensive responsibilities and substantial influence ensure that it will remain the recipient of a continual and voluminous flow of demands from innumerable sources. The quantity and variety of material printed by and for Congress indicates more than a polite acknowledgment of or voracious appetite for such information. It suggests a strenuous effort to weigh the merits of those appeals that reach its chambers and to document that legislators have accorded them reasonable consideration.

Legislative communications are aimed at those in a position to mold or make decisions that affect the enactment or implementation of public policy. Their purposes may be to suggest, urge, or require that new policy be considered, planned, or instituted or that existing policy be evaluated, continued, or revised. The audience may be composed of legislators, the president, administrators, judges, private citizens, officials of local or foreign governments, or some combination thereof. The range of its authority and activity affirms that Congress is an influential and informative author.

These circumstances, coupled with its decentralized organization, account for the fact that Congress is also a prolific author. However, to speak of Congress as an author obscures its key characteristic in this regard, namely, that it is actually many autonomous authors. Messages are constantly being delivered or exchanged, both internally and externally, in the form of bargains, recommendations, requests, criticisms, warnings, and demands. As a consequence, discerning whose views are being articulated can be difficult. From this standpoint, Congress may be observed and studied as a communications network and the legislative process as an information medium.

The two principal factors in this information environment concern the internal and external aspects of a communication. The former refers to the relationship between components that are framed to inform and persuade. The educational function of Congress is an inevitable result, rather than a deliberate goal, of its legislative activity. This fact does not impair the informational utility of congressional publications, but means that it is necessary to look beyond the printed word if a complete grasp of their import is desired.

The analysis of any congressional publication, in addition to its substance, should also include the relationship between its source and audience. Official sources are both houses of Congress acting jointly, one chamber, or a committee. Unofficial sources are party organs, informal groups of legislators, or individual members. The difference between these two types of sources is not due to their potential influence but to the formality of their communications. Those of the former appear as official documents, those of the latter do not, if they are written at all. The mutual impact of both sources, though not always evident, is taken into account by an intended audience.

In a technical sense, communication between a legislative source and an audience is based on the scope of formal jurisdiction. However, while the authority to act may be legally prescribed, the ability to exert influence is not. The levers of influence that may be manipulated by political agents condition the clarity and intensity of the signals communicated. Statements are accorded respect to the degree that they can alter the competitive status of political interests. Despite the force or zeal behind a congressional publication, its content is normally expressed in moderate terms. Legal authority tempered by political prudence serves to avert resistance or hostility that can ultimately produce legislative stalemate or defeat.

Congressional publications is a term that conceals as much as it reveals. It possesses a surface clarity that belies its actual complexity. Its apparently unambiguous nature stems from a distinction between official and other documents. Though this is a valid way to verify existence, identification is merely an initial step. A complete bibliographic citation only confirms the name of the issuing agency. In the realm of politics and policy this constitutes a rather meager supply of useful data.

The nature of corporate authorship also serves to veil desirable and pertinent information. Legislative bodies are inclined and expected to draw upon all sources where public needs are concerned. Congressional publications are a unique species that will yield their more valuable assets only to those with the appropriate experience or perspective. Even in the absence of conscious efforts to shield origins or transactions they oblige readers to acquaint themselves with the overall climate and principal customs of legislative life.

COMMUNICATION FRAMEWORK

Every potential governmental action will normally either benefit or burden at least one identifiable political interest group. That group will, accordingly, express itself more strongly about the issue than most other groups or the mass of voters. Since all implications of any public choice cannot be discerned in advance of its implementation, the best means of ensuring that possible consequences are detected is to encourage access to the policy process. Intensity of concern can only be gauged by the extent of acceptance or objection of those who express themselves in ways that public officials are obliged to acknowledge or respect. Access is the opportunity for or capacity of a political entity to attract the attentive interest of a relevant policymaker regarding a possible authoritative decision affecting the entity's welfare.

For an interest to make itself heard is not the same as to be heard effectively. The latter refers to the ability to exert a continuing and perceptible influence in a certain sphere of public activity. It may mean that some public official can expect to suffer adverse consequences if the petitioning group is denied the opportunity to present its view in a public forum or is not otherwise placated. It may also denote that the frequency of elections, volume of workload, and need for information prompt public officials to offer access to strengthen their position or enhance their reputation.

There are several general conditions that enable most of those who seek some form of access to succeed in their endeavor. One is the wide distribution of political resources. Hardly any group is entirely lacking in some that may be employed within its particular issue area. Another is the multiplicity of access points. This enables interests neglected or rejected at one site to seek and gain a more sympathetic response at another. A third condition is the numerous methods of transmitting views. These include joining or forming politically active organizations, publicly expressing political preferences through the media, possessing political or technical information of value to others, or having allies with some influence over certain communication channels. There also remains the alternative of investing resources in the electoral process or indicating a willingness to do so to attract attention or win support.

Access to Congress for citizens and issues is a crucial feature of the political process. Failures or frailties that stem from this stage of action affect all subsequent developments. The framework of conditions that influence access have at least two significant consequences. First is the level of participation by those who might affect the process of change. This directly reflects governmental responsiveness to citizen needs. Second is the capacity of officials to provide a forum for matching the needs of respectable groups with the store of available resources. This serves to promote political cooperation and facilitate feasible decisions.

There are at least a half dozen major factors that affect the opportunity for and availability of access. Representation as reflected in electoral margins and personal convictions determine a legislator's sensitivity to external demands. The various obligations and objectives of individual members, combined with the numerous and competing interests that seek recognition, affect the ability to register views. The electoral timetable that limits the life span of a Congress to two years contributes to a short-term focus and limited attention span. The persistence necessary to form a favorable consensus often requires a mobilization of resources that extends beyond time limits imposed by the electoral calendar. Procedural arrangements affect the perception of legislative prospects and influence institutional receptivity.

The access offered by a legislature of 535 members tends to facilitate the accommodation of those interests able to exert some political leverage at any one of many decision points. The decisionmaking process serves to expand the range of options submitted for consideration, which accentuates participation, and to narrow the number of options seriously and thoroughly evaluated, which emphasizes protection. The ideal result would be the adaptation of values and coordination of choices that contributes to political stability despite dissatisfaction with any particular policy judgment. The normal openness and ample publicity of congressional access afford citizens the opportunity to petition government, to compete with and criticize others, and to influence the composition of the legislative agenda.

Legislative representation is the articulation and communication of demands of particular publics in the process of political decisionmaking. It forms the basic link between an electoral body and its various constituencies. The two types of representation reflected in the composition and organization of Congress are the geographical and the functional. The former depends on elections for its efficacy, while the latter denotes the enterprise of lobbying. The relationships between legislators and their geographical constituencies tend to determine the manner in which they respond to functional interests.

Functional representation of specialized constituencies in the form of clientele groups supplements that of electoral representation. While the latter is a built-in feature of the constitutional structure, the former is a natural outgrowth of the political order. The formation and operation of interest groups serve to promote greater citizen participation in public affairs than can periodic visits to the polling booth. The wider representation that necessarily ensues better enables Congress to fulfill its role as an arena within which political conflicts can be regulated and reconciled. While elections require legislators to pay attention to the unorganized multitude, lobbying offers access for members of organized groups.

The influence that interest groups are able to exert is due to several factors. Since events and conditions are invariably subject to different interpretations, it is difficult for legislators to be sure about what constituents will favor or support. On any given issue, constituency opinion may be ambiguous, incongruous, or barely discernible. Few constituents have the inclination or understanding needed to express their preferences in a timely and effective manner. Legislators may have little choice except to represent their own conception of their constituents' views or attempt to anticipate them and act accordingly. The passivity of the general public tends to enhance the potential influence of specialized and attentive publics.

Another key factor is the absence of policy-oriented national parties that can enforce conformity to a party platform and threaten the status of members who disregard it. The decentralized structure of congressional elections enables groups with active members in electoral constituencies to gain access to legislators. Such groups are also important sources of information and support that may be used for electoral or policy purposes. By giving voice to the various segments of the general electorate and numerous concerns of attentive publics, Congress represents the diverse elements and tendencies of a heterogeneous and competitive society. Because legislative representation entails participation by relevant interests between the inception and implementation of policy, the success of Congress in this endeavor depends on extensive deliberation to accommodate perspectives and adjust perceptions.

The quality of representation is necessarily determined anew for each matter that comes before Congress for consideration. Each legislative election must be individually and collectively interpreted as an authorization to use judgment or an instruction on one or more issues. The basic questions for each legislator are whether and with what intensity to participate and whether to advocate or mediate. The corporate answer indicates which entities are viewed as the relevant publics. Some of the choices are to represent the interests of those who would be affected, the opinion of those who communicate their concern, or the views of those who must make the decision. Of course, even within each of these general categories declared positions are rarely uniform. Thus, it is always possible for effective representation, in the form of responsiveness to public demands, to produce irreconcilable differences or ineffective results.

Because many people do not hold an opinion on many issues and because the views of those who do may diverge, there is frequently no majority opinion in the community on an issue. The less than scientific means of interpreting the nature of election mandates and of ascertaining the state of public opinion produce results that are less than conclusive. It is the responsibility of legislators to translate the views of those who are articulate and intense into practical policies that also meet the expectations of those who choose to remain indifferent or inactive. The election of partisans creates a climate of cooperation among those who campaign under the same party label. This disposition can be converted into a consensus for legislative action despite the indeterminacy of general opinion and variety of stated positions. Through an exchange of views and recognition of needs, legislators collectively reach decisions that broadly represent interests in the community and that elicit broad political support.

The relative ease of access also involves some political and legislative drawbacks. Competition and bickering among many interested parties may cause inordinate delay in the enactment of critical legislation. The extensive deliberations needed to coordinate action may result in the intensification of problems or lost opportunities for settlement. Concessions to many groups may lead to an agreement that is internally inconsistent and of doubtful effect. Continuous compromise reduces the likelihood of coherent and cogent laws while it increases the possibility of patchwork and ambiguous legislation.

For participants to accrue the benefits afforded by access demands success in the task of political aggregation, or the formation of policy coalitions. The defects associated with access, however, tend to result in less legal integration, or clarity of policy declarations, than might otherwise be the case. In any given situation it is always possible that the negative features of access may undermine the acceptability of some goal or outcome. This is one way of noting that the strengths and weaknesses of access are opposite sides of the same coin.

The two pivotal dimensions of legislative access are participation, or adequate opportunities, and protection, or reasonable safeguards. The former covers action to promote or prescribe that which is deemed beneficial or appropriate, while the latter denotes efforts to prevent or remedy that which is viewed as undesirable or inequitable. Congressional credibility is linked to the capacity to ensure participation and offer protection to those willing and able to invest their resources in political ventures. To the extent that citizens may and do engage in public affairs and to the extent that such activity provides assurance against adverse private or public action, government decisions will be accepted as valid expressions of community opinion.

INFORMATION FRAMEWORK

For legislators to influence the process of community change requires knowledge of those societal forces and group activities that shape the course of probable events. This implies more than an ability to discern and readiness to explore emerging issues. It also involves the faculty to anticipate the likelihood of certain conditions or consequences. To define the proper role of government and suggest possible courses of action is to determine what information is important and undertake efforts to acquire it.

Information about issues and people in the context of conditions that need attention and improvement is useful, but cannot be conclusive. Objective data provide only the starting point from which to devise and assess policy alternatives. This is because facts about the future exist only as estimates or projections. Since policymaking is directed at the future and the future is always uncertain, argument tends to focus on what constitutes valid evidence. Even description and analysis conceded to be impartial and instructive involve assumptions and implications that may provoke criticism.

The quantity and quality of messages received by an organization depend on such external factors as the pace of significant change in its environment, the status of its relationship with other public and private bodies, and the existence of legal or other deadlines. Internal factors include the size of its membership, the distribution of authority, and the capacity to respond. This means that the formal and informal methods used by an organization to collect, select, and transmit information are critically important determinants of its output.

A legislator desires several types of information about any given issue. Substantive information refers to the means and ends of a proposed policy as well as the effects of past governmental action in a policy area. Political information concerns the relative strength of those who support or oppose a proposal and the possible consequences of alternative actions for a legislator's future. Procedural information relates to the legislative rules and practices that may be used to control a measure's progress. Either or both substantive and political merits tend to govern the choice of procedures.

Legislators are called upon to make hundreds of decisions each year that affect vast numbers of people and whose consequences cannot be clearly foreseen. These decisions include recorded and unrecorded votes as well as many other choices that do not involve voting or documentation. Members of Congress are expected to be familiar with and make intelligent judgments about all areas and facets of governmental activity. Even if legislators were inclined to keep themselves fully informed in regard to all such questions, it would not be feasible to do so. No single individual can possibly master more than a very few matters on the legislative agenda at any given time. Limitations imposed by time, capacity, and interest compel legislators to simultaneously cope with an excess and an absence of information.

The sheer volume of potentially useful information is too great for any legislator to absorb without neglecting other responsibilities and priorities. Time is needed not only to collect and collate information, but to explore whether it may be used for purposes other than those for which it was originally created or acquired. Sources of information outside of Congress include constituents, the executive branch, interest groups, the media, state and local government officials, and professional specialists. Within Congress members may receive or solicit information from party leaders, committee members, legislative staff, state delegation members, highly respected colleagues, or auxiliary research units.

The volume of available information is no indication of its utility or validity. First, it is impossible for a legislator to obtain all the technical information that would be needed to make a rational decision on the merits of every issue. Second, even if it were remotely possible, it would be unrealistic to expect a legislator to incur the costs in time and effort that would be necessary. Since the costs of making an uninformed decision can also be high, the question becomes one of how to make intelligent choices without having to expend an inordinate amount of limited resources when reliable information is scarce or unrefined.

Time is another key factor that significantly influences the flow and use of information. The dimensions of an issue that will be presented for decision, the precise nature of the decision, and whether a decision will be necessary at all cannot be anticipated with certainty. Since valuable time may be wasted in acquiring and analyzing information, efforts to do so are commonly not undertaken until it is too late to do it in a systematic and thorough manner. Also of importance is that the length of the interval between the receipt of information and the need for action determines the time available to investigate possible options and make political calculations.

Each legislator seeks means that enable a reasonable and justifiable decision to be made on both substantive and political grounds. One approach to this problem is to apply a combination of values and goals to aid in the selection and synthesis of desired information. The dominant characteristic of legislative perception may be constituency opinion, policy objectives, political competition, or personal ambition. The perspective that prevails depends on the nature of an issue or subject, which includes its salience for various political participants and its potential for creating political leverage.

Another approach is to identify specific sources whose ability to offer sound advice has been confirmed over time. Again, the reliability of a source would be judged in relation to the matter in question. A stock of personal convictions and network of established cues enable legislators to adjust to their information environment. Constituents and colleagues are the sources most relied upon when legislators invest a significant portion of their resources in a public question. Other sources are consulted to the degree that they can provide information compatible with a plausible position or preconceived opinion.

The legislative process may be viewed as an amalgam of strategies and techniques devised to locate, acquire, assess, organize, retain, and transmit information. Political interests and intentions determine whether to accept, affirm, supplement, ignore, question, or refute circulating information. Since legislators are obliged to state positions and make decisions in public, their need for reliable and relevant data is evident. The extent of efforts devoted to the mobilization and manipulation of information is a sign of political competition and salience. Though information is plentiful, its presentation in a persuasive fashion and on an opportune occasion is an infrequent occurrence.

To demonstrate effectiveness in the access to or control of information enhances the ability to exert political influence. This applies with particular force to the capacity to restructure units of available information so as to form a new product or use an existing one for new goals. To create resources of value to other political participants places one in a strong position to attain desired objectives. Legislators who possess valuable information know that the manner and timing of its release can significantly shape actions and outcomes. Since most policy proposals affect far more people than those aware of their existence, information dissemination influences both the size of a potential audience and the level of political activity. Information resources tend to be used to further the purposes of those in a position to control them.

Conditions peculiar to the arena of public policy formulation ensure that information, regardless of its source or content, cannot be divorced from political considerations. It is costly to obtain, analyze, and communicate. To undertake these activities means that resources must be diverted from other possible uses. Also, information can reduce, but not eliminate, uncertainty.

All relevant data are never available, particularly those which would enable individuals to accurately predict the consequences of alternative courses or even of one option.

The pace of communal change and complexity of social relationships limits the utility of even the best substantive information. Under these circumstances even the recent past becomes a relatively poor guide for prospective choice. The inability to isolate or verify causes with sufficient certainty discourages solid confidence in social and policy forecasts. That certain political interests must be placated to promote social stability further reduces the possibility for framing legislation based exclusively or even primarily on objective data.

The means for keeping legislators apprised of social reality, however defined, is the process of public debate and political argument, with all of the changes of course and opinion that being exposed to different points of view may entail. An open institutional process that is neither bound by restricted sources of information nor permits an aloof attitude among members is also one that raises questions about the availability of channels and weight of messages. The flow and form of information in the congressional environment reflects legislative efforts to adapt to a fluid polity and dynamic society.

AGENDA FORMATION

Though the area over which legislative power may be and has been exercised is quite vast, several factors serve to limit its use and scope. Though these factors might be viewed as organizational deficiencies, they reflect conditions that inhere in the legislative process. An adequate conception of the capacity of an elected assembly such as Congress must take account of the unwritten but unavoidable restrictions on its potential actions. These limitations can be described in terms of a barrage of competing demands and pleas combined with tension between institutional and member needs. The requisite time and information needed to accord each matter its proper proportion of legislative attention cannot be determined by neutral standards or granted by political fiat.

A process of petition and persuasion precedes any effort by legislators to devote personal and institutional resources to one matter rather than another. This involves the questions of how issues arise and become salient. Political entities outside Congress, in collaboration with allies within, must exercise initiative to bring a subject to the point where public concern can be translated into legislative consideration. Major issues that receive serious and sustained legislative attention usually undergo an initial political trial outside the halls of Congress. This ordeal entails efforts by proponents to publicize benefits and justify practicality and by opponents to discredit assumptions and question implications.

A political demand is a claim made by an entity on the available or potential resources of the community. It is an expression of opinion that those in authority should pursue a particular course of action or acknowledge the importance of certain values. Demands may take the form of policy options that ensure preferable results, of a right to participate or share in decisionmaking, or of an idea that merits consideration. They may be classified in terms of those that relate to goods and services or to behavior and status. The first category entails direct governmental action to provide tangible benefits, while the second involves the regulation of private conduct to promote social equity.

Claims arise from conditions viewed as unreasonable or inequitable by those unable to prevent or avoid them. They are voiced to redress a grievance or address a problem perceived as adversely affecting relative autonomy or opportunity. To publicly state a demand is to try to convince others that a largely private matter should be regarded as a public one. It is the beginning of an attempt to influence public opinion, public officials, or both, since each can sway the other. Existing communal values and resources initially determine the type and number of demands viewed as sufficiently credible and creditable to merit earnest public discussion.

A demand is usually associated with a single source and may not be taken seriously by other political participants. The emergence of an issue signifies that a matter rates wider interest and has reached a discussion agenda. In the course of transforming one or more demands into an issue, several phases of public and political persuasion can be discerned. First, there is a need to generate agreement that a problem exists and adversely affects an identifiable group. Second, a sizable or influential segment of the polity must be convinced that remedial action is desirable and necessary. Third, it is imperative to foster a perception that the matter is within the purview and capacity of government. Finally, public officials are prompted to place it on an institutional agenda to enlist political support for their own policy views or redress what they consider to be a legitimate grievance.

Proponents of governmental action strive to transfer public questions from a discussion to an operational agenda. This latter is a set of subjects that policy-makers have selected as meriting constructive attention during a given period of time. Other than exploiting the electoral calendar or emergency conditions, the route to the legislative agenda is generally a prolonged exercise in issue definition. Political conflict is clearly evident in differing perceptions of an event or situation and the campaign to define a resultant issue from a particular perspective. Competing definitions reflect efforts to choose the terrain on which a contest will take place which, in turn, affects who will participate and on which side. Public debate on an issue will address both its substantive and governmental aspects, the latter referring to the proper role of public officials and scope of public action.

As issues arise, competing definitions of a problem are advanced by different groups, with each definition implying a different approach or solution. Issue publics cannot be assumed to know the exact nature or dimensions of a given situation, nor can they be expected to offer useful and impartial analyses of existing policies or possible options. They express concern about or prescribe remedies for a problem without always having diagnosed it in detail or presenting verifiable data based on extensive research. Their information activities are designed to marshal evidence for a traditional point of view or attract the attention of potential political allies.

Those who seek to alter public policy may use one or more of several strategies to advance their cause. They may attempt to relate issue impact to a wider audience than those immediately affected as a means of mobilizing political support. Another option is to define an issue in terms of an existing governmental activity, which serves to link their position with a valid precedent. Advocates may emphasize that issue resolution is compatible with sound policy based on its intrinsic or other merits. Those who desire an affirmative governmental response endeavor to present a clear and convincing definition of the issue and nurture the credibility of a political rationale for timely action.

Competitors may successfully redefine an issue to give the impression that governmental intervention would raise more problems than it would remedy or would be unlikely to produce satisfactory results. Adversaries of public action may deny that a public problem exists or claim that a proposed response is aimed at the wrong cause. As legislators attempt to cope with an already congested agenda, the consideration of any new issues, regardless of their merit, may have to be deferred. The fluid nature of the political environment, in terms of either discernible trends or imminent crises, may abruptly displace a matter under consideration.

The major obstacle that confronts advocates of any significant change in public policy is that the type and number of issues recognized by most active political participants as appropriate subjects of legislative action are limited by the status quo bias of every political system. First, the range of views to receive serious scrutiny will be limited by the demonstrated capabilities of existing institutions to adequately address them. Second, the number of policy options to be thoroughly evaluated will be limited by the level of resources that can be mobilized to effectively implement them.

Some combination of the various issue positions is usually forged to engender both substantive and political harmony. Since the degree of uncertainty regarding social causes and policy consequences ordinarily precludes any single opinion from being considered clearly superior, political competition encourages each participant to present the strongest possible case and to willingly or grudgingly disclose policy premises and preferences. That all relevant views are submitted for consideration may generate widespread contention. However, the availability of information facilitates the effort to adopt some definition so that government may proceed to address the matter.

The opportunity for and ability of public officials to produce a credible and authoritative definition of an issue and impose it on the confusion caused by competing issue publics may be more fruitful than trying to find or form the one right definition, which probably does not exist. Thus, it is logical and predictable that officials will attempt to influence the redefinition of an issue in directions in which they are best prepared or most willing to travel. The transition from defining a public problem to formulating a proposed solution indicates that an essentially competitive situation has become a more cooperative enterprise in which officials are more inclined to invest public resources.

Legislators enjoy substantial discretion in choosing the issues to which they wish to respond and in weighing the factors they will consider in deciding how to proceed. Two key reasons for this latitude relate to the nature of the polity and of the issues. First, the number of entities urging action commonly serve to either neutralize each other or expand both the temporal and substantive boundaries within which officials may develop a response. Second, issues usually encompass a cluster of questions whose salience tends to wax and wane over time as conditions or officials change. The strategic position of legislators enables them to bargain over which issues will be addressed and the form in which they will be considered. The price for an issue to be placed on the legislative agenda may be a modification of its definition, which determines the difficulty and manner of its treatment and resolution.

The process of forming an agenda involves making choices about which decisions to consider. There are always more matters that merit attention that can be profitably or prudently addressed at any one time. This means that congressional decisions are a scarce resource in the political community. Placement on the agenda is only a first, though crucial, step on the route to a formal response. Because time is equally as valuable a resource for group proceedings as it is for individual action, congressional politics reflects a perennial struggle to control the legislative agenda.

Several enduring conditions guarantee that a large number of questions will be presented as meriting agenda status. The impact and intricacy of the economy entail a continual need to determine whether and what type of legislation is appropriate. Social diversity and competition generate demands and counter-demands for redesigned public policy. The interrelationship of society and government requires that the functions and activities of the latter be adapted to changes in the former. The scale and complexity of many issues mean that government is the only institution capable of effective action.

Once an item reaches the legislative agenda, it must still survive a winnowing process. Factors that limit the potential number of legislative decisions include the two-year life of a Congress, various commitments and convictions of individual legislators, numerous and competing interests that seek official policy statements, comparative ease of delaying rather than advancing legislation, difficulty in securing timely and reliable information, and persistence necessary to form a favorable consensus. The number of major bills that can clear all such barriers during any congressional cycle is quite limited.

An important distinction for agenda purposes concerns items that are subject to discretionary action and those that are not. Recurring business in the latter category includes the budget and appropriations processes and numerous housekeeping chores. Nondiscretionary matters that arise with less regularity are reauthorizations of expiring programs and emergencies or crises. The resources consumed by these affairs control the discretionary agenda, which is more likely to consist of proposals that are reinstated and familiar, rather than novel and weakly supported.

There are three phases in the development of the legislative agenda. The first centers on issue salience and involves political initiative, or the ability to make an issue a subject of public and congressional concern and debate. An issue is any matter that generates political controversy over the allocation of or access to public or private resources. External entities actuated by specific events, including elections, tend to predominate during this phase. The president, federal agencies, political parties, judicial opinions, constituencies, and interest groups are the main determinants of congressional business.

The leading actor at this juncture is expected to be the president. His national perspective and constituency, combined with vast informational and communications resources, when skillfully and vigorously used, enable him to promote policy goals by influencing public opinion and building political coalitions. However, the open competition that characterizes this phase precludes any individual or group from consistently dominating it. The interplay of conditions and interests within the confines of the legislative process determines which issues are certified for congressional consideration.

The second phase of agenda activity concerns issue definition and structure. The key agents at this point are congressional committees and subcommittees. These panels are legislative laboratories that test and digest the proposals under their jurisdiction. Should the advantages of or necessity for legislation become apparent, committee responsibilities for issue analysis and consensus formation assure them of several options, which translates into political power. The value of information as negotiations are commenced, alternatives assessed, and bargains concluded cannot be overemphasized.

The basic decisions on the type and level of resources to be committed are made during this period. A consequence of wielding the power of virtual life or death over bills also enables committees to assume an entrepreneurial role. Placing problems on the agenda for which there are no satisfactory solutions creates demands and opportunities for such remedies. An unsatisfactory response may even be advanced as a means of stimulating a search for something better. The ability of committees to control substance and to facilitate legislative transactions places them in a commanding position to influence the form and flow of the legislative agenda.

The final phase of agenda development is issue disposition. Party leaders play the primary role as they endeavor to coordinate the functional areas of the committee system and manage each chamber's legislative workload. Decisions on the arrangement of a legislative schedule reflect efforts to reconcile political demands and institutional efficiency. The results of negotiated agreements and chosen options are brought before the two houses of Congress. Most proposals are ratified because of a combination of committee competence and chamber deference. A sure sense of timing and parliamentary skill are also important.

When action by the parent body is imminent, the different scheduling needs of legislators become a principal problem. Majority party leaders require flexibility to regulate the volume of floor business and to assemble majorities for certain bills. Minority party leaders demand an opportunity to offer legislative alternatives and debate substantive issues. Committee members insist on retaining discretion to control the measures reported by their panels. Individual legislators desire a predictable timetable so that they can plan their activities with certainty. The conditions or procedures that serve the needs of one group often conflict with the needs of others.

The manner in which the agenda evolves significantly affects the legislative output. Minor and routine legislation is usually passed earlier in a session, while major and controversial bills require more time for their content to be refined and support aligned. For these latter proposals, the legislative process progressively narrows the range of available alternatives at each successive stage of action. In informational terms, this involves the segregation of facts and the integration of values.

Because facts are specific and stubborn, their interpretation can easily lead to disagreement and deadlock. Those which cause or have the potential to cause such results must be filtered out for legislation to advance. Because values are general and adaptable, they can be expressed so as to appeal to competing interests. Those which contribute to the necessary degree of political inclusiveness are carefully incorporated into a bill. These two aspects of information management form the foundation of any legislative strategy.

Each phase of the legislative agenda generates information about prerogatives, priorities, and procedures. Certain types of information accrue to certain legislators owing to their positions. When and how they communicate this information is as important as its substance. Access to information in the legislative process is a necessary, though not sufficient, condition for favorable legislative action. The drive to reach desired goals provides the incentive to share information, for communication is the essential prerequisite for legislative progress. How general information is transformed into political currency and the latter into public policy are underlying themes of this book.

REFERENCES

Anderson, James E. *Public Policy-Making*. New York: Praeger, 1975.

Cobb, Roger W., and Charles D. Elder. *Participation in American Politics: The Dynamics of Agenda-Building*. Boston: Allyn & Bacon, 1972.

Eyestone, Robert. *From Social Issues to Public Policy*. New York: John Wiley & Sons, 1978.

Jones, Charles O. *An Introduction to the Study of Public Policy*. 2nd ed. North Scituate, Mass.: Duxbury Press, 1977.

Kingdon, John W. *Congressmen's Voting Decisions*. New York: Harper & Row, 1973.

Pomper, Gerald M. *Elections in America*. New York: Dodd, Mead, 1968.

Saloma, John S. *Congress and the New Politics*. Boston: Little, Brown, 1969.

Schattschneider, E. E. *The Semisovereign People*. New York: Holt, Rinehart and Winston, 1960.

Truman, David B. *The Governmental Process*. New York: Alfred A. Knopf, 1951.

U.S. Congress. House. Commission on Administrative Review. *Scheduling the Work of the House*. House Document No. 95-23, 95th Congress, 1st Session. Washington, D.C.: U.S. Government Printing Office, 1977.

Walker, Jack L. "Setting the Agenda in the U.S. Senate," in *Policymaking Role of Leadership in the Senate*. A Compilation of Papers Prepared for the Commission on the Operation of the Senate. Committee Print, 94th Congress, 2nd Session. Washington, D.C.: U.S. Government Printing Office, 1976.

Young, Roland. *The American Congress*. New York: Harper & Brothers, 1958.

2
Legislative History

Decisionmaking is the conversion of information into action. A necessary consequence of choice is the effort to seek and sift useful data. The concrete nature and potential role of available information are the factual and political data that permeate and delimit legislative proceedings and production. This chapter explores how the decisionmaking process influences the range of political options and the message of policy statements. The campaign to transform political conflict into expedient agreement is seen as the most significant factor affecting the text of bills. The evolution of legislative language and formation of legislative majorities are inseparable aspects of congressional performance. A consensus on content and a coalition for passage reflect successful efforts to coordinate substance and strategy.

The first part of this chapter examines the roots and attributes of legislative language through an overview of Congress's lawmaking function and decisionmaking process. The first subsection describes the general nature of legislative negotiation, or the accommodation of diverse values. This produces agreement on how an issue should be addressed. The second subsection reviews the general nature of legislative decisionmaking, or the aggregation of competing interests. This generates agreement on how a proposal should be approved. The third subsection outlines the general nature of legislative pronouncements, or the assimilation of various provisions. This fosters agreement on how a policy should be expressed. All three activities proceed simultaneously and all involve public argumentation, private consultation, political adaptation, and policy implications.

The second part is a general survey of the functions that comprise and the ethos that pervades each major stage of the legislative process. This indicates the types of information, such as how priorities and alternatives are influenced, offered by printed sources that stem from or deal with the key decision points in a bill's journey. The articulation of demands, discussion of issues, mobilization of opinions, and formulation of proposals are all factors that enter into and emerge from a prominent congressional decision. The mosaic of elements that constitute a public law engender assorted explanations of its tenor and target. One approach to clarifying the logic of congressional choice is to focus on how participants cope with the problems of incomplete and uncertain information. This involves an account of the basic assumptions and attitudes that shape arrangements and alternatives. Policy decisions are collective judgments that combine public expectations, political relationships, established practices, and reasonable purposes. These features yield a practical rather than a logical result.

While the first two parts provide background on legislative words and deeds, respectively, the third focuses directly on legislative history. The precise definition of this term tends to vary with the purposes or perspectives of those who influence or monitor congressional business. In this study *legislative history* means the facts and views communicated by legislators through the documents officially cited or issued by them during the course of enactment. A complete legislative history should not only include material on the actions and comments that had a substantive impact, but also recognize the ongoing relationships among past, pending, and expected decisions. The organic and documentary histories of legislation cover more than congressional consideration and authorization. In this part the various dimensions of legislative history are introduced and distinguished.

Lawmaking and representation are the two principal functions of Congress. While the former reflects the desire for regulation, the latter denotes the demand for deliberation. Though these functions are not incompatible, their orientations differ. The emphasis of lawmaking is on problem solving and the effectiveness of the legislative product. The focus of representation is on communication and stresses the responsiveness of legislative proceedings. It is the interaction of the power to govern and the duty to confer that mainly accounts for the structure and process of the congressional environment. The mutual impact of discussion and decision endows public policies and legislative histories with their distinctive qualities.

PUBLIC POLICY CONTEXT

ELEMENTS

Political participants find that tangible benefits and desired objectives are controlled or influenced by others. To acquire or attain them it is necessary to offer or promise something that the others consider desirable. The number and nature of goals being sought means that some will coincide, some will conflict, and some will be complementary. This state of affairs underlies a general opinion that accomplishment depends on cooperation, which requires that participants adjust to each other's preferences. The pattern of conduct through which parties try to rearrange their relationships and reconcile their goals is bargaining.

Bargaining is an interaction in which two or more parties seek to advance their interests by devising inducements, forging commitments, offering concessions, or threatening deprivations. It is a form of negotiation used by participants to reach agreement on the basis for collection action. Bargaining entails a voluntary exchange of political assets or favors that results in mutual gain. Persuasion, on the other hand, is an attempt to mobilize support for one's own position without having to modify it. When political advantages or disadvantages are perceived as relatively certain or minor, or the existence of an obligation is acknowledged, persuasion is more likely to succeed.

Several factors form the preconditions or serve as incentives for parties to engage in bargaining. One is that each concede that the others have the right to make the demands or decisions that they are making. Intense concern combined with recognized status warrants a group's participation in the resolution of an issue. Another is the equivalence of skills and resources available to be invested in a given situation or undertaking. This reduces the opportunity to employ persuasion or otherwise induce compliance. A third factor is the assumption that a public question can be resolved in terms of *more or less* or *now or later*. Such an appraisal indicates that participants are likely to derive some benefits within a reasonable interval.

Since most parties need to collaborate on many matters over an extended period of time, there is also a need for acceptable ground rules. The existence of bargaining norms enables parties to calculate better the anticipated reaction to their claims and proposals. Among the more important norms are that an agenda should be formed and followed, that partial agreements should not be repudiated, that concessions should be reciprocated, and that motives should not be impugned. On the whole, these norms are observed because participants recognize the need for mutual trust as a prerequisite to agreement. Bargaining tends to prevail and succeed when the costs of an attempt to enlarge any one domain of influence appear greater than the uncertain gains that might accrue.

Once assumptions and attitudes have been articulated, communication and bargaining ensue in earnest. Differences of opinion on policy make bargaining necessary, shared views on civic values make it possible, diversity of demands and issues makes it continuous, and the common stake in political stability makes it expedient. Because of fragmented political influence and partitioned legal authority, bargaining is the only alternative to constant vetoes. Acquiescence or agreement among strategically located minorities constitutes the single realistic course that can avoid political frustration or stagnation.

Once negotiations commence, intentions and capabilities are probed and possible settlements assessed. Strategy and preferences may be modified as the exchange of information reveals that the facts are different from what was assumed or that certain objectives would have undesirable consequences. In the course of defending their interests, the minimum needs of each party and the limits of what is acceptable are disclosed. This sets the boundaries within which concessions and commitments are discussed and confirmed. As negotiations proceed from the terms demanded, to those sought, to those accepted, tacit understandings are also reached about what is received and owed.

Discussion remains an important technique for clarifying one's preferences in a competitive environment. It serves as a relatively swift and simple way to present and explore proposals and to elicit and analyze responses. This process helps to shape one's own preferences because the experience of others may be relevant for oneself. One cannot always be certain of preferences until one can forecast the reaction of other interested parties. That the preferences of others are always an influential factor means that many participants cannot refine and explain their position until bargaining has begun.

The key to legislative progress is early and ongoing efforts at consultation and coordination to control the breeding of factionalism and cumulation of discontent. Adherence to bargaining contributes to understanding and enhances the stability of a system in which major contestants have made heavy investments. Thus, the price of cooperation in the service of meeting joint needs is the acceptance of restraints. The outcome is composite policymaking, which synthesizes the best features of plausible proposals. It is a response to the fact that no alternative is obviously superior or can readily attract majority support. In the absence of a comprehensive and integrated policy framework that is politically and practically feasible, the result avoids the risks of inaction and the costs of imposition.

The impulse to compromise signifies that flexible preferences are accorded priority over fixed principles. Compromise is always possible where choices are not mutually exclusive in the sense that one party can only secure gains at the expense of others. Compromise is always necessary where one group is unable to mobilize the resources and support to realize its values through the medium of persuasion. Thus, interests are obliged to form alliances on matters of common concern or to engage in logrolling by exchanging support for each other's proposals. Both types of arrangement become essential in a political environment characterized by a diffusion of power and a need for majority coalitions.

A political dispute resolved without disproportionate sacrifice demanded or intolerable inequities imposed may be termed a compromise. Parties adjust and revise their positions through adaptation and amalgamation until agreement is reached. This approach enables all relevant interests to be accommodated as their values are incorporated into an authoritative decision. Political and substantive goals are balanced against each other as well as against communal and governmental capabilities. The question of how much weight should be given to which values is answered as an issue is redefined. The result is to broaden support for and promote acceptance of an emerging agreement.

The general factor that renders compromise instrumental is that of constraint. Imperfect knowledge means that not all problems have satisfactory solutions. Keen competition between equally valid views precludes an ideal response. Scarce resources mean that the costs of some solutions may be prohibitive. Existing priorities may prevent a problem from being considered in a timely manner. The collaboration of parties and consolidation of demands are essential to cope with constraints. A practical outcome is one that resolves disagreement by the use of options to address current and assess future developments.

Specific conditions that foster compromise solutions include an absence of intense conflict, an absence of an intractable problem, precedents for cooperative action, and precedents for governmental involvement. Even when one or more of these conditions is initially absent, the adroit use of language can define them into existence. First, the serial nature of political decisionmaking provides the time to pursue interests and satisfy demands. Second, the scope of many issues requires debate to be moderated for goals to be perceived as sufficiently complementary to form coalitions.

The coordination that leads to compromise may assume one or more of the following forms: voluntary cooperation, or mutual action in the pursuit of related goals; tacit agreement, or unilateral action that takes other views into account; or reciprocity, which may be mutual or unilateral action that discharges an existing obligation, creates a new one, or both. Compromise ensures a short-term settlement and presumes the possibility of future reconsideration. The fluidity of political conditions and flexibility of policy decisions accord participants considerable leeway to interpret available options and actual outcomes.

The compromises considered necessary for legislative success may be classified as prepackaged, progressive, postponed, or potential. The first type refers to an agreement reached among interested parties before a bill is introduced. The second indicates that accommodation is achieved through the incorporation of judicious amendments at key stages of consideration. The third denotes that action would be more expedient following an approaching election or the mitigation of political intensity. The last covers instances in which agreement is contingent on the occurrence of foreseeable and probable events. Compromise smooths the road to enactment by reducing the number of recorded votes that legislators may be called upon to cast and explain to their constituents.

Compromise through negotiation is considered as the most feasible and profitable approach to arriving at desirable decisions. Though no group or interest may receive all or exactly what it seeks, each derives sufficient gain to enable majorities to form and the institution to function. All disagreement is depersonalized as much as possible to allow bargaining to continue and so that new alliances with former adversaries may be arranged on other bills. Negotiations may involve the exchange of benefits or commitments. The former case tends to focus on a single measure composed of different but related provisions that appeal to each of several entities. The latter is more likely to entail an agreement to support a forthcoming bill in return for enabling another to advance at present.

The legislative process is characterized by multiple points of access, fragmentation of power, varying motives of legislators, and lack of central coordination. For a bill to become law requires the explicit or implicit approval of different units or alliances at each of the several stages through which it must pass. The chain of decisions that affects the progress of legislation offers many opportunities for delay, modification, or defeat to those able to influence the fashion in which any link is forged. To aggregate portions of power possessed at each decision point and convert them into successive majority coalitions necessitates a process of continual bargaining. Only through a series of negotiated compromises can the various organizational units and diverse political elements within Congress be sufficiently coordinated to produce a major legislative decision.

The formal grant of authority or informal accumulation of influence does not guarantee that decisions will eventuate or be effective. The skill and will to bargain produce different levels of involvement and leadership. The exercise of discretion denotes the ability and ambition to compromise on goals and priorities. This entails the allocation of public products and duties in a manner that addresses a cross section of political concerns broad enough to ensure majority support. Legislation becomes a vehicle for mobilizing interests and modifying opinions in the service of communal progress and institutional success.

The bargaining and compromise required by a decentralized and fragmented political environment accounts for the relatively slow pace of legislative proceedings, but it also permits the adjustment of positions and accommodation of purposes to proceed until agreement is reached. Extensive deliberations facilitate the formation of majority opinion as passage through each stage generates gradually wider acceptance and progressively narrows the scope of contention. Those engaged in this maze of maneuvers require the consent of others to attain any of their objectives. For each measure that receives sustained congressional attention there must exist a temporary combination of incentives that fosters cooperation among autonomous islands of influence.

INTERESTS

Decisionmaking in and the decisions of Congress are shaped by its decentralized character and concomitant diffusion of influence. The key factors responsible for this condition are elections, bicameralism, committees, and rules. Legislators are primarily accountable to their constituents rather than their colleagues. The diversity of geographical localities produces many differences of opinion about appropriate policies. That there are two houses of Congress means that the personal and political views of senators and representatives can often clash. Different perspectives and practices also lead to legislative competition between the chambers as a whole. The use of committees enables Congress to cope with a large and complex agenda by distributing its workload among specialized panels for study and recommendation. This division of labor along functional lines creates the need to coordinate policy proposals that intersect and overlap the boundaries of committee jurisdiction. The rules and customs of the House and Senate have evolved to promote stability and prevent domination of the legislative process by any internal element or external entity. As a result, procedures may be employed or invoked to impede action and maintain the status quo.

A bill must avoid numerous congressional vetoes long before the possibility of a presidential veto. Greater effort is required to shepherd a bill through the legislative process than to arrest its passage, which can be accomplished at any one of several points. Because different entities or perspectives tend to predominate at successive sites of action, earlier decisions reflect efforts to anticipate and affect later ones. The potential for discord or deadlock exists between and within political parties, between and within congressional committees, between the chamber and a committee, between the chambers, between policy blocs, and between the legislative and executive branches.

Since a chamber decision is a composite of several formal and numerous informal choices and since a different set of legislators exerts influence at each stage, supporters of a given bill must build a series of majorities to succeed, while opponents need only assemble a single majority to prevail. Not only must majorities be formed at successive sites, but it is first necessary to gain support from strategically located minorities before the process of majority building can proceed with reasonable prospects of success. Proponents must ascertain whether legislative coalitions can be formed on the basis of policy goals, political benefits, acknowledged obligations, institutional loyalty, or some combination thereof. It must also be determined which grounds to stress at which stage of action.

Any organization with as many veto points as Congress should be naturally resistant to innovative proposals and normally oriented toward the status quo. In addition to structural barriers, legislative action may be deterred or thwarted by lack of time, knowledge, interest, or skill. Despite these hindrances and handicaps, hundreds of public laws are enacted each Congress, some of which are political or technical breakthroughs. The characteristics and consequences of the legislative process provide most of the explanation as to how Congress copes with social change and political friction. Institutional viability and vitality stem from forms of cooperative endeavor that foster political consensus and produce feasible responses.

Despite actual and potential controversy or apathy, the wide range of legislative incentives and discretion enables proponents of change to achieve a measure of success. Incentives that serve to overcome institutional inertia or evasion include the evident disadvantages of inaction, opportunities for legislative accomplishment, pressure from external agents, and the integrity of Congress. Deteriorating social conditions and resulting adverse consequences foster a climate in which detachment is equated with negligence. Elected officials are always alert for situations that enable them to enhance their standing with constituents and attentive segments of the public. The president, interest groups, media campaigns, or emergency situations, either singly or in combination, may create an irresistible impetus for change. The desire to maintain or improve the political status of Congress in a highly competitive environment contributes to a more receptive institutional posture.

The legislative process does not provide the opportunity for a united majority to justify its position and sweep aside opposition. It is a means that permits majority opinion to form as political elements adapt to external demands and internal needs. Progress involves the propitiation of relatively small groups induced to cooperate with each other to advance their interests. Legislative majorities are temporary entities composed of several minorities. The scope of most issues means that participants agree for different reasons and that each is at least partially satisfied with the results. This entails a method of reaching decisions in cases where the possible alternatives do not represent the first choice of potential members of a majority coalition.

Potential coalition partners must perceive themselves to have views that, though different, are not incompatible. This is because specific concerns can only be satisfactorily addressed through combined action. Coalitions forged around shared values tend to be more stable than those based on mutual interests. However, most majorities coalesce on the basis of complementary interests that characterize the multiple dimensions of broad and complex issues. When the alternative is that potential members of a majority coalition are guaranteed to receive something for their cooperation or no one achieves anything, participants are encouraged to accede to each other's demands to ensure the passage of legislation.

Agreement on the need for and shape of major policies denotes a temporary accommodation among private and public entities pursuing different objectives. The progress of policy proposals entails the consolidation of competing political claims as various concessions are made to garner essential support. Though it may be generally acknowledged that legislation is necessary, commitments to accept or not oppose a specific bill are usually the result rather than the cause of legislative action. Enactment may be regarded as a process in which policy is approved by a group somewhat or considerably larger than that which originally proposed it. Those who advocate a policy change must persuade or induce others to consent so that agreement will be wide enough to render a decision both possible and effective.

Congress needs a decisionmaking structure that is both effective and efficient. Effectiveness refers to the substance of policies intended to serve as social remedies or provide tangible relief. Efficiency relates to the volume of output necessary to maintain political stability and institutional influence. The capability and credibility of Congress depend on the result of legislative efforts to moderate external competition and neutralize internal contention despite complexity, uncertainty, opposition, and division. There exists a recognized need to weave all pertinent political strands into a policy fabric that can adequately cover the concerns of those responsible for its creation and subject to its application.

Most policymaking is routine in that regularized procedures and acceptable outcomes have conferred legitimacy on the vast majority of government programs. Change requires a favorable response from legislators who can exercise a veto in their domain of influence. It also involves an acknowledgment that certain basic public activities and the policy consensus they reflect should not be disturbed. Policymaking entails the choice of appropriate means within a framework of prevailing values to realize desirable ends. Because drastic departures from established communal commitments are likely to generate intense resistance, the most likely result is a proposal that embodies marginal or gradual change to meet new needs or address unforeseen contingencies.

That the quantity of interests that may participate in the process can be relatively large places limits on the quality of potential decisions. The volatile nature of the policy arena requires time and tact to engender agreement on the reasons for and language of a proposal. Strategies are adjusted to meet the existing political and technical requirements of a given policy problem. Majority coalitions involve different interests with different objectives at different points in time. Thus, different strategies may be necessary at different stages to build majorities for the same measure. Negotiated settlements that support a given bill based on its relationship to the goals and priorities of numerous legislators tend to be modest in scope.

The legislative process cushions conflict in several ways. The many points through which a bill must pass and the numerous procedures that may affect its content contribute to incremental change. To institutionalize and routinize is to reduce speed and strife. The serial nature of decisionmaking enables an issue to be viewed from multiple perspectives and divided into manageable parts. The process possesses a self-critical and self-corrective character that permits values or interests ignored or denied at one point to be acknowledged or accepted at another. The key question at each point is What substantive choices will enhance political appeal without impairing policy quality? However, the fundamental commitment is that the integrity and utility of the decisionmaking mechanism receive priority over the quality of specific decisions when a choice must be made between the process and the product.

A decisionmaking structure that progressively narrows the number of choices available to policymakers is a labor-saving and economical device. First, the need for substantive and political decisions to be compatible reduces the range of options to manageable proportions. Second, policy anxiety is limited by linking a demand for change with a desire for continuity. Third, legislative proceedings reorient political argument among competing interests from the more provocative question of desirable ends to the more pragmatic one of available means. Collective choice entails efforts to devise or detect bases of harmony that can submerge or straddle disagreement which stems from different assumptions or aspirations.

An examination of congressional performance entails important distinctions between sources of influence, especially that between power and knowledge. The recourse to formal prerogatives denotes the use of authority, while the opportunity for informal leadership reflects the role of ability. Both involve political discretion and are necessary to mobilize sufficient resources to facilitate legislative progress. Formal rules establish requirements and assign responsibilities for prescribed proceedings. Informal practices complement written procedures by enlarging or restricting the range of options. Though the official code may confer status and afford opportunities, legislative gains and losses are equally due to applied parliamentary skills.

Any government, due to the source and nature of its authority, is bound to exercise power on debatable grounds or in disputed areas. In the case of democratic government, a clear distinction exists between the goal of public policy and the role of institutional authority. Support for the latter needs to be based on some means for fostering agreement on the validity of the right to decide. When consensus on the matter of what is a public question or on the merits of what should be done about it cannot be attained, consensus on a process for reaching decisions is an alternative to the decisive resolution of given issues. Confidence in a political mechanism can offset occasional dissatisfaction with substantive results.

A willingness to accept the validity of the procedures and arrangements through which decisions are reached is facilitated by the recognition that the costs of a failure to do so would exceed the benefits. The conviction that a policy can be devised that would be acceptable to most, if not all, concerned parties because it permits group interests to be pursued regardless of the immediate outcome, serves as a positive basis for political settlement. The forbearance of demands and tolerance of rivals that characterize political interaction enables participants to justify their claims based on their contributions to agreement. Such an approach reduces intensity and promotes moderation by permitting public decisions to be made through a process of competition and cooperation.

Government decisions regulate the allocation of tangible and intangible resources and modify incentives for their acquisition. The status of Congress as a legitimate political body is based on the congruence of communal values and public choices as manifested in organizational action and output. It denotes a quest for political feasibility, which is the likelihood that policy will be sufficiently acceptable to various segments of society so that it can be translated into effective results. The legislative process is designed to diagnose the needs and validate the claims of numerous and competing interests in a manner that fosters the equitable distribution of benefits and burdens.

AVENUES

The choice among alternative conditions is always between that which exists and that which might exist. Any proposal for change involves the status quo as the necessary starting point. The status quo may be defined as a persistent pattern of action and stable set of beliefs. It consists of an interrelated network of mutually shared expectations that sustains the polity and structures its components. Its political significance is the initial advantage it gives to those who favor its preservation.

The enactment of legislation may reflect anxiety about or acceptance of social change. Change may stem from impersonal communal trends or organized political ventures. It may be defined as any variation in interaction patterns that affects competitive status or preferred objectives. Whether designed to serve as a restraint on or agent of change, legislation takes the form of a prospective rule of behavior applicable to stated conditions or persons or both.

Visible differences between the real and ideal continually prompt concerned parties to frame proposals for social innovation. Different perceptions of actual conditions and potential improvements spur political participants to advocate change or caution. Some principal causes of change are the cumulation of knowledge, evolution of values, redistribution of resources, and transformation of competition. Since it is neither feasible nor desirable to control them, the question is whether innovation will be resigned to chance or subject to choice.

Lawmaking always involves matters regarding the propriety of commitments and restrictions on conduct. Because changes in public policy alter social opportunity, they inevitably affect the framework of political influence. Debate focuses on the efficacy of efforts to control or promote change as reflected in the components of legislative prescriptions and the conditions for citizen compliance. Even when change is considered desirable or inevitable, there always remain questions about its scope, pace, direction, and manageability. The major task of modern legislation is to cope with change as policymakers attempt to anticipate, recognize, understand, and evaluate it.

The apprehension and instability generated by incessant change trigger demands that ensure a continuous cycle of legislative adaptation. Policy formation is a perpetual process and not a single act that settles a matter with finality. Decisions involve successively closer approximations to a more widely acceptable approach. Most policies, because of the heterogeneity and interdependence of social and economic units, are both partial and temporary. They embody choices that remain subject to negotiation and adjustment as these units react to events and results and as their goals and influence evolve over time.

The two key components of public policy are a customary style of decision-making and a fairly stable pattern of decisions. Any particular policy is the result of a consistent series and cumulative impact of official actions, which means that a course of inaction is also a policy. In this sense *public policy* may be defined as a specified set of conditions that officials endeavor to bring about in a given area of concern. The somewhat elastic nature of this definition reflects the fact that policymaking itself is a process of determining whether certain conditions or concerns are or should be within the purview of policymakers.

Lawmaking is the effort to erect a basic legal order for the various objective classes of people and organized groups that comprise society. Statutes may assign jurisdiction to designated social, economic, and political entities or stipulate methods of settling jurisdictional conflicts among them. To establish a pattern of conduct that enables citizens to puruse desired and desirable ends requires that specific rights and duties be defined and sanctioned. The enactment of a public law represents an attempt to steer and blend personal and group needs so as to promote the achievement of individual and communal goals. A policy is a legislative mandate that proclaims civic objectives and authorizes certain means.

Statutes may create functions, confer privileges, impose obligations, or prohibit conduct. Major legislation, which adjusts relationships and allocates resources, usually combines two or more of these purposes as it tries to balance the tangible and symbolic gains and losses to be experienced by those to be affected. Public laws are a means to minimize or mitigate societal conflict and encourage or engender communal harmony. They enunciate goals that are intended to justify the regulation of activities between citizen and government, citizen and citizen, or government and government. Legislation empowers federal agencies to enter designated policy spheres in response to conditions acute enough to affect the welfare of a significant number of people or of government itself.

Political problem solving combines strategic and substantive considerations. Because of scarce resources, political controversy, technical complexity, and time constraints, legislative action serves to alleviate rather than eradicate problems. The success of conflict management stems from estimates of the arrangements available and knowledge of the conditions conducive for fostering agreement. In a fluid political environment, policy mediation becomes an acceptable alternative to issue solutions. In anticipation of further developments, a legislative response represents an invitation to continue the debate under different terms.

The raw material of legislation includes factual data and historical events, immediate political aims and ultimate policy ends, existing legal mandates and estimated budgetary constraints. Since a legislative policy statement is a mixture of facts, values, assumptions, intentions, expectations, and imponderables, the emphasis accorded any particular factor or element is a political question. The number, variety, intensity, and strength of competitors must be balanced against the causes, scope, urgency, and portent of an issue. Seen from this standpoint, statutes are temporary expedients that reflect a political optimum at a given moment in time and can become the basis for long-term solutions.

The basic nature of a statute is derived from the relationship between its general orientation and specific objectives. Its goals may be substantive or symbolic, innovative, or adaptive. Substantive legislation may cover changes in values or conduct or both. It may address a development that is without precedent or test a fresh approach for familiar conditions. Symbolic measures tend to be the product of intense pressure and inadequate information or resources. They ordinarily express views without specifying definite effects or state goals without stipulating methods or deadlines. Innovation and adaptation describe whether a policy embodies drastic or marginal change. The greater the magnitude of change imposed by legislation the more likely its provisions will be phased in over a period of time to permit gradual adjustment to its requirements.

Formal congressional responses may be classified under four broad types of action. A statute may authorize government to monitor and study particular matters to assure concerned citizens that their interests are receiving adequate attention. Legislation may require that recommendations or alternatives be formulated to address specific issues or events so as to be prepared for likely contingencies. A public law may establish guidelines for governmental intervention and contain instructions for prospective action. A policy mandate may consist of a systematic and immediate plan to alleviate certain conditions or ensure certain opportunities. These intentions reflect views about estimates of salience, scope of action, clarity of purpose, and commitment of resources.

One aspect of the general character of a statute is whether its language is compulsory or conditional, expressed via crisp commands or delegated discretion. Another aspect is whether it employs negative sanctions or positive inducements, relying on the deterrence of penalties or eligibility for benefits to influence conduct and evoke compliance. All legislation is intended to guide or limit the choice of officials or citizens. The policy approach denoted by a public law that is substantive, innovative, compulsory, and reinforced by sanctions tends to generate greater controversy than one that is symbolic, adaptive, conditional, and based on inducements. Of course, it is always possible to try to balance the members of each of these pairs of characteristics against each other in the same bill.

Statutory goals may be minimal or ambitious, simple or complex, general or specific, inexpensive or costly. To the degree that the latter member of each of these pairs is emphasized, they are more likely to be controversial and to serve as constraints on decisionmaking. Where controversy cannot be avoided or muted and legislation is considered necessary, objectives may be vaguely defined, intentionally competitive, deferred, symbolic, nonoperational, or nonexistent. Goals may be set low to keep expenditures down or reduce opposition to passage; they may be made easily achievable to satisfy one or more constituencies or in contemplation of eventual program expansion.

The selection and formulation of goals is conditioned by the anticipated reaction of those whose support will be needed for their approval and whose status will be affected by their adoption. As a result, goals tend to be flexible, multiple, and incremental. Goal flexibility refers to indefinite time frames for or different methods of measuring achievement. The existence of several goals deliberately obscures whether they are complementary, inconsistent, or independent and postpones the question of assigning priorities among them. Their incremental nature serves to reassure those who may feel threatened by any departure from the status quo. The number, clarity, and relationship of goals are questions that remain to be settled by the way in which policy is implemented.

Major bills enacted into law during any given session of Congress have usually received legislative consideration during earlier sessions. For most communal change to be ratified or regulated by legislation, support must be accumulated over a number of months or years. A lengthy gestation period is needed to accustom the public and officials to the political and practical feasibility of significant policy innovations. Since the consequences of controversial issues tend to be clearer than their causes, time is also required for a consensus to develop regarding whether and how to address either or both.

In a narrow sense public policy involves the enactment of legislation that is recognized as binding by virtue of its official promulgation. The substantive aspect of lawmaking concerns the formulation of general rules that may be stated for the first time, may combine old and new stipulations, or consolidate existing provisions into a refurbished mandate for action. Though Congress may prescribe or proscribe, encourage or discourage, conduct, the willingness of citizens to obey the law is based as much on access to decisionmakers and a sense of fair play as on constitutional prerogatives and legal forms. The procedural aspect of lawmaking pertains to the prior knowledge and acceptance of the process by which policy is designed and enacted. The authority of law stems from a combined perception of the legality of legislative power and the legitimacy of the legislative process. A successful legislative endeavor skillfully combines formal consent and informal consensus.

LEGISLATIVE PROCESS

INITIAL ACTION

Preliminary congressional business covers the interval from the drafting of a bill by its proponents to its receipt by a committee for potential consideration. During this period a political preference or substantive presumption is converted into a concrete legislative proposal. To translate policy opinions and public objectives into legal language and embody them in a prescribed format is to apply for a position on the congressional agenda. This phase concludes with the referral of a bill to the panel with jurisdiction over its subject matter. Though decisions are mostly routine or somewhat shrouded, they suggest the general outlines of a likely legislative strategy.

The advantages of traveling the legislative route relate to the binding nature and popular approval of a law. It provides a source of legitimacy on which to draw and build and a platform from which to command attention. The disadvantages of the legislative process are its unforeseen contingencies, which may lead to a statute with unsuitable or undesirable provisions. The failure to enact legislation may also foreclose the possibility of successfully pursuing other courses.

Any individual or group may draft a bill either on their own initiative or at the request of or in collaboration with a legislator. The initial form of a draft may range from a general outline of policy goals to a specific statement of program functions. A bill whose text is expressed in general terms serves as an invitation to commence or continue a dialogue whose results will be shaped by evolving conditions and perceptions. Proponents recognize the need to foster substantive and political agreement as a prerequisite to drafting a more acceptable and adequate measure. A bill written as a virtually finished product may imply that widespread approval renders its passage a foregone conclusion or that its sponsors wish to communicate a clear message to other political participants.

To introduce a bill is to formally submit a written proposal for consideration and approval. Introduction is the most common means by which a matter is officially brought to the attention of Congress. The decision to seek a congressional response or remedy requires that legislators be persuaded to commit public and personal resources. The former concerns the appropriate level of funds and personnel needed to administer a policy. The latter refers to the time and effort that legislators are urged to invest in a given undertaking.

The period that immediately precedes or follows the introduction of a major bill involves strategic efforts to stimulate legislative interest. The key question is whether the substantive and political aspects of an issue are sufficiently compelling to warrant congressional consideration of a proposal to address it. The most effective way to ensure legislative action is to secure presidential support. White House access to and coverage by the media enables the president to publicize and dramatize the need for legislation. Prearranged groundwork and accompanying public statements constitute an attempt to till the legislative soil so as to produce a particular political harvest. Once the need for institutional action is acknowledged, many entities must coordinate their intentions and resources to devise a viable legislative strategy. Since the congressional agenda is always congested and the outcome uncertain, the decision to endorse and advance a given measure is of much significance. This is because a bill is not merely a proposal for action, but is itself a form of action.

The political participant best able to influence the congressional agenda is the president. His prerogatives place him in a superior position to persuade legislators that the time has arrived to address a given matter. The president's annual legislative program, which constitutes a comprehensive and consistent package of proposals that cover a wide spectrum of social and economic issues, always invites him to frame legislative priorities. Though this responsibility can be traced to the Constitution and has been supplemented by statute, there is little doubt that its incorporation into regular governmental operations stems from the realization that it aids Congress to perform its legislative function.

From a congressional perspective the president's program is a welcome and convenient starting point for action. It provides legislators with an early notice of administration priorities, an immediate workload for standing committees, and an opportunity for members to gain publicity by supporting or opposing particular proposals. Members of the president's party in Congress are relieved of much of the burden of formulating a policy agenda, while members of the other party are given targets at which to aim. A proposed program enables legislators to orient themselves individually for political purposes and to organize themselves collectively for legislative objectives.

Of the large number of bills introduced during any Congress, only a small percentage have the potential to be enacted into law. Some general criteria for gauging such potential are that a bill not ask for too much or too little, since the former tends to breed opposition and the latter induce neglect. It should also embody a feasible course of action that will enable legislators to claim credit for their endeavors. More specifically, those proposals drafted in the White House or a federal agency or by a prominent interest group, supported by the majority party leadership in one or both houses, introduced by a committee or subcommittee chairman, and addressing an issue on which public and congressional opinion have crystallized to the degree that legislative action is deemed advisable if not essential, are always candidates for serious consideration and likely to make some progress.

Most bills, however, are introduced for reasons unrelated to their anticipated enactment. They are intended to generate favorable publicity for election campaigns and demonstrate that a legislator is diligently promoting constituency interests. Others are used as vehicles to advance novel ideas and pave the way for their eventual acceptance by citizens and officials. Many bills are simply a means to relieve pressure from or discharge a debt to one or more political groups. Some are calculated to affect the progress of measures introduced earlier or about to be introduced. Bills may be divided into three categories based on their origin and content. There are those with insufficient support to proceed beyond referral to a committee. Another class consists of routine measures considered necessary or desirable and whose passage is expedited. Major proposals, drafted or favored by the executive branch, an influential private group, or a significant congressional bloc, consume most of the resources devoted to legislative business.

To draft an authorization bill poses the question of whether to amend an existing law or frame a new one. The former course gives the impression of a routine revision, but may involve complications by attempting to incorporate inconsistent provisions. The latter approach allows for a unity of purpose that may provoke greater opposition. This type of legislation also entails a choice between a limited and an indefinite authorization. The former has greater appeal for those who have doubts about its efficacy and welcome the opportunity to review its impact. The latter is favored by proponents to protect the law against political opponents who could cause it to expire through legislative inaction.

Another choice is that between an omnibus bill, each of whose parts might be a separate measure, or a less ambitious proposal. The advantages of the former are that it can accomplish a great deal if enacted and provides ample bargaining room to form the coalitions needed for passage. Its disadvantages are that it may generate bickering among interested parties and its scope may be perceived as too threatening to existing relationships. More modest bills may be drafted with greater ease and result in greater harmony among their advocates. However, they may also be more difficult to modify satisfactorily if opposition develops or may be viewed as too narrow to justify priority or support.

A significant factor associated with introduction is the choice of a chief sponsor. The selection involves either a request submitted to a member of Congress by an external entity or a consensus based on a legislator's participation in the formulation and advocacy of a proposal. The rules of both houses permit an unlimited number of members to cosponsor bills. Introduction or cosponsorship by a member of the majority party leadership or a committee or subcommittee chairman normally ensures that a measure will at least receive a hearing. Multiple sponsorship, which serves notice of bipartisan or majority support, can encourage committee action on a bill should its chairman not be among its original sponsors. Cosponsorship is also an early means of attracting legislative attention and building political momentum.

The standing rules of each house specify the subjects under the jurisdiction of each committee. Based on these formal guidelines, supplemented by compiled precedents and prior legislation, the large majority of all introduced bills are referred to a single panel and subject to its exclusive judgment. Most bills are drafted so as to ensure their referral to the committee most likely to proceed favorably. Discretion for referral by the presiding officer is greatest when measures cover subjects or propose programs that have not developed any legislative history. This may be due to social innovation or familiar issues that are being redefined.

Major legislative proposals frequently overlap the jurisdiction of two or more committees. The jurisdictional boundaries of the committee system cannot be drawn so as to prevent authority for broad or new areas of knowledge and policy from being at least partially subdivided. To cope with competition between panels and the scope of some bills, each chamber uses the device of multiple referral. This procedure simply recognizes the fact that it is neither politically nor objectively possible to isolate many public issues within the purview of a single committee or to address them as if they were insulated matters.

Three forms of multiple referral are identical in each house. Joint referral to two or more committees involves simultaneous panel consideration. Sequential referral entails consecutive action by designated committees. Split referral denotes which subdivisions of a measure are to be examined by which panels.

Each of these options may stipulate a time limit within which each or all committees must complete action. Multiple referral may reduce or increase friction among committees and may assist or hinder the legislative process. The increased participation and input it fosters does not and cannot guarantee agreement or action.

Two key points at this stage concern anticipated pace and drive. One aspect of legislative strategy involves the question of whether to act at the outset of Congress to maximize the time available for passage or wait until an election year when partisan competition plays a larger role. While the former course provides antagonists with more time to organize opposition, the latter offers the opportunity for adversaries to employ dilatory tactics as adjournment approaches. Another facet of parliamentary planning is whether to seek introduction and action in both houses simultaneously to demonstrate broad support or concentrate on one chamber and use its approval as leverage for passage in the other. If both houses are prepared to proceed, it is considered expedient to launch the campaign for enactment in the chamber that will pass a stronger bill. Paradoxically, the body more inclined to act may be reluctant to do so if it perceives that its efforts will be nullified through inaction by the other.

The elements of initial action comprise a relatively controllable process. There is little need to appeal or protest adverse decisions since matters are mainly in the hands of policy proponents. The political discussion and calculation that characterize this stage overshadow its formal features. It is during this phase of proceedings that advocates expand and refine an educational campaign within and outside Congress. A basic aspect of the internal legislative effort is to identify natural allies, known opponents, and undecided members. In this context, to educate is to activate allies, neutralize opponents, and gain the support of those without a clear position. Another aspect of this enterprise is to notify all key legislators sufficiently in advance so as not to gratuitously alienate those whose status or judgment can be crucial.

COMMITTEE CONSIDERATION

From an overall standpoint the committee system represents a division of labor by major governmental function that relies on specialized competence to evaluate policy proposals as a prelude to informed legislative decisions. A standing committee is a panel of legislators created and elected by its parent body for an indefinite period and authorized to submit recommendations on those subjects over which it is assigned jurisdiction. In a formal sense, committees serve merely as subsidiaries of the House and Senate and provide assistance as needed. However, to perform as congressional counselors demands much more than routine or ministerial action.

Considerable discretion is required to determine whether, when, or how to deal with any given political situation. That such action demands acute and prudent political judgment is a fact recognized by the responsibilities that committees have assumed with the informal approval of their corporate creators. Each chamber consciously, if not formally, grants virtually complete autonomy to its committees and exercises only sporadic surveillance over them. As long as committee activities and objectives are consistent with widespread legislative expectations and inclinations, their performance will not be closely supervised or their decisions significantly revised by the parent chamber.

Committees serve as the eyes and ears as well as the agents and advisers of Congress. The former role requires receptivity and sensitivity, while the latter demands prudence and coherence. Though the standards for panel input and output necessarily differ and may cause some political tension, they tend to contribute to a more balanced and plausible result. By serving as stable political channels for national concerns and as legislative testing grounds for proposed policies, committees help to relieve pressures and solve problems.

Committees are the crucibles of survival for bills, where most succumb to neglect. While the ability of committees to delay, modify, or kill bills is formidable, their commanding position is not due solely to obstructive powers. Many reasons other than panel neglect can thwart legislation, but the committee imprimatur is essential, if not indispensable, for its passage. At the outset of proceedings committee organization facilitates access to policymakers by concerned citizens, while the outcome is subject to chamber reconsideration of proposals that may be unresponsive to some interests. It is usually within the confines of a committee that the concessions and compromises that precede the formation of a majority coalition must be designed or endorsed.

The factors most responsible for committee prominence are access, expertise, workload, and negotiation. Citizens, regardless of their political status, require a visible and official entity to which their views and demands can be conveniently communicated. The scope and complexity of contemporary issues require subject matter specialists to master their substance. The large volume of business that confronts each Congress means that someone must decide which matters will receive attention. A forum is needed to facilitate bargaining and compromise among constituency, functional, party, and ideological interests. Committees are the only agents capable of meeting all the needs suggested by these conditions. They do so by endeavoring to coordinate the key functions or roles that contribute to political accomplishment.

Composed of officials elected by legally defined constituencies and possessed of responsibilities for given subjects, committees necessarily serve a representative function. All panels have a capacity and propensity to respond to certain political interests and to acknowledge the validity of their claims. Legislators seek membership on particular panels because of their political preferences or objectives. Membership confers a status that enables legislators to establish or improve relations with other individuals or groups by serving as an attentive and sympathetic audience. The opportunity for and willingness of citizens and officials to state their case before a committee indicates the vitality of its representative role.

As repositories of policy history and sources of legislative expertise, committees underpin the institutional memory of Congress. They perform an intelligence function that includes the acquisition, evaluation, and dissemination of information and data. Only panel members and staff have the time to thoroughly familiarize themselves with the substantive aspects and political implications of those matters under their jurisdiction. Whether a committee is serving as an information bank or broker or analyzing and verifying data, its responsibilities should be discharged so as to frame an issue in a manner that maximizes the credit for and minimizes the risk of legislative approval. The reputation and influence of a panel depends on the level of confidence inspired as it informs the opinion and guides the action of its parent body.

Committees use their political and informational resources to recognize or engender opportunities for legislative action. Should the advantages of or necessity for legislation become apparent, panels must formulate legislative strategy. This planning function begins with the formation of a committee agenda and estimation of legislative timetables. Because the political climate rarely remains static for any period of time, plans must be continually revised to meet contingencies. Committee skill in operating as a congressional gatekeeper, which involves systematic preparation and shrewd timing, covers the questions of whether or when to proceed, at what pace, and under what conditions.

Having devised a plan, a committee should be prepared to implement it. The exchange and distribution of information that accompanies this undertaking is the basis of an advocacy function. This involves more than simply conducting a publicity campaign and submitting recommendations to its parent body. It includes the coordination of activities, mobilization of support, and negotiation of agreements in pursuit of policy consensus. It is a responsibility of committees to monitor and mold legislative language and to facilitate and maintain legislative majorities. As conduits between the polity and parent chamber, committees are in a strategic position to influence the form and flow of information and, thus, the political and practical viability of policy responses.

Though committee functions have been discussed separately, they actually overlap and reinforce each other. Because the activities involved in all of them proceed simultaneously, a weakness in any one area can seriously affect overall performance. Two elements that are common to all committee operations relate to resource management and member satisfaction. A natural resource is the time and talent of its members and staff, while an acquired resource is substantive and political information. The manner in which both are employed and expended determines a panel's legislative effectiveness. The importance of its proceedings and acceptance of its pronouncements is due to the perception of committee views as an accurate political barometer. For individual legislators, panel membership affects the opportunity to attain such goals as reelection, chamber influence, policy enactment, or other elective or appointive office.

The scope and subject matter of a committee's jurisdiction is a source of both opportunities and limitations. It is a condition that determines whether a panel will find it desirable to initiate action or necessary to react to proposals originated elsewhere. Members may choose to focus on whether existing law is adequate or whether its enforcement warrants reconsideration. Jurisdiction is also a factor that foretells much about the number and strength of those interests with which a panel must contend. In this respect the committee must judge whether some matter under its purview has been preempted by another political entity. The degree of latitude and range of controversy associated with those issues within its sphere of influence governs the intensity of political conflict. Though jurisdiction may confer formal authority, the nature of a committee's policy environment is shaped by power relationships.

One of the keys to understanding committee behavior is the nature of panel constituencies. The entities with which a committee most frequently and earnestly interacts reveal much about its political status. Panels with jurisdiction over foreign and fiscal policies and federal agency operations maintain comparatively extensive communications with officials in the executive branch. Those responsible for questions that tend to generate intense partisan conflict, directly affect certain geographical areas, or concern chamber operations receive the most attention from congressional colleagues. Committees whose purview covers volatile or intractable social and economic issues are the target of numerous and diverse demands from the general public and organized interests. These three broad jurisdictional categories are not mutually exclusive.

The character of a committee's orientation is based on the traditional goals sought by its members. Some panels are mainly concerned with societal problems and statutory solutions. They endeavor to enact sound policy grounded on substantive assumptions and intentions. Other committees are more inclined to identify with the needs and desires of constituents. They serve certain groups based on panel member loyalties or aspirations. Still other committees are responsible for the performance and status of Congress as an independent branch of government. They address institutional developments and operations from the perspective of legislative integrity and influence. Yet other panels are preoccupied with party prospects and electoral results. They pursue partisan gain by attempting to manipulate political conditions or exploit policy contingencies. Action by any committee usually reflects at least two of these general orientations.

Panel workload may be described in terms of volume or salience. Though the range of responsibilities assigned to a committee may remain stable over time, emerging social trends or evident political conflict can significantly affect the quantity and quality of its business. The level of contentiousness and intensity of demands that stem from certain jurisdictions render some committees and subjects less manageable than others. The heterogeneity and competitiveness of a panel's policy environment serve as both a sanction for and hindrance on the role its members may wish or be able to play.

Another key to the legislative influence of each panel centers on the capacity to function cohesively. The two major factors in this respect are committee-subcommittee and majority-minority relations, with the former reflecting the degree of harmony among majority party members. The responsibilities assigned to subcommittees and responsiveness to minority-member sentiment determine how expeditious and effective committee action can be. The level of political friction indicates how thoroughly committee recommendations will be reviewed by its parent body and whose support needs to be cultivated. A panel's eminence and performance affect the perception and reception of its proposals and the methods and resources that will be employed as legislative strategy is devised and refined.

Since committee unity is such an important factor in its success, intrapanel bargaining over legislative language is common. Though a chairman may have the votes to adopt or defeat amendments, uncertainty may exist as to whether panel action can be sustained at future stages. Members search for amendments that can enhance the appeal of a bill without sacrificing committee goals. They must also estimate the most propitious time to compromise, since excessive haste may result in undesirable concessions, while extended delay may allow positions to become too hardened to modify.

If efforts to integrate political and substantive information have not been initiated earlier, then such an undertaking begins or continues in committee. A panel decision to commence action indicates that proponents have successfully used their opportunity for access. The bargaining that characterizes this stage shapes member estimates of legislative receptivity. At the same time, committee debate is intended to generate support, induce acquiescence, or otherwise permit action to proceed. While panel members can regulate the flow of information into and out of their domain, the timetables they set are always subject to pressures or events beyond their control. The relative flexibility of committee procedure enables members to identify the questions that they consider worthy of attention and to readily incorporate new information or adapt to changing conditions in the course of framing specific and convincing recommendations. An adverse decision can be appealed to the full committee, the full chamber, or another standing committee in the same or other house.

In the aggregate, committees dominate the regular decisionmaking process in Congress. One major reason for their power is due to legislative expertise, which combines subject-matter specialization with prudent political judgment. Another reason is the formation of stable relationships, both informational and political, with entities inside and outside the legislative branch. The legislative environment, which places a high value on reciprocity and deference, encourages panels to exploit the resources available to them so as to foster conditions for favorable and creditable congressional action.

FLOOR SCHEDULES

One of the crucial features of any legislative body is the manner in which its daily agenda is formed. Because proposals not cleared for floor action are deferred or discarded, control over the flow of chamber business confers a power to arrest or sustain legislative progress. Each house of Congress has the constitutional authority to decide for itself which issues it will consider, in what form, and when. Legislators generally agree that there are some matters on which they must act for legal or procedural reasons and others on which they should act for policy or political reasons. Responsibility for decisions that frame the legislative schedule can be just as controversial and demanding as those that shape the text of bills.

The scheduling function is mainly composed of calendar transactions that cover designated classes of bills and negotiated compacts that apply to single measures. Though both methods are governed by procedural requirements and political expedients, the former emphasizes formal rules and serves to expedite routine legislation that enjoys extensive support or evokes negligible opposition. The latter involves intensive congressional negotiation over critical bills that must be passed despite vehement resistance or major proposals whose controversial nature produce more than the usual political conflict and legislative uncertainty.

House rules grant privileged status to certain measures deemed essential to congressional operations and the fulfillment of its constitutional obligations. The authority for managing its agenda is lodged in the Speaker and his colleagues in the majority leadership. Their prerogative to schedule floor business is reinforced by a majority of the Rules Committee that is usually responsive to leadership interests, a body of rules that limits debate and facilitates majority rule, and precedents that give the presiding officer considerable control over the recognition of members during floor proceedings. These conditions enable party leaders to establish an agenda that will be observed by all members, though disapproved by some.

House calendars, special orders from the Rules Committee, and classes of privileged business are intended to increase the efficiency of chamber decision-making. The last category covers measures deemed sufficiently important to warrant access to the floor simply by virtue of their being reported from committee. By reducing the amount of floor time consumed by minor legislation, these devices lengthen and structure the time available for major bills. Rather than each member being asked to render a political judgment on every measure, House rules and customs establish a hierarchy of positions that enable their incumbents to make reasonable choices after careful consideration of relevant factors. While this course may exclude the views of some interested legislators it also serves to relieve those who are politically indifferent or reluctant from grappling with thorny problems. Though these practices are logical when viewed against an immense workload and large membership, any approach to decision-making questions of a political nature yields results that are not neutral in their effect.

The floor agenda of the House is governed by the application of standing rules and the adoption of special rules. Through these two options a prospective agenda is formed from the potential agenda of bills that have been reported from committee and placed on either the Union Calendar or House Calendar. Though standing and special rules may entitle certain bills to receive chamber attention, they do not determine the order in which they will be considered. The conversion of an agenda of privileged measures and other matters into a daily and weekly schedule for the order of business is a responsibility of the majority party leadership. Because various kinds of business are or become privileged, the Speaker enjoys wide discretion as to whom to recognize for the purpose of offering a motion to proceed to the consideration of a given proposal.

Every measure that cannot be considered in the House by unanimous consent must become privileged business to reach the floor. Each special rule reported by the Rules Committee recommends that the House consider a measure on the floor out of its regular calendar order. Special rules accord privileged status to measures so that the formal order of business may be interrupted for bills that merit, but are not formally entitled to receive, chamber priority. The powers of the Rules Committee are both procedural and political. Procedurally, the panel determines which nonprivileged bills will reach the floor and what amendments may be proposed to them. The first decision affects the general issues on which the House acts, the second affects the range of choice available for addressing them. Politically, the panel's recommendations reflect majority party interests and inclinations and serve to strengthen the party's continuing control over essential chamber operations.

The Senate delegates the right to frame its floor agenda to the majority leader. He proposes what he believes he can persuade other members to accept. His colleagues expect prior notification of his intentions and his attentiveness to their preferences. The discretion enjoyed by the majority leader to schedule legislation depends on his inclination to seek and take account of the views and needs of interested senators. His success as a legislative manager is directly related to the level of confidence the members have in his professional ability and personal character.

Since the majority leader attempts to make the most productive use of available floor time, he is hesitant to schedule business without some reasonable assurance that the Senate will reach a vote on final passage. Thus, the overwhelming majority of measures advance to the chamber floor via unanimous consent. This is because the tangible resources of the majority leader are limited and the formal procedures of the Senate are ineffectual. To function satisfactorily, the Senate must circumvent its written rules and resort to transactions that require the explicit or implicit concurrence of every senator. If individual preferences are not accommodated by informal cooperation, they will be pursued by taking advantage of formal procedures.

To expedite or ensure chamber action on essential matters, the Senate uses several unique devices. The unanimous consent agreement, which is a counterpart to the special order in the House, is negotiated informally among all interested senators and then approved on the floor by unanimous consent. Though not as detailed as a special order, it provides all members who so desire the opportunity to express themselves within reasonable time limits. The Senate has developed a track system that permits different bills to be considered concurrently by specifying certain periods during which each will receive attention on a given day. Thus, if one is making little or no progress owing to intentional delay, action on other important measures may proceed on a different "track." Another way for the majority leader to manage the daily agenda is to recess rather than adjourn at the end of a calendar day. The continuation of a legislative day, which extends from the time of an adjournment until the Senate next adjourns, by a series of recesses, avoids an interruption in the consideration of business that would be required by the beginning of a new legislative day.

The written rules of the Senate, which permit unlimited debate, assure the opportunity for indefinite delay. This possibility is sufficient to influence the formation of its agenda. The anticipation of extended debate affects scheduling decisions in two ways. First, it discourages the majority leader and the Senate from attempting to consider bills to which some members strongly object. Second, it encourages negotiations over substantive changes in bills to meet such objections. Thus, for all but indispensable legislation, simply the threat of a filibuster can prompt bill proponents to agree to changes that will enable it to be scheduled and debated without the risk of confronting a filibuster.

The same political factors condition the negotiations that produce both special orders and unanimous consent agreements. Both are a means of arranging for the timely and orderly disposition of important business. The more formal and centralized approach of the House is due to its being more than four times larger than the Senate. The more adaptable and inclusive process followed in the Senate also denotes the fact that party leaders cannot easily enforce contested decisions and are vulnerable to member defiance should they try to do so. The size of the House contributes to a more structured operation and also requires a more detailed body of rules to govern its proceedings. Though Senate rules are less elaborate, they also tend to be more awkward, which encourages members to rely more on mutual cooperation to conduct business. The result is that special orders and unanimous consent agreements are necessary to supplant or supplement chamber rules.

The floor agenda is a combination of the overall session workload and expedient daily schedules. It is shaped by a continual balancing of individual prerogatives, collective preferences, external pressures, political opportunities, institutional customs, and statutory requirements. The legislative performance of the Senate depends on the sensitivity of its leaders to the needs of members and the acquiescence of members to the needs of the institution. That of the House depends on fair play for the minority party and assignment of priority to chamber obligations and operations rather than individual-member or small-group predilections. While the Senate majority leader can only propose an agenda, House leaders, supported by a majority party, may impose one. Though the Senate scheduling process is more flexible and open than that of the House, it is also more lengthy and fragile.

It is at this stage that cooperation between party and committee leaders is most important. While committees can delay or inter bills and party leaders strive to form chamber majorities or encourage the use of procedures to overcome disagreement between the chamber and a panel, the resulting friction is recognized as inimical to legislative performance by all concerned. The questions of timing, method, and sequence that inhere in the scheduling process offer many grounds on which to conduct negotiations and conclude agreements. It is more important that all key legislators be consulted at this stage than that they completely approve of the results. Demonstrated regard for status, views, and aims tends to avert the resort to obstructive tactics.

The apparent abdication of responsibility by each chamber to its committees is conditional rather than categorical. The legislative process requires continual interaction between party and committee leaders for satisfactory results. Committee members rely on party leaders for desirable procedures and timing in regard to scheduling legislation for chamber action. Party leaders also serve as communication links between committee members and other legislators, particularly as to the views and voting intentions of the latter, and how such opinion might affect the decisions of the former. The party leadership depends on panel leaders for the approval and substance of legislation, the timetable needed to report it, and the transmittal of party and chamber preferences to committee members. The subject expertise of committee leaders must be coordinated with the strategic information of party leaders to yield favorable legislative action.

Their position at the center of each chamber's communication network is one of the key factors that enables party leaders to exercise a controlling hand in scheduling bills for floor action. Though the number of crucial choices at this stage is relatively limited, their impact is of much consequence. This is because bargaining cuts across several issues and involves commitments based on estimates of committee proceedings that entail eventual allocation of floor time. Workload management covers questions of political priorities and chamber accomplishment and the results are one of the principal criteria for judging party responsibility. The relatively larger role of partisan and limited role of procedural considerations that regulate the flow of business to the floor contribute to the fact that this stage tends to be less publicly visible than others.

CHAMBER CONSIDERATION

The nature of debate significantly differs in the House and Senate. The factor most responsible for the difference in floor environments is chamber size. The comparatively large membership of the House demands more formal and less flexible procedures and fosters reliance on more forceful leadership and hierarchical organization to conduct its business. The relatively small number of senators contributes to the use of less formal and more flexible procedures and results in a more collegial approach to the management of its workload. The principal means employed to govern legislative debate is the control of time. The larger membership of the House has led it to allocate time in equal amounts to proponents and opponents under rules and practices that impose or permit numerous limitations. The smaller size of the Senate has induced it to grant an unfettered opportunity, despite possible abuse, for members to convince or challenge their colleagues.

Floor debate is conditioned by different, but complementary, values in each body. The paramount operational factor in the House is majority rule, while in the Senate it is minority rights. The relatively expeditious nature of House proceedings means that deliberations are usually confined to one bill at a time and its consideration infrequently extends beyond a single day. This action reflects the discipline of stronger party organization as decisions are rendered by a preponderance of numbers. The more adaptable nature of Senate proceedings means that business may alternate from one bill to another and consideration of a measure may extend over days or weeks even without a filibuster. The contingency of unlimited debate encourages its deliberations to emphasize freedom of individual and political expression while its verdicts are reached through a consensus of opinion. The chief consequence of this difference in parliamentary styles is that major committee recommendations are always subject to a more thorough review in the deliberation-oriented Senate than in the decision-oriented House.

The ideal functions of floor debate are to inform and persuade. However, for a bill to reach the stage of chamber action means that most legislators have already passed judgment on it. The opportunity to enlighten and advocate refers to member comments intended to satisfy or influence nonmembers. That a majority may terminate debate in the House whenever it is so inclined, and a minority may prolong debate in the Senate for an extended period, has an unmistakable impact on the strategies available in each chamber to obtain ample time to state one's case. The most significant result of the fact that the House is governed by majority rule and the Senate sanctions minority rights is that legislation becomes the product of complementary modes of parliamentary action.

The key feature of House debate is that it is restricted. Either a standing or a special rule provides for the allocation of a specific amount of time for the consideration of a bill, while parliamentary motions may be adopted that limit debate even further. Extensive deliberations are subordinated to decisions of the majority. Limited debate encourages members to be pointed and prompt in their remarks, since amendments and other motions are brought before the chamber relatively quickly for disposition. The principal consequence of these time limitations is to enhance the influence of standing committees.

The basic form of virtually all legislation is shaped in committee and the burden of proof is on those who would modify the panel's product. Proponents of major amendments in House debate are always at a disadvantage because the conviction exists that a bill ought to be carefully framed in committee and not inexpertly written on the floor. The comparatively large size of House committees and the policy specialization of their members fosters the expectation that the key deliberations on a measure should occur prior to floor action. Because the rules reinforce this view, it is extremely difficult to successfully challenge a committee on the floor.

The result is that panel recommendations tend to be routinely ratified by the parent body and it is seldom that debate results in more than marginal changes in a reported bill. Since it is not feasible to employ the practice of individual consultation as in the Senate, decisions about scheduling and debate are mady by party and committee leaders independent of individual member preferences. The strongly expressed views of large groups of members, though, will be taken into account. The combination of committee influence and impersonal arrangements contributes to debate that largely consists of prepared speeches aimed mainly at external audiences.

In the Senate, floor action is viewed as an extension of committee consideration rather than a new and different decisionmaking arena. As members of a smaller body, senators have larger and more diverse constituencies to represent and more committee assignments with correspondingly less time to specialize than House members. Because senators have less time to devote to bills prior to chamber consideration, a greater number of controversial matters have to await resolution until they are debated on the floor. Minimal restrictions on debate encourage senators to explore all implications of a measure. These conditions foster the coordination of policy through discussion between committee and non-committee members and serve to harmonize the recommendations of committees with overlapping jurisdiction.

Most Senate business is transacted under some form of unanimous consent and a senator need not be recognized to object to a request for such consent. Objections are quite rare because they would upset a schedule carefully planned by party leaders and a motion to undertake the same matter is likely to be approved. However, a single member is in a position to bring business to a virtual standstill for short periods of time, while a group can frustrate action indefinitely. The possibility of such an occurrence prompts party leaders to assure members that every effort will be made to accommodate their scheduling and political needs. The combination of greater demands on the time of senators and the opportunity to affect floor action means that the Senate functions as a more collegial body than does the House.

Senate committee members are more willing to share their influence with colleagues who are not members of the panel that reported a bill. Mutual recognition by senators of the needs and prerogatives of other members is reflected in the political bargaining and policy decisions that can occur during the amending process. It is most vividly demonstrated by the privilege of senators to modify their own amendments without chamber approval, either by personally revising it or accepting language proposed by a colleague. Because all members have the opportunity to express their views on the floor and to have them considered, Senate debate is more likely than its House counterpart to produce a genuine exchange of ideas, with the result that committee proposals are always subject to extensive review.

The most conspicuous difference between the chambers at this stage concerns the decision to close debate. The three methods available in the House are special orders, motions for the previous question, and unanimous consent. The first two are provided for by the rules and are the procedures most commonly employed. In the Senate deliberations conclude when discussion expires of its own accord, through a unanimous consent agreement or a motion to invoke cloture. The first two courses, though beyond the reach of Senate rules, are the means on which it regularly relies. Other than stipulations contained in a unanimous consent agreement, there are no methods in the Senate for bringing deliberations to a close or arranging for a timely vote.

Committee expertise is a factor that looms large in chamber consideration of legislation. Not only are panel members thoroughly familiar with the subject matter, but their anticipation of floor action prompts them to sample the views of other legislators and prepare reasoned explanations imbued with cogent political appeal. If a committee recommendation is unanimous, such a fact will further incline nonmembers to accept or defer to it. Some committees are better able or more willing to reach agreements that accurately reflect the balance of political forces in the full chamber. The increased legislative participation that characterizes floor action, while it may not involve the articulation of unexpected views, may result in familiar interests that appear in unexpected proportions. Though chamber proceedings may confront a committee with a challenge it neither contemplated nor adequately prepared for, on the whole its proposals tend to be ratified essentially as reported.

Because the reciprocity norm in the House is most apparent in the respect that all members accord to the expertise of legislators who serve on other committees, obstructive action must focus on panel proceedings; for once a bill reaches the floor preventing passage becomes very difficult. Obstruction in the Senate can be accomplished more easily on the floor through objections to unanimous consent requests, filibusters, or innumerable amendments. Reciprocity in the Senate is more a matter of mutual deference to individual legislators and is most visible in regard to members who wish to advocate original or unpopular views or share in the exercise of decisionmaking influence. House practices subordinate, while those of the Senate elevate, the influence of individual members as a means to enhance chamber effectiveness.

Party and committee leaders predominate during the stage of floor consideration. While chamber discretion is ostensibly unlimited, in reality the limited time and information of most members incline them to defer to committee recommendations. Debate is aimed at attentive publics in an effort to justify contemplated legislative action. Access to proceedings by non-committee members is relatively open in the Senate and confined in the House. The length of the amending process indicates the degree of satisfaction with the results of earlier access. As the most visible stage of action these proceedings are also subject to the most procedural requirements. Such restraints are necessary to maintain order in the face of potential participation and intense opposition. They also enable legislators to finesse their way to a preferred conclusion and sidestep difficult choices. A chamber decision denotes an initial compromise among those who were entitled to and gained adequate access. Dissatisfaction with the outcome of floor action must be appealed to the other body.

BICAMERAL RELATIONS

Each house of Congress prefers to act independently of the other whenever possible. This course enables each chamber to assert its constitutional prerogatives and pursue desired political objectives. Though rendered permanently interdependent by their shared legislative powers, in many ways the House and Senate are conspicuously different bodies. Representatives and senators are accountable to different constituencies at different intervals. Inherent differences in their composition and orientation generate differences in chamber organization and parliamentary style.

The bicameral structure of Congress is one of the many checks and balances that characterize the U.S. constitutional system. The formal aspects of bicameralism relate to the size of constituencies, number of members, and length of terms. These differences between the Senate and House ensure that the political views and values that pervade each body will often diverge. As a result, political interests will experience different degrees of access and acceptance in each chamber, and those dissatisfied with the results in one body will appeal to and seek a more favorable response from the other.

Another difference of considerable consequence concerns the nature of decisionmaking in each house as reflected in different procedures and perspectives. Among the more prominent features that distinguish the two chambers in this respect are the dissimilar number and jurisdictions of their committees. When constitutional and organizational differences are combined with contrasting policy propensities and priorities, each chamber will pass its own version of a bill. That each house commonly includes certain provisions mainly for the purpose of bargaining with the other is a clear manifestation of the bicameral temper.

Since each body can regularly anticipate political differences with the other, both have procedures or follow practices that are intended to mitigate disagreement before and facilitate agreement after the stage of bicameral negotiations is reached. The manner in which each chamber may deal with bills passed by and received from the other is one of the two basic elements from which bicameral strategies are forged. The other concerns the question of whether to initiate action in both houses simultaneously or to arrange for one chamber to defer action until the other has passed a bill. This choice involves an estimate of which route will produce a more positive result in the sense that each body is inclined to respond to the legislative decisions of the other so as to preserve institutional comity.

Relations between the houses manifest the same features of cooperation, competition, and conflict that characterize relations between the legislative and executive branches. The nature of institutional differences between the chambers may be magnified by differences in policy preferences or partisan control. The absence of any central coordinating authority also contributes to the potential for bicameral friction. The basic issue is the relative autonomy of each body. However, collaboration is clearly necessitated by the constitutional requirement that both chambers must pass the same measure in identical form before it can become law.

As the Senate and House forge their respective legislative agenda, liaison between them tends to be informal and flexible. The process is shaped by such factors as the relations among party leaders of both houses, the significance of proposed legislation, partisan political calculations, and time constraints. Without a formal mechanism to coordinate legislative affairs, bicameral relations take the form of fairly regular interchanges and consultations. Interhouse communications between party and committee leaders and their staffs is usually confined to particular and pending proposals rather than general or extensive plans.

Bicameral cooperation is facilitated by the fact that a substantial proportion of the annual legislative agenda is recurrent and predictable. Concerted action in regard to other matters is guided more by political than institutional conditions as adjournment approaches and choices must be made among the measures to be considered in the remaining available time. Several external factors contribute to chamber cooperation despite the lack of systematic internal coordination. Among the more prominent ones are economic exigencies, international events, media investigations, and presidential initiative.

The conference committee is a practical and effective device for eliciting agreement when each house confronts the prospect of a bargained settlement or an unwelcome deadlock. It permits free discussion and negotiation in a relatively informal environment, in contrast with formal floor action by one body on the bill or amendments of the other. Positions can be explored, options digested, and trade-offs proposed without foreclosing any possible compromises or being compelled to make public and irrevocable commitments. A successful conference yields a comprehensive legislative agreement supported by a politically congenial rationale. Its report is a single package with a legislatively balanced appeal.

It is common for conferees of one house to try to persuade those of the other that their chamber is more strongly committed to a provision and should be allowed to prevail. This is often the reason why floor managers desire a recorded vote during floor action on amendments of little controversy. If a recorded vote was not taken in regard to a matter on which one side is adamant, its members may express a willingness to return to their house to seek a vote that will uphold their viewpoint. The voluntary limitation of discretion represented by a recorded vote serves to reduce the range of alternatives that conferees might otherwise be disposed or obliged to consider. Thus, the sacrifice of flexibility can, on occasion, be a bargaining advantage rather than a weakness.

From an overall perspective, conference negotiations might be viewed as a vehicle used by each side to convey the impression that its options are limited. To succeed in such an effort would leave the other side with the choice between a relatively unfavorable settlement or none because of impending adjournment or expiration of a law. The emphasis on recorded votes, eventuality of soliciting instructions, and evidence of prior public commitment are all means of demonstrating that concessions are incompatible with chamber expectations. There also remains the possibility that one side will threaten to expand the bargaining arena by appealing to or advising those formally excluded from conference negotiations. Tenacity and resistance are ways of altering the perceptions of competitors and maintaining one side's integrity that may affect matters other than those under immediate consideration.

Though conference committees are technically constituted to consider a single bill, the membership of House and Senate delegations tends to be fairly stable over a given period of time in regard to measures covering similar subjects. The familiarity of conferees with each other and the issue occasionally enables an accord to be reached before a conference formally convenes, in which case it simply ratifies the agreement. When conferees serve or expect to serve on two or more conference committees, either simultaneously or consecutively, with considerable overlap among members of both delegations, they may negotiate and reach understandings that apply to all the bills for which they are responsible. Should one conference report result in language that is closer to one chamber's version of a bill, another can be written to more closely correspond to the terms embodied in the other's version. The anticipation or existence of multiple measures in conference on related matters increases the scope of bargaining and the prospects for agreement.

The political climate of bicameral relations is also conducive to mutual cooperation and chamber ratification of the results. Since the first house to consider a bill usually invests more time and effort, it is prepared to accept some changes adopted by the second rather than lose the measure through an inability to reach agreement. Amendments approved by the second chamber reflect further refinement based on the views of those disturbed by the legislation as it passed its body of origin. The additional allies secured by such changes, assuming that other support is not alienated, also induces the first house to be receptive. When a bill is about to become law, both houses wish to be in a position to claim their share of the credit for its enactment.

Legislators responsible for reconciling bicameral differences are in a position to exercise somewhat greater control over access to their proceedings than is possible at earlier stages of action. One reason is the tempo of congressional action, which means that time is usually in short supply. Another is that though formal action is conducted in public, it is ordinarily not scheduled until informal agreement has been reached. If political momentum carries a bill this far, the incentive to conclude a matter, even if only provisionally, is sufficient to produce a settlement. Conference reports embody the ultimate congressional compromise and, despite their occasionally difficult format, exemplify the essence of the legislative process.

FINAL ACTION

Constitutional duties, statutory mandates, political competition, and policy conviction all combine to thrust a major role in legislative affairs upon the president. While it is obvious that the incumbent cannot personally keep track of the numerous measures that might reach his desk or are salient for his program, this task is the responsibility of political, legislative, and agency advisers. From a period preceding the introduction of a major bill they will have been active in regard to its substance and strategy as well as the factor of public perception. This last refers to attempts to sway attentive and general opinions in the direction of the administration perspective so as to make such views available to support the president's eventual decision.

At prior stages of the legislative process the president may have actively participated or have been preoccupied by other matters. If there is no longer any dispute over a bill by the time it reaches the White House or if the president's action is a foregone conclusion, there will be little attempt to influence him. If controversy has not subsided and doubt about his decision still exists, the White House now becomes the focal point of political argument. The president is rarely a passive register of the pressure and propaganda generated by others. He may encourage one or another group whose voice has been muffled to offer its views and test its support. Or he may prepare the groundwork for the course of action on which he plans to embark.

In the case of public bills, members of the White House staff or executive-branch appointees will have been monitoring congressional action and exchanging information with legislators and their staffs. Presidential influence in the form of a coherent policy and consistent strategy is usually the primary means of overcoming the decentralized nature of legislative decisionmaking. The entire process is conditioned, to some degree, by the known or presumed position of the president. In comparison with earlier parliamentary votes, the one cast by the president is reasonably clear and normally decisive in effect. To exercise effective leadership requires the White House occupant to balance expectations that meet political obligations and respect congressional prerogatives.

Though both Congress and the presidency represent national majorities, those groups to which each is more responsive are not necessarily those that elect the other or influence the exercise of its authority. The political interests most influential in the presidential selection process tend not to be the same ones responsible for the composition of a congressional majority. Furthermore, those to whom the president is sympathetic may not have established a working relationship with those members of Congress in a position to condition the exercise of legislative influence. Thus, neither institution can claim an inherent superiority in articulating the public interest. While the president represents the unity of communal aspirations better, Congress reflects more accurately the diversity of societal needs. Their complementary posture and coequal status means that each may justifiably compel the other to compromise.

Presidential relations with Congress are characterized by collaboration with certain groups of legislators, each of which subscribes to a traditional position on the efficacy of a given policy or strategy. The president realizes that legislative cooperation is necessary if he is to achieve other, and perhaps more important, purposes than those embodied in a bill he finds debatable, but not necessarily objectionable. While the political party forms the main bridge between the executive and legislative branches, it is not a homogeneous entity. Party identity enables elected officials to supplement their formal affiliation with those explicit and implicit transactions that comprise the legislative process. Of course, where party control of the White House differs from that of either or both houses of Congress, other bases of communication and accommodation need to be explored and established.

The president is in a position to form a more comprehensive view than any one member of Congress or group of legislators, with somewhat greater latitude to choose among competing interests. This provides the opportunity to assume leadership in promoting policies affecting a wide geographical or broad substantive area. Each president enters office with his own agenda. In the absence of compelling conditions he is understandably reluctant to condone or encourage the investment of legislative resources on matters that divert attention from his preferred objectives. The incumbent is free to use any combination of public statements, private conversations, legal prerogatives, political strategies, legislative tactics, and policy adjustments to advance his views.

Presidential discretion, however, is not unlimited. Its scope and course are subject to constraints that stem from previous commitments. These may take the form of pledges made prior or subsequent to his election, actions undertaken by his predecessors, agreements made by subordinates, or existing law. Thus, in a real sense the process of presidential decision begins long before a bill arrives at the White House. General approval or recommendation does not ensure that the president will sign any measure. To advocate or endorse legislation on a given subject or policy is not a commitment to accept whatever bill may be passed. Not until the last stage of the legislative process is completed can the actual language of a bill be known.

Where the president is not publicly or personally committed to support a bill, he is free to imply or state that a veto is possible if it is not framed to his satisfaction. Knowledge of the presidential position may result in legislation that includes provisions that he both approves and disapproves, with the former intended to carry the latter over the final hurdle to enactment. The president may feel obliged to accept a bill rather than risk the failure of Congress to pass more suitable legislation within a reasonable period of time. If the president deems certain legislation questionable, disapproves of only portions, or opposes enactment but realizes a veto will be overridden, he can allow a bill to become law without his signature. Congress may also pass legislation for which its members can claim credit despite a certain veto, just as a president may wield a veto that is certain to be overridden.

There is a presumption in favor of almost all bills that manage to reach the White House. In the large majority of cases political positions have hardened and policy objectives have crystallized. Many of the factors and forces that contribute to congressional passage operate on the presidency as well. The question becomes one of whether to sanction or challenge the purposes of those behind its passage. Those with superior access to the president enjoy an obvious advantage, since if opposed to a bill they need only gain the assent of a single person and, if in favor, need not depend on or persuade a congressional majority. For any given bill, the president may symbolize public opposition to legislative judgment, may have engineered the formation of a successful legislative coalition, or may have been subject to the same conditions that influenced House and Senate action.

The presidential veto is another means to prevent or postpone governmental action. Its rationale may be to preclude the enactment of imprudent or deficient legislation or to insist on the recognition and assimilation of a national perspective. The incumbent may threaten or exercise a veto for several reasons. He may consider a bill to be unconstitutional, an infringement of presidential prerogatives, or a pronouncement of unwise policy. The strength of the veto is its likelihood of success. The two-thirds majorities needed to override a veto in both houses of Congress almost always give the advantage to those who support the president. The weakness of the veto is its wholesale character. Its use indicates that all efforts at persuasion and negotiation have failed.

In its most technical and legal sense the veto is only a power to restrain. However, in the hands of a forceful incumbent, it may be used as a tool to guide and shape legislative action or as leverage for bargaining purposes. The frequency of its use is not a true index of its importance or influence. Its potential use is a constant factor in congressional deliberations. Legislative intentions generally reflect the disposition to forge bills that the president will be willing to sign. In some instances a president may agree to approve a bill he might otherwise veto based on a promise by congressional leaders that the legislation will be amended to meet his objections.

The veto is not merely an obstructive weapon in the legislative process, but may serve several constructive political purposes for the president. It may be used to occasionally remind legislators that the White House occupant cannot be taken for granted, to build support among or impose unity on executive branch policymakers, to reaffirm his commitments and protect or promote his constituencies, to publicize party or institutional differences on policy priorities, to launch or energize an appeal to the nation at large, or to enhance an image of leadership. Any of these reasons may outweigh the disadvantages incurred.

Excessive or imprudent use of the veto may strain relations between the president and Congress to a degree that inhibits cooperation on matters that would not ordinarily generate disagreement. It is a last resort whose effectiveness depends on its perceived potentialities.

Though the veto, as a constitutional device, applies equally to all legislation passed by Congress, in reality its use reveals definite variations. For some types of measures, the veto is ineffective. This occurs when congressional majorities are overwhelming or a bill is indispensable. For other legislation, the veto is final. Such instances cover measures passed by narrow margins or those with limited political appeal. For another class of bills the veto is politically or legislatively doubtful. In these cases sharp public controversy over an issue renders the eventual outcome uncertain. Every president has numerous allies in Congress, some of whom occupy key positions. Thus, the incumbent may actually exercise a veto or try to do so long before a bill reaches the White House. The use of the veto may be confined to controversial or deleterious bills, as defined by the institutional presidency, or exercised as part of an overall legislative strategy.

A vetoed bill is privileged business and an attempt to override may be made immediately or deferred to a specified day. The bill may also be held at the presiding officer's desk or referred to committee, with the timing of its consideration to be determined. To proceed immediately on a bill returned by the president means either that those who favor it have the votes to override or the lateness of the session does not permit action to be delayed. To defer consideration with the intent to schedule a vote indicates that legislators desire time to amass the extraordinary majority needed. Should a veto be sustained through either inaction or a vote, the bill may be quickly repassed minus the provisions that prompted presidential disapproval or some portions may be added as amendments to subsequent bills that are likely to become law.

Both the presidency and Congress are institutions occupied by policymakers who represent a national electorate. They are legally and politically entrusted with wide-ranging responsibilities and share, to some degree, a common party label. However, their differences, which significantly affect their scope of choice and policy priorities, ensure institutional competition. Those interests or perspectives neglected or rejected by one branch can usually obtain a hearing from the other. Continual interaction between the executive and legislature not only facilitates governmental action, but conserves political resources by reducing misperceptions and miscalculations. Though the level of institutional rivalry will vary, the presidency and Congress remain mutually dependent on each other to meet their common responsibilities. Figure 1 presents the key steps in the enactment of a law.

First Chamber

1. Bill introduced and referred to committee
2. Committee hearings planned and held
3. Committee mark-up scheduled and bill analyzed*
4. Committee report drafted and filed*
5. Bill referred to chamber calendar
6. Terms of floor consideration framed and approved*
7. Bill scheduled for chamber action
8. Bill debated and amended*
9. Final passage*
10. Bill transmitted to other house

Second Chamber

11. Committee and chamber consideration* (see steps 1-8)
12. Bill approved as received* (to step 22) or
13. Bill approved with amendments* or
14. Chamber substitutes its own bill*
15. Bill returned to body of origin

Bicameral Action

16. First chamber agrees to amendments* (to step 22) or
17. First chamber amends amendments and returns bill to second chamber* or
18. First chamber disagrees to amendments and requests a conference*
19. Conference negotiations and agreement
20. Conference report drafted and filed
21. Conference report debated and approved by each chamber*
22. Bill delivered to the White House

Subsequent Action

23. President signs or vetoes bill
24. Congress overrides or sustains veto*
25. Vetoed bill enacted in revised form*

---

*Indicates steps that may or usually involve roll-call votes.

Fig. 1. Key steps and decision points in the enactment of a law.

DOCUMENTATION

OVERVIEW

Legislative history comprehends three distinct but interrelated factors. First is the totality of actions taken regarding a particular policy proposal. This covers the evolution and ecology of public policy as manifested in the political dynamics of parliamentary consideration. Second is the collection of congressional publications that provide an account of formal decisions and explain their verbal elements. Such material suggests the manner in which relevant documents are affected by prior choices and how they affect later ones. Third is the interpretation and meaning of judgments and statements whose causes, content, form, and aims may differ. To construe the final terms of settlement and their implications signals a search for a credible version of legislative intent.

The authoritative explanations of statutory language that comprise legislative history may embrace general policy objectives, the conditions to be addressed or problems to be remedied, a range of possible responses, and authorization of particular resources. *Legislative intent* refers to the definition of specific words or the application of specific provisions. It concerns concrete cases and questions that arise in the course of policy implementation. The competitive nature of legislative proceedings produces differing views on what should be, can be, is being, and will be done. Standards for separating the substantive wheat from the political chaff are less than clear and convincing. The expression of legislative intent, which is a blend of the short-term purpose of passage and the long-term purpose of interpretation, is an exercise in the accretion and adaptation of language.

Legislative intent may be derived from the meaning of words, the relationship of words, the nature of the subject matter, the historical background of an issue, or some combination of these factors. Because the history of one provision may illuminate the meaning of others, it may be necessary to trace a particular purpose or interpretation as it evolves and emerges at the final stage of the legislative process. As the several stages through which a bill must pass to become law are interdependent, so are each of its major subdivisions. While the latter tends to be explicitly noted in the printed record, the former tends to be only implicitly addressed.

Even in the absence of political and technical complexity, limitations of language preclude that clarity of expression which would produce anything approaching unanimity on the meaning of all provisions of significant public laws. Bills require scrutiny in regard to existing law, technical provisions, floor amendments, and political implications. Their drafting is not simply a technical operation that demands legal skill, but is an integral part of the process of policy formulation. Compromise language may be inserted into the text of bills, into phrases that appear in accompanying documents, or in both. Drafting requires dexterity in the use of language to convey or, when necessary, obscure meaning. The textual cogency that denotes a formal report is often incompatible with the strategic harmony that sustains a proposed statute. An innate feature of the legislative process is that language considered politically astute is not always legally acute.

Legislative history per se consists of two types of publications. Primary sources are the official record and include committee reports, hearings, the *Congressional Record*, bills, and other documents issued or used by Congress, either house, or a committee. Secondary sources, which include government and non-government material, may digest, index, annotate, classify, or restate primary sources. Either source may identify reports by government agencies or private entities as well as judicial opinions from which statutory or supporting language was derived or adapted. Despite the value and utility of those publications that form a legislative history, several features of the legislative process affect quality and quantity in ways that increase the difficulty of compilation and application.

Though Congress is a permanent institution, its constitutional life span consists of separate two-year periods. While this segmentation simplifies the identification of action and output, it also introduces complications when legislative consideration extends beyond a single Congress. In addition to those publications issued during the Congress in which a bill is enacted into law, legislative history also includes relevant material generated during prior Congresses. Recourse to previous documentation may be necessary to disclose those factors that temporarily delayed passage and those that contributed to eventual enactment. Since most legislation amends existing statutes rather than creates entirely new policies, a similar search offers the surest clues to the reasons for such revisions.

Major measures are in a state of continual development as they advance toward enactment and their content is subject to change at each stage of consideration. The meaning of most provisions, or what is construed as such, must be derived from the entire process and cannot be assumed to be limited to a single document or phase of proceedings. The serial nature of congressional decisionmaking regularly generates rival views and uneven results. How much weight is to be accorded statements that originate at each stage or how to discern a clear corporate opinion are difficult questions.

In an ideal setting, statutory standards would cover the objectives to be achieved, the extent of administrative discretion, the criteria for making decisions, and the controls to be exercised. Furthermore, new policies would be coordinated and integrated with existing laws and relationships. However, consensus on public policy usually focuses on broad generalities rather than on details that can aggravate political differences of opinion. Modern legislation tends to generate general agreement on ends and disagreement on means. Political conditions conducive to passage of a major bill ensure that it will not be a model statute. Its language will be phrased in terms less than explicit and precise, if not deliberately ambiguous and vague, to maintain the support necessary for its enactment. A major statute is a collective articulation of shared interests that combines facts and values so as to promote its approval rather than clarify its provisions.

Statutory solutions represent the results of competition among numerous groups and goals. The ambiguous nature of legislative language signifies that political friction has been moderated or averted and enables entities with differing interests to work together harmoniously. Legislation embodying indefinite or flexible objectives is the means used by Congress to simultaneously satisfy its many constituencies. Should a bill be written in plain and clear terms, its content or sponsor would be more likely to invite attack than attract support.

Though equivocal expressions may ensure continuous debate, they provide the leeway for accommodation where all parties with a demonstrable stake in the outcome are afforded the opportunity to have their positions publicly recorded. A consequence of political bargaining is that different groups of legislators will support a given measure for different reasons. The inclusive or inconclusive nature of legislative terminology reflects the translation of negotiated compromises into acceptable provisions.

That the volume of the printed record may be large or small does not always indicate the actual importance of a measure. Where a majority is sure of its strength its members may not feel the need to offer a thorough explanation, while those in the minority may not wish to employ their resources in a futile effort. Of course, such conditions do not preclude either camp from engaging in an extensive discussion of a proposal for political or other purposes. It is where proponents and opponents are uncertain of the legislative outcome or of political consequences that the use of all available arguments and evidence about an issue ensures that the printed record will be most complete.

To secure passage of many bills, it is necessary to avoid alienating or antagonizing certain legislators. This has two notable consequences for the content of congressional publications. First, those parties that fail to have their views incorporated into a measure's legislative history at one stage may succeed at another. Such a development may occur despite or because of contrary statements that appear in earlier parts of the printed record. Second, words that do not appear in print may be as important as those that are included. This covers provisions rejected or deleted as well as matters consciously given the silent treatment.

A statute is a rule of uniformity or a statement by Congress of its judgment as to how far circumstances render uniformity possible. Vagueness or omission commonly leaves many questions about the scope and shape of policy unanswered. The implications of many statutory provisions are intentionally or unavoidably obscured by the nature of legislative decisionmaking. For these reasons the debate on purposes and meaning is not concluded, but merely reoriented, by the passage of legislation. The legislative cycle is an organic process with a tentative culmination rather than a definite termination.

There are several aspects to the significance of legislative history for public officials and private citizens. It enables individuals, with or without legal advice, to better understand the laws under which they live and the personal consequences of legislative enactments. It serves to guide federal executives as they endeavor to apply the law to specific situations or designated groups in the implementation of programs. It supplements the language of statutes to provide judges with explanations that facilitate the adjudication of cases under particular provisions. It furnishes material needed by scholars, journalists, lobbyists, and students to educate themselves or enlighten others about public policies and governmental decisionmaking.

From the standpoint of observers a statute may be viewed as an allocation of resources among certain groups, a legal mandate binding on some citizens, a statement of goals desired by the polity, or an opinion in the form of public policy. From the perspective of participants in the political process a statute may be judged somewhat differently. Legislators may deem it a compact or a settlement to be observed until modified; the president may consider it a tool or a means to better superintend public business; agency administrators may regard it as a license or an authorization to engage in certain activities; and affected publics may treat it as a law or a rule to be obeyed, exploited, evaded, or opposed.

A legislative history may be as brief as the single most authoritative document, as determined by a user, that applies to a given statute or as massive as every relevant word printed during the progress of a measure from bill to law. The scope of material included in a legislative history depends on its intended use. In regard to official purposes, legislative history is consulted when statutory language is susceptible of more than one interpretation or where primary sources offer inadequate guidance. Though helpful and welcome, legislative history is not a completely satisfactory alternative to clear statutory language. While there will always exist some question about the degree of discretion consistent with certain legal phraseology, it always carries more weight than that of extrinsic aids.

Congress is an arena in which politics and law meet and merge to form public policy. Legislative success depends on factors of policy, procedure, politics, and personality. Official printed sources only address the first of these. Efforts that concern enactment cover a variety of strategies, agreements, motivations, and explanations. Pertinent legislative documents only address the last of these. Policymaking is not the sole preserve of legislators, and their inclination to act need not be expressed through the passage of a law. To what extent and at what point along a policy continuum Congress becomes involved are equally important for estimating legislative influence. For researchers, the prime drawback of the legislative process is that Congress is rarely able to speak with a single and clear voice. The great advantage is the accessibility of published material owing to the open and inclusive nature of its decisionmaking process. Despite their value, there is more to the policy process than can be gleaned from congressional publications alone.

ORIGINS THROUGH REFERRAL

1. Committee Prints. Though these publications vary widely in content, for the purposes of this survey the most important type are monographic studies on current issues or legislative proposals. While they are authorized by and prepared for the use of a given committee, they may or may not have the approval of panel members in regard to their orientation or interpretation. Prints may be written by committee staff, congressional support agency specialists, or private consultants. They provide background information on events and topics that fall within committee responsibilities and that will or have become the focus of legislative attention. This research is not always related to contemplated legislation, but many prints are intended to assist committee members in addressing problems or formulating policies. Special reports on particular subjects or questions can often furnish significant clues as to why certain statutory or substantive options were or were not pursued. The existence and character of prints can be most readily ascertained through *CIS/Abstracts*.

2. Presidential Messages. These documents may address salient issues, convey general recommendations, urge immediate action, or request the passage of specific measures. Regardless of their major purpose, they often contain the text of draft legislation. The explanations that accompany such proposals, especially those enacted without significant change, become key elements of legislative history. All presidential messages transmitted to Congress are cited in the *Congressional Record* on the day of their receipt, assigned the prefix *PM* and numbered sequentially for each Congress, referred to the appropriate committee, and printed as a Senate or House document. Though perusal of the *Record* is one way to keep current on these communications, more convenient sources are the Congressional Quarterly *Weekly Report* and *Weekly Compilation of Presidential Documents*, which notes the Senate or House document number.

3. Bills. Once the need for legislative action is conceded or confirmed, efforts are devoted to the political architecture of a bill. Since only members of Congress may introduce a bill, the actual reason behind it or the identity of its original source may be obscured. Though the link and path between a germinal idea and a formal proposal can be difficult to ascertain, it can be of particular importance when a bill is enacted with the same basic language as it was initially drafted. When the phrase *by request* appears on an introduced bill, a member declares that the action is on behalf of an external entity. Information about origins and background, including the purposes of and arguments for a bill, is available when a member makes a statement on the floor at the time a bill is introduced. These remarks will then appear in the *Record*.

There are three other possibilities that provide the opportunity to retrieve information on the genesis and authorship of bills. One is when a measure that has failed to pass in a prior Congress is reintroduced in the current one. The best source for this development is a committee report, otherwise it is necessary to communicate with the committee staff. Bills may also be introduced as a result of hearings held on two or more related measures or on a certain subject or event. To locate these printed hearings one can consult the chart at the end of this chapter. Identical measures introduced in each house are known as companion bills. If introduction in one chamber offers no clues as to history and objectives, such information may be available about its companion. The *House Calendar, Congressional Record Index,* and *Digest of Public General Bills and Resolutions* all note the existence and numbers of companion bills.

Committee members are rarely surprised by the referral of a bill to their panel. One reason is that legislative courtesy and political tact predispose nonmembers to give advance notice to key members. Another is that most of the important measures referred to a committee are introduced by its own members. The individual who knows most about the origins and intentions of a proposal is its chief sponsor, whose name appears first on the printed copy of an introduced bill. When published sources fail to provide any or enough background information, one must contact the office of a sponsor for the facts or advice on where to obtain them.

HEARINGS THROUGH REPORTS

The division of labor and subject specialization represented by its committees denotes that Congress is a committee-centered information system. Only panel members have the time to thoroughly familiarize themselves with the subjects under their jurisdiction. This advantage is reinforced by extensive, poorly indexed and delayed printing of hearings, unanimous or near unanimous committee reports that avoid expressing diverse views, expeditious routing of proposed legislation to the floor, and domination of chamber debate by committee members. However, unless panel decisions and proposals violate traditional legislative norms and goals, their endeavors will receive the approval or induce the acceptance of the parent body.

Committee decisions about the initiation and organization of hearings as well as the reporting and amending of bills are of immeasurable importance. The framework within which further deliberations proceed tends to be firmly set by panel action. Hearings indicate how well a matter has been addressed and reports how well it has been assessed. The former denotes adequate collection and the latter systematic analysis of relevant information. Hearings and reports not only emphasize the rigor of committee scrutiny and standards, but it is through these publications that an attempt is made to alter the perceptions and influence the alignment of those legislators yet to act. Though these documents may be neither the first nor last to issue from the legislative process, they serve as the twin cornerstones of any legislative history.

1. Hearings. A thorough public hearing given to those with a substantial interest in or knowledge of a proposal is needed to help a committee forge a bill capable of surmounting the obstacles with which the road to enactment is paved. Hearings provide an opportunity to gauge whether the investment of additional legislative resources would be politically profitable. It is through these proceedings that panels determine which interests will have access to the policy process, a crucial judgment that profoundly affects the substantive impact of Congress on the end product. The readjustment of societal relationships and reallocation of communal resources entailed in the formation of new policies and programs prompt widespread efforts to participate and persuade. The hearing is a legislative tool designed to elicit information, focus attention, encourage compromise, and foster consensus among competing political elements.

    Hearings are a key source for understanding or establishing the general thrust of a bill or the circumstances that produced the perceived need for legislation. Should other material be scarce, silent, nebulous, or divergent, hearing testimony may provide the fullest and clearest statements of legislative purpose and intent. Hearings offer a forum to bill proponents and drafters who are not members of Congress. The testimony of executive branch officials or private citizens with first-hand knowledge of a bill's origins and objectives enhances the value of hearings for legislative history purposes. The remarks of an administration spokesman on an administration-supported proposal may be treated as the testimony of a drafter. The comments of private parties may also be accorded considerable weight when they represent entities that have reached an agreement that is embodied in legislation and sanctioned by members of Congress. The emphasis given oral or written testimony that is subsequently incorporated or cited in a committee report leaves little doubt about its prominent place in a legislative history.

2. Committee Prints. These are section-by-section analyses of bills or comparative versions of legislation. The former contains detailed explanations of provisions with citations to current statutes. The latter presents parallel columns of different proposals or of a bill and existing law. The format and content of prints are consciously designed to illuminate statutory objectives and legislative intent. However, their unofficial nature and limited quantities render them difficult to identify and obtain. Information about their preparation and availability must usually be sought through committee staff attorneys.

3. Mark-up Transcripts. Committee mark-up sessions are the equivalent to floor debate in the full chamber. However, the transcripts of mark-up proceedings are rarely published. When available in printed form, their importance stems from information provided on committee amendment of an introduced bill. Mark-up action is occasionally summarized in a committee report. Though of genuine value for documenting legislative history, their general inaccessibility raises questions about who can or should make use of them and the validity or propriety of such usage. Further discussion of mark-ups appears in chapters 4 and 8.

4. Committee Reports. These documents are considered the most reliable and persuasive component of legislative history because they reflect the considered and collective judgment of those legislators most deeply involved in studying and drafting proposed legislation. The report that accompanies a bill outlines its overall purposes and provides a detailed explanation of each major provision. It contains the findings and recommendations that stem from the committee's interpretation of an issue and distillation of its evidence. The aim is to elucidate and generate support for the panel's position regarding the political, substantive, and administrative feasibility of the reported measure. Even the views of opponents that appear in a report may be useful to demonstrate that there was general agreement on a particular construction or that a certain position was clearly rejected.

    Committee reports also serve as the best introduction to floor consideration of a bill. They supplement the legal language of bills through factual and political analysis and argument intended to present the strongest possible case for favorable legislative action. The concise discussion of substantive and legislative history establishes the contours of debate and is the key to understanding the views expressed and amendments proposed. For controversial measures, reports function as handbooks for advocates during chamber proceedings, while their contents enable routine legislation to be accelerated through to enactment with little or no debate. Senate and House deliberations generally disseminate and elaborate the arguments and explanations of proponents and opponents that appear in a committee report.

SCHEDULING THROUGH PASSAGE

Article I, Section 5, of the Constitution requires each house to keep and publish a journal. Though maintained throughout each session, they are printed and bound only at its close. The chronological contents of these volumes are the official record of legislative proceedings, and should there be a discrepancy between either journal and the *Congressional Record*, it is the latter that is corrected. Each journal contains, as does the bound *Record*, a history of bills and resolutions and a detailed subject index. All parliamentary motions and their disposition are included, while floor debate and extraneous information are excluded. The succinct summary of actions and results that comprise the body of each journal simplifies the search for desired information and, when used in conjunction with the *Record*, can facilitate access to the latter, just as the *Record* can supplement the account of the former.

1. Scheduling. Because the decisions that shape the daily order of business are controlled by the majority party, there is a lack of formal documentation regarding this function. Special orders in the House are noted and unanimous consent agreements in the Senate are printed in the chamber's calendar and their texts also appear in the *Record* and journal of each house. A summary of each chamber's scheduled business for its next daily session is inserted at the end of the *Daily Digest* section of the daily *Record*. Friday issues of the *Daily Digest* contain a section entitled "Congressional Program Ahead," which outlines the plans of each house for the coming week. A more informative description of the forthcoming legislative program usually appears at the end of the "Proceedings" section of Friday editions of the *Record*, where party leaders announce and reply to questions about the agenda. Since formal documents provide information only about final results, journalistic sources must be consulted to ascertain reasons and strategy.

2. Debate. The House and Senate each control the content of their portions of the *Congressional Record*. It is not an exact transcript of the proceedings and debate in each chamber, but a "substantially verbatim" account. Members of both houses are allowed to edit the reported copy of their speech before publication. Also, House members may be permitted, by unanimous consent, to revise and extend their remarks when their time to speak has expired, while senators may receive approval to insert any unfinished remarks at the point where, for whatever reason, they stopped speaking. Large black dots known as bullets are used in the Senate Proceedings section to identify statements in the *Record* that were not delivered during actual debate, while the House uses a different style of type in its portion of the *Record* to distinguish such remarks.

For the purposes of legislative history, prepared statements tend to be accorded more weight than extemporaneous remarks; explanations given by sponsors of floor amendments are usually considered of more consequence than statements made by other members about intended effect; a colloquy or other comment by the floor manager is of prime importance when ambiguities or other inadequacies are discerned in a bill after it has been reported. Issues or questions not addressed or merely alluded to by a committee report are often discussed at some length during floor debate and here the views of individual members may be material in creating legislative history or helpful in clarifying legislative intent.

3. Amendments. In legislative parlance, the word *amendment* has two distinct meanings. Its more common usage refers to a proposed change to a pending bill. Most bills are also proposed amendments to existing law. The context of deliberations, including the stage of legislative action, language of parliamentary motions, and citation of specific documents avoids potential confusion about which meaning is relevant. In unofficial discussion or public debate an amendment, whether to a bill or law, sometimes becomes known by the name of the legislator who sponsored it. This form of journalistic shorthand used by the media can serve to readily identify legislative proposals that lack formal titles or official numbers.

   The disposition of amendments is the most critical aspect of chamber action other than the vote on final passage. Floor decisions on one or more amendments may determine whether there is a vote on final passage or render such a vote a mere formality. In terms of providing relatively clear legislative history, the key documentation covers committee amendments accepted and other amendments rejected. To the degree that panel amendments are defeated and floor amendments adopted, legislative history becomes more difficult to interpret. Further information on amendments and the amending process is contained in chapters 5, 6, and 8.

4. Voting. From a legislative history perspective, there are several salient facts about a chamber vote. They are whether or not a proposition is voted upon at all; whether approved or disapproved, the precise language of the motion or measure; whether the motion or measure approved or disapproved was substantive or procedural; and when approved, the timing or its sequential relationship to other votes on other propositions. These and other aspects of voting receive detailed treatment in chapter 7.

CONCURRENCE THROUGH ENACTMENT

Depending on the length of time that elapses between action on a bill in each house and the extent of differences involved, the publications of the second chamber to act serve as an implicit or explicit reply to those of the first. Criticism tends to be muted and indirect and expressed in terms of a discussion of the omission or inclusion of specific provisions and the purposes thereof. Regardless of differences, the nature of legislative language and objectives generally allows ample latitude within which both houses may negotiate satisfactory compromises.

1. Substitutions. When a bill is received by one house from the other, and the former has already begun action on a companion or similar bill, it will frequently proceed to consider and pass its own bill. At this point the second chamber may call up the bill passed by the first, amend it to read identically with its own bill just passed, and pass it in lieu of its own bill. By this procedure both houses place their versions under an identical bill number, which prepares the path for bicameral interaction and agreement. In reference to documentation, all publications in the second chamber that pertain to its own version become legislative history for the bill under its new number once the substitution occurs.

2. Amendments. When it is decided by party and committee leaders that the two chambers should resolve their differences by the process known as amendments between the houses, each body acts separately in succession on changes proposed by the other to a given measure until agreement is reached. Other than floor debate and amendment action there is no official document that covers these proceedings and decisions. In the absence of a formal and separate publication, memoranda drafted by the staff of the committees having jurisdiction and that explain the text agreed upon may be inserted in the *Congressional Record*.

3. Conference Reports. These documents are considered especially persuasive evidence of legislative intent because they represent the final word on the final version of a bill. It is clearer for legislative history purposes when conferees adopt a provision as it was passed by one house rather than rewrite it to resolve chamber differences. Two common forms of conference agreement are silence and ambiguity. These devices enable each side to advance a favorable interpretation or preserve desired options. Though such action may yield inconsistent efforts in the interpretation of law, legislators recognize the uses of political and administrative flexibility. All interested parties gain something with the implicit understanding that the solution is tentative pending actual experience and results.

4. Vetoed Bills. Since the president does not disapprove bills for trivial reasons, his objections to a measure returned to Congress without his signature contain significant statements of interpretation derived from analysis within the executive branch. Subsequent floor debate on the bill may reveal that the executive view is precisely why it should be enacted over a veto or represents a spurious reading of legislative intent. In either case, further light is shed on legislative history should the veto be overridden. If a veto is sustained, the bill may be repassed at the same or the next session in revised form. In this instance, the veto message,

which appears in the *Congressional Record*, becomes an integral part of a bill's legislative history.

CHARTING A COURSE

The preceding discussion of the role of congressional publications in the formation and implications of legislative history is in the nature of an overture. A systematic survey and intensive investigation are presented in chapter 3 through 9. The purposes of this subsection are to clarify two important distinctions in the realm of legislative history, to introduce the more convenient ways to approach the pursuit of legislative history, and to provide a comprehensive overview of legislative history documents.

There is a significant difference involved depending on whether a legislative history project is contemporaneous or retrospective. In the former case, it is necessary to consult those publications issued at least monthly, especially if the goal includes acquisition of the material. In the latter case, annual sources, many of which cumulate their daily, weekly, or monthly issues, will meet most needs. The appropriate type and level of effort also depend on whether the purpose is to compile or employ legislative history or both. A retrospective approach can rely more on secondary sources and is more likely to satisfy the needs of an impartial inquiry. The need to use such information for professional or political purposes entails more dependence on primary sources, including those more difficult to identify and obtain.

The bound *Daily Digest*, issued at the close of each session of Congress, is the single most complete source of facts on legislative business because it covers both chamber and committee proceedings. It is arranged chronologically, with entries for each day on which any formal congressional activity occurred. Under the heading "Chamber Action," it identifies bills introduced, reported, considered, and passed. For those measures acted on, it describes the amendments adopted and rejected and notes the method of voting and vote totals. References to the appropriate pages of the bound *Congressional Record* are included. Under the heading "Committee Meetings," it distinguishes among full committees, subcommittees, and conference committees. If the meeting was a hearing, the names of witnesses are listed. The subject, bill number, and status of the legislation are given for hearings, mark-ups, and conferences. This information enables one to follow the progress of measures during the all-important stage of committee consideration. A subject index cites bill numbers and separately identifies action on each measure in terms of hearings, mark-up, report, chamber action, conference consideration, and public law or veto. Its concise format and thorough coverage make it an excellent place from which to begin tracing legislative history.

The *Legislative Histories Annual*, published by Congressional Information Service, identifies all pertinent printed items, including material issued during earlier Congresses. It is arranged by public law number with a citation to the *Statutes at Large*. The publications listed for each history are committee prints, hearings, committee reports, the *Congressional Record*, House and Senate documents, the *Weekly Compilation of Presidential Documents*, and the slip law. There is also a concise summary of the purpose(s) and provisions of each law and cross references to *CIS/Abstracts* for congressional publications. For major legislation, the following additional information is included: full *CIS/Abstracts*; citations for all relevant bills; *Record* citations for all chamber debate on the enacted bill, including companion and predecessor measures in the current and prior Congresses; and citations to related congressional publications. An index of subjects and names provides access by the topical content of laws, by the names of agencies and organizations created or affected by laws, and the names of political and geographical entities affected by laws. A second index offers access by bill number. The first *Annual* appeared in 1985 for calendar year 1984. Prior legislative history information for the years 1970 through 1983 was included in the annual *CIS/Abstracts*. Its publications perspective and inclusive presentation make it an excellent place from which to begin assembling a legislative history.

Committees occasionally issue committee prints that cover the enactment of a major law under their jurisdiction. These convenient and useful publications contain most key documents that comprise a legislative history. If a specific one cannot be located through *CIS/Index*, a person can contact a committee to learn if such a compilation was prepared and whether a copy is available. For essential information inadequately covered by legislative material, the indispensable source is the CQ *Weekly Report* or the annual CQ *Almanac*. The journalistic account provided by both fills in many information gaps that characterize formal documents because of their official nature and political intent. Figure 2 is designed to serve as an orientation device rather than an optimal resource. It is a companion aid to the bibliographic guide in chapter 8 and a graphic adjunct to the Document Index.

	Basic Features					
	Body			Index		
Source	Frequency	Arrangement	Cumulated	Frequency	Entries	Cumulated
CIS/Index	Monthly	Author Subject Title	Annually	Monthly	Author Subject Title	Annually
CQ Almanac	Annual	Topical			Committee Name Subject	
CQ Weekly Report	Weekly	Topical		Weekly	Committee Name Subject	Quarterly
Congressional Record (Final Edition)	Annual	Chronological			Name Subject	
Congressional Roll Call	Annual	Chronological			Subject	
Daily Digest (Final Edition)	Annual	Chronological			Subject	
Digest of Public General Bills and Resolutions	5-6 issues per session	Bill/Res. No.	Annually		Name Subject	Annually
House Calendar	Each day House is in session	Bill/Res. & Public Law No.	Each issue	Each Monday	Subject	Monday and final editions
House Journal	Annual	Chronological			Name Subject	
Legislative Histories Annual	Annual	Public Law No.			Name Subject	
Monthly Catalog	Monthly	Issuing Agency		Monthly	Committee Subject Title	Annually
Senate Journal	Annual	Chronological			Name Subject	

Document Coverage

Key - Access by: Author (A); Bill/Resolution No. (B/R); Public Law No. (P); Subject (S); Title (T)

Committee Prints	Presidential Messages	Hearings	Mark-up	Committee Reports*	Debate	Voting	Bills & Resolutions	Public Laws	Status Tables
A/S/T	A/S/T	A/S/T	A/S/T	A/S/T			B/R S/T	P/S/T Popular Name	
	Text of all					S			Annual (P)
	Text of all					B/R		Periodical Listing	Weekly (Selective)
	A/S			B/R/S	B/R/S	B/R/S	B/R/S	B/R/S	Annual (By B/R)
						S			
		S	S	S	S	S	S	S	Annual (P)
				B/R/S	B/R/S		B/R/S/T	P	Cumulative & Annual (By B/R & P)
				B/R/S	B/R		B/R/S	B/R/P/S	Cumulative & Annual (By B/R & P)
	A/S B/R			B/R	B/R/S	B/R/S	B/R/S	B/R	Annual (By B/R)
B/P/S	B/P/S	B/P/S	B/P/S	B/P/S	B/P/S	B/P/S	B/P/S	B/P/S	
A/S/T	A/S	A/S/T	A/S/T	A/S/T				S/T	
	A/S B/R			B/R	B/R/S	B/R/S	B/R/S	B/R	Annual (By B/R)

*Includes conference reports.

Fig. 2. Comparison of major bibliographic sources.

REFERENCES

Berman, Daniel M. *In Congress Assembled.* New York: Macmillan, 1964.

Dahl, Robert A. *A Preface to Democratic Theory.* Chicago: University of Chicago Press, 1956.

Edwards, George C., III. *Presidential Influence in Congress.* San Francisco: W. H. Freeman, 1980.

Fenno, Richard F., Jr. *Congressmen in Committees.* Boston: Little, Brown, 1973.

Folsom, Gwendolyn. *Legislative History: Research for the Interpretation of Laws.* Charlottesville, Va.: University of Virginia Press, 1972.

Froman, Lewis A., Jr. *The Congressional Process.* Boston: Little, Brown, 1967.

Gross, Bertram M. *The Legislative Struggle.* New York: McGraw-Hill, 1953.

Jewell, Malcolm E., and Samuel C. Patterson. *The Legislative Process in the United States.* New York: Random House, 1966.

Keefe, William J., and Morris S. Ogul. *The American Legislative Process.* 3rd ed. Englewood Cliffs, N.J.: Prentice-Hall, 1973.

Lindblom, Charles E. *The Intelligence of Democracy.* New York: The Free Press, 1965.

Mitchell, Joyce M., and William C. Mitchell. *Political Analysis and Public Policy.* Chicago: Rand McNally, 1969.

Morrow, William L. *Congressional Committees.* New York: Charles Scribner's Sons, 1969.

Oleszek, Walter J. *Congressional Procedures and the Policy Process.* 2nd ed. Washington, D.C.: Congressional Quarterly Press, 1984.

Rieselbach, Leroy N. *Congressional Politics.* New York: McGraw-Hill, 1973.

Ripley, Randall B. *Congress.* 3rd ed. New York: W. W. Norton, 1983.

Ripley, Randall B., and Grace A. Franklin. *Congress, the Bureaucracy and Public Policy.* 3rd ed. Homewood, Ill.: Dorsey Press, 1984.

U.S. Congress. House. *Constitution, Jefferson's Manual and Rules of the House of Representatives.* House Document No. 98-277, 98th Congress, 2nd Session. Washington, D.C.: U.S. Government Printing Office, 1985.

U.S. Congress. House. *How Our Laws Are Made.* House Document No. 97-120, 97th Congress, 1st Session. Washington, D.C.: U.S. Government Printing Office, 1981.

U.S. Congress. Senate. *Enactment of a Law.* Senate Document No. 97-20, 97th Congress, 2nd Session. Washington, D.C.: U.S. Government Printing Office, 1982.

U.S. Congress. Senate. *Senate Procedure.* Senate Document No. 97-2, 97th Congress, 1st Session. Washington, D.C.: U.S. Government Printing Office, 1981.

Vogler, David J. *The Politics of Congress.* 4th ed. Boston: Allyn and Bacon, 1983.

Wayne, Stephen J. *The Legislative Presidency.* New York: Harper & Row, 1978.

Young, Roland. *The American Congress.* New York: Harper & Brothers, 1958.

3
Policy Research

Policy research is one means by which legislators keep themselves informed of existing and proposed policy developments. Though the theory that underpins this form of information assumes a value-neutral environment, the political context in which it is prepared and applied significantly affects its content and utility. This chapter examines the ideal and practical aspects of policy research, with particular emphasis on the role of the four congressional support agencies: the Congressional Research Service, General Accounting Office, Office of Technology Assessment, and Congressional Budget Office.

Major policy proposals may originate as, or eventuate in, congressional bills. In either instance, they frequently engender prominent studies and analyses that are designed to probe substantive and political premises and purposes. To explore the research background of legislation is to focus on how public policies are initially framed and legislative objectives provisionally formulated. The usefulness and limitations of policy research depend on the degree to which its sponsors or consumers believe it can help to bridge the gap between ideal solutions and political realities.

Policy research covers a variety of material that cannot be succinctly described or readily identified. It may be prepared by a governmental or non-governmental body; it may be issued by an administrative or legislative entity; it may or may not be printed; its availability may be restricted; it may be an original study or a compilation of previously published material; it may be descriptive or analytical, conceptual or practical, objective or subjective. The reasons for this lack of regularity in sources, accessibility, and content relate to chronology and knowledge.

Though policy research generally precedes legislative action, it is not a mandatory part of the legislative process. Its prelegislative origin usually coincides with views on a given issue that are still in a formative stage. The preliminary nature of its issuance and observations account for the discretion and diversity that characterize its authorship, substance, and distribution. Its appearance as or in a congressional publication or its use by legislators can confer a status equivalent to more formal documents.

RESEARCH AND POLITICS

The nature of policy research can be clarified by comparing it with professional research. The latter focuses on the formulation and consequences of public policy, is intended to advance knowledge in a given field of study, and is aimed at members of a profession. It tends to be structured by empirical data, with its content insulated from personal motives or desires and its validity established by objective criteria. Policy research focuses on matters that extend beyond a specific subject area, is intended as a guide to action, and is aimed at a set of political decisionmakers. It is inevitably affected by external factors, with its content subject to the values and goals of particular clients and its validity established by a process of competitive negotiation.

Policy research may simply incorporate professional research in the form of analyses of the original objectives or unintended consequences of existing government programs, studies of the implications of possible policy adjustments or major reforms, and evaluations of the strengths and weaknesses of proposed alternatives. Professional research may also be used as a base to develop original approaches that include novel and analytical techniques that can be applied to societal problems, the integration of concepts from the fields of politics, economics, administration, and law to illuminate the evolution and effects of public policies, or the examination of seemingly unrelated matters that are actually different dimensions of a larger issue.

To enhance the acceptability of a research product, it is necessary to identify the needs and desires of those entities likely to be affected by a proposed policy and to obtain information about and from them. This undertaking is designed to disclose and neutralize the natural biases of various sources and to accommodate the views of interested parties. Policy research combines disciplinary expertise with insights from the sphere of political dynamics to highlight the interactive processes that are an integral part of an issue and its resolution.

A generalization that can be made about policy research concerns its purpose. Whether authorized or adopted by legislators, it is intended to help crystallize opinion on the merits of an idea or appropriate governmental action. Thus, it is one form of political input and influence that may address a proposal from the standpoint of credibility, desirability, feasibility, or necessity. Such efforts reflect an ongoing contest to set the legislative agenda and affect the activities of political participants.

Complexity and competition are the two factors primarily responsible for the decision to undertake policy research. Policymakers are rarely confronted by conditions or problems with obvious causes or solutions. The scope and impact of contemporary issues must be defined and refined before realistic proposals can be devised. Efforts to generate agreement on the existence and nature of a problem are not merely intended to clarify a specific situation. Analyses sponsored by concerned parties also attempt to foster common perspectives so as to influence public debate and the policy climate.

The purposes of policy research may involve efforts to identify an issue or problem, assess whether legislative action is feasible, accumulate factual data and clarify underlying values, ascertain available alternatives, and provide a technical evaluation of the consequences of alternatives and correlate such consequences with desirable goals. Political factors may intrude at any time depending on the strategy or solution favored by groups of legislators. Some may wish to limit the research focus to the exploration of a possible legislative decision, others may seek to facilitate a timely decision, while still others may desire to support chosen positions. In any case, only legislators can undertake a political evaluation of the consequences of alternatives and foster the consensus necessary to adopt a preferred policy.

Though policy research is a legislative tool of acknowledged value, any given situation usually produces at least one barrier to its unreserved acceptance by all parties involved. The competing goals of legislators can prevent a question from being described with the precision necessary before it is assigned to another entity for further study; objective research may not generate information desired to advance a legislator's personal ambitions or a committee's policy preferences; politicians tend to address only those aspects of an issue that can be exploited to their advantage; legislators prefer to commit resources for application to immediate matters rather than invest in an uncertain future when they may no longer be in a position to exert influence.

Even when legislators are receptive to research input, there exist impediments to its use. Many policy decisions are necessitated by fixed timetables or dictated by unforeseen events. The lack of sufficient time to explore an issue thoroughly often means that all relevant information cannot be obtained. A fluid environment that continually affects the ranking of public priorities, combined with time constraints, generally limits research output to partial and tentative proposals. If technical analyses are inconclusive or inconsistent, a political decision remains the only recourse. For complex policy problems the effort to develop criteria needed to isolate and compare costs and benefits is never complete or definitive and always remains subject to challenge regarding data and interpretation. Since contemporary issues are too indefinite and far-reaching for research alone to offer conclusive verdicts about correct choices, disagreement often ensues about the timing of formal statements or the initiation of other legislative actions.

Congress is an arena of advocates in which legislators who have different roles, constituencies, objectives, and abilities endeavor to advance political viewpoints. Since policymaking occurs in an adversary environment, decisions must be the result of negotiations. The process of formulating and adopting policy receives more attention than its consistency or objectivity. In this climate, disinterested analysis is inseparable from legislative advocacy because plain facts affect political fortunes. Thus, all legislators who support a bill rarely do so for the same reasons and just as rarely for reasons compatible with research criteria.

The several stages of the legislative process require bargaining and compromise to form successive majorities regardless of factual or verifiable evidence. The utility of results is determined by parties engaged in the process of conflict and cooperation. The quality of the research product cannot restrict or override the values or interests of potential users. Political participants who disagree about the need for congressional action on a certain subject may be motivated by the substance of factual and analytical inquiries or by the conviction that such a course will produce a favorable outcome.

Since policy research is not always the only or most important kind of information on a given issue, it must compete with other types. The major alternative to such research is the broad range of policy options generated by parties who do not claim to be objective. The vigorous pursuit and direct clash of concrete interests serve to test various assumptions and aims against one another. Research results can encourage the reconsideration of premises and purposes as the legislative process, which accentuates the aggregation of interests rather than the analysis of information, proceeds. Though the legislative and research processes are not natural allies, they can complement each other.

Policy research can facilitate and guide discussion among political competitors who may not be able to agree on fundamental values or policy forecasts. Research material contributes to the success of political negotiations when it establishes contours and focuses arguments so as to increase the intelligibility of policy options and reduce the resistance to possible decisions. That the validity of policy research is based upon its utility to those attempting to achieve desired goals does not nullify its value, for as with legislation itself, its legitimacy is determined by its acceptability.

CONGRESSIONAL SUPPORT AGENCIES

All policymakers need continuous access to sources that can provide timely, accurate, systematic, and comprehensive information and analyses. The availability of data poses the problem of information management rather than its acquisition. The volume of information is too great for legislators and their staffs to examine and organize in a timely and concise manner. Thus, they must often rely on others to process the information upon which legislative decisions will be based. Since policy research entails investing facts with their political significance, the perspective of those units responsible for accumulating and processing information is a key factor.

Though Congress uses the studies of administrative agencies and private organizations, it has chosen to establish research units to exclusively serve its own needs. The main reason it has done so is to redress the balance of policy initiative between the executive and legislative branches. Congress requires a constant flow of factual, descriptive, analytical, and interpretive information. An independent staff capability to analyze and assess issues and legislation reduces congressional dependence on other political entities in deciding upon the feasibility, purposes, methods, and implications of existing and proposed policies.

Congressional committees are the principal consumers of policy research, which is used to aid them in the performance of legislative and oversight functions. These panels play a pivotal role in policy formulation but seek outside assistance only when they are unable or unwilling to meet demands on their resources. Because most committee staffs are comparatively small and preoccupied with pending decisions, they lack the time for extensive research projects. The result is that policy research, though a regular feature of the legislative process, serves an auxiliary role.

The cost of collecting information tends to increase and its value decrease the longer the process continues. By entrusting a project to a capable and responsive unit, a committee conserves its resources and, by avoiding a commitment to act, keeps its options open. The guidelines stipulated by the committee ensure that the research methods used and form of presentation will be adapted to its needs. The desired result would be a disinterested study whose attributes are attuned to the realities of the legislative environment.

Standing committees are the units among which Congress distributes its workload and through which it promotes policy expertise. Committee members are expected to combine subject specialization with political judgment in preparing and submitting recommendations to their parent bodies. Though this arrangement enables nonessential information to be screened and essential information to be processed, it does not foster the ordering of priorities or the consistency of policies. Committee autonomy tends to insulate related areas of policy from one another. The broad and complex issues generated by social and economic conditions do not fit neatly into the jurisdictional compartments of the committee structure.

Legislative policymaking requires the coherent consideration of several different functional policy areas, each of which is the responsibility of a different committee. The integrated and coordinated nature of policy research serves to partially overcome the diverse and divergent elements that comprise the organizational and political environment of Congress. A comprehensive approach that identifies all relevant factors may also function to counterbalance the views of political interests that have access to committee members.

Anticipatory or long-range studies can identify matters likely to require eventual congressional attention. The collection and analysis of information about such potential problems can proceed in advance, unaffected by political controversy and unhurried by urgent need. Developments can be monitored by specialists without consuming legislative resources until the need for action is manifest. When a legislative decision becomes necessary, a foundation will have been laid that provides an opportunity for Congress to address a subject more quickly and confidently. This promotes a more orderly schedule for the legislative consideration of issues and reduces the possibility of immediate action preceding adequate preparation.

A manageable fund of digested data helps to offset the segmented and fitful nature of the legislative process, which inhibits the accumulation and availability of all pertinent information needed for imminent decisions. Major issues can be diagnosed early enough to permit information resources to be fully mobilized and held in readiness for expeditious application. The employment of specialized skills to identify and analyze conditions and alternatives that can be only dimly perceived on the political horizon enables Congress to more precisely address substantive questions.

Congress confronts the difficult task of trying to forge an effective link between policy specialization, as typified by its organizational features, and policy integration, as demanded by the complexity and scope of contemporary issues. One response of Congress to this matter has been to enlarge the responsibilities of two support agencies, the Congressional Research Service (1970) and General Accounting Office (1970; 1974), and to create two others, the Office of Technology Assessment (1972) and Congressional Budget Office (1974), to meet the short-term policy research needs of committee decisions and deadlines as well as the long-range needs of congressional attention and alternatives.

These four research staffs can ensure the equal availability of information and introduce common frames of reference to both houses and all committees, insulate the analytical phase of research from political biases to produce a more credible product, reallocate resources more easily as changing conditions and congressional needs warrant, and apply information generated for one type of response to other types. Legislative support agencies also have access to, and may enlist the aid of, entities or individuals in the academic or industrial communities with expertise in particular methodologies or subjects. They can pursue information originating outside the legislative arena and adapt it to the needs of congressional clients.

When acting as agents for congressional committees, all four support agencies are empowered to obtain information from any federal agency. Most such requests cause no friction or are resolved through committee-agency negotiations. An impasse, which may reflect political conflict between Congress and the president, may lead to committee issuance of a subpoena or passage by one house of a resolution directing that the information be transmitted. Thus, information that agencies may withhold from the public cannot be easily denied to the legislative branch. Its release to legislators may then result in its public dissemination through congressional publications.

All four congressional support agencies confront the situation of providing information within a political context. Despite their nonpolitical modes of operation, their subordination to a political body means that impartial preparation of research material cannot preclude its interpretation and application from being subject to political preconceptions. Since each legislator has geographical as well as functional constituencies, each is more concerned about the specific effects of public policies rather than their overall relation to the national welfare. Policy research will find greater legislative acceptance when the substance of an issue is perceived as highly technical in nature and its impact is viewed as general in nature.

CONGRESSIONAL RESEARCH SERVICE (CRS)

The CRS is an operationally independent unit within the Library of Congress whose primary function is to provide Congress with research assistance on public issues. It responds to committee requests to judge the advisability of enacting particular proposals, to estimate the probable results that would follow enactment, and to assess alternative means of accomplishing intended objectives. Its studies endeavor to provide a systematic and comprehensive investigation of the practical options and potential consequences within a given policy area. These analyses focus on the specific needs or purposes pertinent to approaching decisions.

Congressional committees use the CRS to help them prepare for hearings and analyze legislation. The former activity embraces the review of new policy concepts and their relation to the legislative process, evaluation of reports issued by and about federal agencies, synthesis of technical information in committee jurisdictions, critiques of interest group positions, summary and analysis of court decisions covering particular areas of public policy, and preparation of subject surveys on federal and state legislation. The analysis of legislation encompasses background reports on the evolution of policy issues; legislative histories of bills or subjects under consideration; in-depth analyses of proposals that address national and international problems; pro and con analyses of potential legislative solutions; section-by-section comparisons of related measures; and memoranda that summarize a bill's purpose and effect, describe other bills of similar purpose previously introduced, and recapitulate all prior action taken by Congress on each such proposal.

The CRS serves as a communication channel between the legislative process and various fields of knowledge, including sources in academia, industry, and government, to keep itself and its clients informed of new forms and uses of information. The agency enters into contracts for research projects when it lacks the expertise or time necessary to meet deadlines. The criteria for approving such contracts include knowledge of an institutional viewpoint, competence in the application of a research or analytical technique, and availability of special facilities. For those issues that overlap committee jurisdiction, its projects are interdivisional in preparation and interdisciplinary in content. In these cases, task forces composed of specialists in different but related subject areas pool their efforts to produce more comprehensive studies that cover the mutual impact of various or possible government actions.

CRS research products are not readily available to the public. This is due to a combination of its legal status and the fact that many requests from congressional committees are considered confidential. Complete lists of these studies are distributed only within the congressional community. However, there are two sources that can be used to identify most, if not all, of its unclassified output. A semiannual publication available from the Government Printing Office is entitled *CRS Studies in the Public Domain*. It cites all CRS research that has been issued as committee prints or House and Senate documents or inserted into printed hearings or the *Congressional Record*. The CRS Annual Report, available from the Joint Library Committee, contains a more inclusive list of its reports and other material. Both catalogs are organized by subject and specify the type of output, such as report, issue brief, information pack, bibliography, research guide, or overview. Some CRS printed products can also be found in the *Monthly Catalog* and *CIS/Index*. Once an item has been identified, the most convenient way to obtain it is to contact the office of one's congressperson or senator. Responding to such requests is part of the regular business of constituent service.

GENERAL ACCOUNTING OFFICE (GAO)

The basic research activity performed by the GAO is program review, or the analysis and assessment of agency programs and operations to determine their compliance with applicable laws and regulations, the economy and efficiency with which resources are managed and consumed, and the costs and benefits that stem from the pursuit of statutory objectives. In addition to conducting its own appraisals, the GAO also evaluates program reviews completed by federal agencies. In its role as the principal congressional monitor of federal programs, it seeks to ensure that existing laws are appropriate, effectively administered, and serving to achieve intended purposes.

Regular GAO audits of agency activities enable it to identify overlap and duplication among programs, inadequate coordinating arrangements among interdependent programs, and inconsistent approaches to programs having related goals. This examination of results not only generates recommendations for changes but also largely determines what type of remedial action is most appropriate. The major difficulty associated with program evaluations is that neither authorizing legislation nor agency regulations establish explicit standards or specify clear goals against which administrative performance can be judged. Not only are measurement techniques almost always less definite than desired, but agreement is often absent regarding a program's precise purposes. In addition, differences between the policy goals of Congress as a whole or a congressional committee and those of the president or an executive-branch agency impede agreement on whether objectives have been met.

Though analyses of agency affairs may be undertaken by the GAO at the request of congressional committees, in practice most reports are self-initiated and based upon a perception of congressional interests and needs. The criteria used to decide whether to investigate a program are its social and economic impact as measured by actual or potential political controversy, public criticism by professional groups or other levels of government, or the recency of GAO or other evaluations. Studies focus on the reasons for a sudden or sharp increase in program costs, alternatives to existing programs, economic evaluations of proposed programs, or cost-benefit analyses of program inputs and outputs. Though a typical report contains an intensive examination of an identifiable problem or operational area, collectively they can provide a comprehensive view of an entire program, issue, or agency.

One section of the GAO Annual Report summarizes its recommendations for legislation contained in its studies and is arranged by subject, with cross references to public laws and congressional committees. A biannual booklet entitled *General Accounting Office Publications* is a list of the agency's reports submitted to Congress during the preceding year. A monthly publication entitled *GAO Documents* is a more up-to-date listing that includes abstracts of reports prepared for Congress. All of the titles contained in these three items would also be found in the *Monthly Catalog*. GAO proposals and studies not issued as separate reports and that may appear in printed committee hearings can be identified in *CIS/Index*.

OFFICE OF TECHNOLOGY ASSESSMENT (OTA)

The OTA was created to provide Congress with policy research on subjects principally relating to science and technology, with emphasis on the broader economic, environmental, social, and political implications of scientific and technological developments. Its studies are designed to serve as an early appraisal of the potential applications and probable impact of technological changes and programs. By relating technology to policy and exploring the possible consequences of alternative technological choices, its reports are intended to offer a thorough and balanced analysis that can facilitate the effective social management of such innovations. This prognostic capability is calculated to orient legislative effort in appropriately curbing, counteracting, controlling, or channeling technological trends in the public interest.

The specific informational responsibilities of the OTA are to identify the existing or probable effects of technology or technological programs, establish cause-and-effect relationships where possible, determine alternative technological methods of implementing programs, ascertain feasible programs for achieving desirable goals, estimate and compare the consequences of alternative methods and programs, and identify areas where additional research or data are required to adequately support estimates and comparisons. Such information is needed by legislators to anticipate, understand, debate, and evaluate existing or emerging problems and to formulate viable policies. A systematic effort to identify and project developments, as well as to analyze policy options before the pressure of events requires immediate action, aids in the legislative assessment of matters where the government is considering support for or regulation of technological applications.

To accomplish its purposes, the OTA is authorized to conduct surveys of existing and proposed government programs with a high technology content, to report on the activities or responsibilities of agencies in affecting or being affected by technological change, to monitor the natural and social environments to detect the effects of technological developments, and to recommend or undertake technological assessments. The value of a possible research project is judged by whether the subject already is, or is likely to become, a major national issue, the significance of a policy's effect on the distribution of economic and social resources, whether a technological impact is imminent or irreversible, the availability of sufficient knowledge to assess the technology and its consequences, or a study's potential for reinforcing or supplementing previous assessments.

OTA research appears either as separate office reports or in the form of committee prints issued by those Senate and House panels having responsibility for such subjects as energy, health, information technology, international security, natural resources, and transportation. Its Annual Report to Congress contains a synopsis of each assessment completed during the year, including policy options, legislative recommendations, and suggestions for further study and analysis. OTA periodically issues a list of publications and its output can also be readily identified through the *Monthly Catalog* and *CIS/Index*.

CONGRESSIONAL BUDGET OFFICE (CBO)

The CBO was created to improve the flow and quality of information needed in the discharge of legislative budgetary responsibilities required by the annual consideration and formulation of the federal budget. Such research applies to the content and passage of budget resolutions, appropriation bills, revenue measures, and other authorizing legislation involving budget authority. As a prerequisite to providing such information, the CBO monitors the performance of the economy and estimates its impact on government activities and analyzes the probable effects of alternative budgetary decisions. Its research products are intended to facilitate the establishment of priorities, in terms of spending totals, allocated among major functional areas of government.

The CBO is required to prepare an annual report on fiscal policy and budget options. Part 1 of this document presents projections of federal revenues and expenditures that would occur if current laws and policies remain unchanged for the next five years. It also examines the state of the economy and the economic outlook for the coming five years. Part 2, which appears as a separate publication, provides a more detailed analysis of the most pressing or prominent budget issue. It discusses alternatives that might be chosen and the likely impact of each on national economic growth and development. Both parts are designed to suggest some criteria against which Congress can consider possible policy changes as it formulates the budget for the next and later fiscal years. As part of the annual budget process, it also issues an analysis of the recommendations contained in the president's budget and compares executive and legislative economic forecasts.

For public bills under consideration by committees, the CBO prepares cost-implementation and financial-effect analyses that appear in committee reports. It also issues periodic reports on the status of congressionally approved budget authority, appropriations, revenue, and debt legislation. This information cumulates the amounts and changes for these fiscal categories as the figures appear in separate bills and compares them with the total in the most recent budget resolution. Through these reports Congress is kept informed about how its individual decisions affect its overall fiscal policy goals.

The priority for claims on CBO resources are first, the Budget committees; second, the Appropriations, House Ways and Means, and Senate Finance Committees; and third, other committees. Its reports and analyses are either issued separately by the office or appear, in whole or in part, in publications originating mainly with the budget committees. The CBO occasionally issues a list of publications and maintains an index of available information to facilitate public access to its material. At this time, the latter is a strictly chronological listing of items which may be examined only by an in-person visit. Thus, the *Monthly Catalog, CIS/Index*, and *American Statistics Index* are the best means of access to its research output.

INTERIM BODIES

Situations arise when it is impractical or inappropriate to commit proposals requiring congressional attention to standing committees. Some of the reasons that permanent panels may fail to address important issues are an unusually heavy workload, inadequate staff resources, meager member interest, or uncertain political consequences. Whether the reasons for inaction or ineffective action are substantive, political, practical, or procedural, there is a legislative response that is applicable in all cases. Temporary units are a flexible instrument that can overcome some deficiencies in legislative organization and the indifference of standing committees.

Two such panels, which owe their existence to legislative authorization, are select committees and advisory commissions. These interim bodies are formed to investigate an issue or problem and submit recommendations to Congress, the president, or both. They expire after a specified period of time or upon submission of their final report. Common reasons for their creation are that they enable all major political interests affected by a given situation to be represented by appointment, focus public attention on a matter by publicizing it, and are a means for according priority to the consideration of complex and critical developments. Their formation also implies a judgment that a problem exists, it is important, some action is necessary, and federal action is justifiable.

Select committees are especially useful to counteract the difficulties posed by an issue whose subject matter overlaps the jurisdiction of two or more standing committees. Advisory commissions seem most appropriate when the technical nature of a question and the expertise needed to address it are beyond the capabilities of legislators and their staffs. In the process of gathering and analyzing information these entities can also serve as a forum for reaching a compromise among numerous parties with various purposes. That they are usually in a better position to perform in a visibly fair and politically neutral manner increases the perceived caliber and efficacy of their eventual product.

While these entities can place new issues on the governmental agenda and contribute to public education, they may be formed to deflect political pressure or unfavorable attention from existing organizations that are unable or unwilling to cope with certain situations or subjects. Their creation may also be a dilatory tactic intended to mollify one or more interests by demonstrating that a matter is receiving its rightful quota of consideration while a concrete response is discreetly deferred.

Their major functions are to conduct investigations of specified matters, evaluate the performance of government or reality of conditions, prepare and issue reports, and submit recommendations or alternatives. The printed products may include hearings, staff studies, background papers, preliminary reports, legal analyses, and statistical surveys. The *Monthly Catalog* and *CIS/Index* provide the best bibliographic coverage of these publications.

FEDERAL AGENCIES

Another way for legislators to keep informed of developments that affect their responsibilities is to have government executives prepare and transmit reports to Congress. Research studies may be required or requested of federal agencies through legislation, resolutions, committee reports, hearings, or informal agreements. In whatever form the call is conveyed, its recipient may be the president, an agency administrator, or any other executive-branch official, and may provide that the document be submitted to Congress, either house, or one or more committees.

Prescribed reports may focus on administrative activities, decisions, findings, plans, or any other aspect of policy formulation or implementation. Reporting requirements may range from the known utility of a concise presentation of certain facts and figures to an extensive and detailed account of conditions and alternatives that may generate considerable controversy. The content and timing of reports depend on such factors as the legislative agenda, the political climate, substantive needs, and agency resources. These also determine whether a report will be legally mandated or otherwise demanded.

The prerogative to assign reports enables Congress to specify at a relatively early stage of deliberation the type of information it needs to address a given subject or problem. Such a requirement allows or compels an agency to commence and complete a study and state its views. This approach combines administrative expertise with the legislative desire to respond to political matters. For legislators who may lack other resources or opportunities, sponsoring a report may be a more realistic and effective way to participate in the policy process than introducing legislation.

Reports also serve as vehicles to stimulate or supplement public debate. They can and do inform the general public and particular publics about the nature of issues and capabilities of government. These documents also contribute to the education of legislators who may be able to use them as an information base on which to forge their own proposals. By commanding or inducing agencies to issue reports Congress pursues increased legislative knowledge and influence at the same time that it promotes broader public understanding and participation. The basic goal is to strengthen the political and policy position of the legislative branch as it competes with the vast information resources of the executive branch.

An annual publication entitled *Reports to Be Made to Congress* is issued as a House document and lists all such items mandated by law that federal entities, including the president, must submit. A biennial volume entitled *Requirements for Recurring Reports to the Congress* is published by the General Accounting Office. It includes statutory and nonstatutory requirements as well as voluntary submissions and contains an abstract of each report cited. Since some of these products may not be printed or, if printed, may be incorporated into various congressional publications, not all of them will be listed or clearly identified in the *Monthly Catalog* or *CIS/Index*.

PRIVATE ENTITIES

There are two principal ways to classify private-sector organizations that issue research products which legislators may use. Three basic categories emerge from a classification by purpose. One includes organizations that conduct research without regard to its potential impact on public policy. The primary emphasis is on objective or scientific inquiry as a means to advance knowledge or surpass competitors. Another is composed of units whose research is intended to influence policy decisions but that refrain from direct political activity. They advance some version of the public interest and endeavor to foster a climate of opinion conducive to its reception. Finally there are those whose research is part of the effort to represent or benefit particular constituencies or clients. They advocate opinions and cultivate legislators as they seek to have specific proposals enacted into law.

A threefold division is also derived from a classification by type. One covers nonprofit corporations, which include research institutes, scholarly and technical societies, and academic institutions. Another consists of profitmaking firms, which may range from the small consulting office to immense industrial enterprises. Lastly there are interest groups in the form of professional and trade associations. While a clear correlation exists between the units described under the third purpose and third type, other relationships between purposes and types tend to be less consistent.

The research produced by these organizations may take a variety of forms. Nonprofit corporations may prepare self-initiated studies or reports under contract. These projects may appear as articles in scholarly journals, pamphlets printed by the unit itself, or books published commercially or by the unit of origin. Profitmaking firms issue annual reports, prospectuses, and advertising brochures. Such publications discuss problems and resources, results and plans, and products and services. Interest groups circulate newsletters, position papers, and magazines. This literature serves to explain and justify an industrial or occupational viewpoint.

There is no single source that can be consulted for the names of all organizations whose research output may influence public opinion and policy formation. However, there are two particularly useful annual directories that provide much valuable information. Both are comprehensive in scope though their content is confined to the national capital area. They identify and describe private and public sector organizations that directly or indirectly influence public policy. The *Washington Information Directory* is published by Congressional Quarterly and *Washington 87* is issued by Columbia Books. The former is organized exclusively by major subject area, while the latter combines a subject arrangement with some classification by purpose and type. Each has an extensive organization/subject index.

STANDING COMMITTEES

As with proposed legislation, all policy research is funneled through standing committees. Limits on time, expertise, manpower, and funds usually mean that panels request and review rather than create research products. However, occasions arise when it is considered more appropriate for committee staff to undertake a project than to have it prepared by an external entity. In this case the panel has several options to augment its resources for the task.

Either house of Congress may authorize a committee to pursue a specific inquiry and grant it additional funds for such a purpose. Panels may also make use of the contingent fund of each body to let contracts for the temporary services of consultants. The first case requires the full chamber to adopt a resolution, while the second needs the consent of the Senate Rules and Administration or House Administration committee. Both instances involve the formal approval of colleagues and indicate the relative importance of the enterprise.

Committees may also arrange to borrow staff from the Congressional Research Service, General Accounting Office, or federal agencies when technical mastery or policy acumen is essential. Fellowship and internship programs exist that can also provide trained professionals and subject specialists from other areas of government or the private sector. These means are mainly used to supplement the assistance obtained through other channels or sources. In seeking research support, it is often necessary to employ different skills at different stages of the operation.

In the legislative environment, time becomes a more critical element in the research process than in other settings. This is because whoever can first produce a thorough and cogent study is in a strong position to shape the course of public and political debate. Thus, a research strategy is needed that is consistent with the intended use of the results. Criteria and procedures should be established in advance for each phase of the project. Time must also be allowed for contingencies that compel adjustments to or deviations from the original plan.

A research work conceived and composed by a standing committee eliminates two steps in the effort to frame legislation. First, it obviates the need for a fresh review of findings and recommendations; second, it averts the effort required to translate proposals into appropriate legislative language. In addition, arrangements exist to expedite the issuance of congressional publications by the Government Printing Office. Tighter control over the scheduled completion and distribution of these inquiries can be the deciding factor in the choice of a primary author. Committee research may appear as nonlegislative committee reports, committee prints, printed hearings, and Senate or House documents.

REFERENCES

Coleman, James S. "Policy Research in the Social Sciences," in *Policy Analysis on Major Issues*, A Compilation of Papers Prepared for the Commission on the Operation of the Senate. Committee Print, 94th Congress, 2nd Session. Washington, D.C.: U.S. Government Printing Office, 1977.

Johannes, John R. "Statutory Reporting Requirements: Information and Influence for Congress," in Abdo I. Baaklini and James J. Heaphey, editors, *Comparative Legislative Reforms and Innovations*. Albany, N.Y.: State University of New York Press, 1977.

Schick, Allen. "The Supply and Demand for Analysis on Capitol Hill," in *Policymaking Role of Leadership in the Senate*, A Compilation of Papers Prepared for the Commission on the Operation of the Senate. Committee Print, 94th Congress, 2nd Session. Washington, D.C.: U.S. Government Printing Office, 1976.

U.S. Congress. House. Commission on Administrative Review. *Final Report*. House Document No. 95-272, 95th Congress, 1st Session. Washington, D.C.: U.S. Government Printing Office, 1977.

U.S. Congress. House. Commission on Information and Facilities. *Congressional Budget Office: A Study of Its Organizational Effectiveness*. House Document No. 95-20, 95th Congress, 1st Session. Washington, D.C.: U.S. Government Printing Office, 1977.

U.S. Congress. House. Commission on Information and Facilities. *Information Resources and Services Available from the Library of Congress and the Congressional Research Service*. House Document No. 94-527, 94th Congress, 2nd Session. Washington, D.C.: U.S. Government Printing Office, 1976.

U.S. Congress. House. Commission on Information and Facilities. *Inventory of Information Resources for the U.S. House of Representatives — Part II: Other Resources in the Legislative Branch*. Committee Print, 94th Congress, 2nd Session. Washington, D.C.: U.S. Government Printing Office, 1976.

U.S. Congress. House. Commission on Information and Facilities. *Inventory of Information Resources and Services Available to the U.S. House of Representatives — Part IV: Private Organization Resources*. Committee Print, 94th Congress, 2nd Session. Washington, D.C.: U.S. Government Printing Office, 1976.

U.S. Congress. House. Commission on Information and Facilities. *The Office of Technology Assessment: A Study of Its Organizational Effectiveness.* House Document No. 94-538, 94th Congress, 2nd Session. Washington, D.C.: U.S. Government Printing Office, 1976.

U.S. Congress. House. Commission on Information and Facilities. *Organizational Effectiveness of the Congressional Research Service.* House Document No. 95-19, 95th Congress, 1st Session. Washington, D.C.: U.S. Government Printing Office, 1977.

U.S. Congress. House. Committee on Rules. *Guidelines for the Establishment of Select Committees.* Subcommittee Print, 95th Congress, 1st Session. Washington, D.C.: U.S. Government Printing Office, 1977.

U.S. Congress. House. Committee on Science and Technology. *Technical Information for Congress.* 3rd ed. Committee Print, 96th Congress, 1st Session. Washington, D.C.: U.S. Government Printing Office, 1979.

U.S. Congress. House. Select Committee on Congressional Operations. *General Accounting Office Services to Congress: An Assessment.* House Report No. 95-1317, 95th Congress, 2nd Session. Washington, D.C.: U.S. Government Printing Office, 1978.

U.S. Congress. Joint Committee on Congressional Operations. *Congressional Research Support and Information Services.* Committee Print, 93rd Congress, 2nd Session. Washington, D.C.: U.S. Government Printing Office, 1974.

U.S. Congress. Senate. Commission on the Operation of the Senate. *Congressional Support Agencies,* A Compilation of Papers Prepared for the Commission on the Operation of the Senate. Committee Print, 94th Congress, 2nd Session. Washington, D.C.: U.S. Government Printing Office, 1976.

U.S. Congress. Senate. Committee on Government Operations. *Congressional Oversight: Methods and Techniques.* Committee Print, 94th Congress, 2nd Session. Washington, D.C.: U.S. Government Printing Office, 1976.

U.S. General Accounting Office. *Analysis of Requirements for Recurring Reports to the Congress.* Washington, D.C.: General Accounting Office, 1980.

4

Hearings*

Committees are the instruments through which Congress chooses to screen and process proposals to change public policy. A committee decision to hold hearings, except for the annual appropriations and budget process, indicates that a matter has crossed the threshold of political salience. These proceedings serve to focus public and political attention and may be a prelude or an alternative to legislation. This chapter explores the multipurpose nature of hearings, examines their structure and procedure, and discusses their contents. The aim is to offer a framework within which to analyze and assess the printed product.

Committee hearings play a crucial role in the life of legislation. The result of these proceedings determines whether a bill will advance beyond committee consideration and, if so, what revisions, if any, the committee deems necessary. Hearings form a bridge between a bill's referral to committee and a committee's recommendation to its parent body for favorable legislative action. Both the House and Senate have rules that apply to hearings and all committees have additional rules that supplement those of each chamber. These stipulations are few in number and narrow in scope. This encourages political participation and informal negotiation before access to committee members becomes more restricted and procedures more formal during later stages of the legislative process.

PURPOSES

To schedule hearings is an option entirely within the discretion of a committee or subcommittee. Since time is one of a legislator's most valuable resources, the decision to invest it in hearings is evidence that an issue will receive serious consideration. Hearings may be held because committee members express much interest in a proposal or subject, great concern is manifested by other major political actors or a combination of both factors. They may reflect the state of public opinion, or of certain interested publics, as perceived by legislators, or they may be planned to influence the way in which an issue is perceived by the public.

---

*This chapter derives from an article, "Congressional Committee Hearings," by Jerrold Zwirn, in *Government Publications Review*, Vol. 7A, pp. 453-61, © 1980 Pergamon Journals, Ltd. Reprinted with permission of Pergamon Journals.

Hearings are a means of collecting and conveying factual and political information. As a communication medium that provides the opportunity for several goals to be pursued simultaneously, not all of which are necessarily consistent, they serve as a versatile legislative tool. They enable legislators to judge whether further committee or congressional action is necessary or to demonstrate that such action is or is not warranted. This entails preparing a foundation for recommending that legislative action be legally binding, politically compelling, advisory, or deferred.

Legislative and oversight proceedings constitute the two basic types of hearings. The latter are mainly retrospective and involve a review of existing laws from the standpoint of policy priorities, program effectiveness, or administrative discretion. The former are mainly prospective and may focus on one or more introduced bills, a bill about to be introduced, or a subject on which legislation is contemplated. Since most public policies can be modified by either administrative or legislative action, these differences are more a matter of emphasis than substance. It is not unusual for oversight hearings to indicate that a legislative remedy might be appropriate or vice versa.

The ideal function of hearings is to enable legislators to obtain those facts needed to make informed and rational policy decisions. However, technological and political developments have contributed to an environment in which the prevailing condition is a surfeit, rather than a scarcity, of information. Its availability has transformed the hearing process into a central clearinghouse for ideas and opinions needed by all participants in the political arena. Hearings are an integral part of any overall strategy designed to enact a bill into law.

All significant legislation hearings are a political necessity. Only by subjecting a bill to extensive and intensive scrutiny can a committee produce a measure that can survive the challenges that await it at each stage of the legislative process. Hearings provide one of the earliest opportunites to ascertain whether the compromises that are an indispensable ingredient of all major bills are likely to materialize. They tend to generate agreement on the main outlines and major provisions of a measure while identifying secondary or divisive features whose elimination would facilitate its passage.

Hearings may last one day or several weeks depending upon the nature of the matter addressed or committee purposes. Proceedings may be prolonged to generate public and congressional interest and support or may be brief in an effort to forestall the mobilization of opposition. A large number of witnesses may mean that, rather than giving a proposal thorough consideration or being too lenient in permitting testimony, a committee is engaged in a delaying action. Such a tactic is employed to obstruct legislation by leaving insufficient time for a bill to pass through all stages of the legislative process prior to congressional adjournment.

The duration of hearings, though usually planned in advance, is always subject to unforeseen conditions. After one or more sessions they may be adjourned without plans to reconvene, with plans to reconvene at a definite time, to reconvene at an unspecified time pending the availability of certain testimony, or to await developments that may warrant further proceedings. Given a preferred outcome, legislative strategy and political expediency combine to determine which course will be followed.

Though hearings may be held on a measure there always remains the possibility that a committee will conclude that legislation is unnecessary or inappropriate. One of these situations occurs where a hearing provides a forum for viewpoints denied other outlets. This function can be quite important when it serves to ameliorate social or economic tensions by giving aggrieved parties an opportunity to publicly present their case. There are also occasions when the nature of legislation suggested by hearings is viewed with apprehension by the parties that would be affected. This development encourages an extralegislative reconciliation of differences rather than the acceptance of an imposed solution. In both instances the results will often obviate the need for legislation. A similar result ensues where a committee holds hearings on a bill that its members know will not advance any further. The purpose is to attract attention and introduce colleagues, other political actors, and the public to a matter so as to place it on the political agenda and prepare the ground for its eventual passage.

Oversight hearings are a means of monitoring the administration and effectiveness of programs that have been enacted into law. Appropriations and budget hearings are held on an annual basis. The latter is a review of broad governmental functions that overlap agency jurisdictions. It constitutes an assessment of national priorities and the direction of current or proposed activities considered essential to attain policy objectives. Other than the president's budget message, budget committee hearings provide the only occasion for a regular and comprehensive overview of public business and purposes.

Though appropriations hearings always precede appropriations legislation, their nature corresponds more closely to an oversight proceeding. Their focus is on administrative decisions as these affect the economy and efficiency of agency operations. The chief topics covered are financial administration and the status of specific projects. These are discussed from the standpoint of the agency's budget estimates for the coming fiscal year. Appropriations hearings entail a detailed examination of everyday matters and provide many insights into the nuts-and-bolts aspects of government.

Legislative oversight is conducted by the same committees that are usually occupied with the consideration of bills. Thus, oversight by these panels tends to be irregular because it rarely generates the interest and publicity that attends new legislation. When these committees are sufficiently motivated they will hold hearings to determine whether the programs under their jurisdiction are achieving intended purposes. Some of the reasons that lead to such hearings include adverse media coverage, constituent or clientele complaints, admission of difficulties by executive branch officials, a program that results in continual litigation, critical reports by private research organizations, or leaks by agency personnel about mismanagement or malfeasance. A trend toward more frequent legislative oversight involves placing more programs on an annual authorization basis. Such reauthorization hearings on bills that would extend or amend existing statutes inevitably result in a form of program oversight.

All oversight hearings serve to keep committee members informed of significant administrative developments, provide for an exchange of views to clarify the nature of particular problems, and afford an opportunity for legislators to evaluate the capabilities of administrators. An oversight hearing may address the validity of assumptions underlying existing policies or programs. Such an evaluation of the necessity or adequacy of statutes may elicit information that convinces committee members of the need for remedial legislation. However, these proceedings are usually concerned with either legislative intent or the propriety of particular decisions, both of which stem from the discretion conferred on administrators by all important public laws.

Both legislators and administrators continually seek to reconcile legislative intent with administrative discretion. Legislators endeavor to influence decisions that result from the need to delegate authority, while administrators undertake to apply policy in a manner that will enhance their professional or political status. Since personnel changes in both committees and agencies occur with some regularity the interpretation of legislative intent and the use of administrative discretion are likely to vary over time. Thus, oversight hearings may be employed to reinforce or reemphasize committee messages conveyed at prior hearings, by committee reports or through informal channels. The occasion may also be used by legislators to insist upon, or by administrators to explain, the adoption of different criteria or procedures for implementing programs. By emphatically expressing their views committee members attempt, in a public forum, to extract policy-oriented commitments from not always reluctant executive branch officials.

When oversight hearings focus on specific agency decisions they may expose questionable or inefficient practices or function as a disciplinary proceeding for an administrator. In this instance a legislator or a committee in its corporate capacity either anticipates or has experienced some political embarrassment because of agency action or inaction. The aim of committee members would be to either reverse a decision or ensure that it did not recur. It should be recognized that congressional dissatisfaction with agency performance may reflect disagreement with presidential intentions. This attention to discrete decisions whose effects can be directly linked to the political reputations of elected officials gives these proceedings a somewhat narrower cast than those discussed in the preceding paragraph.

Hearings may represent an effort to expose the weaknesses and sophistries of some plausible proposal being advanced by a narrow or partisan interest. A committee may wish to discredit such a faction so that a constructive search for policy alternatives may proceed without distortions that impede agreement on a viable approach. In this case legislators must communicate with the public to counteract the effects of political oversimplification. This is not to imply that legislators are always impartial judges seeking only to advance the public interest. Hearings may denote a genuine quest for facts and views or a staged proceeding designed to support a previously reached conclusion. They can be a sincere search for a reasonable course of action that commands wide acceptance or an attempt to confer an aura of respectability on a policy decision of questionable efficacy. Hearings also enable undecided legislators to gauge public opinion by noting who supports or opposes a proposal and to calculate the political advantages or disadvantages of their own position.

Hearings are also an occasion for interested groups and knowledgeable individuals to present their views and versions of the facts. The desired result would be the encouragement of mutual understanding and accommodation that promotes development of a consensus. These proceedings are tangible evidence of citizen access to the policy process. By furnishing a forum for all prominent perspectives a committee precludes the allegation of biased judgment and demonstrates that it has discharged its duties in a responsible manner. Balanced and thorough hearings serve as a source of legitimacy for subsequent committee decisions.

Two factors that influence hearings and are vital to an understanding of their effects are climate and content. The former refers to the political environment of an issue and includes such elements as the primary locus of influence in a given policy area and the nature of committee relationships with other political entities. The latter concerns the political complexion of a bill and involves such matters as the degree of controversy engendered by its provisions and the ability of committee members to negotiate satisfactory compromises among competing interests. These considerations often provide a key to explain subsequent committee or congressional action, such as the length and pace of legislative proceedings and the number and nature of proposed amendments.

Committee hearings may be scheduled to transmit technical or political information, to assess the political feasibility of policy proposals, to influence public opinion or administrative action, or to promote or impede legislation. They provide a permanent public record of the views advocated by the various parties interested in a given issue and afford evidence of committee diligence and integrity. Though hearings are not the only means that may be used to accomplish each of these purposes, they are the only means that can be used for all of them. The variety of goals that may be pursued via hearings are closely related but sufficiently distinct to allow their results to be interpreted differently by most interested parties. They can consume much time and effort yet yield an uncertain product. Hearings ultimately represent an attempt by legislators to acquire information and exert influence, which confirms the observation that information is power.

STRUCTURE AND PROCEDURE

Considerable committee staff work is a prerequisite to constructive and productive hearings. These activities pertain to subject matter and witnesses. All pertinent printed materials are consulted and concisely summarized. Prospective witnesses, including executive branch officials and representatives of major private organizations, are regularly sent questionnaires regarding the matter under consideration. These individuals often welcome the opportunity to express their views and prepare the ground for their possible testimony. It is then necessary to systematize this information after determining which specific topics will be addressed. After taking into account the views of committee members, staff members formulate questions designed to elicit the responses considered necessary to yield optimal results.

The gathering of information, including synopses of secondary materials, acquisition of official documents, analysis of questionnaires, and related correspondence, generally leads to compilation of a briefing book. Along with an introductory memorandum written by staff members, this collection of material is used to familiarize legislators with the details of the bill or subject and enables them to prepare for their participation in the hearings. While hearings are in progress the committee staff usually prepares a digest of each day's testimony to clarify what ground has been covered and what remains to be surveyed.

A coordinate phase of the preparation process involves the number, selection, and order of witnesses. Except for government officials, whose testimony is considered essential on matters affecting the jurisdiction of their agencies, key committee and staff members decide who will be invited or permitted to appear.

In most cases all organizations with a substantial interest in the issue will be offered the opportunity to testify. Two aspects to the order in which witnesses appear are status and substance. The former pertains to the positions of individuals, who are usually given priority as follows: members of Congress, executive branch officials, private organization representatives, non-government specialists, and others. The latter concerns the overall order of witnesses, which should be planned so as to present a logical development of the subject.

While there is no right to testify, all major viewpoints should be represented to meet the criteria of thoroughness and fairness. The rules of each house of Congress also entitle minority party members to invite witnesses to testify on at least one day during hearings held on any proposal. It is not uncommon for committee staff to meet in private with prospective witnesses prior to their public appearance. A review of projected testimony and planned questions minimizes the possibility of surprise or embarrassment and promotes cooperation and communication. This practice is also intended to preclude the possibility of an adversary proceeding.

Since most legislation or oversight covers ground that committees, to at least some extent, have previously tread, it can be anticipated who will wish to testify and what positions will be taken. The combination of staff preparation and member familiarity with the subject of hearings usually averts unexpected developments. However, what cannot be foreseen with equal clarity is the public impact of and response to all testimony, especially when an issue is dramatized by the plight of ordinary citizens or the confrontation of major public figures.

A well-organized hearing involves observance of certain preliminary procedures. These relate to providing adequate advance notice to all interested parties, informing prospective witnesses of the questions or subjects the committee would like them to address, and obtaining written copies of statements from those who wish to submit them. The rules of each house stipulate that committees make a public announcement of the date, place, and subject matter of any hearing at least one week in advance, unless there is sufficient cause to begin sooner. The rules also urge committees to require submission of written statements by witnesses and to limit oral presentations to a brief summary of such statements.

Despite adequate preparation and sound procedure hearings may be used to either generate support for or opposition to a proposal. This can be done by the manipulation of their timing and length, the selection and order of witnesses, and committee member questions. Hearings may constitute an attempt to advance the views of certain witnesses when members, who share such views, ask helpful questions. They may also represent an effort to harm the prospects of other witnesses when members, who disagree with their views, pose hostile questions. Though testimony from various viewpoints may help to bring an issue into sharp focus, much of it can be propagandistic and intended to score political points.

The House has a rule allotting five minutes to each committee member who wishes to question each witness before any member may proceed to use more time. The Senate has an informal ten-minute rule. This traditional format, though it can be expedient for some legislators and functional for the entire committee as indicated by the earlier discussion of purposes, does not promote extended exchanges between members and witnesses. Comparative analyses of different viewpoints or intensive exploration of specific concepts or conclusions are unlikely to emerge.

To induce results that are more informative and incisive a committee may organize a panel discussion in lieu of or in addition to hearings held in the customary manner. This approach is similar to a seminar, with the invited participants and committee members jointly discussing prescribed topics while the committee chairman serves as a moderator. For the consideration of complex or controversial economic or social issues this arrangement has some advantages over the usual procedure of witness testimony accompanied by committee member interrogation.

It enables advocates of one view to directly challenge proponents of a competing view. Exposure of each presentation to criticism from diverse perspectives can highlight areas of accord and promote a synthesis of opinions. The invited panelists, as specialists, are in a better position to evaluate proposals advanced by other specialists than are committee and staff members who tend to be generalists. Thus, the committee is relieved of some of the burden of assessing technical testimony and discerning emerging agreement.

These discussions also enhance the educational value of hearings by contributing to an improved grasp of the subject by legislators, staff, and other interested parties. Panel members normally submit research papers to the committee which are printed prior to the hearings. This allows all prospective participants to prepare in advance and focus on points in dispute or on those that need elaboration. That this form of hearing is not more widely used can probably be attributed to the fact that it limits the ability of committee members to exercise control of the proceedings. Also, since panels are usually scheduled in addition to regular hearings, there is the matter of being able to fit them into the legislative timetable.

Regardless of the format, all hearings begin with an opening statement from the presiding legislator, who is a committee or subcommittee chair. These remarks, which are written in advance of the hearings, review the subject to be covered and the questions to be explored. The specific situation or reason that prompted the hearings and an outline of what the committee expects to accomplish are also offered. On occasion the committee press release announcing the hearings and describing the ground rules under which they will be conducted is inserted into the official transcript. Each witness begins testimony with a brief summary of the major points included in his or her written statement. The remainder of this chapter is devoted to a description of the contents and uses of the printed record.

THE PRINTED TRANSCRIPT

The original transcript of testimony is usually available for examination in the committee office soon after the conclusion of hearings. Its printing is at the discretion of the committee, but is almost always ordered when legislation is under consideration. Except for appropriations hearings, they are seldom printed prior to floor action on a bill. The time lag between the presentation of testimony and its availability in print may be minimal or it may be months depending upon committee workload or strategy. The length of this interval is relatively unimportant for most legislators, who would not have the time to read the volumes and who primarily rely on the concise committee report for written information that they need on proposed legislation.

The printed record is not a verbatim transcript for three reasons. First, committee members and witnesses are routinely given the opportunity to edit their remarks. Second, the presiding legislator may make and permit others to make off-the-record statements. Finally, confidential matters are discussed at sessions closed to the public and this testimony is not included, though it is usually noted, in the record. However, these practices only rarely detract from the value of what does appear in print. (See figure 3 for an example of a printed hearing.)

The cover page of a hearing will normally note the subject, subcommittee and full committee name, Congress and session, bill number, and hearing date. Though hearings are not a formal series, some committees for their own convenience assign alphabetical or numerical serial designations to them throughout each session or Congress. When hearings are extensive they are issued in numbered parts, a practice that apprises readers of the existence and sequence of the other volumes.

Though all hearings contain valuable material, they are not always edited or printed in a form that facilitates access to their contents. All appropriations hearings have running subject headings and subject indexes. Since these proceedings tend to be the most voluminous, such aids are essential to locate specific parts of the text. However, their appearance in other hearings is irregular. For most, the only finding aid is the contents, which may be arranged alphabetically or chronologically by organization or individual. While some contents are convenient guides to witnesses, organizations, committee member statements, and supplementary material, many are barely adequate and none can substitute for a subject index. It should be recognized that preparation of such an index requires time that cannot always be so invested owing to other committee priorities. In many instances the titles of hearings are either inconsistent, even though the subject matter is identical, or they do not adequately describe their contents. Most of the difficulties posed by these shortcomings have been eliminated by *CIS/Index.*

Hearings do not consist of coherent essays that lead to logical conclusions. As a phase of the policy process they routinely reflect the untidy and fortuitous nature of the political environment, including exaggeration and opportunism. Composed of dialogue that frequently shifts between related or unrelated subjects and numerous insertions of supplementary material, hearings exhibit a somewhat disjointed text. Objective information is available from the statements and reports of neutral sources and may be gleaned from the record by comparing and contrasting the views and data presented by parties in disagreement. Even an instructive hearing, because of the form of its proceedings and format of its transcript, tends to yield its substance with some reluctance.

Equally as important as oral testimony is material prepared either in advance of or subsequent to a hearing and inserted into the record. Printed hearings are regularly used as a means of presenting supplementary material that would not otherwise be published or made readily available. Such information may be placed at the rear of the volume, distributed throughout the text, or organized by a combination of these methods depending upon its relationship to oral or written testimony. The various types of such material are discussed in the following pages.

URGENT RELIEF FOR THE HOMELESS ACT

HEARING

BEFORE THE

SUBCOMMITTEE ON
HOUSING AND COMMUNITY DEVELOPMENT

OF THE

COMMITTEE ON BANKING, FINANCE AND URBAN AFFAIRS
HOUSE OF REPRESENTATIVES

ONE-HUNDREDTH CONGRESS

FIRST SESSION

ON

H.R. 558

A BILL TO PROVIDE URGENTLY NEEDED ASSISTANCE TO PROTECT AND IMPROVE THE LIVES AND SAFETY OF THE HOMELESS, WITH SPECIAL EMPHASIS ON FAMILIES AND CHILDREN

FEBRUARY 4, 1987

Printed for the use of the Committee on Banking, Finance and Urban Affairs

Serial No. 100–3

U.S. GOVERNMENT PRINTING OFFICE

68–633 O   WASHINGTON : 1987

For sale by the Superintendent of Documents, Congressional Sales Office
U.S. Government Printing Office, Washington, DC 20402

Fig. 3. A committee hearing.

1. Prepared statements are submitted by witnesses in advance of the hearings and address questions that were derived from committee staff analysis of the subject under consideration. Since hearings often result in frequent changes of focus owing to the fluctuating attendance and varying interests of committee members, it is advisable to read the prepared statement before turning to the discussion that embraces an individual's oral testimony. Witnesses also have the opportunity to submit additional supporting material for the record. Included are the written statements of those who did not have the opportunity to appear in person. These remarks do not become a part of the record and thus, publicly available, until approved by a committee or staff member. They may be omitted or rejected based on either content or length.

2. When panel discussions are held the papers submitted by panelists are arranged and printed by topics in the order in which they are scheduled for discussion.

3. Administrative documents and directives include internal agency papers that describe and analyze decisions and operations. Though presented in support of agency actions, such material offers an inside view of how policies are implemented.

4. A committee may request the General Accounting Office or contract with a private organization to evaluate an agency's performance. The resulting management analysis or cost-benefit study will usually appear in the record.

5. Staff studies prepared by committee or agency personnel or by private entities that specialize in a subject or policy area are commonly made part of the record.

6. Upon the conclusion of hearings there may be several reasons for the insertion of additional questions and answers into the record. During the course of testimony questions raised by legislators, but not addressed by witnesses, are answered afterwards; some legislators unable to attend the hearings have written questions distributed to certain witnesses; some who do attend do not have the time to ask all the questions they have and also submit written ones; and review of oral testimony by committee members and staff often results in further questions to clarify statements or obtain more data.

7. Committee correspondence includes exchanges of information or views with agency personnel or with non-government representatives regarding agency policies or plans.

8. Pertinent newspaper or journal articles are regularly collected and incorporated into the record.

9. Two multiple insertions peculiar to appropriations hearings relate to budget justifications and spending decisions. The former is composed of detailed descriptions of each program administered by an agency and is prospective in nature. This material includes much statistical data and comparative figures of funds expended in the current fiscal year and the amount requested for the coming fiscal year. The latter consists of explanations of the circumstances involved in the commitment of funds for particular purposes and is retrospective in nature. This material includes information that supports the continuation or expansion of programs and discusses their scope and effects. These two insertions provide a comprehensive and itemized accounting of all aspects of an agency's activities and functions. A major portion of each appropriations hearing is comprised of documentation submitted by the agency being scrutinized.

10. One other type of insertion, as rare as it is valuable, is the contents of a committee briefing book.

For legislative history purposes one would proceed from subsequent committee or congressional action as expressed in committee reports, floor debate, or versions of a bill to those pertinent comments or more elaborate explanations that appear in the printed record. Significant components of legislative hearings are (1) the text of the bill or bills under consideration, (2) a detailed discussion of the implications of a measure's provisions, (3) agency analyses of bills and suggested amendments, and (4) examination of amendments from other sources. Hearings are especially valuable regarding the origins and background of amendments to a bill as it is reported by the committee. It should be noted that in reaching decisions, legislators are free to ignore testimony delivered at hearings or to apply information not presented at such proceedings.

A mark-up session is scheduled when committee members conclude that they have all the information they need or can obtain or that further action cannot be delayed. At this meeting, or series of meetings, the panel frames its final decisions on the content of a bill. The measure is read line by line, with each word, phrase, or clause open to discussion and analysis. Interpretations and amendments are proposed and debated, with decisions reached by consensus if possible and by vote if necessary. The consequences are significant for both the pace of panel action and substance of the bill. When these proceedings are printed, which is seldom, they may appear in the same volume with hearings or as a separate publication in hearing form. (See figure 4 for an example of a hearing and mark-up.)

There are at least three occasions on which a bill or program is considered by more than one committee and is the subject of more than one hearing. A comparison of these separate but related proceedings provides information about the evolution of legislation, which committees emphasize which aspects of a proposal, and those parties impelled to press appeals because of dissatisfaction with the results of earlier hearings. One situation arises when hearings are held on the same bill by the corresponding committees in the House and Senate. Another instance occurs where an appropriations committee considers an appropriate allocation of funds for an agency or program after it has been authorized by a legislative committee. A less common development involves those bills whose

INCREASE AMOUNT OF FEDERAL PAYMENT

HEARING AND MARKUP

BEFORE THE

COMMITTEE ON
THE DISTRICT OF COLUMBIA
HOUSE OF REPRESENTATIVES

NINETY-NINTH CONGRESS

SECOND SESSION

ON

H.R. 4479

TO AUTHORIZE THE ANNUAL FEDERAL PAYMENT FOR FISCAL YEAR
1987 OF $444,500,000

———

MAY 6, 1986

———

Serial No. 99–18

———

Printed for the use of the Committee on the District of Columbia

U.S. GOVERNMENT PRINTING OFFICE

61-590 O   WASHINGTON : 1986

For sale by the Superintendent of Documents, Congressional Sales Office
U.S. Government Printing Office, Washington, DC 20402

Fig. 4. A combined hearing and mark-up.

provisions overlap the jurisdiction of two or more committees in the same chamber, in which case each panel may consider the entire measure or only specified portions.

An investigation is a proceeding that is closely related to a hearing. The major difference between them is that investigations are precipitated by the failure or frustration of the customary communications process. Because their primary purpose is to compel the disclosure of information they tend to be adversary in nature. Investigative procedures are, thus, more numerous and more formal since the committee may issue subpoenas to compel the attendance and testimony of witnesses and the production of papers, an action that can lead to legal proceedings. In regard to the printed record all that applies to hearings is equally applicable to investigations except for the lack of discussion and material directly related to legislation.

Hearings disclose the alignment of and the rationale for positions maintained by political contestants and illuminate the congressional decisionmaking process. The development and enactment of public policy invariably involves the readjustment of societal relationships. It is in the context of a potentially altered status that many parties design and deliver their testimony. Thus, to strengthen their case, those who would be most affected by congressional action attempt to link their interests to general communal goals and values. The hearing is an institutionalized mechanism employed to regularize and canalize the multilateral bargaining that always accompanies major legislation. An examination of the printed record in conjunction with related materials reveals that, though legislators make the formal decisions, others often make substantial contributions to the ultimate result.

The printed record is a valuable compilation of material on the nature and impact of an issue and testifies to the fact that information is rarely neutral because of the different interests and values that affect how it is perceived. A hearing or its transcript may be viewed from at least three perspectives. For committee members it is an instrument used to shape and justify immediate actions and a yardstick for future hearings. For participants in the political process it is a reservoir of argument and an agent for devising strategy concerning the proposal under consideration. For students of government it is a source of the most up-to-date information on a given policy, program, or subject and a guide to further research.

REFERENCES

Berman, Daniel M. *In Congress Assembled.* New York: Macmillan, 1964.

Goodwin, George, Jr. *The Little Legislatures.* Amherst, Mass.: The University of Massachusetts Press, 1970.

Griffith, Ernest S. *Congress: Its Contemporary Role.* 4th ed. New York: New York University Press, 1967.

Gross, Bertram M. *The Legislative Struggle.* New York: McGraw-Hill, 1953.

Jewell, Malcolm E., and Samuel C. Patterson. *The Legislative Process in the United States.* New York: Random House, 1966.

Keefe, William J., and Morris S. Ogul. *The American Legislative Process.* 3rd ed. Englewood Cliffs, N.J.: Prentice-Hall, 1973.

Kofmehl, Kenneth. *Professional Staffs of Congress.* West Lafayette, Ind.: Purdue University Studies, 1962.

Morrow, William L. *Congressional Committees.* New York: Scribner's, 1969.

U.S. Congress. Senate. Committee on Government Operations. *Congressional Oversight: Methods and Techniques.* Committee Print, 94th Congress, 2nd Session. Washington, D.C.: U.S. Government Printing Office, 1976.

5

Committee Reports*

The importance of committee reports in the legislative process stems from their inseparable link to congressional bills. Reports are agents of action whose contents are historical, factual, analytical, and political in nature. As retrospective documents they present a concise prelegislative history of issues and legislative history of bills. As prospective documents they explain the purposes and provisions of measures so as to maximize potential support. The implicit and explicit political considerations interwoven with the account of facts, events, expectations, and intentions that comprise reports are all essential for an understanding of federal legislation.

United States statutes are neither self-explanatory nor self-executing. Their passage normally represents the culmination of a lengthy process that begins with conception and concludes with enactment. During this period of time proposed laws develop a history that elucidates their means and ends. Such information is most cogently and methodically conveyed via committee reports. This chapter presents a detailed examination of reports, focusing on the purposes, content, format, and uses of those that accompany public bills. The underlying theme is the relationship between reports and bills and how this relationship affects the nature and status of reports.

TYPES AND PURPOSES

Though reports originate in committees they are officially termed House and Senate Reports. Since bills are of the foremost importance and are treated as official documents of each chamber, the reports filed with them are designated in a corresponding manner. Reports are the formal means employed by committees to communicate with their parent body. Their contents constitute an explanation by an agent of the manner in which it has discharged the responsibilities delegated to it by its principal. They comprise a separate and distinct class of publications through which committees convey information and submit recommendations for the consideration or approval of each house.

---

*This chapter derives from an article, "Congressional Committee Reports," by Jerrold Zwirn, in *Government Publications Review*, Vol. 7A, pp. 319-27, © 1980 Pergamon Journals, Ltd. Reprinted with permission of Pergamon Journals.

Reports can be divided into two major categories—legislative and non-legislative. The latter category includes those that are exclusively housekeeping in nature and those with policy implications. The housekeeping variety primarily concern the printing of documents or committee expenditures and include legislative activity reports issued by each committee. Reports that are nonlegislative but may affect or lead to legislation include studies or investigations by committees of programs, agencies, or subjects within their jurisdiction; those that accompany concurrent resolutions in conjunction with the congressional budget process; and those filed with resolutions which realign committee jurisdictions, create new panels, or amend the rules of either house. A nonlegislative type that is unique to the House is filed by its Rules Committee and invariably consists of a single sentence recommending adoption of a resolution. The resolution prescribes the rules and conditions that will govern floor consideration and debate of bills previously reported by other committees. Also nonlegislative in purpose are those in the Senate that accompany treaties and nominations and are designated as Executive Reports.

Special reports may be either legislative or nonlegislative in nature and originate in two ways. Either house may instruct a standing committee or create a temporary panel to study or investigate a given situation or subject. Also, certain standing committees are expected to submit recurring reports to keep their parent body informed of developments in an area of continuing interest. These reports may contain specific legislative proposals, general recommendations for legislative action, or simply may present the results of an inquiry.

The category of legislative reports can be subdivided into those accompanying public bills and those filed with private bills. While public measures embody proposals to establish general policy, private measures provide specific relief for individuals or organizations from the effects or requirements of existing policy. Private bills are usually based entirely on a factual situation, while public bills involve value judgments and the allocation of resources as well as facts.

Public measures take the form of either authorization or appropriation bills. Authorizations create or continue programs or agencies and set the maximum level of funds that may be appropriated therefor. Appropriations, which normally follow authorizations, authorize agencies to expend specified amounts of public funds for specified purposes. Authorization bills, by repealing law, and appropriation bills, by denying funds, may terminate or suspend the operation of an agency or program. This chapter will focus on the reports that accompany authorization and appropriation measures.

A committee may report a bill favorably, unfavorably, or without recommendation. The overwhelming majority of measures are reported favorably. Those that cannot attract the support of a majority of committee members rarely receive committee attention. While a bill is a proposal that would mandate a change in public policy, its accompanying report advances the case for favorable legislative action by marshaling arguments to justify the change. Reports are an essential supplement to bills because the latter, as potential law, consist only of commands and do not offer explanations as to why such commands are desirable or how they should be construed.

Reports present findings and recommendations that are derived from and refined through committee hearings and deliberations. If a bill is brief, simple, and uncontroversial, its report will reflect such circumstances and will not contain much more than some general comments and the committee's recommendation for passage. Controversial or significant measures will entail the preparation of detailed and lengthy analyses that highlight committee reasoning on all major points.

The factor most responsible for the content and format of a report is its primary audience—the membership of Congress. It is a relatively concise presentation of the political issues involved and decisions reached during a bill's consideration. Reports are designed to provide members of Congress with sufficient information to evaluate a measure by emphasizing the political context within which the committee acted. The purposes of a bill are addressed from both an overall perspective as well as from an analysis of the objectives of each major provision. This explanation of the relationship between the whole and its parts is intended to elucidate the committee's position and to generate support for the proposal. For busy legislators, reports tend to be the main written source of information on bills because they are presented in a politically useful form.

The degree of committee unity is one of the key factors that affects a committee decision to report a bill favorably to its parent body. The closer a panel is to unanimity, the greater the possibility that its proposal will be approved as reported. It is considered embarrassing and distressing for committee members when their recommendations are rejected, reversed, or revised by floor action. The desire to avoid this outcome motivates each panel to accommodate its members without unnecessarily weakening a bill. This disposition accounts for language in a committee report that may appear inconsistent with the language of the bill. In this case the risk of erroneous interpretation, which can be rectified, is subordinated to political solidarity, the absence of which can cause more serious problems.

Agency administrators who will be responsible for the execution and enforcement of a bill once it is enacted into law are also a group that reports are meant to influence. Executive branch officials are expected to regard the directives, suggestions, criticisms, and general advice included in reports as having almost, if not the full, force of law. Legislators intend such statements to serve as instructions or guidelines for administrative decisions. If ignored the result may be the use of more formal instruments of control, such as investigations, more detailed and restrictive statutes, or reduced appropriations. Thus, while reports are not legally binding, they are regularly consulted by administrators when questions arise about the meaning or purpose of particular statutory provisions.

There are two major reasons for placing some committee dicta in reports rather than in legislation. One is that legislators recognize the need for administrative discretion if programs are to be effectively implemented and should report statements prove to be inapplicable or inimical they can simply be disregarded. Another is the greater time and difficulty involved in attempting to draft legal language to cover the various situations that may confront an administrator. When executive branch officials decide to act in disregard of a report, they are expected to seek prior approval of key committee members.

Another audience at which reports are aimed is comprised of members of the judiciary. In litigation that concerns the application and interpretation of statutes, judges require information that can clarify legislative intent. Reports are almost always consulted in such cases.

The rules of each house of Congress stipulate that, for a standing committee report to be valid, a committee majority must be present at the meeting that authorizes it to be filed, though the actual number of members voting to report may be less than a majority of the full committee. The rules of both houses also provide that each report accompanying a public bill, except for appropriation measures, must contain:

1. The total number of votes cast for and against the motion to report when such decision is made by a roll call vote. In the Senate, the vote of each committee member must also be noted.

2. A comparative print of those provisions of the reported bill and any statutes it would amend or repeal, showing by appropriate typographical devices the proposed changes. Where a bill amends a law by adding a provision, the report must quote the section of the law immediately preceding the proposed amendment. In the House this is known as the Ramseyer rule and compliance with it can only be waived by a floor vote. In the Senate it is known as the Cordon rule and a committee may dispense with its requirements by stating in its report that such action was necessary to expedite Senate business.

3. A detailed statement, where applicable, concerning new budget authority or new or increased tax expenditures authorized by the measure.

4. An estimate prepared by the Congressional Budget Office relating to the costs that would be incurred by implementation of the measure and a comparison of such estimate with any presented by the committee or a federal agency (if submitted in time for inclusion).

5. Supplemental, additional, or minority views concerning the reported bill when committee members give proper notice of their intention to file such views. The inclusion of these views must be noted on the first page of the report. This requirement also applies to appropriation bills.

House rules require the following information to appear in its reports:

1. The findings and recommendations of the committee regarding the administration and effectiveness of those laws within its jurisdiction that relate to the reported measure.

2. A summary of any findings and recommendations made by the Government Operations Committee pertaining to the reported measure (if submitted in time for inclusion).

3. An estimate prepared by the committee concerning the costs that would be incurred by implementation of the measure and a comparison of such estimate with any submitted by a federal agency.

4. An inflation impact statement that analyzes the potential effect of the measure on the national economy.

Senate rules provide that its reports must contain an evaluation of the regulatory impact of a measure, consisting of:

1. An estimate of the numbers of individuals and businesses that would be affected.

2. A determination of the groups and classes of such individuals and businesses.

3. The probable effect upon personal privacy.

4. The anticipated volume of additional paperwork that would result and costs that would be incurred.

In the absence of such information, a statement of the reasons why compliance with the rule was impracticable must be included.

Though both houses have rules that require all reports accompanying public bills to be printed, the Senate permits its committees to dispense with *written* reports to expedite chamber business. However, the force of custom restricts the use of such discretion to very few occasions.

Information required by House and Senate rules amounts to only a limited portion of most reports and reveals nothing about format. Over time, reports have assumed a form which, though not invariable, has consistent features presented in a regular order. The descriptions below represent a group portrait rather than a picture of a typical member. Differences among reports reflect such factors as previous committee or congressional consideration of the subject, the degree of controversy engendered by the issue, the form and content of the bill itself, or committee member preferences.

AUTHORIZATION REPORTS

Reports that accompany authorization bills may consist of as many as eight distinctive parts. (See figure 5 for an example of a committee report.)

1. Introduction: This part always includes the number and session of Congress, body of origin, report number, succinct statement of the bill's subject, date reported, committee member responsible for submitting the report, committee that considered the measure, bill number, brief description of the bill's purposes, a statement as to whether the measure is reported with or without amendments, and a recommendation that the bill be passed. When applicable, it will note that supplemental, additional, or minority views are included and there may be a table of contents. The introduction is the most standardized portion of any report.

Calendar No. 157

| 100TH CONGRESS
1st Session | SENATE | REPORT
100-64 |

THE CIVIL RIGHTS RESTORATION ACT OF 1987

JUNE 5, 1987.—Ordered to be printed

Mr. KENNEDY, from the Committee on Labor and Human
Resources, submitted the following

REPORT

together with

MINORITY VIEWS

[To accompany S. 557]

The Committee on Labor and Human Resources, to which was referred the bill (S. 557), to restore the broad scope of coverage and to
clarify the application of title IX of the Education Amendments of
1972, section 504 of the Rehabilitation Act of 1973, the Age Dis-
crimination Act of 1975, and title VI of the Civil Rights Act of
1964, having considered the same, reports favorably thereon with
an amendment in the nature of a substitute, and recommends that
the bill as amended do pass.

I. INTRODUCTION

On May 20, 1987, the Committee on Labor and Human Resources, by a vote of 12-4, ordered favorably reported S. 557, "The
Civil Rights Restoration Act of 1987." Senators voting in favor of
the bill were Senators Kennedy, Pell, Metzenbaum, Matsunaga,
Dodd, Simon, Harkin, Adams, Mikulski, Stafford, Weicker, and
Cochran. Voting against were Senators Hatch, Quayle, Thurmond,
and Humphrey.

The bill is sponsored by Senator Edward M. Kennedy, Chairman
of the Committee, and cosponsored by Senators Weicker, Metzenbaum, Packwood, Cranston, Stafford, Adams, Baucus, Bentsen,
Biden, Bingaman, Bradley, Breaux, Burdick, Chafee, Chiles, Cohen,
Daschle, DeConcini, Dodd, Ford, Fowler, Glenn, Gore, Harkin, Hol-

91-109 O

Fig. 5. A committee report.

2. Committee Amendments: When the text of amendments is included it will usually follow the introduction. Such text will most often appear when a committee reports a substitute, which is an amendment in the form of a rewritten bill covering the same subject as the introduced version, with only the original bill number being retained. If separate amendments are adopted, the precise place in which they are to be inserted is specified by reference to the page and line number of the introduced bill. Should amendments not appear here, their text may be derived from part 5 below.

3. Body: There are several components of this subdivision, whose content and order is subject to greater variation than any other part.

   a. Summary and Purpose—A brief presentation of the general objectives of the bill.

   b. Background and Need—A historical survey of the issues involved along with a discussion of existing programs and policy options. Executive branch communications requesting the introduction and consideration of a measure are likely to be quoted. Where a bill primarily proposes amendments to a statute, there may be an analysis of how well its purposes have been fulfilled.

   c. Major Provisions—An exposition of the bill arranged topically by its principal purposes, including discussion of the rationale for committee decisions. This portion may cite references to hearings, court decisions, and government studies.

   d. Legislative History—An account of committee and congressional action in prior Congresses on the same or similar bills, which will usually be identified by their numbers. Committee actions in regard to the measure being reported would also be discussed, if not presented separately.
   Two components that appear with less frequency are:

   e. Committee Amendments—A discrete treatment of their substance will most often appear when the bill being reported originated in the other house or was initially considered by another committee in the same chamber. A comparison of the significant differences between the two versions is customarily presented. The committee of original jurisdiction may also discuss its amendments under this heading, but such discussion is usually incorporated into the Major Provisions subsection.

   f. Hearings—A summary of the testimony which notes the issues raised and the positions taken. The main arguments in favor of and in opposition to the bill, as presented by agency and organization spokesmen, as well as a committee analysis of and response to each major point, may be offered. The information contained under this heading is usually incorporated into either or both the Major Provisions and Legislative History subsections.

These components are not always clearly labeled or distinguished and some may be combined in different proportions, but they can be identified by a cursory examination.

4. Section-by-Section Analysis: This is a detailed explanation, in nontechnical language, of the purpose of each section in the order in which it appears in the bill. It is the most authoritative interpretation and forceful presentation of legislative intent. Included are definitions of all important terms and most of the statements aimed at administrators and judges. General committee expectations, which may be communicated under a separate heading immediately preceding or at the very beginning of this part, would serve as additional guidance for executive and judicial officials.

5. Comparative Print: This is the text of the differences between a reported bill and the law it proposes to amend as required by the Ramseyer or Cordon rule. Of course, if the measure would not change existing law this part is omitted.

6. Agency Views (or Executive Communications): Committees almost always solicit the views of those agencies that would be responsible for a proposed law or program as well as agencies that have government-wide responsibilities, such as the Office of Management and Budget and the General Accounting Office. These views may be conveyed in a letter that summarizes the agency viewpoint or by a report that provides an agency analysis of each major provision of the introduced bill. Since agency personnel regularly appear at committee hearings, these views may be incorporated into that part of the committee report which covers such proceedings.

7. Supplemental, Additional, and Minority Views: Though the rules of each house provide only for these three views, most committees will approve the use of other headings to distinguish the views of individuals or combinations of individuals from one another when several reasons are advanced for differing with the majority. Other common headings include concurring, separate, individual, dissenting, and opposing views. Some of these views can be differentiated as follows:
   - Supplemental views reflect an endorsement of the legislation for reasons other than those offered by the majority.

   - Additional views indicate general agreement with the majority except for specified provisions.

   - Minority views are reserved for use by minority party members who disagree with the aims or methods or both that are embodied in a bill.

   - Dissenting views usually express strong disagreement by majority party members.

All views, except those of the majority, are signed by the members expressing them. The body and section-by-section analysis constitute the majority view.

8.   Appendix: Two types of information would appear in this part. One is either excerpts or the quotation in full, from government documents that relate to the matter addressed by the bill. The other is statistical or other data compiled by the committee staff to facilitate consideration of the measure by committee members.

All authorization reports will have an introduction, body, and section-by-section analysis, with the inclusion of other parts and the length and detail of any part subject to conditions previously mentioned. The content of a report will often depend on whether the same or a similar bill has been previously reported, either in the same or the other house. If a significant amount of time has elapsed since the earlier report, the later one will usually serve as an implicit or explicit reply. In addition, the subsequent one may contain only abbreviated subsections covering background and need and legislative history, if it does not omit them entirely.

Should the subject matter of a bill overlap the jurisdiction of two or more committees it may be simultaneously referred to each for consideration. A report will be filed jointly and if the panels are unable to reach agreement on the substance of the bill to be reported, the report will communicate this fact. It will also state that the alternatives recommended by each committee will be offered as amendments when the bill reaches the floor to allow the parent body to decide which to accept. Such broad-gauged bills may also be referred sequentially to two or more panels, in which case the last to consider it forges the final form of the reported version. In the Senate all reports by different committees on the same bill have different report numbers. In the House all such reports bear the same number, but are designated as different parts of the first report to be filed.

When numerous bills on the same subject are introduced and referred to the appropriate committee, the panel may decide to combine the provisions of several into a single measure. A committee member will then introduce this legislation as a new bill, which will be referred to the same committee and reported as a clean bill. This procedure avoids reporting a bill with many amendments, each of which would have to be considered separately by the parent body. The report will mention when this has been done and will identify the numbers of those bills that were amalgamated into the reported version.

Though most language in authorization reports is issued as if it originated with the committee, this is not always the case. Commentary and phraseology may be solicited from or offered by any entity concerned with the legislation. Regardless of the source or its adaptation, once language receives the committee imprimatur it becomes the official statement of legislative intent. Though an author may not be acknowledged, the originator is always pleased to have the panel adopt a written presentation. This practice also conserves committee resources when such drafts are consistent with panel views and goals.

APPROPRIATION REPORTS

Reports that accompany appropriation bills differ sufficiently from those filed with authorization bills to warrant separate treatment. The primary reasons for these differences are (1) appropriations must be enacted each year if government agencies are to continue to function; (2) by custom, these measures originate in the House and are reported as original bills, which means that they are drafted in committee rather than introduced by a legislator and referred to a committee; and (3) their text allocates specified sums of money to specified agencies for specified purposes. At present there are thirteen general appropriation bills that provide the spending authority for all except those few agencies that are self-sustaining.

House and Senate rules each contain a similar stipulation relating to reports filed with general appropriation bills. Senate reports must identify each committee amendment that proposes an appropriation not necessary to implement the provisions of an existing law or treaty. House reports must contain a statement describing the effect of any provision in the bill that would change the application of existing law. Both requirements are aimed at the same practice, which is the inclusion in appropriation bills of provisions that impinge upon the jurisdiction of other committees. Since conditions may render this practice necessary or desirable, the rules instruct the appropriations committees to highlight each such provision so that the parent body may consciously pass upon its expediency.

Reports that accompany appropriation bills may consist of as many as six distinctive parts.

1. Introduction: Except for minor differences derived from the fact that the House Appropriations Committee is reporting an original bill, this part is identical to that for authorization bills.

2. Body: There are usually three components of this part, which appear in the following order:

   a. Summary — A brief description of committee recommendations, including a tabular recapitulation.

   b. General Discussion — A review of significant matters that were elicited at committee hearings and a brief account of the major factors affecting governmental expenditures covered by the bill.

   c. Major Provisions — A commentary arranged by bill title, with the budgets of larger agencies discussed in terms of their subdivisions. The authorizing legislation under which each agency or program operates is usually cited. The extensive annual hearings held by appropriations subcommittees represent the most regular and thorough review by Congress of the administration of the laws it enacts. Report statements that focus on the use of administrative discretion illustrate the committee's attention to detail and concern with economy and efficiency. Senate committee reports normally reflect the results of appeals made by agencies of decisions reached by the House committee and where differences exist between the two figures, they will be specifically addressed.

3. General Provisions: These are stipulations that apply to all of the appropriations made in the bill, to more than one of the agencies covered by the bill, or to all of an agency's appropriation rather than to a single account.

4. Limitations and Legislative Provisions: This part notes those provisions, mentioned above as being required by the rules of each house, that would amend existing law.

5. Supplemental, Additional, and Minority Views: This section is identical to that for authorization bills.

6. Expenditure Tables: One table compares permanent budget authority for the current fiscal year, which does not depend upon congressional action, with the level of such authority contained in the budget estimates submitted by the president for the coming fiscal year. This table is arranged by agency and by program thereunder. A second table compares new budget authority that was enacted for the current fiscal year with new budget authority recommended in the bill. The Senate committee report has additional columns comparing its figures with those of the House bill. This table is arranged by bill title and corresponds to the Major Provisions subsection. There will occasionally appear a third table showing the proposed allocation of funds by function or organizational unit and geographical area.

Two other types of appropriation measures are supplementals and budget rescissions. The former provides additional budget authority beyond the levels prescribed by the general appropriation bills owing to new programs authorized since their passage or an urgent need that cannot be postponed until the next general appropriation act. The latter revokes previously enacted budget authority prior to the time it would lapse. The submission of formal presidential requests initiates the consideration of both types of measures. Reports that accompany supplementals and rescissions identify, by their House and Senate document numbers, the presidential messages that prompted committee action. All reports on appropriation bills will always include an introduction, body, and tables.

MODIFICATION

Committees may file supplemental reports any time prior to floor consideration of a bill and these would be designated as successive parts of the original report. One of the reasons that leads to submission of a supplemental report is the need to correct an error that was overlooked during the process of drafting and proofreading. Another reason would be to complete a report whose original version failed to include all information required by the house rules. A final reason stems from a change in the situation a bill is designed to address, which results in a recommended revision of the measure and a corresponding revision of its accompanying report. Should a typographical error appear in a printed report, it will be reprinted with a star in the lower left-hand corner of the first page to indicate it is a corrected copy.

Once a bill reaches the floor it may be recommitted, or returned to committee by the parent body, for one of two reasons. If a bill is ruled out of order on the floor because its accompanying report fails to meet all requirements of the house rules, it is automatically recommitted. The parent body may also express its disapproval of a measure by voting to recommit it. In both cases the reports are nullified and must be filed anew for the bill to be considered. A subsequent report is treated as a new and separate report and is assigned a new number, but it will identify the previous report by number.

Though reports are formal statements whose importance often rivals the bills they accompany, the fact that they consist of argument and explanation and do not have the force of law means that they are not themselves acted upon by the parent body during floor consideration of a bill. Thus, a report cannot be formally amended by legislators who may disagree with some of its contents. However, there are ways in which reports can, in effect, be amended. One method is to amend that portion of a bill to which a particular report statement applies. To the degree that a measure is significantly amended on the floor, the value of a report for construing its provisions decreases. Another approach is to have language included in a subsequent report that neutralizes language contained in an earlier one. This may be accomplished by the insertion of a restrictive or contrary statement or by omission of the disputed words. One other way is to engage in floor debate about the interpretation of specific report comments with the intention of clarifying or limiting their application.

CONFERENCE REPORTS

The final report that would be submitted on a bill is a conference report (see figure 6). Conference committees are ad hoc panels whose members are appointed from among the members of those standing committees that considered a bill in each house. Their purpose is to reconcile the differing versions of a measure as it was passed by each chamber. Authorization and appropriation conference reports will not be differentiated since, except in one particular, their form is identical. For a conference report to be valid a majority of the conferees from each body must sign it.

A conference report is a combined bill and report. The first, or bill, portion is the conference report proper and contains the text of all changes to the measure agreed upon by the conferees. The second part, which is equivalent to a report, is termed the *Joint Explanatory Statement*. It describes the legislative effect of the changes adopted. Unless otherwise indicated, further mention of a conference report will refer to the joint statement. To the extent that they differ from or omit language appearing in either standing committee report, the latter is superseded.

The introduction to a conference report includes a brief statement of the bill's purposes, the bill number, and a summary description of the manner in which the conferees resolved their differences. Its body corresponds to the section-by-section analysis of an authorization report or the major provisions subsection of an appropriation report. The precise format of the body depends upon the manner in which the second chamber amended the bill.

100TH CONGRESS *1st Session*	HOUSE OF REPRESENTATIVES	REPORT 100-426

HOUSING AND COMMUNITY DEVELOPMENT ACT OF 1987

NOVEMBER 6, 1987.—Ordered to be printed

Mr. ST GERMAIN, from the committee of conference,
submitted the following

CONFERENCE REPORT

[To accompany S. 825]

The committee of conference on the disagreeing votes of the two Houses on the amendments of the House to the bill (S. 825) to amend and extend certain laws relating to housing, and for other purposes, having met, after full and free conference, have agreed to recommend and do recommend to their respective Houses as follows:

That the Senate recede from its disagreement to the amendment of the House to the text of the bill and agree to the same with an amendment as follows:

In lieu of the matter proposed to be inserted by the House amendment insert the following:

SECTION 1. SHORT TITLE AND TABLE OF CONTENTS.

(a) SHORT TITLE.—This Act may be cited as the "Housing and Community Development Act of 1987".

(b) TABLE OF CONTENTS.—

79-029

Fig. 6. A conference report.

Either house may amend a bill that originated in the other by deleting its entire text and inserting the text of a bill on the same subject that has been reported or passed in the second chamber. This form of amendment is termed a substitute. In this case the conference report will usually contain a descriptive summary of the comparable House and Senate provisions and refer to the derivation of each change adopted. By providing an explanation of how differences in language were resolved and stating whether the conference provision is identical to that of the House or Senate version or a combination of both, it is determined whether a standing committee report or the conference report conveys the conclusive interpretation of any particular provision.

Where the second chamber passes a bill of the first with separate amendments, which can number in the hundreds, the conferees normally trade on most of them, with the first house acceding to some and the second receding on others. Those remaining in disagreement will then be compromised. It is these latter changes that are discussed in the conference report. Amendments that are purely technical or clarifying in nature are simply identified as such and not discussed further, even if they involved compromises. Each amendment is identified by a number that is assigned to it based upon the order in which it appears in the bill and each is discussed in numerical sequence.

Appropriation bills are invariably sent to conference via the second method outlined above. When the Senate changes the amount or language of a House-passed appropriation bill, it inserts a numbered amendment into the text of the measure. These amendments are numbered consecutively and are cited in the conference report by their number. Thus, it is necessary to use the text of the Senate-passed bill to follow the conference report. At their close, conference reports present the totals agreed upon and compare them with prior fiscal year figures, budget estimates submitted by the president, and the House and Senate versions of the bill as it was sent to conference.

Though dissenting views may not be included, a phrase following a signature in a conference report may note exceptions taken by certain conferees. Those conferees who disapprove of the entire report can only decline to sign it. Statements expressing disagreement would be inconsistent with the basic purpose of a conference, which is the resolution of differences between the two houses. Formal expressions of dissent must await floor consideration of the conference report proper.

A substitute amendment that reaches conference results in either complete agreement or disagreement. Separate amendments sent to conference may also produce partial agreement. The number of each amendment remaining in disagreement appears at the end of the bill portion of the report. In this case the report may discuss the reasons for the lack of total accord and recommend actions to each body that would promote agreement. If the conference report proper is approved by each house, the status of the amendments reported in disagreement remains unaffected. The authority of a second conference would be limited to those matters not disposed of by the first.

When the conference report proper is recommitted or rejected by either house the bill reverts to its preconference status. A second conference would have authority to consider the measure as if it had not been previously sent to conference. A subsequent conference report on the same bill, whether due to partial agreement, recommitment, or rejection of the earlier one, is assigned a new number and treated as a new and separate report. This latter report will identify the previous one by number. A conference that is unable to reach any agreement will file a report consisting of only the joint statement, explaining why differences could not be reconciled. In this instance there also remains the possibility of another conference.

REFERENCES

Kirst, Michael W. *Government Without Passing Laws.* Chapel Hill, N.C.: University of North Carolina, 1969.

Kofmehl, Kenneth. *Professional Staffs of Congress.* West Lafayette, Ind.: Purdue University Studies, 1962.

U.S. Congress. House. *Constitution, Jefferson's Manual and Rules of the House of Representatives.* House Document No. 98-277, 98th Congress, 2nd Session. Washington, D.C.: U.S. Government Printing Office, 1985.

U.S. Congress. House. *Procedure in the U.S. House of Representatives.* 4th ed. 97th Congress, 2nd Session. Washington, D.C.: U.S. Government Printing Office, 1982.

U.S. Congress. House. Committee on Rules. *Legislative Reorganization Act of 1970.* House Report No. 91-1215, 91st Congress, 2nd Session. Washington, D.C.: U.S. Government Printing Office, 1970.

U.S. Congress. House. Committee on Science and Technology. *Legislative Manual.* 4th ed. Committee Print, 99th Congress, 1st Session. Washington, D.C.: U.S. Government Printing Office, 1985.

U.S. Congress. Senate. *Senate Legislative Procedural Flow.* 95th Congress, 2nd Session. Washington, D.C.: U.S. Government Printing Office, 1978.

U.S. Congress. Senate. *Senate Procedure.* Senate Document No. 97-2, 97th Congress, 1st Session. Washington, D.C.: U.S. Government Printing Office, 1981.

U.S. Congress. Senate. *Standing Rules of the Senate.* Senate Document No. 99-22, 99th Congress, 2nd Session. Washington, D.C.: U.S. Government Printing Office, 1986.

6

Debate

Though the *Congressional Record* contains a detailed account of floor proceedings, it does not elucidate the purposes that inform or the procedures that influence the structure and substance of legislative debate. The differences derived from contrasting parliamentary environments are as important for understanding House and Senate deliberations as are their similarities. Independent majorities in each chamber determine what action is necessary or desirable and when action is imperative or appropriate. In this sense, a distinct congressional agenda does not exist. The House and Senate each form their own agenda and, though comparable, they are not identical.

The scheduling of business for chamber action entails efforts to balance institutional efficiency and political considerations. Such plans need to be consistently stable to enable legislators to organize their activities, yet sufficiently flexible to meet public exigencies. The key question concerns how each house can coordinate the functional areas of its committee system and manage its legislative workload in a manner that ensures fitting and timely decisions. The schedule for and structure of legislative business are matters as vital as its substance. These arrangements involve methods and options geared to accord with the practical and political convenience of members of Congress, both individually and collectively.

Floor action is the most formal stage of the legislative process. The body of House and Senate rules and customs is intended to assure systematic and comprehensive consideration of proposed legislation. This requires the application of numerous and complex procedures to promote orderly deliberations and facilitate reasonable decisions during proceedings in which all members are eligible to participate and which serve as the basis for final disposition of a bill. House rules reflect the majority party views on how the chamber should be governed, while those in the Senate are instrumental for minorities who wish to protect their interests or protest majority intentions.

Both houses rely to a considerable extent on unanimous consent requests to conduct their business. Such requests are used to expedite chamber proceedings where the written rules are silent, prescribe a time-consuming procedure, or expressly prohibit an action. The resort to consent indicates that the rules, if scrupulously followed on all occasions, would often inhibit timely, effective, and smooth action when all or most members agree on the need for it. Unanimous consent requests usually apply to minor matters over which there exist no sharp differences of opinion or serve to simplify, in a manner satisfactory to all parties concerned, the consideration of major measures. While any legislator by merely objecting to such requests can seriously skew the chamber timetable, it is rarely done, for two reasons. One is the realization that the integrity of the legislature could be impaired and the other is that the member may sacrifice his or her own legislative effectiveness.

The core of congressional debate, around which most discussion revolves, is the amending process. This chapter examines the nature of floor debate, describes the distinctive features and consequences of House and Senate proceedings, and explains the rules and practices that govern the consideration of amendments. As at other stages of action, proponents and opponents each use available parliamentary tools to their own advantage. Debate invariably reflects and reviews all previous congressional action on a proposal. Therefore, a complete picture of the contents of the *Congressional Record* also requires an account of the essential elements that affect the context of debate.

PURPOSES AND PRACTICES

SCHEDULING

Since the majority in each body is held accountable for its legislative output, regulating the flow of business to the floor is a party responsibility. Majority party leaders in the House apprise minority party leaders of the floor schedule in advance and usually entertain any objections or suggestions received. While the majority may stress speed and order in floor deliberations, a minority whose views are rejected or ignored can disrupt and delay, though it cannot obstruct indefinitely. The minority continually presses for predictability to avoid the possibility of parliamentary intrigue or abrupt action, while the majority wishes to avoid the appearance of arbitrary or abusive behavior. In the Senate both parties are on a more equal footing since the minority is in a position to thwart majority designs interminably and bring chamber action to a virtual standstill.

Majority party leaders always seek to widen available options as they attempt to discover or create the most propitious moment for chamber proceedings. Minority party leaders demand an opportunity to offer legislative alternatives and debate substantive issues. When the wishes of committee members and individual legislators are taken into account, it becomes clear that the conditions or procedures that serve the needs of one group often conflict with the needs of others. How and when bills reach the floor indicate whether they will be routinely ratified, thoroughly reviewed, or tenaciously opposed. The scheduling process may be simple or complex depending on a bill's substance, the time available to consider it, the degree of controversy it engenders, and the personal relationship between party and committee leaders.

Upon completing favorable consideration of a bill a standing committee reports it to the parent chamber. In this way a panel formally submits its recommendations for action and approval. All reported measures are referred to a calendar in the chronological order in which they emerge from all committees. A calendar is a legislative docket that provides information on pending business, including bills awaiting or undergoing floor action. Assignment of a calendar number to a measure, though an official recognition of its eligibility for chamber consideration, is a routine administrative matter. Calendar status neither requires action by the parent body nor limits its discretion to act.

Calendars reveal only the formal aspects of how minor measures reach the floor of each house. Where major legislation is concerned, calendars serve merely as a starting point for determining chamber priorities. Except for noting the date on which a bill is reported, the routine procedure of calendar status tends to veil more significant scheduling plans. The earlier a measure is scheduled during a Congress or session, the greater the time available for proponents to negotiate the compromises necessary for passage. Should proponents delay scheduling until later in a session, when members are eager to adjourn, they may be able to pass a bill that could not withstand extensive scrutiny. This strategy also places opponents in a position to kill a bill through dilatory tactics unless granted concessions.

For calendar transactions, the terms under which bills may be considered are stipulated by chamber rules. Each piece of major legislation, however, is unique in regard to the nature of its provisions and alignment of competing political forces. It cannot be brought to the floor by a regular parliamentary route because opponents would use the rules to veto such a move. Neither can it be scheduled for chamber action in the absence of a definite arrangement agreed upon in advance. To avoid legislative paralysis or futility each house has developed a mechanism for framing the ground rules under which controversial measures can be cleared for floor proceedings in a manner that satisfies all or most interested parties.

The means used by both houses involve more than simply establishing a framework for legislative deliberations. Prior to the formulation of conditions to regulate debate, the bills to be advanced must be selected and assigned priority. Among the more visible and typical factors taken into account during the discussions that precede these decisions are committee and chamber workloads, action by the other body, adjournment plans and the proximity of elections. Other considerations that relate to whether an issue has become politically ripe for legislative action include the extent of previous congressional attention, the need to acknowledge and accommodate committee efforts, the positions and activities of external political entities, and the state of professional and public opinion.

DEBATE

The primary functions of floor action are to review the recommendations of committees, legitimize collective pronouncements, and justify individual positions. From this standpoint, legislative debate produces a spontaneous exchange of views that provides an explanation of the practical and political merits of a bill, with proponents presenting the case for its passage and opponents arguing for its defeat or modification. Such discussion is intended to enlighten legislators so as to enable them to arrive at clear and definite policy decisions. In the course of proceedings the reasons that underpin these decisions should be clarified so that interested citizens may reach sound conclusions regarding rationale and results. However, the conditions under and means by which these purposes are pursued suggest that floor action be viewed in terms other than strict accountability of committees to the chamber or of legislators to the electorate.

By the time a major bill reaches the floor of either house most members have committed themselves to support or oppose it, while others, owing to lack of information or interest, are unfamiliar with its provisions. Thus, debate mainly serves to reinforce the conclusions of legislators who have already reached a decision or to rationalize the positions of those whose vote is based on considerations other than substance. Deliberations tend to reflect solidified sentiments and only occasionally serve to make converts. Though political discussion prior to floor action often means the latter becomes a mere formality, chamber debate does have two important general purposes. One is to present intelligibly arguments likely to receive extensive media coverage. This enables attentive citizens to judge better the policy questions that affect their welfare and prepares the ground for widespread public acceptance of legislative output. The other is an extension of the ongoing campaign to build a record concerning a bill's provisions. This effort is aimed at those responsible for administering and interpreting the law and who would be expected to consult such remarks for elucidation or guidance.

Debate is less an assessment of options than it is a variety of efforts to resist or strive for change. In addition to its wider aims, floor action also serves several strategic and tactical purposes. It may be used as a means of communication among allies on a given bill in regard to the timing of actions or nature of amendments. Debate may be employed to delay a vote so as to enable one side to try to alter the balance of opinion on the floor through superior argument or increased attendance. It may serve as a means to make explicit and formalize unwritten agreements reached during earlier stages of the legislative process. Chamber proceedings may also provide momentum for a bill prior to its consideration in the other house, in conference between the houses, or at the stage of presidential action.

While the previous paragraph applies to legislators as members of political coalitions, debate also serves individual objectives. By publicizing views that may have received inadequate attention earlier, legislators can and do contribute to a public dialogue and citizen education. Floor statements can be instrumental for member instruction as well, especially when knowledge about a proposal is not widespread, when a bill does not present partisan or ideological issues, or when amendments raise unanticipated questions. In these cases a forceful and factual speech may offer legislators a compelling reason or defensible justification for their vote. Finally, for legislators who are not completely enthusiastic about or unalterably opposed to a bill, debate offers an opportunity to express the intensity of their approval or disapproval for consumption by those whose support is valued.

All floor action is formally initiated and guided by the power of recognition exercised by the presiding officer. No appeal is permissible from a decision to grant or deny recognition. However, it is standard practice for the majority leader and floor manager to receive preference when they wish to be recognized. For the former, such instances cover all matters that concern the daily agenda, while the latter is accorded priority to address all questions that affect the disposition of a bill. When a measure is under consideration the presiding officer regularly maintains an informal list of those to be recognized, including the names, order, and purposes of each member, with party and committee leaders entitled to precedence whenever they rise.

For each bill that reaches the floor a member of the reporting committee, usually either the chairman or a subcommittee chairman, is designated as its floor manager. As the principal spokesman for the bill this individual replies to questions, rebuts criticism, and manages or monitors the time available for debate through allocation or limitation. This person must judge when committee amendments should be offered or deferred, when floor amendments should be accepted, modified, or opposed, and be prepared to explain the meaning and purpose of all amendments proposed. The custom that the floor manager be recognized to speak on all key occasions strengthens the role as the primary parliamentary strategist responsible for guiding legislation through to final passage.

The formal factor of type and the informal one of source are basic elements of the amending process. The four types of amendments embrace the parliamentary motions to insert, to strike out and insert, to strike out, and to substitute. The first and second are known as perfecting amendments and their consideration takes precedence over the other two types. The difference between the second and fourth is that the former applies to only a portion of the pending text, while the latter may apply to an entire subdivision or bill. When a substitute for an entire bill is offered, both the bill and substitute are open to perfecting amendments. After a perfecting amendment is offered, another or second-degree amendment may be proposed to the first, but amendments in the third degree are prohibited. Second-degree amendments enable proponents of a measure to propose modifications to counteract the appeal of amendments offered by opponents. This practice enables each camp to perfect its proposal prior to a final chamber decision.

The three sources pertain to those amendments reported by a committee in its corporate capacity, those offered from the floor by committee members who disagree with their panel's recommendations, and those proposed by non-committee members. In deference to committee specialization and effort, panel amendments are accorded a privileged status and must be disposed of prior to any that may be offered from the floor. However, floor amendments that apply to pending committee amendments are in order and a committee amendment that is a substitute for an entire bill will not be acted on until all floor amendments have been considered, for the approval of a substitute would preclude any other amendments. With these exceptions, committee amendments are debated in the order in which they appear in the reported version of a bill.

Since committees may be divided when major legislation is reported, those panel members who differ with the majority are often authorized to offer floor amendments as alternatives during consideration of committee proposals. Committee amendments are recommendations that are not officially incorporated into a bill until formally adopted by the parent body. The rejection of a committee amendment that deletes or modifies a portion or all of an introduced bill has the effect of restoring the original text. Once an amendment to some part of a bill has received chamber approval, it is no longer subject to amendment. This restriction, however, can be circumvented in two ways. First, words may be added to a previously adopted amendment or an amendment to a later section of a bill may be approved even though inconsistent with the provisions of an earlier amendment. Second, an amendment broader in scope than the one previously adopted that encompasses the earlier text as well as other provisions may be approved.

A common reason advanced by committee members to oppose floor amendments proposed by non-committee members is that such proposals should have been made while the bill was in committee and more time was available for thorough consideration. Proponents of such amendments often argue that committee membership is not representative of the entire chamber and the amending process broadens the range of interests that may exert influence on legislation. Though both contentions are generally valid, it should be noted that most floor amendments are offered by those who wish to weaken or kill a bill. Opponents may propose controversial amendments intended to reduce the support enjoyed by a bill or ones whose purpose is to nullify its principal provisions. Amendments originated by those in favor are designed to strengthen it or to neutralize hostile amendments.

Since amendments may be proposed to refine, as well as undermine, a measure, floor managers must decide whether to accept, modify, or oppose them. Legislative experience and subject-matter expertise may incline the floor manager to accept an amendment to accommodate one or more legislators rather than because of its intrinsic merit. There is a preference to defeat or deflect amendments on procedural grounds. Such action is less personal and leaves the matter open for future consideration under other circumstances. In some instances the preparation and offering of an amendment involve efforts similar to introducing a bill, including the selection of a prominent sponsor, assembling of cosponsors, and coordination of political activities.

Amendments may be offered to placate an external entity, stall for time while further negotiations are undertaken, test political sentiment for a proposal, or score political points. Members who propose amendments to important legislation can often attract more attention than introducing bills unlikely to reach the floor. The amending process generally comprehends endeavors by floor managers to repulse attempts to defeat or dilute the committee product. A legislative tendency to support the committee or majority party when in doubt enhances the ability of the floor manager to engineer coalitions favorable for maintaining panel recommendations intact.

HOUSE PROCEEDINGS

SCHEDULING

In the House all public bills are referred to either the Union Calendar or House Calendar. The former lists those measures that directly or indirectly raise or appropriate funds or dispose of public property, while all other public bills are assigned to the latter. The chief sponsor of a bill on either calendar may, by filing a written request with the clerk, have it placed on the Consent Calendar. This procedure is reserved for uncontroversial measures whose consideration may be expedited on two days each month and whose passage requires unanimous approval. Objectors' committees are designated by the majority and minority leaders to screen bills on this calendar. The informal rules generally applied by objectors are that a measure not involve more than one million dollars, not change national or international policy, and not be inconsistent with the president's program.

A House procedure that corresponds to a calendar is suspension of the rules. Though any bill, whether or not it has been introduced or reported, may be placed on a suspension list, in practice only those measures on a calendar are so treated. A letter from a committee chairman to the Speaker serves to request that a bill be considered under suspension procedure. The guidelines that govern the use of this legislative route are that a bill not involve funds in excess of $100 million and that there exist little or no opposition, particularly from the executive branch. Suspension of the rules is in order on two days each week and during the last six days of a session.

It is entirely within the discretion of the Speaker to recognize members for the purpose of making the motion to suspend the rules and, thus, to determine which bills will be brought to the floor in this manner. Because this procedure requires a two-thirds vote for passage its use is usually limited to relatively uncontroversial measures or those that cannot pass under unanimous consent. Though basically a means of expediting routine or minor business, it can be applied to emergency legislation. Only those amendments included in a motion to suspend the rules and pass a bill are in order under this procedure and debate is limited to forty minutes, equally divided between those who favor and oppose the bill.

These expedited procedures have been adopted in response to the fact that regular procedures do not ensure that certain measures progress from introduction to conclusive floor action within relatively short periods of time. Their use relieves some of the pressure on the agenda by enabling the House to act on more bills than would otherwise be possible if more elaborate methods were followed on all that were reported. In effect, the majority is willing to sacrifice a certain degree of agenda control over bills that matter less in return for greater control over those that matter more.

All House measures not accorded a privileged status under the rules and those that evoke organized opposition must be channeled through the Rules Committee to reach the floor. While the total number of such bills constitutes a relatively small proportion of chamber business, it includes most of the major proposals on the Union Calendar and House Calendar. To ensure its responsibility to and facilitate its cooperation with the majority party, the Speaker is empowered to appoint all majority members of the Rules Committee. The majority, to strengthen its control, also maintains at least a two-to-one margin on the panel despite the overall party ratio in the House.

The Rules Committee is authorized to report resolutions that apply to any bill whether or not it has been introduced or reported. In practice this discretion is confined to measures on the Union Calendar and House Calendar. The resolutions, formally termed *special orders* and informally known as *rules*, enable those bills to which they apply to be given precedence for chamber action. Such special rules are privileged business and confer a similar status on measures whose calendar number would prevent them from reaching the floor before congressional adjournment (see figure 7 on page 116). On the surface, it would seem that the Rules Committee simply discharges a procedural responsibility. However, any organ that enables some rather than other bills to receive House attention wields substantial influence over legislative output.

The request for a rule is initiated by the chairman of a committee that has reported or is about to report a bill. In deciding whether to draft a rule, a poll of House members is conducted by the party leadership to ascertain membership opinion on the bill. Special orders suspend the standing rules regarding a given measure and prescribe the terms under which it will be debated. In effect they are special rules formulated to meet the prevailing parliamentary and political circumstances. The major provisions of these resolutions cover length of debate, points of order, and floor amendments. Time limits relate to the number of hours or days allotted to general debate or to a particular day or time beyond which debate may not extend. The waiver of points of order involves the prohibition of challenges from the floor to the effect that the contents of a reported bill violate the standing rules of the House.

The most significant portion of a special order is that which pertains to permissible amendments. It may incorporate the text of only those amendments that will be in order, it may name those members only who are authorized to offer amendments, it may prescribe the order in which amendments are to be considered, it may allow amendments to only certain parts of a bill, it may prohibit or permit all amendments. Most bills receive an open rule, which enables any germane amendment to be proposed. Some are given a modified open rule, which provides that only specified amendments may be considered or offered to certain subdivisions of the bill. A few are granted a modified closed rule, which limits the amendments to be in order to those authorized and proposed by members of the committee of jurisdiction. A closed rule, which is requested by the reporting committee, prohibits all amendments and is rarely granted. It is justified on the basis of extremely complex or technical legislation that would be impaired by dubious amendments or because of the need to expedite emergency measures.

Though the Rules Committee does not possess the power to amend bills, proponents of a measure may agree to offer an amendment on the floor that a Rules Committee majority deems desirable so as to ensure favorable panel action. The Rules Committee may also compel another standing committee to accept certain amendments stipulated in a rule as the price for having its bill reach the floor. In addition, it may report a special order that contains provisions contrary to those desired by the panel that framed the bill. Rules Committee action may make in order for consideration an amendment in the nature of a substitute which might not otherwise be in order. This provides the House, or significant groups of its members, with a choice between alternative approaches to an issue.

A bill may be denied a special order and prevented from reaching the floor owing to opposition from the party leadership, another entity in the House, members of the Rules Committee, or some combination thereof. The panel's power to deny or delay a rule may prove useful for party leaders opposed to a particular measure or in favor of one that might not pass if brought to the floor too soon. Legislators badgered by conflicting demands from external political interests may prefer to avoid a vote and persuade the Rules Committee to refrain from further action. Bills may be denied clearance for chamber consideration because of strategic or substantive reasons or the combination of a heavy workload and time constraints.

A special order is more than simply official clearance for chamber action. It combines the power of the Rules Committee to alter the order of business and to report revisions to the standing rules of the House. Special orders prescribe the

IV

House Calendar No. 29

100TH CONGRESS
1ST SESSION

H. RES. 179

[Report No. 100-113]

Providing for the consideration of the bill (H.R. 1934) to clarify the congressional intent concerning, and to codify, certain requirements of the Communications Act of 1934 that ensure that broadcasters afford reasonable opportunity for the discussion of conflicting views on issues of public importance.

IN THE HOUSE OF REPRESENTATIVES

MAY 28, 1987

Mr. HALL of Ohio, from the Committee on Rules, reported the following resolution; which was referred to the House Calendar and ordered to be printed

---

RESOLUTION

Providing for the consideration of the bill (H.R. 1934) to clarify the congressional intent concerning, and to codify, certain requirements of the Communications Act of 1934 that ensure that broadcasters afford reasonable opportunity for the discussion of conflicting views on issues of public importance.

1   *Resolved,* That at any time after the adoption of this

2 resolution the Speaker may, pursuant to clause 1(b) of rule

3 XXIII, declare the House resolved into the Committee of the

4 Whole House on the State of the Union for the consideration

2

1 of the bill (H.R. 1934) to clarify the congressional intent con-

2 cerning, and to codify, certain requirements of the Communi-

3 cations Act of 1934 that ensure that broadcasters afford rea-

4 sonable opportunity for the discussion of conflicting views on

5 issues of public importance, and the first reading of the bill

6 shall be dispensed with. After general debate, which shall be

7 confined to the bill and which shall not exceed one hour, to

8 be equally divided and controlled by the chairman and rank-

9 ing minority member of the Committee on Energy and Com-

10 merce, the bill shall be considered for amendment under the

11 five-minute rule, and each section shall be considered as

12 having been read. At the conclusion of the consideration of

13 the bill for amendment, the Committee shall rise and report

14 the bill to the House with such amendments as may have

15 been adopted, and the previous question shall be considered

16 as ordered on the bill and amendments thereto to final pas-

17 sage without intervening motion except one motion to recom-

18 mit.

HRES 179 RH

Fig. 7. A special order or "rule" from the Rules Committee.

terms of debate for a specific bill and temporarily suspend any standing rules that conflict with such terms. The standing rules accord a privileged status to special rules, which may be considered on the floor at any time except on the same day they are reported. This restriction may be waived by a two-thirds vote and does not apply during the last three days of a session.

One other standard feature of special orders is that the bills to which they apply be debated in the Committee of the Whole House on the State of the Union, otherwise known as the Committee of the Whole or simply as the Committee. This entity, as are all other committees, is a creature of the House, but unlike other committees, all members are eligible to participate in its proceedings. The Committee of the Whole is the House in a guise that facilitates the consideration of major bills. The significant differences between the House and the Committee are that the latter requires a quorum of only 100, rather than an absolute majority of 218; several motions that can be used to delay business are not in order in the Committee; and amendments in the Committee are debated under a rule that allots five minutes each to a proponent and an opponent, as compared with an hour rule that governs debate in the House.

DEBATE

House debate is organized into three identifiable segments when controversial legislation is considered. The initial phase concerns approval of a special order reported by the Rules Committee. Ostensibly a procedural action, the framing of and floor deliberations on such measures focus on the substance of a bill and the amendments that will be in order. Debate is limited to one hour and time is equally divided between and controlled by two members of the Rules Committee, one who supports and one who opposes the rule. If a special order is strenuously debated, amended, or defeated, it is due to the legislation to which it applies. When a rule cannot command a majority, the bill itself probably cannot, though the adoption of a rule does not guarantee passage of the bill.

Once the House resolves itself into the Committee of the Whole upon approval of a special order, the second segment of chamber deliberations begins. This phase is known as general debate and is normally limited to one to four hours by the rule. At this point, because the quorum requirement is smaller, many legislators may leave the floor, which means that members of the reporting committee constitute a significant proportion of those who remain to debate and vote on amendments. A special order will name those individuals authorized to control the time for general debate, which is invariably divided equally between proponents and opponents of the bill. The leaders of each side are the floor manager for those who support the measure and the ranking minority party member of the reporting committee or subcommittee for those who oppose it.

The customs of the House constrain the presiding officer to recognize the two leaders in preference to others. These legislators alternate in their opening remarks, with the floor manager speaking first, and then apportion time in small amounts at their discretion, primarily to other members of the committee that reported the bill. General debate provides an occasion to explore and explain the major purposes and provisions of legislation. It is characterized by those arguments likely to receive extensive media coverage and appeal to interested parties outside the chamber. This phase also enables floor leaders to assess member sentiment as a prelude to the timing and nature of parliamentary motions and strategic maneuvers. Motions that concern the disposition of a bill are not in order during these proceedings and the floor manager has the prerogative to make the closing statement as general debate expires.

The third phase of House deliberations commences upon the conclusion of general debate. This is the consideration and disposition of amendments under the five-minute rule. During these proceedings the presiding officer alternates recognition between a member who offers and one who opposes each amendment. House rules require that bills be read in their entirety, which is usually section by section, for purposes of amendment under the five-minute rule. Amendments to each subdivision are not in order until that part of the bill to which they apply has been read by the clerk. While the purpose of this requirement is orderly discussion and focused debate of complex and lengthy measures, departures from it through unanimous consent requests can save time and allow for some flexibility. The object of pro forma amendments, which are superficial in nature and not intended to alter a bill, is to obtain additional time for debate. They can be recognized by motions to *strike the last word* or to *strike the requisite number of words*.

A committee and its floor manager are always in a position to take advantage of the priority accorded the consideration of panel amendments. Instead of reporting a bill with numerous amendments, which would give opponents several opportunities to modify it, a committee can report a clean bill or a substitute amendment, which places the burden on those who wish to revise a "finished product" on the floor. If separate amendments are reported, the floor manager usually obtains unanimous consent to have them debated and voted upon as a package, making it necessary to vote against all to reject one, a practice that favors the committee version.

Upon the conclusion of debate under the five-minute rule, whether in regard to an amendment or a bill, further amendments may be offered but may not be debated. The only information available is from the reading of an amendment or from informal discussion among members on the floor. This situation tends to favor committee recommendations since members are reluctant to support amendments without sufficient reason, which is difficult to establish in the absence of debate. After the final subdivision of a bill has been read or debate has been limited, a substitute for the entire measure may be offered. This allows for the consideration of a complete alternative to the pending proposal.

It is also common for special orders to state that amendments printed in the *Congressional Record* at least one day prior to chamber action on a bill must be debated under the five-minute rule regardless of any time limitations. The purpose of this procedure is to prevent arbitrary attempts to end debate when important amendments are to be proposed and to inform legislators in advance, who might not be inclined to support changes with which they were unfamiliar. However, these amendments will not be considered unless offered from the floor and may not contain provisions that would not otherwise be in order.

At the conclusion of the amending process the floor manager makes the motion to rise and report. A majority vote in favor is a command to the chairman of the Committee of the Whole to deliver an oral report to the House, the Committee is dissolved, and a quorum reverts to 218 members. The most common situation is for the chairman to report that the Committee has reached a resolution, with or without amendments, as directed by a special order. The special order regularly proscribes any further debate in the House. Only those amendments approved by the Committee are reported and may, on the demand of any member, be voted upon separately. This procedure is another advantage enjoyed by standing committees. Should an amendment opposed by the floor manager be approved in the Committee of the Whole, a separate vote in the House affords a second opportunity to defeat it, while its proponents rarely have a second chance if they lose in the Committee. When the House rejects an amendment adopted in the Committee of the Whole the effect is to restore the original text of the bill. The usual practice is for all amendments adopted by the Committee to be approved en bloc by the House.

Special orders that apply to bills on the House Calendar, rather than the Union Calendar, prescribe that they be debated in the House, rather than in the Committee of the Whole. Because these measures tend to be less controversial, only general debate is permitted and is normally limited to one hour. Where such bills reach the floor without a rule the length of debate is set by unanimous consent and rarely exceeds an hour. The floor manager and opposition leader divide control of the available time and amendments may not be offered by other members unless one of the leaders yields the floor for that purpose. Unanimous consent is usually obtained to dispense with the reading of a bill and amendments may be offered to any part of the text at any time by a member who has the floor.

The floor manager may move to close debate any time after it has begun under the five-minute rule in the Committee of the Whole or under general debate in the House. Such action is the means used by proponents of a bill to prevent what they consider to be undesirable amendments or dilatory tactics. However, this prerogative must be exercised with caution, for if it is perceived as an attempt to unfairly suppress debate and voted down, priority in recognition passes to those opposed to the bill. Where the risk that this may occur is too great, proponents will offer the motion to rise in the Committee of the Whole and to adjourn in the House. The parliamentary result is simply to suspend proceedings, while the political effect is to enable proponents to regroup their forces.

There are few occasions in the House when debate is not required to be germane to the matter under consideration. The three general criteria of germaneness are subject matter, fundamental purpose, and committee jurisdiction. The subject matter test usually pertains to specific portions of a bill, while that of fundamental purpose normally applies to an entire measure. The standard of committee jurisdiction means that a proposal must fall within the purview of the panel that reported the bill. Whenever any doubt exists, it is the responsibility of proponents to demonstrate that an amendment is germane. Though an amendment may meet all three criteria it may still be ruled out of order based on a complex constellation of parliamentary precedents.

Any member may question the germaneness of an amendment by raising a point of order against it on which the presiding officer must rule. A special order from the Rules Committee that waives points of order against committee amendments does not apply to points of order that challenge floor amendments on germaneness grounds unless it contains a provision to that effect. Points of order are not always raised because of inadvertence, members favor the amendment, or a special order waives them. In general, amendments that would narrow the scope of a provision or bill or add a new section are more likely to be ruled germane than those that would enlarge its scope or modify an existing section. The relevance of amendments is considered necessary to prevent proposals that have not been adequately analyzed in committee from becoming law.

SENATE PROCEEDINGS

SCHEDULING

The Senate has only a single calendar for its legislative business. However, party leaders maintain two informal calendars for scheduling purposes. One, which lists routine measures, serves as a consent calendar and notes bills reported since the last time the calendar was called. It enables senators to familiarize themselves with the bills so as to facilitate passage with little or no debate. This is accomplished under a call of the calendar, which is privileged business one day each week but is usually undertaken by unanimous consent whenever it is convenient for the chamber as determined by the party leaders. For measures that reach the floor in this manner, senators are permitted to speak for only five minutes on each and amendments may be offered.

Calendar committees from each party, equivalent to objectors' committees in the House, monitor bills under this procedure. A senator will object to passage if requested to do so by a member of his party, if the proposal is deemed to be too important to be approved without debate, if an amendment is considered necessary, or if it otherwise lacks merit. A measure blocked by objection retains its original position on the calendar, to be disposed of as circumstances allow. An objection may be overruled by a majority vote, which enables consideration to proceed without the five-minute speech limitation. Under this procedure minor measures are passed, defeated, or passed over with minimal debate so that the Senate's time may be conserved for action on major legislation. It is these latter bills, to which the chamber is obliged to devote most of its time, that are noted on the other informal calendar.

When legislation is reported out of a Senate committee the chairman informs the majority leader and discusses its scheduling prospects. The majority leader then brings the matter to the attention of his party's policy committee, of which he is the most prominent member. This panel surveys the Senate's workload and the party program prior to reaching general decisions about the timing, sequence, and other conditions for scheduling major bills. Responsibility to structure the arrangements and settle the details is left with the majority leader.

The majority leader is obliged to consult with the minority leader, the committee chairman, and all other senators who express a strong interest in the bill. These extensive negotiations are necessary because the goal is a unanimous consent agreement (see figure 8). As its name implies, this form of action can only be successfully pursued if no senator objects to it. The unanimous consent agreement is an informal mechanism that is a counterpart to the special order in the House. It is informally negotiated and drafted outside the chamber and requires unanimous approval when offered as a binding contract from the floor. Its use enables the Senate to expedite its business by avoiding the inconvenience and delay that would attend strict adherence to its standing rules. By suspending formal requirements, unanimous consent agreements assure timely and orderly debate of major bills.

UNANIMOUS CONSENT AGREEMENTS

S. 490

1.—*Ordered,* That the Majority Leader, after consultation with the Minority Leader, may at any time after 2:00 p.m. on June 23, 1987 move to proceed to the consideration of S. 490, a bill to authorize negotiations of reciprocal trade agreements, to strengthen United States trade laws, and for other purposes.

Ordered further, That upon the completion of the amendment process on the bill, the Senate proceed to make a nondebatable motion to proceed to the consideration of a House bill without any further debate, action or motion, and that it be in order to make a nondebatable motion to strike all after the enacting clause and add the text of the Senate bill, as amended, if amended, and proceed immediately to its passage without intervening debate, action or motion. *(June 17, 1987.)*

S. 1174 (ORDER NO. 120)

2.—*Ordered,* That during the consideration of S. 1174, a bill to authorize appropriations for fiscal years 1988 and 1989 for military activities of the Department of Defense, for military construction, and for defense activities of the Department of Energy, to prescribe personnel strengths for such fiscal years for the Armed Forces, and for other purposes, the amendments listed below be in order under the following time limitations, with the time to be equally divided and controlled in the usual form:

Lautenberg—Religious Headgear—1 hour, 30 minutes.
Hatfield-Kennedy—Nuclear Testing—2 hours, provided that if a tabling motion fails, the time limitation falls.
Hatfield—Chemical—1 hour.
Pryor—Chemical—1 hour, 30 minutes.

Ordered further, That a vote occur on or in relation to each amendment upon the expiration or yielding back of the time.

Ordered further, That no second degree amendments or amendments to the text be proposed to be stricken be in order.

Ordered further, That when the Senate resumes consideration of S. 1174 on Thursday, Sept. 24, 1987, the pending amendment, No. 712, be temporarily laid aside for consideration of an amendment to be offered by the Senator from Arizona (Mr. McCain).

Ordered further, That after 6:00 p.m. on Thursday, Sept. 24, 1987, the first rollcall vote be limited to 15 minutes, and each succeeding rollcall vote be limited to 10 minutes each. *(Sept. 18, 23, 1987.)*

S.J. RES. 187 (ORDER NO. 308)

3.—*Ordered,* That notwithstanding Public Law 99-177, the Senate temporarily postpone consideration of S.J. Res. 187, a joint resolution complying with the requirements of section 274(f)(1) of the Balanced Budget and Emergency Deficit Control Act of 1985, until no later than the close of business on Thursday, Sept. 24, 1987, and that it be in order to consider the resolution under the statute, notwithstanding Sec. 254(a)(4)(A) of the Act. *(Sept. 22, 1987.)*

H.R. 2907 (ORDER NO. 315)

4.—*Ordered,* That the Majority Leader, upon consultation with the Minority Leader and the managers of the bill, be authorized to lay before the Senate H.R. 2907, an act making appropriations for the Treasury Department, the United States Postal Service, the Executive Office of the President, and certain Independent Agencies, for the fiscal year ending Sept. 30, 1988, and for other purposes, there be 1 hour on the bill, to be equally divided and controlled in the usual form.

Ordered further, That no amendments be in order, except the committee reported amendments.

Ordered further, That no motions to recommit, with or without instructions, be in order. *(Sept. 23, 1987.)*

H.J. RES. 362

5.—*Ordered,* That the Majority Leader, upon consultation with the Minority Leader and the managers of the resolution, be authorized to lay before the Senate H.J. Res. 362, the Continuing Resolution, and that there be 1 hour on the resolution, with the time to be equally divided and controlled by the Chairman and the Ranking Member of the Appropria-

Fig. 8. A daily schedule of business printed in the Senate *Calendar.*

The general provisions of such an agreement may specify the order in which bills will be considered, state when measures will reach the floor, and stipulate the time at which a vote on final passage will occur. Because of deference to the personal and political needs of individual senators, the time frame established is more flexible than in the House. Whether a time limit is fixed for the conclusion of debate or omitted, Senate consideration of a bill usually extends over several days as chamber business is juggled to accommodate institutional and member needs.

The more detailed aspects of unanimous consent agreements relate to amendments and other motions. Limits are set to the amount of time that may be consumed for the debate of each motion and amendments are required to be germane to the bill under consideration. Such stipulations are necessary because Senate rules are either silent or inadequate in regard to these points. Any amendment authorized by a unanimous consent agreement is considered germane irrespective of its actual relationship to a bill. This development reflects the need to propitiate all senators who insist on being heard.

Those bills not disposed of in the Senate by unanimous consent requests, passed during a call of the calendar, or scheduled under unanimous consent agreements are brought before the chamber by a motion to proceed to their consideration made by the majority leader. Such motions to consider bills out of their regular order are debatable and, if adopted by a majority vote, action on the bill continues until completed or regularly scheduled business intervenes. In the latter instance the measure may be returned to the calendar, its consideration may be extended by unanimous consent, or, if not, it may be brought before the Senate another time under the same procedure. This route is reserved for relatively uncontroversial bills that cannot be conveniently reached under a call of the calendar or controversial proposals on which unanimous consent agreements cannot be fashioned.

For those measures not regulated by unanimous consent agreements and not subjected to filibusters, party and committee leaders strive to devise informal arrangements for the conduct of debate. These are proposals on which senators agree that passage is necessary or desirable, but on which most wish to express their views or offer amendments. Unanimous consent agreements cannot always adequately cope with situations that combine significant legislation, complex parliamentary procedure, and extensive participation. Instead of multiple calendars and special days the Senate regulates and reorients its floor schedule through unanimous consent requests to lay business aside temporarily, which suspends action on but does not displace the matter under consideration. Both the negotiation of satisfactory floor plans for and actual chamber action on a given bill can consume considerable time.

DEBATE

Senate deliberations are less structured and more spontaneous than those in the House. Its rules do not contain provisions relating to the allocation of time, but only provide that a vote by sixty members can terminate a filibuster, a majority that is difficult to assemble. In the absence of a unanimous consent agreement, debate can only be restricted by successfully invoking cloture and need only be germane during the consideration of general appropriation bills.

Otherwise there are no limitations on time, germaneness, or amendments. Though the Senate does have a mild germaneness rule, it is rarely observed or enforced. Unlimited debate is the usual practice, subject to whatever agreements are necessary or can be arranged to bring deliberations to a close.

A filibuster is an attempt by opponents of a bill or amendment to have it withdrawn or modified. It is not simply prolonged speech by one or more senators, but the use of all rules and procedures to delay, modify, or defeat legislation. Because bills are vulnerable to such tactics at several points in the legislative process, the possibility of a filibuster pervades all action on major proposals. Bargaining is encouraged because any senator may object to requests for unanimous consent and any group may exact concessions for not obstructing business. The use or threat of a filibuster during the closing days of a session virtually compels a measure to be abandoned. A numerical majority is insufficient to advance legislation if an intense minority is opposed.

A unanimous consent agreement designates those members responsible for controlling the time available for debate and a senator is not entitled to recognition unless yielded to by another exercising such control. After opening remarks by the floor manager and opposition leader and the disposition of committee amendments, a bill is open to debate and amendment at any point. General debate and the amending process are not treated as formally distinct phases. Those senators in control of the time arrange as to who will make the closing speech. Under a unanimous consent agreement that limits the time allotted for debate, subsidiary unanimous consent requests for considering amendments or specifying the time for voting on them may be made.

Unless a unanimous consent agreement specifically excludes the consideration of other business until the bill to which it applies is finally disposed of, other matters may interrupt at any time at the discretion of party and committee leaders. A provision that sets a vote on final passage of a measure at a specified time will not be affected by such interruptions. Such a stipulation also precludes any early motions that would adversely dispose of a bill or any that would delay a vote on final passage. When it is stated that a vote is to be taken on a certain amendment, motions to alter or reject it are not in order prior to such vote. If amendments are to be voted on after a certain hour without debate, they may still be proposed, but may not be debated.

It is common for a unanimous consent agreement to adopt a committee substitute for a bill or all separate panel amendments. Under this procedure the amended bill is then considered as original text for the purposes of floor action. This facilitates the amending process by allowing both first- and second-degree amendments, the latter of which would be precluded if committee amendments were considered as being in the first degree. The floor manager, acting with committee approval, may modify panel amendments after the bill has reached the floor. Unless specifically excluded, committee amendments come within the time limitations established by a unanimous consent agreement, which can result in little time for the consideration of floor amendments if panel recommendations are not adopted without debate.

After the disposition of committee amendments there is no prescribed order in which amendments may or must be offered. Thus, senators tend to jockey for position and a satisfactory sequence may be formalized in a unanimous consent agreement or informally arranged by party leaders and amendment proponents. Amendments may be drafted any time after a bill is introduced. Though the

Senate rules are silent about the printing of amendments, most are printed separately prior to floor action on the pertinent bill and may be submitted to the committee of jurisdiction or held at the presiding officer's desk. As with House amendments printed in the *Congressional Record*, this practice makes the proposals available to other members in advance of debate. Legislators are more likely to approve amendments that they have had the opportunity to consider beforehand. Printed amendments have no official status until offered from the floor.

Debate that is undertaken without the restraints imposed by a unanimous consent agreement invites the offering of nongermane amendments. This means that any proposal, regardless of whether it has been introduced or considered by a committee or whether it is related to a pending bill, may be offered as an amendment. The text of one bill may be proposed as a substitute for or as an additional subdivision of another. The effect is to immediately bring any legislative proposition to the Senate floor. A nongermane amendment may simply be offered to extract a commitment that hearings will be held on its subject, in which case the sponsor will withdraw it from consideration. Though such amendments may be offered by any senator, they usually need the support of some party and committee leaders to have a chance for adoption. However, the possibility of a nongermane amendment tends to preclude committee action that defies the wishes of senators who have a strong interest in certain legislation but are not members of the panel of jurisdiction.

In the absence of a unanimous consent agreement debate can only be restricted or terminated by the resort to cloture. Sixteen senators must sign a cloture petition to close debate when the Senate is prevented from proceeding with its business because of a filibuster. This is presented to the presiding officer, who is required to state the motion to the Senate immediately. Two days later the presiding officer submits the matter to the chamber for a roll-call vote. A motion to invoke cloture requires sixty votes to close debate on all questions that pertain to the consideration of legislation. Without a unanimous consent agreement or sufficient support for cloture, a vote on final passage may be indefinitely delayed as party leaders try to negotiate an end to a filibuster. However, it may not be possible to arrange for such a vote in the event of determined opposition.

BICAMERAL PROCEEDINGS

CONVENTIONAL CONCURRENCE

Because a bill must be passed by each chamber in identical form before it can be presented to the president for approval, the means of reconciling differences between them is of paramount importance. Bicameral cooperation is a fundamental prerequisite for institutional effectiveness. There are two ways in which the houses may adopt identical versions of the same bill without recourse to a formal conference. The more expeditious course is where each passes a companion bill as it was introduced or one passes a measure as it was received from the other. Though this outcome requires complete agreement either before or soon after the legislative process begins, it is not uncommon in view of the fact that most legislation is routine and uncontroversial.

Another route for the resolution of bicameral variations is known as amendments between the houses. Under these proceedings each chamber acts separately in succession on the amendments adopted by the other until agreement is reached. Regularized communication across the Capitol among party leaders and staff is necessary to facilitate this process. There may also be some collaboration between the members and staff of corresponding chamber committees before either panel reports a bill. This enables one or both to frame legislative language that will pave the way for a satisfactory compromise on matters in which one committee anticipates some difficulty on the floor. Because amendments between the houses can become awkward and time consuming, this route is usually reserved for bills of a less complex and controversial nature.

Senate bills received in the House are held at the Speaker's table if a committee is working on a companion bill or referred to the appropriate panel if such action has not commenced. Senate measures that are substantially the same as House bills favorably reported and that do not require consideration in the Committee of the Whole are also held at the Speaker's table. These proposals are privileged business and may be brought to the floor as soon as a motion to do so is authorized by the committee of jurisdiction and a panel member is recognized for that purpose. Senate bills that are not so privileged may reach the House floor via special order, suspension of the rules, or unanimous consent. House bills transmitted to the Senate are treated in a similar manner with the exception that none are officially accorded a privileged status.

At this stage of proceedings efforts may be made to bypass committee consideration in the other chamber. All House-passed bills delivered to the Senate may be placed directly on its calendar without being referred to committee, a procedure that any senator may invoke. This course is followed when a companion Senate bill has been favorably reported or when Senate committee action on the companion or House measure appears doubtful or likely to be unfavorable. House committees may be bypassed by a nongermane Senate amendment to a House-passed bill. In this instance, the Senate amendment is a separate measure that may be held at the Speaker's table for House action. A Senate-passed bill referred to the House and substantially the same as a measure on a House calendar provides an opportunity to evade the authority of the Rules Committee to grant approval for consideration of the House bill.

The success of such strategy indicates that party and committee leaders in one house prefer the version of a bill passed by the other to that passed by their own. When the type of informal cooperation necessary between members of each house to bypass a committee or otherwise expedite action is not feasible, another procedure is available. Where the second chamber holds a bill transmitted by the other instead of referring it to a committee, the option exists for the second chamber to pass its own version of the measure and then substitute its text under the number of the companion bill received from the first house. This practice eliminates the need to consider separate amendments to the other chamber's bill and facilitates anticipated bicameral negotiations.

Amendments between the houses occurs when the second chamber to act on a bill adopts amendments and returns it to the body of origin for further consideration. For both houses to reach agreement on an identical version of a bill under this procedure requires one or more of the following developments: the body of origin may (1) accept the amendments of the second chamber, (2) insist on its version and persuade the second chamber to recede from its amendments, or (3) amend the amendments with the subsequent concurrence of the second chamber. Informal negotiations between members of Congress and their staffs are an essential aspect of this process.

When one house amends a bill originated by the other such an amendment is considered as original text for the purposes of amendment. The body of origin may then amend the amendment and the second chamber may further amend it, which would be a second-degree amendment and preclude additional amendments. At some point in this process either chamber may formally disagree to the amendments of the other. The stage of disagreement is reached when one house adopts a motion to that effect. Each house has similar procedures that govern the disposition of its own bills returned from the other with amendments. In both chambers such business is accorded privileged status and the question of its consideration on the floor is not subject to debate. Party and committee leaders determine when and how these measures will be scheduled for floor action.

Throughout these proceedings each house retains the option to agree or disagree to some or all of the amendments of the other. Amendments may be debated and voted upon separately or collectively as seems most likely to foster agreement. Should amendments between the houses fail to produce total or partial agreement or if lack of agreement is anticipated, either house may, at any time after a bill passed by the other has reached its floor, request a conference. Amendments between the houses is a procedure that, if prolonged, can become cumbrous and irksome to the degree of jeopardizing the possibility of bicameral agreement. Thus, if differences cannot be settled within an expected period of time, a conference is proposed as a more desirable alternative.

CONFERENCE COMMITTEES

When significant differences exist between the houses regarding their respective versions of a bill covering the same subject, a conference is invariably held to reconcile them. A conference committee is a temporary ad hoc panel composed of a delegation from each chamber. The members of each delegation are expected to maintain the position of their house as expressed in the measure and to arrive at a result that will be acceptable to both. Conferences simultaneously seek bicameral agreement and bipartisan support. They enable each body to avoid the stigma of either hasty retreat or intransigence in its relations with the other. For one house to refuse a conference either kills a bill or compels the other to accept an imposed version. Since neither alternative is politically palatable, conferences become the congressional court of last resort for controversial legislation.

Though one house need only ask for and the other agree to a conference, the matter is not always so straightforward. The chamber that receives a request for a conference determines whether one will be held and the scope of its jurisdiction. The body that originates the request customarily acts last on the conference report, a course that cedes one of its options. The house that considers a report first may approve, reject, or recommit it to conference, while the second chamber to act cannot recommit it since approval by the first officially dissolves the conference. Thus, a slight advantage attends being the last house to act before a conference and the first to act afterward. These possibilities may lead to some maneuvering or delay by either or both houses. The desired result would be for one house to induce the other to concede without a conference or to secure an advantage as affairs proceed.

When either house amends a bill received from the other, it may return the measure and allow the body of origin to request a conference or, in anticipation of disagreement, it may ask for a conference at this time. The motion to request a conference is not in order until a motion to agree or disagree to the amendments of the other chamber or to insist on its own has been voted upon. The usual procedure is for the body of origin to disagree to the amendments of the second house and request a conference, while the other body insists on its amendments and agrees to a conference. These preliminaries are regularly disposed of by unanimous consent requests made by floor managers, who have monitored the progress of the bill in the other house and have agreed to call for a conference.

In the House the authority to appoint conferees is lodged in the Speaker, while the presiding officer of the Senate is routinely authorized to do so by a motion or unanimous consent. Though members of conference committees are formally named in this manner, in reality the Speaker and presiding officer invariably accept the recommendations of the chairman of the committee that reported the bill. The party ratios on each conference delegation normally reflect that of the entire chamber. The number of members on each tends to vary from three to seven, though the total may be larger. The latter situation is common where more than one committee considered a bill in one house. In this case conferees are chosen from each, but their authority to negotiate is confined to those provisions for which their committee alone is responsible.

Prior to the first conference meeting each delegation will try to reach agreement on which provisions of their chamber's bill to firmly insist upon and which of those adopted by the other body to resolutely resist. These political preparations initially determine which amendments or sections are subject to being bartered, compromised, or reported as still in disagreement. Many actions that occur during earlier stages of the legislative process can be explained by the fact that legislators often plan their strategy with the expectation that a conference will be necessary to resolve bicameral differences and to reconsider decisions made by their own house about which they have serious reservations.

A standing committee may report a bill with language its members realize might not be approved on the floor, while floor managers are inclined to accept some amendments to ensure passage of a bill. In the first case committee members may endeavor to have certain provisions restored in conference, while in the second they may try to have portions of the text deleted. Floor amendments may be adopted to placate a particular constituency, with the tacit understanding that they will be discarded in conference because their substantive effects are inconsistent with constructive legislative objectives. This tactic enables legislators to claim political credit for a popular but deficient proposal without assuming the responsibility for enacting it into law.

In anticipation of a conference each house may modify or delete provisions strongly supported by the other or adopt expendable amendments. These actions are intended to provide leverage in the conference bargaining process where some amendments can be sacrificed in exchange for retention of those parts of a bill each chamber considers more important. Eventual conferees must decide whether to seek a recorded vote on certain amendments since this will affect their flexibility in conference negotiations. Though an unrecorded vote permits greater discretion, a recorded vote can strengthen their bargaining position. Thus, the judgment of floor managers must often extend beyond immediate considerations to an estimate of what can contribute to favorable conference results or survive the process.

House rules permit separate consideration of Senate amendments to a House bill embodied in a conference report that would have been ruled out of order as nongermane if offered in the House. The significance of this procedure is the leverage it gives House conferees, who can argue that the inclusion of such amendments will jeopardize the report, since the rejection of a part results in rejection of the whole. Conversely, if Senate language does not include nongermane amendments, Senate conferees can argue that their version should be accepted by their House counterparts because Senate procedures enable a single member to obstruct legislation. In this case there would seem to be less of an obstacle to obtain House approval for concessions to the Senate than vice versa.

The filing of a conference report, which is formal notice in each chamber that conferees have completed their deliberations, is a privileged matter. In the House a conference report must be printed in the *Congressional Record* for at least three legislative days before it can be brought to the floor, but this rule is waived during the last six days of a session. The Rules Committee may also report a special order providing for the debate of a conference report on the same day it is filed. House action may also proceed under suspension of the rules or unanimous consent. A conference report may be considered in the Senate by motion or unanimous consent on the same day it is filed. Though the question of whether to consider a report is not debatable in the Senate, a unanimous consent agreement may be necessary to limit the length of debate or exempt report language from points of order. The privileged status of conference reports, the small number of individuals involved in scheduling decisions, and the lateness of the session all combine to produce relatively expeditious action once they are filed.

When points of order are raised in either house the floor manager may argue that report language does not violate chamber rules or, if it is conceded that such is the case, it was necessary to reach agreement. The thrust of this reasoning would be that the situation offered a choice between the conference version as it stands or no bill at all. Should conferees anticipate points of order that would jeopardize approval of the report, they may try to use debate to accomplish their purposes. This is done by omitting certain language from a report and by expressly stating an interpretation that has not been formally incorporated into it.

Should a conference report embody only a partial resolution of differences, each chamber would first vote on the report and, if approved, the amendments reported in disagreement may be disposed of separately in the order in which they appear in the report, collectively or through appointment of another conference. When a report states that no agreement has been reached, each house may proceed in whatever manner it deems appropriate, just as before the conference. If one house rejects a report, the resolution of differences would require that either body recede from its disagreement with the other, propose a further amendment that is accepted by the other, request another conference, or pass another version of the bill. Owing to political factors and time constraints only the second and third possibilities are realistic options.

Since the decisions of conferees normally become the judgment of Congress, negotiations can be lengthy and intense as each side perceives a need to claim success, however it may be defined. Two procedural factors contribute to approval of the overwhelming majority of conference reports. First, because they are not subject to amendment in either house, it is necessary to reject the entire product to express dissatisfaction with a portion. Second, since most reports are filed for action toward the end of a session or Congress, the timing of their consideration creates pressure for passage. The conference process may fail if one house declines to appoint conferees, conferees are unable to reach agreement and do not file a report, one house does not act or rejects the report, or amendments reported in disagreement cannot be reconciled. Despite bicameral rivalry, the desire for accommodation and accomplishment means that very few bills die at this stage of the legislative process.

REFERENCES

Berman, Daniel M. *In Congress Assembled.* New York: Macmillan, 1964.

Froman, Lewis A., Jr. *The Congressional Process.* Boston: Little, Brown, 1967.

Gross, Bertram M. *The Legislative Struggle.* New York: McGraw-Hill, 1953.

Jasper, Herb. "Scheduling of Senate Business," in U.S. Congress. Senate. *Committees and Senate Procedures,* A Compilation of Papers Prepared for the Commission on the Operation of the Senate. Committee Print, 94th Congress, 2nd Session. Washington, D.C.: U.S. Government Printing Office, 1977.

Oleszek, Walter J. *Congressional Procedures and the Policy Process.* 2nd ed. Washington, D.C.: Congressional Quarterly Press, 1984.

U.S. Congress. House. *Cannon's Procedure in the House of Representatives.* House Document No. 610, 87th Congress, 2nd Session. Washington, D.C.: U.S. Government Printing Office, 1963.

U.S. Congress. House. *Constitution, Jefferson's Manual and Rules of the House of Representatives.* House Document No. 98-277, 98th Congress, 2nd Session. Washington, D.C.: U.S. Government Printing Office, 1985.

U.S. Congress. House. *How Our Laws Are Made.* House Document No. 97-120, 97th Congress, 1st Session. Washington, D.C.: U.S. Government Printing Office, 1981.

U.S. Congress. House. *Procedure in the U.S. House of Representatives.* 4th ed. 97th Congress, 2nd Session. Washington, D.C.: U.S. Government Printing Office, 1982.

U.S. Congress. House. Committee on Rules. *A History of the Committee on Rules*. Committee Print, 97th Congress, 2nd Session. Washington, D.C.: U.S. Government Printing Office, 1983.

U.S. Congress. House. Committee on Science and Technology. *Legislative Manual*. 4th ed. Committee Print, 99th Congress, 1st Session. Washington, D.C.: U.S. Government Printing Office, 1985.

U.S. Congress. Senate. *Enactment of a Law*. Senate Document No. 97-20, 97th Congress, 2nd Session. Washington, D.C.: U.S. Government Printing Office, 1982.

U.S. Congress. Senate. *Senate Procedure*. Senate Document No. 97-2, 97th Congress, 1st Session. Washington, D.C.: U.S. Government Printing Office, 1981.

U.S. Congress. Senate. *Standing Rules of the Senate*. Senate Document No. 99-22, 99th Congress, 2nd Session. Washington, D.C.: U.S. Government Printing Office, 1986.

Vogler, David J. *The Third House*. Evanston, Ill.: Northwestern University Press, 1971.

7

Voting

Voting would appear to be one of the clearer and simpler forms of congressional decisionmaking. On both an individual and collective basis, a recorded vote is a conspicuous and concrete fact. However, the structure and strategy of congressional voting, combined with the multiple goals of legislators and legislation, can preclude an obvious or routine verdict. Whether or when to have a vote, on which question, and by which method are decisions that are vital for the progress of a bill. This chapter examines the procedural and political aspects of the voting process and its relationship to legislation.

Though a roll-call vote is the most explicit type of legislative decision, its significance can be subject to varying interpretations. It is not an isolated action and should be viewed in the context of preceding and succeeding votes to be accurately assessed. In addition, voting alternatives are shaped by other decisions in the legislative process that may be more important. The comparative visibility and intelligibility of a congressional vote tend to veil the complexity of its immediate background and ultimate meaning. The parliamentary tactics and political purposes associated with voting affect the passage and form of bills as materially as other legislative proceedings.

The external environment of Congress, including electoral results, presidential action, prominent events, and public opinion, all of which can materialize in a variety of ways, may result in a vote and also determine its outcome. Should a bill reflect partisan or ideological divisions, the party ratio or philosophical cleavage may lead to a predictable result. The continual bargaining that characterizes congressional decisionmaking can contribute to votes that constitute part of the negotiation process. This practice, known as logrolling, involves the exchange of support among those who favor different provisions of the same bill or advocate unrelated bills. Blocs of legislators vote for those portions of or an entire measure important to others in return for reciprocal action. Explanations that focus on the influence of these factors are beyond the scope of this chapter.

PROCEDURAL FACTORS

An examination of congressional voting requires that the stages, types, methods, and forms of voting be distinguished. The initial stage of voting occurs in committee, and each panel must maintain a complete record of all roll-call votes, including the names of those members present but not voting and those using proxies. Proxy voting is the practice of authorizing committee members to cast votes on behalf of absent colleagues. This record is open to public inspection in the committee office, but more accessible sources are transcripts of mark-up sessions printed in hearing form, committee reports, and Congressional Quarterly's *Weekly Report*. Floor votes during chamber consideration and bicameral action are the two subsequent stages.

The types of votes are quorum calls, which establish that the minimum number of legislators necessary for proceedings to be valid is present; procedural votes, which are decisions on matters other than the merits of a measure; substantive votes, which either adopt or reject amendments to a bill; and final passage, which is a series of votes rather than a single ballot. Each of these types applies to each stage, though the unique nature of each stage means that the types manifest themselves somewhat differently.

A judgment regarding which method of voting to employ during floor proceedings can be as crucial for a bill as a decision to take a vote. There are four methods by which to take unrecorded votes, which do not reveal the name or position of individual legislators. When unanimous consent is used, the presiding officer merely states that "without objection" the motion or measure is adopted or passed. A voice vote is based on the volume of sound of those members responding, and the presiding officer determines whether the chorus of "ayes" or "nays" has prevailed. Since most legislation is minor or routine, these two methods are frequently used to dispose of business. For a division vote, the presiding officer counts the members on each side, who either stand or raise their hands. During an unrecorded teller vote, which occurs only in the House, members cast their votes by walking through the center aisle to be counted by other members, known as tellers; the vote total of those for and against is announced. For a division, the result may be conveyed in the same manner or simply by a statement that one side has a majority.

There are also four methods available for conducting recorded votes. On a recorded teller vote, which is peculiar to the House, members cast votes by depositing cards in a ballot box or by electronic means. When a recorded vote in the House reveals the absence of a quorum, the result is an automatic roll call that combines a quorum call and vote on the pending question. A regular roll call is held whenever demanded and seconded by one-fifth of a quorum. Article I, Section 5, of the Constitution provides for a yea-and-nay vote on the request of one-fifth of the members present. In the Senate, there is no difference between the last two methods and electronic voting is not used. A legislative call system comprised of bells or buzzers and lights operates to alert legislators in the Capitol and Senate and House office buildings to the type and method of voting in progress on the floor of either chamber.

The forms of voting refer to the manner in which a legislator may communicate or conceal his or her position. The options are to vote in the affirmative or negative, to be present but not vote, to be absent, to announce at a later time how one would have voted if one had been present, or to be paired. A pair is an unwritten and voluntary agreement between individual legislators that applies to a scheduled roll-call vote. Pairing permits a member to have a position on a given question officially recorded though the member is unable to be present. A legislator who will be absent for a floor session may conclude an agreement with a colleague who will attend and vote on the opposite side. The one who is present refrains from voting to redress the imbalance caused by the absence of a colleague who differs on an amendment or bill.

A "live" pair occurs when a legislator who is present withholds his or her vote and pairs with an absent colleague. A simple pair develops when two absent legislators pair with each other. General pairs are used primarily in the House, where members leave their names with the clerk to be matched with others who have done the same. This indicates only that two legislators would have voted on opposite sides of a question, but does not indicate which side. While pairs are not counted in the vote totals, the names of those paired and their positions, if known, appear in the *Congressional Record*. Though the professed purpose of pairing is to enable legislators to have their positions formally noted in cases of unavoidable absence, it is also a convenient way to avoid a controversial vote. Since pairing is an unofficial practice not recognized by the rules of either house, any errors or misunderstandings that result from the making or breaking of pairs are not matters for chamber notice or action.

When a simple majority vote is necessary to transact business, this means a majority of those present and voting, assuming the existence of a quorum, not a majority of those present or a majority of the entire membership. Legislators present but not voting are counted for the purposes of a quorum. Though a member makes a motion that requires a vote, the member may not be familiar with the technicalities of parliamentary procedure and may use improper phraseology. To ensure that the terminology is correct and consistent with the desired action, a vote is taken on a question as it is stated by the presiding officer. Should it be discovered, after a vote has been taken, that a procedural or substantive error was made, the proceedings are vacated by unanimous consent and another vote is scheduled.

POLITICAL FACTORS

Unrecorded votes enable legislators to take ambiguous or contradictory positions during the consideration of a bill. An equivocal stance, though it can be politically expedient, is not necessarily an attempt to deceive or mislead. A roll-call vote compels complete endorsement or disapproval of a proposal even when a legislator may not be that certain of its merits or defects. A member may agree with the aims of a bill, but disagree with its means. Though major bills contain several subdivisions and have multiple purposes, on final passage a legislator cannot vote for some provisions and against others.

The question of whether a vote is to be recorded can be of some political significance. A roll call requires legislators to publicly declare themselves on matters on which they may have taken an unclear position or maintained silence. They prefer to avoid roll calls when their views conflict with those of their constituents. By delaying a vote until after the roll has been called the first time or until most have been electronically recorded, a legislator may join the majority and claim credit with those who favored the proposal while informing those who opposed it that voting with them would not have changed the outcome. When a member personally favors a measure that constituents oppose, by delaying his or her vote and determining that it will pass anyway, the member can vote against it to please the electorate.

Because of their control of the legislative schedule, party leaders can arrange for votes to occur at those times most likely to produce results consistent with their perception of the party, chamber, or national interest. On less visible votes, mainly procedural or unrecorded ones, party leaders are assured of a higher level of support for the party position. Roll-call votes on the substance of measures are the most visible and tend to attentuate their influence. Leaders closely monitor the tally to determine whether they will need to call upon votes being held in reserve or can release those who would prefer to vote on the other side but have agreed to support the party position if such action would alter the outcome. The presiding officer may exercise some discretion in delaying the announcement of a result to allow time for switches or latecomers to vote. These maneuvers cannot be ascertained from the printed record of a roll call because names are listed in alphabetical order only.

The two major reasons for having an unrecorded vote are to expedite uncontroversial measures or to avoid the publicity of a position. Among the many reasons for desiring a roll-call vote are that advocates of a particular proposal may wish to have those on the other side publicly identified. Also, such a vote may bring more members to the floor and affect the outcome, create a strong chamber position that can be used as leverage during bicameral action, determine the drift of collective sentiment, oblige public demand that a decision be made in the most visible manner, and help gauge the appeal of a proposal as a prelude to further action. Roll-call votes reflect an increase in publicity, partisanship, and participation as compared with unrecorded votes.

HOUSE ACTION

The House may conduct its business either in the Committee of the Whole or in the House. The House, whose quorum is 218, votes to go into the Committee of the Whole, whose quorum is only 100, when it approves a special order reported by the Rules Committee or adopts a motion to consider an appropriation bill. A quorum call is not in order in the Committee of the Whole once it is determined that a quorum is present, unless the Committee is operating under the five-minute rule and a question is brought to a vote.

A motion to rise in the Committee of the Whole is equivalent to a motion to adjourn in the House and, if adopted, the Committee is dissolved and action must proceed in the House. When the Committee rises because it lacks a quorum it may not report the bill it has acted on and the measure retains its status until the Committee reconvenes. If compelled to rise in this situation, it would be necessary to obtain a quorum of the House for the Committee to be granted approval to promptly resume its deliberations.

The primary legislative task of the Committee of the Whole is to consider amendments. Initially the presiding officer, or chairman, puts the question to a voice vote. If the person is uncertain of which side prevails, or if a member on the losing side demands it, a division vote is taken. Twenty members, or one-fifth or a quorum, may require an unrecorded teller vote, while twenty-five members may obtain a recorded teller vote. The order of voting in the Committee of the Whole is always voice to division to tellers; the most important is the last, for if a quorum is present it is the final vote on an amendment in the Committee. Teller votes are usually reserved for key amendments or those decided by close margins on voice or division votes. Because an amendment may be voted upon more than once, it is possible to lose one vote and win another or vice versa. Since many of the most important votes in the Committee of the Whole may be unrecorded, a legislator may support efforts to weaken a bill favored by constituents, while on a roll-call vote on final passage in the House, the legislator may vote for its approval.

Once the presence of a quorum has been established in the House, a point of no quorum is in order only when a proposition is put to a vote. The failure of a quorum to respond on a roll-call vote, followed by adjournment, does not affect the pending question, which is voted upon anew when the House reconvenes. When a quorum fails to vote on any matter and an objection is made for that reason, an automatic roll-call vote by electronic device is ordered. If the number of those voting and those present who decline to vote totals at least 218, this procedure simultaneously verifies the presence of a quorum and decides the pending question based upon a majority of those voting.

The demand for yeas and nays under the Constitution must be supported by one-fifth of those present, while a demand for a roll-call vote under House rules must be seconded by one-fifth of a quorum, or forty-four members. Which form the demand takes depends upon which is more certain to bring about a roll-call vote. A demand for a roll-call vote may be made following the determination that an insufficient number of members second a request for the yeas and nays. A demand for an unrecorded teller vote, if supported by one-fifth of a quorum, must be granted should a request for a roll-call vote be refused. The Speaker makes a count of members in those cases where a minimum number of legislators is needed to second a demand for a vote. The requirement for such a minimum number to sustain the demand for a vote prevents requests that are dilatory in nature and favored by only a few members. A demand for a division vote is not precluded by the fact that a roll-call or teller vote is denied. If a quorum is absent as indicated by the total number of votes cast on a division or unrecorded teller vote, any member may demand a roll-call vote.

Amendments defeated in the Committee of the Whole are not reported to or voted upon by the House, except for the motion to recommit, which is discussed below. After the Committee reports those amendments it has adopted to the House, the Speaker asks all members to identify those on which a separate vote is desired. The remaining amendments are usually approved as a package by voice vote, after which the contested ones are voted upon individually by roll calls in the order in which they appear in the bill. Votes in the House that reverse decisions made in the Committee of the Whole do so for one of two reasons. If the vote in the Committee was unrecorded, it probably reflected the personal views of members, while a roll call in the House denotes the perception that members have of constituent preferences. The larger quorum necessary to transact business in the House means that many members who did not participate in Committee of the Whole proceedings are present for House action. The Speaker or chair of the Committee usually do not vote, but may do so to make or break a tie since a tie vote defeats a proposal.

Two motions are available to opponents of a bill whose purpose is to test voting strength on a measure. One, the question of consideration, is raised in the House when a bill is initially taken from a calendar. In most cases this will be a vote on a special order reported by the Rules Committee. The other motion is an amendment in the Committee of the Whole to strike the enacting clause, which is debated under the five-minute rule. A vote against consideration keeps a bill on its calendar, while the adoption of a motion to strike the enacting clause, if upheld by the House, kills a bill.

The motion for the previous question, whether incorporated into a resolution reported by the Rules Committee or made by the floor manager of a bill, if adopted, closes debate and brings the House directly to a vote on one or more amendments or all authorized amendments and final passage. Final passage in the House begins with voting on the amendments reported by the Committee of the Whole. Next is engrossment and third reading, a purely formal action that is approved by unanimous consent. This is followed by a motion to recommit, usually with instructions, which is reserved for use by those opposed to the bill. It provides an opportunity to offer a complete alternative to the pending measure and may include amendments defeated in the Committee of the Whole. It is a privileged motion that enables the minority to have a roll-call vote on its proposal; the result may be a more accurate reflection of sentiment than the vote on final passage. Some legislators who vote to recommit will, after the motion is defeated, vote for final passage because they believe the bill to be preferable to none at all or because the latter vote is more intelligible to constituents.

The actual vote on final passage is normally by roll call, but if the outcome is obvious and members are anxious to adjourn or proceed to other business, it may be by voice vote. All votes on amendments or bills, except in the Committee of the Whole, are subject to the motion to reconsider and are not considered final until reconsidered. Should a majority approve the motion, the matter to which it applies is once again before the chamber for action. A prompt motion to reconsider, which is made immediately following the announcement of a vote result, disposes of the matter without jeopardizing a bill. The motion, offered by someone who voted with the majority, invariably fails because all members who participated in the original decision are still on the floor. To delay reconsideration provides opponents of a measure the opportunity to persuade others to change their votes and to bring to the floor those members who were absent.

When several roll-call votes on different measures are likely to occur on the same day, the Speaker may postpone such votes to a designated time on that day or within the next two days. This procedure saves time since a normal voting period is fifteen minutes; however, the Speaker is empowered to reduce the voting period to five minutes for all such votes after the first. In addition to promoting efficiency, it is also easier to assemble all members in favor of certain proposals when the exact time of voting can be known in advance. This clustering of votes is also applicable to special orders from the Rules Committee and conference reports.

SENATE ACTION

The Senate has no counterpart to the Committee of the Whole and operates on the assumption that a quorum is always present until a member suggests otherwise or the contrary is revealed by a quorum call or roll-call vote. When less than a quorum responds to a roll call, the results are invalid and the presiding officer orders a quorum call; after a quorum appears, a vote is taken anew on the pending question. A quorum call may be requested by any senator prior to a vote on any motion or measure.

Most quorum calls are used to suspend floor action temporarily for the purpose of constructive delay. This pause permits informal discussions that would be much more difficult to arrange under the formal rules. Under a unanimous consent agreement limiting debate and controlling time, a quorum call is not in order prior to the expiration of time allotted for debate or until all such time is relinquished by those senators entitled to control it.

The three methods of voting used in the Senate are voice, division, and roll call, and once a result has been announced no motions for another vote, as in the House, are in order. The presiding officer may request a division vote whenever in doubt of the results of a voice vote, or any senator may do the same before the results of a voice vote have been announced. A quorum call or a roll call may be demanded by any senator prior to the announcement of the results of a voice or division vote. Thus, the absence of a quorum does not invalidate a voice or division vote if it is not challenged at the appropriate time. If a senator fails to request a roll-call vote in time, the senator may still make a motion to reconsider, which, if adopted, nullifies the earlier vote.

A roll-call vote must be taken when demanded and seconded by one-fifth of a quorum, or eleven members, with the number necessary to support such a demand determined by a show of hands. A quorum call may be demanded when a request for a roll-call vote does not have a sufficient number of senators to second it, after which the request for a roll call may be renewed. Though a roll-call vote must technically be demanded by one-fifth of a quorum, in practice it is rarely denied to any senator who desires one, though the senator may be persuaded to withdraw the request. A roll-call vote is valid when the number of senators voting, plus those present but not voting, constitutes a quorum of fifty-one. The vice-president may vote only in case of a tie, but since a tie vote defeats a proposal, his vote would only be decisive to approve a measure.

Sixteen senators must sign a cloture petition to close debate when a filibuster prevents the Senate from proceeding with its business. This is presented to the presiding officer, who is required to state the motion to the Senate immediately. Two days later the presiding officer submits the matter to the Senate for a roll-call vote. A motion to invoke cloture requires sixty votes to close debate on all questions except those to amend the Senate rules, which require a two-thirds majority of a quorum. Any Senate rule may be suspended by a two-thirds vote, and this procedure is primarily used to permit legislative amendments to general appropriation bills if unanimous consent cannot be obtained.

Should a unanimous consent agreement specify that a final vote on a bill and all amendments thereto shall occur at no later than a certain hour, votes may not be taken at times earlier than stated. The first step in final passage is taken when senators no longer have amendments to offer and the presiding officer orders a bill engrossed and read a third time, a formality that requires only a moment. It is not in order to recommit a bill unless a unanimous consent agreement provides for such a motion. The flexibility of the Senate amending process enables members to propose a greater number of substitute or other amendments than those in the House. Since substitutes are comprehensive revisions of pending measures, they serve the same purpose as a motion to recommit with instructions offered in the House, while other proposals may be offered to test voting strength.

A roll-call vote on final passage is followed by a motion to reconsider. Voice votes may be taken on final passage though a majority of senators may be absent and, except for a motion to reconsider, the action is final unless challenged before the result is announced. In the absence of a unanimous consent agreement or cloture, a vote on final passage may be delayed as party leaders endeavor to negotiate an end to a filibuster. However, it may not be possible to arrange for such a vote in the presence of determined opposition.

BICAMERAL ACTION

When each house passes different versions of a bill, the differences may be resolved through action by each chamber on the language adopted by the other or through appointment of a conference. In the former case the body of origin may vote separately on each or collectively on all amendments approved by the other house. The decision to seek a conference initiates a series of procedural votes covering a request for and an agreement to a conference and the appointment of conferees by both chambers. Conference committee meetings are open to the public unless a majority of the House membership or of Senate conferees decides by a roll-call vote to hold a closed session. Though a majority of the conferees from each house must vote to endorse any agreements reached and to have a report submitted to their respective chambers, the only equivalent to a roll-call vote taken in conference that appears in print is the names of those who sign the report.

A conference report is filed in each house once conferees reconcile all, or are only able to settle some, of their differences. The first chamber to vote may approve, reject, or recommit the report and, if approved, the second may vote only to accept or reject, since approval by the first dissolves the conference. Should a conference report embody only a partial resolution of differences, the first vote is on the report; if approved, the amendments reported in disagreement may be acted on separately, collectively, or through appointment of another conference.

House rules provide for separate votes on those portions of a conference report that are nongermane Senate amendments to a House bill, and if disapproved, the entire report is rejected. Each house may vote to instruct its conferees to insist on retaining language in the chamber's version of a bill or opposing language contained in the other body's version. This procedure, because it cannot influence conferees appointed by the other house and can inhibit the bargaining process, is infrequently employed. All votes that relate to bicameral action are subject to the motion to reconsider.

GENERAL CONSIDERATIONS

All roll calls are assigned numbers in chronological order throughout each session of Congress. In the Senate, roll calls on legislative and executive business are numbered in separate series. Because of occasional errors in the recording of votes and the use of unanimous consent to permit the change of a vote, the most accurate tallies appear in the bound *Record* and the journals rather than in contemporaneous publications. The indexes of these sources cite only the pages on which a given measure received consideration, without specifying where voting data can be found. Thus, use of the journals is more convenient for locating such information since it is not necessary to scan numerous pages of debate, which can easily result in overlooking an unrecorded vote.

Congressional Quarterly issues two annual publications that describe and tabulate several hundred roll-call votes. The CQ *Almanac* includes much more than voting-related information while *Congressional Roll Call* contains only such facts. The voting data are identical in each, and both have separate subject indexes for these recorded votes.

Article I, Section 5, of the Constitution stipulates that a majority of each house is the quorum necessary to conduct business, but the House and Senate interpret this provision to meet the practical needs of managing their workloads. All members of Congress have other demands on their time in addition to attending floor sessions of their respective chambers. Senate proceedings foster a greater frequency of roll-call votes, mainly because of smaller membership and greater collegiality. Also, unlike the House, the Senate does not have a procedure for combining a quorum call with a procedural or substantive vote and has no equivalent to the Committee of the Whole, which facilitates the disposition of amendments through unrecorded votes. The latitude of Senate debate results in a greater number of amendments offered for consideration. Though its rules require a majority of a quorum to demand a roll-call vote, an individual senator is accorded the privilege if insistent. Finally, since the Senate regularly operates without a quorum, any formal notice of this fact leads to a roll-call vote.

When a simple, rather than an extraordinary, majority is necessary to transact business, this means a majority of a quorum. Since a quorum is itself only a bare majority of the entire body, major voting decisions can be made by just over one-quarter of the total membership. In the House, which conducts much of its important business in the Committee of the Whole, where the quorum is 100, only 51 votes are needed to dispose of amendments. A majority vote in either house is sufficient to amend measures that require a two-thirds vote for final passage or to reconsider votes that involved a two-thirds majority. Key votes in the House that affect the substance of a bill are those on special orders, amendments, and recommitment, while Senate decisions on amendments are the crucial votes in that chamber.

When procedural votes determine whether a bill will reach final passage, they are of equal significance to substantive ones and constitute basic elements of legislative history. Upon the determination of the lack of a quorum, only the motions to adjourn or commence a quorum call are in order. The motion to adjourn may be used by proponents of a bill to prevent undesirable action or by opponents to prevent any action. Quorum calls may be resorted to by either side for the purpose of holding a hasty meeting to discuss strategy and tactics.

Though voting is a unique action that is clearly distinguishable from debate, throughout the legislative process the two activities remain closely related. They are two aspects of the same proceeding, with the statements that comprise debate preceding the decisions expressed through voting. The procedural connection is more definite than the relationship between the voting process or a vote result and the content of a bill. The meaning of a negative vote tends to be clearer than an affirmative one, which transforms the multitude of individual views into a corporate expression whose substantive implications are not always evident or consistent. The procedural maneuvers that represent efforts to secure an advantage when the outcome of a vote is uncertain also tend to cloud the meaning of some voting decisions.

It is necessary to mobilize majorities at many points in the legislative process to enact a bill into law. A vote reveals whether a majority exists, what its components are, and suggests other legislative transactions that might be initiated. The strategy for success on floor votes is to have more members present who support one side than the other. This is not necessarily an easy task because of the numerous demands on the time of legislators and the variety of sources that can exert political influence.

Because the order in which votes are taken can have important consequences for the content of a bill, it is a question that can generate some controversy and may be resolved through a special order in the House or a unanimous consent agreement in the Senate. The impact of a vote depends upon its methods, margin, and relationship to other votes. The sequence of voting decisions vitally affects the range of options available for successive votes. Thus, the parliamentary and political factors that influence the legislative timetable can be critical for the qualitative and quantitative results of a vote.

Committee consideration of a bill inevitably has a profound effect upon floor votes. Decisions may be made that preclude a floor vote or produce a unanimous or near unanimous verdict. Since a major bill is in a state of continual revision throughout its life, it is possible that an early vote in favor may, owing to modifications of the measure or changes in the political environment, develop into a later vote against the bill or vice versa.

The number of voting decisions on a given bill generally reflects the level of controversy generated by an issue. One paradox of the legislative process is that a multiplicity of votes tends to obscure their individual and collective meaning. Another paradox is that though a roll-call vote compels legislators to publicly commit themselves and enables constituents to hold them accountable for their actions, it is just such visible commitments that may impede the negotiation process which is essential to produce compromises that can command wide political support.

REFERENCES

Froman, Lewis A., Jr. *The Congressional Process.* Boston: Little, Brown, 1967.

Gross, Bertram M. *The Legislative Struggle.* New York: McGraw-Hill, 1953.

Jewell, Malcolm E., and Samuel C. Patterson. *The Legislative Process in the United States.* New York: Random House, 1966.

Oleszek, Walter J. *Congressional Procedures and the Policy Process.* 2nd ed. Washington, D.C.: Congressional Quarterly Press, 1984.

U.S. Congress. House. *Constitution, Jefferson's Manual and Rules of the House of Representatives.* House Document No. 98-277, 98th Congress, 2nd Session. Washington, D.C.: U.S. Government Printing Office, 1985.

U.S. Congress. House. *How Our Laws Are Made.* House Document No. 97-120, 97th Congress, 1st Session. Washington, D.C.: U.S. Government Printing Office, 1981.

U.S. Congress. House. *Procedure in the U.S. House of Representatives.* 4th ed. 97th Congress, 2nd Session. Washington, D.C.: U.S. Government Printing Office, 1982.

U.S. Congress. Senate. *Senate Procedure.* Senate Document No. 97-2, 97th Congress, 1st Session. Washington, D.C.: U.S. Government Printing Office, 1981.

U.S. Congress. Senate. *Standing Rules of the Senate.* Senate Document No. 99-22, 99th Congress, 2nd Session. Washington, D.C.: U.S. Government Printing Office, 1986.

8

Bills*

Legislative histories usually focus on the political factors and maneuvers that affect the progress of bills or on formal statements that would help to construe their provisions following enactment. A perspective that has received less attention concerns those rules and practices that govern preparation and disposition of legislation. This chapter traces the typical course of a major bill by describing its development and treatment as an official document at each stage of the legislative process. A survey of sources that can be consulted to identify bills and locate their texts concludes the discussion.

Bills are the raw material of congressional business. Considered primarily as political vehicles and potential law, their nature as legislative papers is generally overlooked. The procedures that apply in this latter regard determine when a bill is printed and in which congressional publications it will ultimately appear. For the purposes of what follows, the term *bills* includes joint resolutions, since both are treated in an identical manner and, upon being approved, are law. The only exception is a joint resolution that is a proposed constitutional amendment, which does not require presidential approval upon passage. Otherwise, the major differences between bills and joint resolutions are that the latter are numbered in a separate series and tend to be used for the incidental or subordinate purposes of legislation.

PRE-FLOOR PRACTICES

In the House, printed blank forms on which members have the original draft bill typed are available in the stationery room. All forms must be signed by the legislator whose name appears first thereon before they can be accepted for introduction. Once formally introduced by being dropped into a hopper at the desk of the clerk of the House, bills are assigned a number, beginning with 1, that they retain for the duration of the Congress. The parliamentarian, under the supervision of the Speaker of the House, then designates the committee to which

---

*This chapter derives from an article, "Congressional Bills," by Jerrold Zwirn, in *Government Publications Review*, Vol. 7A, pp. 17-25, © 1980 Pergamon Journals, Ltd. Reprinted with permission of Pergamon Journals.

the bill is referred for consideration. The bill clerk, under the direction of the clerk of the House, prepares a duplicate copy of the draft and forwards it to the Government Printing Office. Upon delivery of printed copies to the bill clerk, the bills are distributed to the document rooms of both houses and the office of the secretary of the Senate. One official printed copy is transmitted to the chairman of the committee to which it was referred, for which the bill clerk obtains a receipt. The original draft is retained in the files of the clerk of the House.

Printed forms are also available in the Senate, where draft bills are presented for processing to clerks at the presiding officer's desk. They are endorsed at the desk to indicate the author and the committee that has jurisdiction. After referral by the parliamentarian, under the supervision of the presiding officer, the bill is sent to the secretary of the Senate's office to be numbered and forwarded, by the bill clerk, to the Government Printing Office. Printed copies are usually available the following morning and distributed as in the House. The original copy is filed in the secretary's records. (See figure 9 for an example of an introduced print of a public bill.) Bills introduced in either house whose provisions overlap the jurisdiction of two or more committees may be referred simultaneously or sequentially to those panels. In the House only, a bill may be divided into parts for referral to different committees.

Members of either house who introduce private bills may themselves indicate the committee to which the bills will be referred. Private bills apply to identifiable individuals or organizations within a legislator's geographical constituency and do not affect the general public. However, the distinction between public and private bills is not always clear, and bills may contain provisions of both a public and private nature, in which case they are treated as public measures.

Legislators frequently introduce numerous bills that are similar in purpose. Under these circumstances, a committee may choose one bill and incorporate the provisions of others. Another option is to amalgamate the best features of several bills and draft an entirely new version, which is then introduced and assigned a new number. This latter measure is referred to as a clean bill. For particularly complex and significant matters, primarily involving appropriations and revenue, the legislation is regularly drafted in committee, the first print is the reported version, and it is termed an original bill. A committee may also report a substitute, which is an amendment in the form of an entirely new bill, with only the original number being retained. Identical measures introduced in each chamber are known as companion bills.

A bill of some length and complexity often occupies a committee for several months. When extended consideration engenders numerous revisions, the panel will have the bill printed periodically to reflect the changes. These drafts, which serve as working papers, are designated as Committee Print No. 1, Committee Print No. 2, and so on. Because they are issued in a limited quantity and their printing is not formally noted, knowledge of and access to these prints tend to be restricted to parties immediately concerned with the legislation. Independent researchers usually do not learn of their existence until granted permission to use committee records after they have been transferred to the National Archives.

The contents of an introduced print are number and session of Congress, bill number, house and date of introduction, name(s) of legislator(s) who sponsored it, committee to which it was referred, type (bill or joint resolution), and the law(s), if any, it proposes to amend. After the member's name there will occasionally appear in parenthesis the phrase *by request*. This denotes that the

II

100TH CONGRESS
1ST SESSION

S. 774

To amend the Internal Revenue Code of 1986 to provide for the deduction of contributions to long-term care savings accounts.

IN THE SENATE OF THE UNITED STATES

MARCH 18, 1987

Ms. MIKULSKI introduced the following bill; which was read twice and referred to the Committee on Finance

---

A BILL

To amend the Internal Revenue Code of 1986 to provide for the deduction of contributions to long-term care savings accounts.

1   *Be it enacted by the Senate and House of Representa-*

2   *tives of the United States of America in Congress assembled,*

3   SECTION 1. SHORT TITLE.

4   This Act may be cited as the "Long-Term Care Savings

5   Account Act of 1987".

6   SEC. 2. LONG-TERM CARE SAVINGS ACCOUNTS.

7   (a) IN GENERAL.—Part VII of subchapter B of chapter

8   1 of the Internal Revenue Code of 1986 (relating to addition-

9   al itemized deductions for individuals) is amended by redesig-

Fig. 9. An introduced print of a public bill.

bill was introduced at the request of a government agency or private organization and that the legislator does not necessarily endorse it. Each line of the text is numbered, beginning with 1, on each page.

The text of a public bill may consist of as many as twelve distinct parts: (1) title—a brief statement of purpose(s); (2) enacting clause—identical for all bills; (3) short title—a descriptive phrase specifying its primary subject; (4) table of contents; (5) declaration of purpose—a statement of conditions the bill is intended to rectify; (6) definition of terms; (7) main body of the text in numbered titles and/or sections; (8) exceptions and provisos; (9) amendments and repeals; (10) savings clause—continues the effectiveness of specified legal obligations to avoid inadvertent lapsing or impairment; (11) separability clause—provides that if any provision of the *act* is declared invalid, the remainder is to be unaffected; and (12) effective and expiration dates. For a joint resolution, 2 is a resolving clause and 5 a preamble. All bills include 1, 2, and 7, though the text, if brief, will not be subdivided.

Printed forms for submitting proposed amendments are available only in the Senate. The key information included is a brief statement of purpose, the Senate or House bill number, name of the member offering it, and the page and line number where it is to be inserted. The bill clerk adds an amendment number. If the bill to be amended is in committee, the amendment is referred there; if it is not adopted, the sponsor may, after the bill is reported, resubmit it for consideration when the bill reaches the floor. At this time the amendment will be printed with the identical calendar number of the bill. This number signifies the bill's readiness for consideration by the parent body. A senator may receive permission for such a printed amendment to be retained at the presiding officer's desk for submission when the bill reaches the floor. These amendments, as well as unprinted or floor amendments, are numbered separately and serially, beginning with 1, throughout the existence of a Congress. Both printed and unprinted amendments are prepared on an identical form and become part of the official bill file.

When a committee has completed consideration of an introduced bill, its staff drafts a copy that incorporates all amendments adopted. It is delivered to the bill clerk, who transmits it to the Government Printing Office. The reported print, as this version is known, contains, in addition to the information appearing on the introduced print, a calendar number, a report number, date reported, name of member reporting it, and amendments, if any. Amendments are printed in lined-through type if they are deletions and in italics if they are additions. These amendments are committee recommendations only and must be approved by the parent body before being officially incorporated into the bill. A bill referred to two or more committees concurrently is reported only once, either jointly or by one of the panels which considered it. Measures referred to two or more committees consecutively, or those divided for referral in the House, may be reported by each panel.

Introduced bills, printed amendments, and reported bills, both prior to and after being printed, are examined for accuracy by the bill clerk. A printed copy found to contain a typographical or other error is stamped *star print*, the error is noted on the print, and the correct matter is inserted. It is then returned to the Government Printing Office and, when reprinted, will have a small star in the lower left-hand corner and the words *star print* on the first page to indicate that the original print has been corrected.

FLOOR PROCEDURES

Once a bill reaches the floor, all amendments offered must be in writing and may be printed, typed, or handwritten. If introduced at least one day prior to floor consideration in the House, amendments are printed in the daily edition of the *Congressional Record* in advance of debate. These amendments are deposited in a separate receptacle at the rostrum or with the official reporters of debates and must bear the member's original signature. In the Senate they may be printed individually or in the *Record* prior to debate. An amendment must include the name of the legislator, the number of the bill to which it pertains, and the precise place in the bill it is to be inserted. Each amendment adopted in the House is initialed by two reading clerks to certify its approval. The legislative clerk in the Senate notes each amendment passed on the desk, or official, copy of the bill. When a bill under consideration is printed prior to passage to show which amendments have been adopted, the official copy remains at the desk for use as further amendments are proposed.

Upon completion of floor action, the bill clerk transmits to the enrolling clerk (who also serves under either the clerk of the House or secretary of the Senate) all papers relating to a bill passed by the chamber. These papers include the official copy of each bill, a separate copy of each amendment adopted, and any supplementary material. The enrolling clerk does not alter the official copy, but prepares a *printer's copy* using cut-outs of the reported print, copies of amendments approved, and any typed instructions regarding the arrangement and format of the text. The printer's copy is edited so that amendments appear in their proper place in the bill. Editing, in this instance, refers to the preparation of a "true copy" of the chamber's action on a bill, including the incorporation of technical and clerical changes where authorized. Such changes usually involve punctuation, cross references, or the renumbering of pages and subdivisions of the text. For particularly lengthy bills, the printer's copy is updated on a daily basis. This process is officially known as the engrossment of a bill.

The edited copy is sent to the Government Printing Office and is now technically termed an Act, denoting that it is an act of one house of Congress. Though a bill is redesignated an Act after it has been passed by its body of origin, the designation of a joint resolution remains unchanged. The final copy of such a measure whose passage has been attested by the signature of either the clerk of the House or secretary of the Senate on its last page is known as an engrossed bill. An engrossed copy is retained in the files of either the clerk or secretary. The official printed copy, prior to being signed and transmitted to the other house, is examined for accuracy by the enrolling clerk. If no errors are found, it is delivered to the presiding officer's desk while the second chamber is in session. An accompanying message contains its number, title, date of passage, and a request for concurrence.

Upon being received by the second chamber, it is referred, but not delivered, to the appropriate committee(s). The bill clerk, after making a copy, transmits the official engrossed bill to the committee and obtains a receipt. The copy is sent to the Government Printing Office, and this version is termed the Act or referred print (see figure 10). It contains number and session of Congress, bill number of the body of origin, house to which it has been transmitted, date it was received, committee to which it has been referred, the law(s) it proposes to amend, and the

II

100TH CONGRESS
1ST SESSION

H. J. RES. 90

IN THE SENATE OF THE UNITED STATES

JUNE 9, 1987

Received; read twice and referred to the Committee on Labor and Human
Resources

JOINT RESOLUTION

To authorize and request the President to call and conduct a
White House Conference on Library and Information Services to be held not earlier than September 1, 1989, and not
later than September 30, 1991, and for other purposes.

Whereas access to information and ideas is indispensable to the
development of human potential, the advancement of civili-
zation, and the continuance of enlightened self-government;

Whereas the preservation and the dissemination of information
and ideas are the primary purpose and function of the library and information services;

Whereas the economic vitality of the United States in a global
economy and the productivity of the work force of the
Nation rest on access to information in the postindustrial information age;

Fig. 10. A House-passed joint resolution referred to the Senate.

date it passed the first chamber. This date is normally a calendar day in the House, while in the Senate the legislative day is noted if it differs from the calendar day. A legislative day extends from the time either house meets following an adjournment until it again adjourns. The Senate often decides to recess, which does not end a legislative day.

Engrossed bills may not be altered by the other house. When action by the second chamber results in passage with amendments, the changes must be transcribed on separate paper, stating which words are to be inserted or deleted and where, by reference to page, line, and word of the bill. However, action on the measure proceeds as in the body of origin, and the reported print will incorporate the text of amendments adopted in committee. Upon final passage, all amendments approved are engrossed and, when printed, are numbered consecutively in the order in which they appear in the bill, beginning with 1, unless there is only a single amendment. The engrossed bill and engrossed amendment(s) are then delivered to the body of origin. An accompanying message requests that the first chamber concur in the amendments.

If an identical or substantially similar measure has been reported in either chamber prior to receipt of an engrossed bill, the latter may not be referred to a committee and printed. It may subsequently be referred or substituted for the reported bill depending upon strategic or procedural considerations. A common action is for the second chamber to pass its own bill and then substitute its text under the number of the companion measure received from the other house. This procedure, which technically involves approval of an engrossed bill in lieu of the measure that was reported in the second house, facilitates anticipated bicameral negotiations.

CONFERENCE PROCEDURES

If the body of origin agrees to the amendments, or if amendments are not adopted by the second chamber, legislative action on the bill is completed. However, if there is disagreement that cannot be resolved by the houses acting separately in succession, the house having custody of the official papers on a bill may request a conference with the other to reconcile their differences. The papers, which consist of the original engrossed bill, engrossed amendments, and all messages exchanged between the chambers concerning the measure, are then delivered to the other body, for in conference procedure a house may only act when in possession of the papers. Upon agreement to a conference, the papers are returned to the house that asked for the conference. The bill clerk of the requesting body then gives the papers to its conferees, or managers, and obtains a receipt.

Prior to the first conference meeting, staff attorneys from the committees of jurisdiction in each house jointly prepare an agenda. This draft, which describes and analyzes the items in disagreement, may take one of three forms. For less complex bills, it may consist entirely of a narrative statement. For more complex bills, a two-column print that permits comparison of the provisions of each measure is preferred. One other option is a combination of the first two. This agenda is usually supplemented by such information as who sponsored which amendments, memoranda on the legislative language approved by each house, and proposals incorporating possible compromises. These unofficial papers are in the same class as the committee prints discussed earlier in this chapter.

The authority of conferees is confined to choosing between or compromising on the amendments in disagreement. They may neither alter the text approved by both houses in identical form nor add provisions not adopted by either body. These restrictions do not apply when the second chamber has adopted a substitute, which is an amendment in the form of a new bill. In this case there is total disagreement, and conferees are free to write an original bill covering the same subject, though its provisions must be derived from at least one of the two versions under consideration. Though new matter is not permitted in conference reports, clarifying language or changes in phraseology to effect legislative consistency are acceptable as long as they do not broaden the scope of the bill beyond the differences committed to conference.

There are several possible outcomes of a conference. Conferees may trade, accepting the language adopted by the other house for one or more provisions if the other body's conferees will do the same; all amendments in disagreement may be compromised; or there may be some combination of these two possibilities. One other result would be the inability to reach agreement on all or any of their differences. If agreement is reached on some, a report is filed disclosing which matters have been resolved and which remain in disagreement. Approval of such a report by each chamber means that the remaining differences must still be settled before the bill can be enrolled.

When the managers reach agreement they file a report which, to be valid, must be signed by a majority of the conferees of each house. The report is drafted by staff members of the committees that considered the bill in each chamber. It is prepared in duplicate, with House conferees signing first on their copy and Senate conferees first on theirs. The managers of the house that requested the conference now give the official papers to the managers of the house that agreed thereto. The latter deliver them to the presiding officer, following which the bill clerk examines the report for accuracy, assigns a number to it, and forwards a copy to the Government Printing Office. Most conference reports are printed in the House only to avoid unnecessary duplication, but occasionally one is printed by both houses, in which case it will have two separate numbers. Should a typographical error be discovered in a printed conference report, it would be reissued as a star print.

A conference report is, in effect, a bill or an amended portion thereof, containing the text of all changes agreed upon, with an accompanying explanation of actions taken. Where the report refers to pages and line numbers, references are to the engrossed bill and engrossed amendments. The report includes the number and session of Congress, the house in which it was printed, report number, subject of the bill, date reported, name of member reporting it, and bill number. It may not be amended by either house acting independently of the other, but only by a concurrent resolution, which is used to coordinate the internal affairs of both houses on matters of mutual interest.

Upon approval of the report by one house, the papers are transmitted to the other with a message communicating its action. Endorsements noting legislative action taken by each house on the conference report, and the dates thereof, are noted on the engrossed bill by the clerk of the House or secretary of the Senate. Rejection of the report by one chamber may lead to another conference, in which case the second report would supersede the first. If both adopt it and, thus, agree upon an identical version of the bill, all papers relating to the measure are delivered to the enrolling clerk of the body of origin.

In the House only, special treatment may be accorded a bill whose subject matter falls within the purview of two or more committees. The Speaker is authorized to appoint an ad hoc panel composed of members from those committees with jurisdiction to consider such a measure, which is known as an omnibus bill. Upon passage its subdivisions are engrossed separately and, in the Senate, are referred to the appropriate committees. When the components of an omnibus bill are returned from the Senate with amendments, or when such amendments result in a conference, each component is considered separately, but agreement must be reached on all components for the bill to be enrolled.

ENACTMENT

An enrolled copy is prepared from the engrossed bill, engrossed amendments, the conference report, and all messages exchanged between the chambers concerning a bill. The procedures for enrollment are identical to those for engrossment. An enrolled bill is the final copy of a bill passed in identical form by both houses. It is printed on parchment and endorsed with the signature of either the clerk of the House or secretary of the Senate to indicate its body of origin, in whose files the official papers are retained.

Bills that originate in the House are examined for accuracy at the enrollment stage by staff members of the House Administration Committee and in the Senate by members of the secretary's staff. Immediately preceding enrollment, members of both staffs compare their versions of a bill that has passed both chambers. When the bill is found to be truly enrolled, it is transmitted to the House parliamentarian, who signs a receipt therefor and secures the signature of the Speaker, who signs the bills first, regardless of its body of origin. The measure is then delivered to the Senate parliamentarian, who also signs a receipt and obtains the signature of the president of the Senate. Following this dual signing, the bill is returned to either the House or Senate parliamentarian, depending upon its house of origin, for presentation to the president of the United States.

If a bill has been enrolled and signed by both presiding officers, or only by the Speaker, and an error is found, the signature(s) are rescinded by a concurrent resolution, after which it is reenrolled. The original enrolled bill is delivered to the White House, for which a receipt is obtained from a presidential staff member. Other than final adjournment, there is no time limit within which an enrolled bill need be presented to the president. Presentation may actually occur after final adjournment if a concurrent resolution authorizing such action has been adopted. Congress may request, by concurrent resolution, that a bill which has been forwarded to the president and found to contain an error be returned for correction and reenrollment. Concurrent resolutions are also used to correct technical and typographical errors in engrossed and enrolled bills. An error in an enrolled bill in the president's possession may also be corrected by a joint resolution. Should an error not be detected until after a bill has become law, it can only be corrected by passage of another bill.

When the president signs an enrolled bill within ten days of receipt, Sundays excepted, it becomes law even if Congress has adjourned, and he so informs the body of origin. If the president neither signs nor vetoes it within ten days, Sundays excepted, and Congress has not adjourned, the bill becomes law and is endorsed by the administrator of General Services. Should the president return a bill to its house of origin with a statement of his objections (see figure 11) and it is repassed by a two-thirds vote, an endorsement is made on the bill by the clerk of the House or secretary of the Senate to that effect. It is then transmitted to the other chamber, where, if it passes with a two-thirds majority, it is again endorsed, the president's veto is overridden, and the bill becomes law. A bill without an effective date becomes law the day it is signed by the president, repassed by Congress over a veto, or endorsed by the administrator of General Services.

If the body of origin fails to override a veto, it notifies the other house by message and refers the original enrolled bill and veto message to the committee that reported the measure. Should the second chamber fail to override, it returns the bill to the body of origin with a message regarding its action. When the president vetoes a bill by withholding his signature following the final adjournment of Congress, the original copy is returned to the house of origin. In these instances, no print is made of the bill in the form in which it reached the president.

The house acting last when a bill is approved over a veto has it delivered to the administrator of General Services. This official receives copies of all enrolled bills that become law. A copy is sent to the Government Printing Office, which prints it in duplicate for the purpose of final revision. Upon the return by the administrator of one of the duplicates, the Government Printing Office prints the law in its final form.

The first official print of a statute appears in pamphlet form and is known as a slip law. (See figure 12 on page 154 for an example of a slip law print of a public bill.) Each print indicates the manner in which the bill became law. Slip laws are published in two series — public and private — each of which is numbered separately, beginning with 1, for each Congress. Where some doubt exists as to whether a statute is a public or private law, the decision is made by editors in the Office of the Federal Register after examining the history, nature, and scope of the legislation.

The heading of a slip law includes the public or private law number, the number of the Congress, bill number, and date of approval. On the last page of each public slip law is a guide to its legislative history that records the committees that considered it and their report numbers, the number of any companion bill, the dates of action and passage by each house, with reference to the *Congressional Record* by volume, year, and date. Also cited is any presidential statement appearing in the *Weekly Compilation of Presidential Documents*. Editorial information in the margins consists of subject headings; citations of laws amended, repealed, or referred to; references to prior or subsequent pages of the statute when its text mentions other sections of it; page numbers of the *Statutes at Large* on which it will appear; and section of the *United States Code* in which it will be inserted. None of this information is part of the law itself. Once printed, slip laws are delivered to the document rooms of both houses of Congress. They are legal documents and may be used as evidence in any legal proceeding.

100th Congress, 1st Session - - - - - - - - - Senate Document 100-10

VETO—S. 742

MESSAGE

FROM

THE PRESIDENT OF THE UNITED STATES

RETURNING

WITHOUT MY APPROVAL S. 742, THE FAIRNESS IN BROADCASTING ACT OF 1987, WHICH WOULD CODIFY THE SO-CALLED FAIRNESS DOCTRINE

JUNE 23, 1987.—Ordered to be printed

U.S. GOVERNMENT PRINTING OFFICE
91-011 WASHINGTON : 1987

Fig. 11. A vetoed bill returned to its body of origin.

PUBLIC LAW 100-12—MAR. 17, 1987   101 STAT. 103

Public Law 100-12
100th Congress

An Act

To amend the Energy Policy and Conservation Act with respect to energy conserva-   Mar. 17, 1987
tion standards for appliances.   [S. 83]

Be it enacted by the Senate and House of Representatives of the   National
United States of America in Congress assembled,   Appliance
                                                                            Energy
SECTION 1. SHORT TITLE.   Conservation
                                                                            Act of 1987.
This Act may be referred to as the "National Appliance Energy   42 USC 6201
Conservation Act of 1987".   note.

SEC. 2. DEFINITIONS.

(a) ENERGY CONSERVATION STANDARD.—Section 321(a)(6) of the
Energy Policy and Conservation Act (42 U.S.C. 6291(a)(6)) is
amended to read as follows:
    "(6) The term 'energy conservation standard' means—
        "(A) a performance standard which prescribes a mini-
    mum level of energy efficiency or a maximum quantity of
    energy use for a covered product, determined in accordance
    with test procedures prescribed under section 323; or   *Post,* p. 105.
        "(B) a design requirement for the products specified in
    paragraphs (6), (7), (8), (10), and (13) of section 322(a); and *Post,* p. 105.
    includes any other requirements which the Secretary may pre-
    scribe under section 325(o)."   *Post,* p. 107.
(b) NEW DEFINITIONS.—Section 321(a) of the Energy Policy and
Conservation Act (42 U.S.C. 6291(a)) is amended by adding at the end
the following paragraphs:
    "(19) The term 'AV' is the adjusted volume for refrigerators,
refrigerator-freezers, and freezers, as defined in the applicable
test procedure prescribed under section 323.
    "(20) The term 'annual fuel utilization efficiency' means the
efficiency descriptor for furnaces and boilers, determined using
test procedures prescribed under section 323 and based on the
assumption that all—
        "(A) weatherized warm air furnaces or boilers are located
    out-of-doors;
        "(B) warm air furnaces which are not weatherized are
    located indoors and all combustion and ventilation air is
    admitted through grills or ducts from the outdoors and does
    not communicate with air in the conditioned space; and
        "(C) boilers which are not weatherized are located within
    the heated space.
    "(21) The term 'central air conditioner' means a product,
other than a packaged terminal air conditioner, which—
        "(A) is powered by single phase electric current;
        "(B) is air-cooled;
        "(C) is rated below 65,000 Btu per hour;
        "(D) is not contained within the same cabinet as a fur-
    nace the rated capacity of which is above 225,000 Btu per
    hour; and

Fig. 12. A slip law print of a public bill.

CALENDARS

The primary function of legislative calendars is to provide information about pending business. The official title of the *House Calendar* is *Calendars of the United States House of Representatives and History of Legislation.* It is printed each day the House is in session and consists of three primary calendars, to which all measures reported by committees must be referred, and two secondary calendars. After a bill or resolution is reported it is assigned a calendar number on one of the three primary calendars. They are the Union Calendar, to which all public bills directly or indirectly raising or spending public funds or disposing of public property are referred; the House Calendar, to which all other public measures are referred; and the Private Calendar, to which all private bills are referred.

The more important of the secondary calendars is the Consent Calendar, discussed in chapter 6. The other secondary calendar is the Discharge Calendar, which is used for motions that remove a measure from the custody of a committee that has not reported it. Once a majority of House members have signed a petition in favor of discharge the motion is in order on designated days. This procedure is rarely used because of the aversion to overriding committee decisions and the availability of other means to bring proposals to the floor. The vast majority of measures acted on are taken from the Consent and Private Calendars.

For researchers, one of the two most informative sections of the House Calendar is its numerical list of bills and resolutions. It contains a complete history of all House and Senate bills, joint resolutions, concurrent resolutions, and House simple resolutions that reached a calendar. For each such measure, where applicable, it also identifies the House Rules Committee resolution that conferred a privileged status on it which enabled the chamber to consider it out of its calendar number order. A second very useful feature is the subject index in each Monday edition. Its frequency provides the most up-to-date access to current chamber activity. Also, under the subject heading of "House Reports" it lists all committee reports not directly related to bills or resolutions and are, thus, not clearly identified elsewhere.

The Senate has only a single *Calendar of Business* for its legislative activity and it is also printed each day the chamber is in session. Its most important section is "General Orders," a list of the measures reported by committees or otherwise placed on the calendar. The name of the committee and whether it reported the proposal with amendments is noted. Two distinct features of the Senate *Calendar* are that it includes House measures substantially the same as those reported in the Senate and contains a cross-reference table that lists Senate and House bills in numerical sequence with their general order number. It also contains the text of unanimous consent agreements, which set the terms under which major bills are debated. In contrast with the *House Calendar*, it is not cumulative and only presents information about business pending on the day it is issued. Thus, the Senate *Calendar* is of limited research value and, in any case, the facts it furnishes can be readily obtained from other available sources.

Certain classes of privileged business are not placed on chamber calendars. The most significant of these are measures amended by one house and returned to its body of origin for further action, proposals sent to or reported from conference committees, and bills vetoed by the president. The status of conference action, though, is included in separate sections of each calendar, with the House document providing more detailed information. Since these matters concern bills or resolutions that have left the custody of the chamber, they cannot again be referred to a calendar upon their return. They are regularly held for disposition at the Speaker's table in the House and the presiding officer's desk in the Senate, which are calendars by another name.

Most standing committees issue approximately six to eight calendars that cumulate data during the two-year congressional cycle. The standard sections of committee calendars include a numerical list of all bills and resolutions and a chronological list of all presidential messages referred to the panel, committee action on and the legislative status of each such measure, and a concise and complete description of all committee publications. An important feature is the identification of all hearings, including those not printed. Along with biennial Legislative Activity Reports that are issued as formal committee reports and appear in the Serial Set, committee calendars are a superior source for information about panel workload. They usually include a detailed subject index that provides the most exhaustive treatment of committee jurisdiction.

BIBLIOGRAPHIC GUIDE

The preceding account applies to the usual route of major and controversial bills which, though few in number during any given session of Congress, generate the bulk of legislative business. Bills are routinely printed upon introduction, when favorably reported from committee and after passage by one house, unless additional printings are specially ordered by either chamber. A routine printing may be omitted if it would unreasonably delay legislative action, a situation that occurs most often during the closing days of a session.

There are numerous exceptions to the usual route that affect the printing of bills, and some of the more common or important ones should be noted. A message from the president requesting enactment of specific legislation will usually contain a draft bill and, when referred to a committee, may serve in lieu of an introduced bill. The initial printing is the reported print for legislation that originates in committee. If a bill is referred from one committee to another, it is reprinted on each such occasion, but there will be only one reported print. An Act print is omitted in the second chamber when one of its committees has reported a bill identical or substantially similar to one subsequently received from the other body. Each house may consider bills passed by the other without referring them to a committee. In this instance, there will not be a reported print in the second chamber, though the bill will be printed with a calendar number.

Most bills enacted into law are not controversial and pass both houses either without amendment or, if amended, are agreed upon without a conference. The vast majority of all bills are, of course, not enacted into law, and most do not progress beyond being referred to a committee following their introduction. The life of all bills expires with the final adjournment of a Congress. Any bill may be reintroduced in a succeeding Congress, but it will be assigned a new number and action on it will begin anew regardless of the stage it reached during its prior consideration. The form in which it is reintroduced will, to some extent, usually reflect any changes it underwent in its earlier life.

The following is intended to serve as a general guide to the more accessible publications that enable one to identify bills and locate their texts. A bill number is its foremost identifying characteristic, but there are several ways to identify the number if not known. Regardless of which source is used, either the number of the Congress or the year needs to be known to narrow the search.

Sources that provide access by subject include the index to the bound *Congressional Record* and that of each chamber's journal, which present information about all bills introduced; the *Digest of Public General Bills and Resolutions* (*DPGBR*), prepared by the Congressional Research Service and normally published in two cumulative issues with periodic supplements and a final edition at the end of each session, which also covers all bills; and the Monday and final editions of the *House Calendar*, which contains information about all bills *reported in both houses*. Each of these items also provides access by bill number.

Sources that provide access by public law number include the *House Calendar*, the end-of-session edition of the *Daily Digest* section of the *Congressional Record, DPGBR, Statutes at Large, Legislative Histories Annual*, and CQ *Almanac*. For access by private law number the *House Calendar* or *Statutes at Large* can be consulted, both of which provide subject access to all bills enacted into law.

Sources that provide access by bill sponsor include the index to the bound *Record, DPGBR*, and the House *Journal*.

When a bill number is known and the public law number is needed, one can consult the *House Calendar*, the bound index of the *Congressional Record, DPGBR*, or *Legislative Histories Annual*. When a public law number is known and the bill number is needed, one can consult a slip law, *Statutes at Large*, and the same sources cited in the previous sentence, except that the *Daily Digest* rather than the *Congressional Record* proper provides the information. A pamphlet entitled *How to Find U.S. Statutes and U.S. Code Citations* enables researchers with partial data about a law to retrieve complete information. It is published periodically by the Office of the Federal Register, National Archives and Records Administration.

Legislative history or status tables reveal the stages of the legislative process through which a bill passed or those which it bypassed. Such information indicates the occasions on which a bill was printed. These tables are normally arranged by public law number. Two that are cumulative throughout a Congress are found in the *House Calendar* and *DPGBR*, while three that are cumulated at the end of each session appear in the final edition of the *Daily Digest, Legislative Histories Annual*, and CQ *Almanac*.

Presented below are sources that can be consulted for the different versions of or changes made in a bill as it progresses through Congress.

1. Introduced print: The primary source is hearings held by the committee(s) that considered the bill. To determine whether such hearings have been printed one can use the *Monthly Catalog* or *CIS/Index*. Both provide access by subject, bill title, and committee; the latter also by public law number, bill number, and popular name of the law or bill.

2. Committee amendments rejected: All committee roll-call votes and the text of amendments voted on are recorded in a minute book. Sources that are more accessible would be the printed transcript of a mark-up session; the supplemental, additional, or minority views contained in the committee report; floor amendments proposed by committee members; and the descriptions of committee action that appear in Congressional Quarterly's *Weekly Report* and other print media.

3. Committee amendments adopted: These are available in printed mark-ups and committee reports. The existence of the former can be determined through use of the sources mentioned in 1 above. Report numbers are listed in the status tables of publications previously discussed. If a committee reports a clean bill, with a new number, in lieu of the introduced version on which hearings were held, this will be noted near the beginning of the report. In the Senate, when more than one report accompanies a bill, each will have a different report number. In the House, all reports on a bill are assigned one number, but are designated as different parts of the same report. In each chamber, all reports on the same bill will have the identical calendar number. The report may also identify by bill number similar or identical measures introduced in prior Congresses. All reports are in the Serial Set but appear in the *Record* only on those infrequent occasions when they are read on the floor or are printed therein by unanimous consent.

4. Floor amendments adopted and rejected: Legislative history tables only cite the date(s) of floor action. Sources that identify pertinent pages in the Proceedings section of the *Congressional Record* are its index and *Legislative Histories Annual*. The *Record* index notes all proposed amendments under the sponsor's name. This includes those amendments not formally offered and those offered but withdrawn before being acted upon. The *Record* history of bills and resolutions cites all amendments offered on the floor of each house.

5. Act print (engrossed bill): Committee hearings held in the second chamber. See 1 above.

6. Committee amendments rejected and adopted: When a committee amends and reports a bill passed by the other house, its report contains an explanation of its amendment(s) and is most likely to include the text if it reports a substitute. See 2 and 3 above.

7. Floor amendments adopted (engrossed) and rejected: See 4 above.

8. Conference report: The text always appears in the *Record* and in the journal of each house. Also see 3 above, except the number is not given in the *Daily Digest*. When one house has passed a substitute, this report contains the entire text of the bill.

9. Vetoed bill: Measures returned by the president with a veto message are listed in the index to the bound *Record,* the *Monthly Catalog, CIS/Index,* and the *Weekly Compilation of Presidential Documents.* The last includes the text of all messages submitted to Congress concerning legislation and all public statements regarding the same. The text of all veto messages, which includes the bill, also appears in the *Record* and the journal of the house of origin. The text of the bill, along with the message, is printed in the Serial Set as either a House or Senate document, depending upon the body of origin. The text of a bill that is pocket vetoed must be compiled from its latest print, plus any amendments adopted that appear in the *Record,* including any conference report.

10. Laws (enrolled bills): These are published in the *Statutes at Large.*

11. Companion bills: Their number is given in the index to the bound *Record, House Calendar, DPGBR, Daily Digest,* and *Statutes at Large.*

12. Concurrent resolutions: These appear in the *Record, Statutes at Large,* and the journal of each house.

Some of the publications noted above have unique features. *Legislative Histories Annual* provides information about bills prior to the Congress in which they are enacted into law; otherwise one must use either a subject or sponsor approach to identify such measures if a committee report does not discuss its history. The *House Calendar* and House *Journal* list all vetoed bills, separately identifying those returned with a message and those vetoed when the president withholds his signature following congressional adjournment. A status table for major legislation, including all general appropriation bills, appears in the CQ *Weekly Report* and on the final pages of the *House Calendar.* The *DPGBR* is the only source that provides a synopsis of each bill, which is presented in the form of both an abstract and a factual description.

Introduced and reported versions of bills are occasionally printed in the *Record,* but the irregularity of this practice means that it must be consulted in each instance. Their text, as well as that of printed amendments, is more likely to appear under Senate proceedings. The dates of introduction and presidential approval are always given in the *Record.*

A very limited number of multivolume sets of bound bills are issued sometime after the final adjournment of each Congress. These contain all introduced, reported, and Act prints of both houses, as well as printed Senate amendments. They are distributed to the House and Senate libraries and the Law Library of the Library of Congress. The Government Printing Office distributes introduced, reported, and Act prints of all bills and printed Senate amendments, in microfiche only, to those depository libraries that choose to receive them.

REFERENCES

Cummings, Frank. *Capitol Hill Manual.* 2nd ed. Washington, D.C.: Bureau of National Affairs, 1984.

Thaxter, John H. "Printing of Congressional Bills." *Library Resources and Technical Services* 7 (Summer 1963), 237-43.

U.S. Congress. House. *Constitution, Jefferson's Manual and Rules of the House of Representatives.* House Document No. 98-277, 98th Congress, 2nd Session. Washington, D.C.: U.S. Government Printing Office, 1985.

U.S. Congress. House. *How Our Laws Are Made.* House Document No. 97-120, 97th Congress, 1st Session. Washington, D.C.: U.S. Government Printing Office, 1981.

U.S. Congress. House. *Procedure in the U.S. House of Representatives.* 4th ed. 97th Congress, 2nd Session. Washington, D.C.: U.S. Government Printing Office, 1982.

U.S. Congress. Senate. *Enactment of a Law.* Senate Document No. 97-20, 97th Congress, 2nd Session. Washington, D.C.: U.S. Government Printing Office, 1982.

U.S. Congress. Senate. *Senate Legislative Procedural Flow.* 95th Congress, 2nd Session. Washington, D.C.: U.S. Government Printing Office, 1978.

U.S. Congress. Senate. *Senate Procedure.* Senate Document No. 97-2, 97th Congress, 1st Session. Washington, D.C.: U.S. Government Printing Office, 1981.

U.S. Congress. Senate. *Standing Rules of the Senate.* Senate Document No. 99-22, 99th Congress, 2nd Session. Washington, D.C.: U.S. Government Printing Office, 1986.

U.S. Congress. Senate. Committee on Rules and Administration. *Automated Legislative Record Keeping for the United States Senate.* Committee Print, 92nd Congress, 2nd Session. Washington, D.C.: U.S. Government Printing Office, 1972.

9

Resolutions

Congressional resolutions are an auxiliary means for expressing legislative policy and influencing governmental action. As formal measures, they may precede, supplement, serve as an alternative to, or constitute an ingredient of legislation. Resolutions may or may not affect public policy, and those that do may have slight or significant consequences. This chapter concentrates on resolutions whose policy implications are both important and intentional. The desired effect of policy-oriented resolutions, in contrast with bills, is more evident in the conditions and motives that lead to their introduction rather than in the content of the proposals themselves. This is because resolutions, by definition, cannot become law. How their uses and results relate to and compare with public bills is a recurring feature of the following discussion.

TYPES AND PURPOSES

The three forms of resolutions are joint, concurrent, and simple, but since the first is equivalent to a bill, the term *resolutions* as used below refers only to the latter two forms. Concurrent resolutions result from the combined action of both houses of Congress, while simple resolutions involve one chamber acting independently of the other. The major difference between bills and resolutions is that the latter do not contain legislation and need not be presented to the president for approval. Procedures for the consideration and disposition of concurrent and simple resolutions, which are numbered in separate series, are essentially the same as that for bills. Their course from introduction through adoption differs only in the length rather than in the route of their journey.

The uncontroversial nature of ceremonial or hortatory resolutions usually means expedited action and an absence of related congressional publications. Three relatively routine uses, however, are of more than passing interest. Resolutions are used to authorize the printing of many Senate and House documents that appear in the Serial Set. Concurrent resolutions fix the date of final adjournment for a session of Congress and necessarily affect which measures can be considered before time expires. They also serve to correct the text of bills, as detailed in chapter 8. Some resolutions having policy objectives are examined elsewhere in this volume. Special orders reported by the House Rules Committee are analyzed in chapter 6; budget resolutions originating with the Budget committees in chapter 10; and resolutions of ratification from the Senate Foreign Relations Committee in chapter 11. Resolutions that have a substantive impact on public policy usually generate some, if not all, of the same types of congressional publications that are issued in the course of enacting laws.

Resolutions are the formal means by which either or both houses communicate with their members and committees. These housekeeping measures may concern chamber rules, congressional investigations, or select committees. Such statements are compulsory in nature and regularly authorize activities, prescribe procedures, and determine purposes. Their direct and immediate effect on legislative organization, operations, and resources can have as much policy impact as any law. Aims that cannot be achieved directly through legislation may be accomplished indirectly via housekeeping resolutions.

Resolutions also confirm executive and judicial nominations, address the flow of information between Congress and the other two branches, and recommend action to other public officials. These legislative devices may expedite or inhibit federal administrative or legal proceedings, demand information from the executive branch or private individuals, or suggest proposals on current affairs to independent political agents. These statements may contain opinions or express purposes of a political or legal nature and may be binding or advisory in their effect. In the latter case, a cooperative response is necessary to render them effective. They are normally reserved for matters where a statutory course is considered inapplicable or questionable.

The distinction between housekeeping and declaratory resolutions does not reflect a difference between those that have policy implications and those that do not. It merely indicates that the former are aimed at members of the congressional community regarding matters exclusively within the authority of either or both houses, while the latter are targeted at external entities whose use of discretion may or may not be limited, but can be influenced by their content. Both types are used by Congress to dispose of nonlegislative business that is an adjunct to its lawmaking power.

Because resolutions may be used in lieu of bills to influence certain policy environments or promote particular policy goals and because few are legally binding, they can be adopted more easily than legislation. Resolutions can conveniently be used when legislators wish to realign their resources, stimulate public debate on a given subject, assert or defend legislative prerogatives or objectives, or issue warnings to other political participants. Whether political aims are pursued by bill or resolution is more of a tactical than a strategic decision and, of course, both means may be used simultaneously.

An examination of three major purposes of housekeeping resolutions is followed by an analysis of an equal number of declaratory ones. The first purpose in each series involves formal procedures that either mandate or prohibit specified actions; the second in each focuses on legislative efforts to obtain information; and the third concerns the nature of guidelines for the use of official authority and public resources, though all three goals may overlap in any particular instance. In terms of exerting influence, the order in which each cluster is discussed represents a progression from a more to a less compelling form of action.

HOUSEKEEPING RESOLUTIONS

The most important housekeeping resolutions are proposals to revise the standing rules of each house. The primary purposes of rules are to allocate authority, confer legitimacy, promote stability, and foster efficiency. Rules designate who is authorized to perform which functions or to act under certain circumstances by establishing positions or units and a corresponding division of labor. Decisions reached in accord with these requirements are considered legitimate institutional actions despite any disagreement with their purposes. The existence of orderly and known procedures means that legislative action can proceed without disputes about the validity of particular decisions. The regularity and predictability afforded by written rules enables legislators to adequately prepare for action and provides mechanisms for legislative coordination.

Because rules prescribe the way things must be done, they often determine what in fact is done. Thus, they are not necessarily neutral statements that affect all parties equally. Revisions of rules tend to alter the advantages of legislators by making it relatively easier for some political interests, but more difficult for others, to reach their goals. In general, existing rules benefit those who favor the status quo since they can usually prevail at any one of the many points at which a bill may be stifled. Political differences generated by proposed changes in legislative rules reflect contests over the distribution and exercise of power.

Some rules merely enable Congress to cope with a large workload in an orderly manner. They may simply increase or decrease legislative alternatives as a means of facilitating regular and routine business. However, under certain conditions almost any rule may be used to serve policy or partisan purposes. As an integral factor of legislative strategy, the rules may be wielded by a majority to advance or a minority to impede legislation. Procedures represent power to those in a position to apply or invoke them and thus become ends in themselves. Because the legislature itself has several functions and each member has individual goals, there will often be controversy over rules that affect whose policy views will be realized.

The interrelationship of rules means that several may address the same purpose or one may relate to two or more purposes. Responsibility for the cumulative and unique impact of these politically sensitive stipulations rests with the majority party in each chamber. Such majorities speak through the House Rules Committee and the Senate Rules and Administration Committee in the form of simple resolutions to amend the rules.

Each house has a rule that authorizes its standing committees to undertake investigations of any subject within their jurisdiction. Inquiries initiated under this grant of authority tend to differ only slightly from regular hearings. Though witnesses and records may be summoned and examined for purposes of uncovering illegality or impropriety, the constraints of a committee's budget generally preclude a full-scale investigation. When such a probe is considered necessary, it is authorized by a resolution that states the reasons for and purposes of the inquiry.

The power of Congress to conduct investigations is derived from its power to gather information and educate its members as a vital aid for intelligent lawmaking. These proceedings increase the capacity of legislators to examine and

IV

House Calendar No. 1

100TH CONGRESS
1ST SESSION

H. RES. 26

[Report No. 100–1]

To establish the Select Committee on Hunger, the Select Committee on Children, Youth and Families, and the Select Committee on Narcotics Abuse and Control.

IN THE HOUSE OF REPRESENTATIVES

JANUARY 7, 1987

Mr. PEPPER, from the Committee on Rules, reported the following resolution; which was referred to the House Calendar and ordered to be printed

---

RESOLUTION

1   *Resolved,*

2   TITLE I—SELECT COMMITTEE ON HUNGER

3   ESTABLISHMENT

4   SEC. 101. There is hereby established in the House of

5   Representatives a select committee to be known as the Select

6   Committee on Hunger (hereinafter in this title referred to as

7   the "select committee").

Fig. 13. A housekeeping resolution.

obtain a firmer grasp of social conditions or governmental problems that may warrant legislative solutions. Other matters on which investigations may focus include the effectiveness of existing legislation and its implementation, along with efforts to inform the public or influence the opinion of certain political entities or to protect legislative integrity from the alleged misconduct of members of Congress or against the assumed prerogatives of executive-branch officials. Investigations are a tool that enables Congress to compete better with the presidential establishment for public attention and political influence.

Simple resolutions authorizing investigations are reported from the Senate Rules and Administration Committee or the House Administration Committee. These panels have jurisdiction over the contingent fund of each house. This is an appropriated sum upon which each chamber may draw to cover the expenses of unforeseen legislative activities. In addition to providing the authority and defining the scope of an investigation, a resolution may assign the responsibility to a standing or a temporary committee.

The basic purposes of a temporary or select committee may be to analyze particular conditions or events to discover causes or clarify consequences, to study designated matters and prepare a comprehensive legislative package for action by standing committees, to evaluate the merits of specific legislative proposals, to encourage coordinated legislative decisionmaking by providing balanced representation among all geographical and other interests, to explore the adequacy of existing laws or administration of certain programs, or to give priority to issues of a compelling nature.

Resolutions creating select committees serve as charters that stipulate the functions to be performed and the matters to be examined, confer authority to obtain information, provide for the selection of members, furnish the needed resources, and prescribe its life span (see figure 13). The form its recommendations are to take, whether public law, revision of federal regulations, agency reorganization, or other administrative action, is usually included. In the House, select committees are established by resolutions reported from the Rules Committee and funded by resolutions that originate in the House Administration Committee. In the Senate, both steps are under the jurisdiction of the Rules and Administration Committee.

DECLARATORY RESOLUTIONS

The most frequent type of declaratory resolution is a resolution of confirmation. The Constitution confers the power to approve presidential nominations solely on the Senate. However, those positions subject to legislative confirmation are, in most cases, designated by law. The key appointees covered by this requirement are cabinet-level and subcabinet executives, major military and diplomatic officers, regulatory agency commissioners, and federal judges. Though the president submits thousands of names for Senate consent, only a small fraction of the total fall into categories that may generate much interest or controversy. Resolutions of confirmation may be reported from any committee with jurisdiction over a given administrative entity or judicial tribunal.

The manner in which a law is applied and construed is directly related to the abilities and attitudes of those responsible for its administration and adjudication. The question of fitness for office, especially senior policymaking positions, is one that cannot be readily or conclusively answered. Though some professional qualifications are imposed by law and tradition, and demonstrated competence in previous endeavors is a natural and normal standard, other criteria are less subject to formal or informal prescription. Legislators are quite aware that if those entrusted with the implementation or interpretation of law are out of tune or out of touch with those who sponsored it, there is the probability that the actual effect of legislation will differ from the intended effect.

Presidential selection is often based on political debts owed to those who helped the president attain office, symbolic representation of particular population groups or geographical areas, the skill to lobby for administration proposals in Congress, or the capability to meet the managerial needs of an agency. The principal consideration tends to be the compatibility of policy views between the president and the nominee. Since the confirmation process by itself cannot always resolve all doubts about individual merit, it is essential that senators have confidence in the integrity of the selection process. Another important factor is that senators may not attach any conditions to a decision to confirm and, after approval, removal is beyond the formal authority of legislators except for impeachment proceedings.

As a routine matter most high-level nominees are informally cleared by the White House staff with appropriate members of the Senate prior to any public announcement of their names. While this practice serves to smooth the path for the large majority of nominees, conditions do not always foster a favorable legislative reception. The political and substantive opinions of nominees undergo a more detailed and thorough scrutiny when the Senate and White House are controlled by different parties, when the position or agency is an object of current controversy, when the official will not be immediately subject to presidential control or removal, and when the president appears to be using appointments to significantly reorient established program operations or prospective policy decisions.

Resolutions of inquiry may be directed at either the president or an agency administrator and may be answered by the latter directly or through the president. They may call for facts or documents in the possession of any executive-branch official or agency. These measures are usually reserved for situations in which desired information cannot be obtained through routine channels. Such requests or demands are based on the constitutional duty of Congress to keep itself informed of the need for new or revised public policy. This course also implies that adverse or more compelling legislative action may follow a failure to comply.

The most common types of questions concern the factual basis for having undertaken or refrained from pursuing certain actions, authority under which specific decisions were enforced, the results of administering a particular program, or the agency directives affecting implementation of a law. Resolutions of inquiry are privileged matters in the House only and may be introduced by any legislator. This means that a committee with jurisdiction is obliged to consider the measure even though it disapproves of its purpose. Failure to act would result in loss of committee control of the proposal. As a result of this procedure, a panel is as likely to recommend that such a resolution be rejected as adopted.

Resolutions of opinion or advice contain recommendations to public officials or private entities over which Congress either lacks or chooses not to exercise legislative authority (see figure 14). The former case covers matters of a traditionally local concern or international situations within the purview of other

III

100TH CONGRESS
1ST SESSION

S. CON. RES. 7

To express the sense of the Congress regarding its opposition to reductions in Veterans' Administration funding levels to pay for health care for certain categories of eligible veterans.

IN THE SENATE OF THE UNITED STATES

JANUARY 14 (legislative day, JANUARY 13), 1987

Mr. MURKOWSKI (for himself, Mr. CRANSTON, Mr. SIMPSON, Mr. THURMOND, Mr. STAFFORD, Mr. SPECTER, Mr. MATSUNAGA, Mr. DECONCINI, Mr. MITCHELL, Mr. ROCKEFELLER, Mr. GRAHAM, Mr. DASCHLE, Mr. SIMON, Mr. BRADLEY, Mr. BINGAMAN, Mr. BURDICK, Mr. LUGAR, and Mr. McCAIN) submitted the following concurrent resolution; which was referred to the Committee on Veterans' Affairs

APRIL 7 (legislative day, MARCH 30), 1987
Indefinitely postponed

CONCURRENT RESOLUTION

To express the sense of the Congress regarding its opposition to reductions in Veterans' Administration funding levels to pay for health care for certain categories of eligible veterans.

Whereas in title XIX of Public Law 99–272, the Consolidated Omnibus Budget Reconciliation Act of 1985, the Congress established three categories of veterans' hospital-care and nursing-home-care eligibility;

Whereas under the above law, the Veterans' Administration is required to furnish needed hospital care and may furnish needed nursing home care to veterans in category A for

Fig. 14. A declaratory resolution.

nations. Though these measures may reach further than bills, they are also less authoritative because aimed at conditions not considered susceptible to statutory remedies. As the least binding type of legislative policy statement they may be used to placate interests unable to engineer passage of more forceful measures or to bring policy views to the attention of other groups that may be inclined to consider their merits.

The more important resolutions of opinion adopted in lieu of a recourse to bills are aimed at the president or a subordinate executive-branch official. Those addressed to the president relate to matters in which he is authorized or expected to exercise discretion. They may urge that a specific situation be given attention, express support for or opposition to contemplated executive action, or request that plans for meeting certain conditions be submitted to Congress for its consideration. Those directed at administrative appointees may clarify the legislative intent of a statute regarding the legal authority of a federal agency under specified circumstances. These measures may emerge from any committee as concurrent or simple resolutions.

JURIDICAL RESOLUTIONS

At any given time, either or both houses of Congress are involved in legal proceedings as defendants, plaintiffs, or third parties. These matters cover the litigation of cases that concern institutional powers, procedures, or personnel. They may be based on the action or inaction of public officials or private citizens. This requires legislators to formally communicate with legal officials in the legislative, executive, and judicial branches of the federal government. The means used to convey congressional approval, denial, or other judgment are concurrent or simple resolutions. For lack of an official or traditional designation they may be termed *juridical resolutions*. Though discussed here as a distinct form of action based on their legal usage, in effect they operate similarly to housekeeping and declaratory measures depending on whether they address individuals within or outside Congress.

Legislative prerogatives and practices may be challenged in court by government officials, private citizens, or even members of Congress itself. In such cases a judicial tribunal may issue a summons or subpoena for the appearance of legislative-branch employees or delivery of legislative-branch documents. Neither officers nor staff members of either chamber may voluntarily, or in response to a court order, provide either oral or written information regarding official functions, documents, or activities of the house without its prior consent. This restriction produces several congressional options.

Either house may adopt a resolution to authorize members of its staff to appear before courts as witnesses in their capacity as legislative-branch employees. The resolution usually states the subject on which testimony may be given or otherwise prescribes limits on its scope. Where papers are concerned, a resolution may authorize full disclosure or stipulate that copies of specified documents be furnished. Congress may prohibit access to persons or records pending a review of whether a subpoena is a valid exercise of court jurisdiction, is material and relevant, and is consistent with the privileges of the legislative branch.

It is not uncommon for legislators to insist that certain information, in the form of testimony or documents, is needed for Congress to meet its constitutional responsibilities. Such instances may be grouped into two general categories. One concerns positive acts, such as bribery or libel, that undermine the integrity of legislative proceedings. The other occurs when individuals refuse to perform acts, such as to testify or produce documents, that the legislature claims authority to compel if it is to fulfill its obligations with respect to the enactment and assessment of law.

The power of Congress to punish individuals for contempt begins with the issuance of a subpoena by a committee. Any person summoned as a witness before a panel and who fails to appear, declines to answer any pertinent question, or refuses to produce particular documents may be cited for contempt of Congress. To enforce compliance with its subpoena the committee must report a resolution certifying the facts in its committee report and recommending that the case be referred to the appropriate U.S. attorney for prosecution. Should the named individual reach an agreement with the panel before legal action has commenced or concluded, another resolution would be needed to recommend that contempt proceedings be discontinued.

Congress may choose to enter into lawsuits brought to its attention because of the bearing they may have on institutional authority. A chamber resolution would direct either the Senate legal counsel or the House counsel to the clerk to intervene as a bona fide party or to file a brief as amicus curiae. Either body may also authorize the appointment of a private attorney to act in its behalf who would be compensated from its contingent fund. The individual so designated would be instructed to assert and defend the rights of the house in any further proceedings in the case, including appeals to higher courts.

In whatever manner it becomes a participant in legal proceedings or whatever the nature of a lawsuit, Congress reserves the right to determine its course or response. In the exercise of its constitutional prerogatives it may cooperate completely with the judicial branch, cooperate to a certain extent, or refuse to cooperate. In cases other than contempt, a juridical resolution is introduced by one or more members of the party leadership in the chamber. In contempt cases it is introduced by a member of the committee that is seeking information.

The easiest way to identify juridical resolutions is by a check of the subject index of the *Congressional Record, House Calendar* or *Journal* of either house under the headings "House" and "Senate." The best way to obtain background information on the matter to which such resolutions pertain is to consult a periodic publication of the House Judiciary Committee. It is entitled *Court Proceedings and Actions of Vital Interest to the Congress* and is issued as a committee print. For each case included in this volume, its first part provides a one-paragraph summary that highlights the key legal principle or most significant issue raised in the litigation. The second part, organized under various subject headings, presents a more thorough discussion of the issues and status of each case. The third part contains the text of available judicial opinions.

BIBLIOGRAPHIC POINTS

Except for confirmations, resolutions to amend the rules are more common than other types. One reason is that the nature of legislative business compels continual adjustment of procedures and schedules. Another is that they are the only alternative to legislation for reaching the intended objective. The purposes for which other resolutions are available may also be realized through hearings, advisory commissions, consultant contracts, congressional support agencies, or informal communications with executive or judicial-branch officials. Despite being a milder form of congressional action than legislation, resolutions can arouse or accompany as much controversy as any bill. This is the key factor affecting the quantity and diversity of congressional publications that may be issued in conjunction with legislative consideration of a resolution.

That resolutions of confirmation are a form of executive rather than legislative business means that those sources one needs to consult for the progress of nominations differ from those required to trace other resolutions. When the president transmits a message to the Senate containing one or more nominations it is assigned a Senate Executive Document number, entered in the *Congressional Record* and *Executive Journal*, and referred to the appropriate committee(s). Upon panel approval, an executive report may be issued and the nomination is placed on the Executive Calendar. Resolutions of confirmation are not assigned a resolution number. They are identified by their Senate Executive Document number or Executive Calendar number. The *Congressional Record* and *Executive Journal* cite the executive report number and cover chamber action, though the latter does not include floor debate.

As with most bills, the text of resolutions appears in printed hearings and is more likely than bills to be included in a committee report. Unlike most bills, all resolutions acted on by either house appear in the *Congressional Record* and its journal. The finding-aids section of the preceding chapter on bills is equally applicable to resolutions, with the obvious exception of those comments concerning laws and vetoes. Where a legislative goal is being pursued by both bill and resolution, these companion measures are noted in the *Record, House Calendar*, and *Digest of Public General Bills and Resolutions*.

REFERENCES

Froman, Lewis A., Jr. *The Congressional Process*. Boston: Little, Brown, 1967.

McKenzie, G. Calvin. *The Politics of Presidential Appointments*. New York: The Free Press, 1981.

Oleszek, Walter. *Congressional Procedures and the Policy Process*. 2nd ed. Washington, D.C.: Congressional Quarterly Press, 1984.

U.S. Congress. House. *Constitution, Jefferson's Manual and Rules of the House of Representatives*. House Document No. 98-277, 98th Congress, 2nd Session. Washington, D.C.: U.S. Government Printing Office, 1985.

U.S. Congress. House. *Procedure in the U.S. House of Representatives.* 4th ed. 97th Congress, 2nd Session. Washington, D.C.: U.S. Government Printing Office, 1982.

U.S. Congress. House. Committee on the Judiciary. *Court Proceedings and Actions of Vital Interest to the Congress.* Committee Print, 99th Congress, 1st Session. Washington, D.C.: U.S. Government Printing Office, 1986.

U.S. Congress. House. Committee on Rules. *Guidelines for the Establishment of Select Committees.* Subcommittee Print, 95th Congress, 1st Session. Washington, D.C.: U.S. Government Printing Office, 1977.

U.S. Congress. Senate. *Senate Procedure.* Senate Document No. 97-2, 97th Congress, 1st Session. Washington, D.C.: U.S. Government Printing Office, 1981.

U.S. Congress. Senate. *Standing Rules of the Senate.* Senate Document No. 99-22, 99th Congress, 2nd Session. Washington, D.C.: U.S. Government Printing Office, 1986.

U.S. Congress. Senate. Committee on Government Operations. *Congressional Oversight: Methods and Techniques.* Committee Print, 94th Congress, 2nd Session. Washington, D.C.: U.S. Government Printing Office, 1976.

10

The Federal Budget

A public budget is a political blueprint. Its formation is the most comprehensive political enterprise in which government engages in any given year. Budgeting involves competition between and within the executive and legislative branches as well as between and among public and private entities. Since funds are limited, while demands are not, budgetary decisions entail crucial choices about potential sources and possible expenditures. In essence, a budget is a plan to achieve stated goals through certain means at a specified cost within a given time period. Because goals, means, costs, and time all represent different values to different groups, the management of public funds requires the exercise of political judgment.

To form a public budget is to distribute financial resources through political processes. Decisions reflect an effort to balance conflicting aims and satisfy competing claims. Since communal commitments cannot be accurately quantified, budget figures serve as the closest approximation to their absolute and relative measurement. Specific dollar amounts attached to proposed federal activities present one view concerning the proper role and scope of government. Despite or because of the controversy it may generate, a budget centers attention on and broadens understanding of public purposes and capabilities. In this sense, it constitutes a formal and concrete agenda for discussion and action.

A public budget is also a multipurpose instrument owing to the number and nature of its perspectives and objectives. It is an amalgam of legal, political, financial, and managerial decisions. Its legal aspects concern prescribed procedures and administrative accountability; its political aspects cover policy preferences and institutional influence; its financial aspects include resource allocation and revenue devices; its managerial aspects involve organizational coordination and efficient operations. The budget is a vehicle used to provide public goods, establish public priorities, address economic problems, and promote effective governance. Prospective accomplishment always confronts the question of the compatibility of goals.

The first section of this chapter discusses the economic, political, and instrumental elements that comprise the federal budget. Its first part reviews those concepts and constraints that shape the contours of budget policy. Its second part examines the substantive and strategic roles of major participants in the process. Its third part surveys the policy options available to meet conditions and pursue goals. The second section is a detailed account of the political and procedural nature of the budget. It reveals why the budget cannot be established by a single act of government, but emerges from a continuous round of choices and duties.

Budgeting may be viewed as the central phase of governmental action. It is preceded by planning, which involves assumptions and projections about political, economic, social, and technological developments and their impact on public business and priorities. It is succeeded by an assessment of how well programs are operating and the degree to which they are achieving intended objectives. The budget is one part forecast, as represented by the contemplated results of proposals, and one part feedback, as reflected by the recommended revision of policies. The wide range of decisions and interests involved in efforts to reconcile an existing with an expected state of affairs creates both opportunities and obstacles for budgetmakers.

Since all national public transactions, whether planned in advance or dictated by events, affect federal finances, budgeting is the most inclusive of governmental functions. Budgetary decisions explicitly or implicitly address such questions as the direction and pace of governmental activities, the appropriate level of governmental involvement in given policy spheres, the relative merits of government programs, who should pay to support and who should benefit from these programs, and the nature of the relationship between the public and private sectors of society. These factors explain the abundant quantity of budget publications and their value as a source of information on any and every aspect of federal business.

BUDGET POLICY CONTEXT

ELEMENTS

The information needed by policymakers to prepare a viable budget flows from the relationship between public finance and economic conditions. The influence of the federal government on the transactions in and performance of the economy cannot be matched by any other institution. Budgetary policies and decisions inevitably and significantly affect the level and tenor of economic activity whether or not public officials plan it. Though general agreement exists on the interdependence of the federal budget and the national economy, the exact nature of the relationship remains uncertain. One of the reasons it is so difficult to gauge the mutual impact of the federal and nonfederal sectors of the economy is the numerous roles played by the U.S. government.

In the field of economic regulation the federal government establishes legal requirements for engaging in economic activity, issues money, regulates the availability of credit, and imposes taxes. In the area of economic security it is responsible for the administration of welfare services, maintenance of full employment, unemployment compensation, and retirement programs. In the realm of economic growth it endeavors to increase the nation's productive capacity and the actual output of goods and services. In the sphere of economic stabilization it strives to foster a favorable business climate and control cyclical fluctuations in production, consumption, employment, and prices.

As the nation's largest employer, consumer, proprietor, and financier, the federal government accounts for more than 20 percent of the gross national product. The effects of the federal budget on the economy are mainly visible through aggregate spending by individuals, businesses, and governments. Federal expenditures would necessarily rise simply because of an increasing demand for government services resulting from normal population growth. However, the continuous, pervasive, and formidable influence of the federal government is also a result of the fact that the economy has been nationalized. The reasons for this policy reflect a significant change in social values since the 1930s regarding the development and distribution of basic communal resources.

The economy, left to private-sector decisions, demonstrates a tendency to alternate between periods of expansion and contraction as well as to engender an imbalance in the distribution of resources. In other words, private economic activity can have serious public consequences when the operation of the market system generates systemic deficiencies and social inequities. Since the Great Depression it has been generally accepted that the federal budget can and should be used to counteract economic fluctuations and relieve economic distress. Governmental intervention represents an attempt to cope with the problems of a modern industrial society and democratic polity. Public finance poses the question of how to simultaneously meet the challenges of the business cycle and the election cycle.

The performance of the economy also affects the budget. The rate of inflation influences the prices that government must pay for goods and services as well as its outlays for many benefit programs. A rise in unemployment can substantially increase expenditures and reduce revenues. The level of interest rates controls the cost of financing the public debt. The overall degree of prosperity determines the proportion of the gross national product that government directly produces or purchases. All such economic developments translate into changes in the general standard of living or the status of certain population groups. Any major economic event or trend will eventually be reflected in political competition and budget policies.

Many difficulties face those responsible for devising a comprehensive, consistent, and credible economic policy package. It involves the coordination of public and private institutions, the choice of appropriate economic targets, the use of effective policy instruments, and the trade-off between aggregate and sectoral effects. Because of the variety of roles that government may assume and goals that it may pursue, different criteria are commonly applied to judge the merits of the federal budget. The most salient factor from one perspective may be a secondary matter from another. Whatever their apparent standards, budget verdicts are based on the priorities of those who pronounce them.

Economic forecasting is a tool used by policymakers to manage the national economy. Forecasts of economic activity serve as the starting point for formulating budget policies. A forecast is a statement about an uncertain or unknown future event or trend. It can be qualitative or quantitative, conditional or unconditional, explicit or silent on the probabilities involved. The utility of economic forecasting is based on the premise that there exist continuities of economic activity that run from the past to the present and on into the future and that such continuities can be extracted from the mass of available data.

Overall economic activity reflects a combination of natural systemic fluctuations and policy-induced oscillations. An economic forecast apprises public officials of what is likely to occur under current economic conditions and government policies. It consists of projections of key components of the national economy and federal budget. This analysis is accompanied by a discussion of underlying premises and the major contingencies related to the projections. Economic forecasts are based on certain suppositions about the course of economic activity. Budget estimates then become a function of the economic assumptions on which they are predicated.

Most of the budget figures in each year's budget documents must be estimated. The only numbers not estimated are those that concern prior fiscal years and current economic conditions. The sensitivity of budget aggregates to economic developments complicates budget planning because forecasting the economy inaccurately leads to forecasting the budget inaccurately and economic forecasting is less than an exact science. Accurate estimates of the government's financial position require accurate forecasts of policy decisions and economic prospects. Erroneous or inaccurate assumptions lead to greater deviations and discrepancies the further they are projected.

Though both policy rationality and political expediency dictate the use of systematic analysis to discern the economic outlook, forecasting is subject to several limitations. First, economic knowledge cannot yet render a consistent or definite explanation of the interrelationships of the major components of the economy. Second, in terms of existing policies, economic conditions and connections tend to change more abruptly or acutely than the regulations that govern them. Third, major noneconomic events, such as natural disasters, weather conditions, and international crises regularly influence economic developments. Finally, there is the impact of the forecast itself, whose feedback effects may be both substantial and unpredictable.

An economic forecast is based on four types of assumptions. If these assumptions should contain any miscalculations or misinterpretations, and these are unavoidable, budget estimates will prove inaccurate. Economic assumptions relate to the performance of the economy, legislative assumptions to the decisions of Congress, administrative assumptions to the actions of federal agencies, and technical assumptions to the data and methods used. This means that a forecast itself may become the center of controversy. A key conclusion to be drawn is that even valid and complete information and analysis can be nullified or undermined by any one of many economic contingencies and political opportunities.

The time frame of an annual budget cycle also introduces some distortion into the perception of events and survey of data. Budgeting involves trade-offs among current policies and between long-term and short-term policies. Because economic policies cannot be isolated from other factors that affect the economy, it is always difficult to determine what they have accomplished or may accomplish. The force and course of economic currents change gradually over time and cannot be readily reoriented. Policy choice may be between long-term economic growth and short-term political costs or short-term political gain and long-term economic costs. Since elections occur every two years, immediate problems tend to receive attention at the expense of underlying economic weaknesses.

Anticipatory policies are required to avoid recurring cycles of inflation or recession or both. Proposed policy changes must be based on forecasts of the economy's direction and effects. The discipline of economics has not yet advanced to the point where it can measure or predict the impact of policies with much confidence or precision. Which budget policies would most contribute to economic health and which programs would be consistent with such policies cannot be definitively determined. Though economists may offer advice on the likely consequences of these choices for the economic climate, the inadequacy of economic analysis inevitably leads to the use of political criteria.

Because budget decisions have political implications and other policy decisions have economic implications, a sharp distinction often cannot be made between the political and economic factors that shape the federal budget. Economic conditions are less visible and volatile than political ones, and elected officials are more familiar with and sensitive to the latter. Accordingly, budgetary decisions reflect the primacy of political over economic judgment. Since political competition and electoral prospects influence major public decisions, politicians tend to be more flexible than economists regarding the means and ends of budget policies. Even if economics were more of an exact science, it would still remain subordinate to the political incentives and intentions that guide the conduct of elected officials.

The budget deficit measures the amount by which government expenditures exceed its receipts. Therefore, it is the sum that must be borrowed to meet its financial commitments during the course of a fiscal year. The public debt is a figure that records the total amount of money owed by the federal government. It is an accumulation of all past borrowing or previous deficits. The authority of the United States to borrow or create debt enables it to finance deficits and fulfill obligations that cannot be funded from current revenue. While the annual deficit affects the debt by adding to it, the debt affects the deficit because of the interest that must be paid on the debt.

The mere existence of a budget deficit is not a reliable or conclusive sign of mistaken public policy. Deficits are considered justifiable when they are incurred to stimulate a sluggish economy or cushion the effects of an economic decline. The injection of new purchasing power into the economy counteracts the effects of an economic slump. The increased level of economic activity generated by federal spending results in additional revenues that can reduce the deficit. In periods of economic stagnation it is also a wiser course for government to borrow rather than tax to fund its operations and services. The former approach does not reduce the income or wealth of persons or organizations during the period when resources are needed, which would only aggravate the economic situation.

However, it is recognized that continually large deficits that increase interest costs to service the growing debt do produce adverse effects. Such a deficit leaves less room in the budget for programs that meet genuine national needs; it breeds greater inequity in the distribution of income since the prime beneficiaries of interest payments are the wealthy; it weakens public confidence in government's ability to pursue sound policies; it diverts funds from private consumption and investment since the federal government is the preferred borrower in all credit markets; and it increases the level of interest rates for all borrowers which, in turn, leads to slower economic growth.

Despite these results there are many reasons why it remains difficult to reduce federal expenditures and shrink the budget. Budget policies and outlays constitute long-term commitments to individual welfare and collective security; they underpin essential communal services; they are a stabilizing factor in an unstable environment; they provide special benefits to specific groups. The major recipients of federal funds are not federal agencies, but state and local governments, contractors, grantees, borrowers, bondholders, and beneficiaries of transfer programs. These are large and influential constituencies who would not be naturally inclined to relinquish current benefits in the absence of compelling conditions.

Though the deficit figure is the best known numerical summary of budget policy, it is misleading to the degree that the results of public priorities are due to changes in the economy unrelated to federal action. During a decline in economic activity, the budget responds automatically to increase the deficit through greater outlays for unemployment compensation, while receipts are reduced because fewer people are paying taxes. In periods of inflation, benefit programs linked to the Consumer Price Index result in larger than expected expenditures, which also increase the deficit. Thus, the size of the deficit is far from being entirely within the control of the federal government. Its existence, though, continually sparks debate about the relationship between financial responsibility and social obligation.

There is one other important perspective from which to consider this topic. Deficits that increase physical assets, preserve natural resources, and improve personal status constitute an investment in the future that should be appraised in more than merely monetary terms. Yet the notion persists that at some point the size of the debt will pose a real threat to economic security and financial stability. The causes, consequences, and control of deficits involve economic and financial as well as political and policy questions. The complexity and magnitude of the issue have thus far prevented the formation of a consensus as to what can or should be done.

INTERESTS

Several reasons account for the fact that budgetary affairs have dominated the political agenda in recent years. Among the more prominent ones are the growth in the scope and spending of the federal government, the conflict over public priorities between the legislative and executive branches, persistent and prodigious budget deficits, and genuine doubt about how to cure general and specific economic ills. Increased efforts devoted to preparing and promoting budget proposals have propelled money matters into the forefront of public debate. From the vantage point of institutional competition, the president enjoys a natural advantage over Congress owing to the structure of the executive branch.

Rivalry exists between and within agencies for available funds. The primary goal is to obtain support for those policies and interests that are within an agency's purview. Agency advocacy is not directed solely to securing the highest possible appropriation in a given year. Attempts to ensure favorable review of its budget request means protecting basic programs against cuts and having its share of increases or decreases proportionate to changes in other agency budgets. To be granted a satisfactory funding level contributes to stability and continuity in its financial status and provides for the possibility of expansion and innovation over time.

Though most agencies seek to develop and maintain clientele group and congressional committee support, the administrative environment in which they function imposes definite restrictions on their independence. The Office of Management and Budget (OMB), as the central staff arm of the institutional presidency, continually monitors the performance and activities of federal agencies. Its extensive authority and bureaucratic expertise serve as constant checks on agency efforts to advance their interests or enhance their position. Despite such constraint, some agencies are better able than others to achieve their aims or avoid executive control. However, a president determined to exercise strong budgetary influence within his own domain possesses the tools to stamp his imprint on the product.

Budget preparation within the executive branch proceeds almost entirely out of public view, with widespread publicity limited to the final results. The desires of political elements whose support the president concludes cannot be gained or is not needed are unlikely to be accorded favorable budget treatment. His position at the apex of the executive hierarchy renders him less vulnerable to numerous and narrow pressures that generate federal spending. This enables him to focus more clearly on total figures and the appropriate alignment of policy objectives. As an exercise that embraces political leadership, policy initiative, economic perception, and managerial competence, budgeting is a true test of the ability to govern.

Formulation and presentation of the executive budget enables the president to publicize his requests to Congress for new programs, changes in existing ones, the management and distribution of federal funds, and sources and methods of revenue. It contains a proposed allocation of resources that would establish priorities and accomplish purposes within the federal sector and facilitate presidential direction of the administrative activities of the federal government. The budget document is also intended to aid and persuade the general public and particular publics to gauge national economic developments and view proposed policies from the presidential perspective. In effect, the executive budget is a studied political argument in the guise of a sober governmental agenda.

Legislative disposition and congressional structure foster the diffusion of power. Budget formation and policy integration require the consolidation of power. Budgeting necessarily involves the incorporation of diverse interests and opinions into a reasonably inclusive and consistent decisional framework. It demands that attention be paid to the relationship between and reconciliation of ends and means, claims and resources, and the parts and the whole. Within Congress different units have been assigned the primary responsibility for each of these components.

Authorizing committees propose substantive legislation that creates or continues an agency or program for an indefinite or specified period of time and may recommend funding methods or levels. The authorization process focuses on the practical and political merits of governmental ends and means. It involves an evaluation of socioeconomic conditions and the needs of concrete interests. Authorizing legislation establishes policy goals and designates areas in which government may appropriately act to remedy problems or confer benefits. Such statutes embody value judgments about what government should do to define and address national needs.

Appropriations committees submit measures that authorize one or more agencies to incur financial obligations and make payments from the Treasury for a specified period of time. The appropriations process emphasizes fiscal responsibility and the prudent use of public funds. It entails an assessment of financial resources and the needs of federal programs. Appropriations legislation grants certain levels of spending authority to particular agencies for stipulated purposes. An appropriations act expresses value judgments about what government can afford to do in view of numerous legitimate demands and limited budgetary receipts.

Budget committees draft measures that provide Congress with the opportunity to consider questions that do not directly arise when authorization and appropriation bills are debated individually. Among the more important issues that become subject to legislative exploration are the proper amount of total federal spending, the allocation of funds among major public purposes, and the implications of these decisions for the government's financial health. To establish national fiscal policy and broad budgetary priorities involves value judgments about the balance between general prosperity and personal welfare.

Every program that has an annual authorization, as well as new and expiring ones, can be subjected to three legislative decisions during a single session of Congress. This is because Congress has three processes for reaching financial decisions and each has its distinctive manner of measuring and reporting relevant data. While the processes are distinct, they cannot be completely disengaged from one another. Though there is some overlap, they do not duplicate one another. Because the boundaries that separate them are not clear cut, issues tend to return for disposition in slightly or significantly different forms.

When the economy performs favorably or as forecast, relative harmony tends to prevail in budgetmaking circles. This means that adequate funds are available to meet plans or appropriate policies are in place to meet events. When the economy is unstable and unpredictable, legislators are compelled to recalculate and revise the budget. As the economy veers from its projected course, budgetary conflict increases between the legislative and executive branches and within Congress. Discrepancies between expected and actual performance generate divergent budgetary behavior within Congress as decisions made in one process are challenged in another.

A major purpose of the congressional budget process is to achieve parity with the president for setting national priorities. Specifically, it enables Congress to correlate aggregate federal revenues and expenditures for the fiscal year in view of existing conditions and commitments, obtain the data necessary to reach rational and feasible decisions on how to balance and integrate fiscal and social policies, and to coordinate the authorization and appropriations processes. It was designed to encourage committees to submerge their differences so as to develop an effective vehicle that could serve as a realistic alternative to presidential recommendations.

In a collegial and accessible institution such as Congress, this effort has produced mixed results. The congressional budget, in contrast to the presidential budget, is formulated in the glare of considerable media coverage. The opportunities offered to claimants by a legislature of 535 members is more likely to result in accommodation of all interests able to exert some political leverage at any one of many decision points. While the executive budget probably reflects a better policy balance, the legislative budget probably embodies a better political balance. The unity of the presidency and diversity of Congress produce different approaches to budgeting whose effects permeate the process.

The arrangements and procedures by which the federal budget is formulated may be judged from both an institutional and an informational viewpoint. The institutional perspective may be subdivided into its internal and external aspects. The centralization of authority in the executive branch is more conducive to producing a plan characterized by agency adherence and policy coherence. That the executive budget appears on the scene first also enables the president to seize the political initiative. The tools and timetable of the process provide the chief executive with a managerial and competitive advantage in the early stages of budgetmaking.

Congress cannot hope to match the orderly and uniform performance of the executive branch. However, the president's budget relieves legislators from having to start from scratch and serves as a useful point of departure. The prominence of the executive package also contributes to somewhat greater legislative solidarity as Congress responds to its major political rival. The administration's issuance of a comprehensive financial plan immediately generates criticism from those interests concerned with budget integrity or direction. Acting afterward suits the capacity of Congress better and provides the opportunity to overcome the initial edge enjoyed by the president.

Because of the relatively greater control that can be exercised within the executive branch, the presidential budget can be framed better to appeal to some external constituencies. As a political instrument, it can be used to discharge political debts, acquire political credits, and invest political capital. Because congressional authority is divided, legislative resources are primarily consumed by efforts to forge a proposal that can unite internal units. The product is an agreement that records the results of numerous political compromises. The institutional result reflects actions meant to maintain a balance of support over opposition that can be mobilized for budgetary or other aims.

The informational approach consists of the substantiation and interpretation of budget figures that denote either of two levels of decision. Priority decisions cover the sum total of expenditures, the allocation of funds among functional areas of governmental activity, the amount of revenue needed to finance all federal programs, and the level of surplus or deficit consistent with sound fiscal policy. Program decisions affect agency resources and operations as they relate to prior and projected achievements. These choices are directly linked to the welfare of clientele groups whose action and vision concern a small portion of the budget.

The responsibility for priority decisions in the executive branch rests with the president, who relies on advice from his Council of Economic Advisers, top officials of the OMB, and Treasury Department. Congress as a whole, acting on the advice of the House and Senate Budget Committees and the Joint Economic Committee, also makes priority decisions. The budget process is designed to identify and clarify the factors and relationships that affect or flow from these policy choices. The role of the president and Congress is to aggregate the demands and integrate the goals of agencies and committees, respectively. Their joint responsibility for the general welfare and common focus on the national scene provide the basis for a cooperative effort to neutralize centrifugal tendencies in the political arena.

Program decisions concern funding levels for existing and proposed governmental activities. These judgments are made in accordance with congressional-committee and federal-agency jurisdictions. The actions of the executive branch and independent federal entities, the OMB in the absence of presidential direction, along with the authorization and appropriations committees, focus on program needs and results. Overall budgetary implications and comprehensive fiscal policy are less important to these participants. Another aim of the budget process is to disclose the mutual impact of and coordinate the strategies embodied in priority and program decisions.

The budget process may be viewed as an attempt to harness the natural tensions that pervade governmental operations. Within Congress friction exists between legislators who authorize and appropriate funds as well as between members responsible for spending and raising revenue. Within the executive branch disputes ensue between administrators who deliver program services and manage financial matters as well as between temporary officials and career staff members. A comparison of the two branches reveals that Congress is more concerned with the production and distribution of resources while the president emphasizes their correlation and productiveness. Variations in authority and constituency relationships mainly account for this continual competition. Though installed to adjust or restrain such differences, the budget process is as much a captive as it is a captain of its environment.

AVENUES

Federal officials may employ one or more of three vehicles to influence economic behavior, conditions, and prospects. Fiscal policy concerns the total level of government spending and revenue and the allocation of resources between the federal and nonfederal sectors of the economy. Monetary policy involves the regulation of the money supply and credit conditions through the national banking system. Structural policy is the use of direct controls on specific economic sectors or ventures. In conjunction with each other, they comprise an economic policy designed to promote prosperity, growth, and stability. After a brief look at the last mentioned option, the remainder of the discussion will focus on fiscal and monetary routes.

Structural economic policies are aimed at particular commercial or industrial relationships and transactions. Their purpose is to control business and financial practices, wages and prices, labor-management relations, and imports and exports. Problems that are both serious and separable are candidates for targeted treatment. The focus is on certain segments of the economy and the contemplated effects are purposefully confined. Taken in their entirety, these constituency-oriented measures exert considerable influence on the overall economic picture. However, it is the scope and impact of fiscal and monetary policies that conspicuously demonstrate the economic role of government and its capacity to manage economic affairs.

Fiscal policy, which is the joint responsibility of Congress and the president, is designed to implement the budget. It consists of a combination of automatic stabilizers and discretionary adjustments. The former are a set of existing programs intended to counteract the effects of economic decline without the need for further governmental action. The two types of stabilizers are transfer payments and the tax code. Transfer payments are funds distributed to individuals or organizations for which goods or services are not required in return. Examples are social security, unemployment compensation, veterans benefits, and public assistance. Different tax rates and exemptions apply as individual incomes rise or fall. These built-in features of economic policy serve to provide immediate relief until discretionary proposals can be formulated, adopted, and implemented.

The twin tools of discretionary fiscal policy are expenditures and taxes, and each plays a different role in the economy. The general purposes of spending are to provide goods and services that, if not provided by government, would not be provided at all or provided inadequately. Reliance on expenditure policies enables the government to allocate more precisely resources between the public and private sectors, react relatively quickly with measures that can produce relatively quick results, and target more effectively the distressed geographical areas. Though increased spending means greater government control it cannot be criticized on the grounds of inefficiency or impropriety if communal resources were otherwise to remain idle or if obvious public needs were being neglected.

Taxation is a compulsory reduction in income or wealth imposed on individuals or organizations. The general purposes of taxation are to finance the cost of government operations and services and to distribute the costs equitably throughout the population. Recourse to revenue policies that reduce taxes enlarges private-sector discretion over the use of resources, requires more time to undertake but also produces more enduring results, and permits a more effective targeting of distressed economic sectors. Decreased tax rates are not the most dependable means for influencing private spending since consumers may choose to increase their savings or use their additional income in ways that do not stimulate the economy. Though public officials can control the use of a fiscal-policy instrument, they are unable to clearly foresee its effects.

Many difficult decisions confront those responsible for the formation of fiscal policy. First, assuming that social causes are known and goals are valid, is the question of whether to emphasize expenditures or taxation or use them in tandem. The selection of a tool or course depends on both economic and political factors. Economic implications concern the level of disposable income to be expected, while political implications concern the level of governmental intervention to be warranted. This cluster of choices centers on the form and content of policy, which covers the balance between and sequence of its components and the potency and duration of its prescriptions.

Another group of problems surrounds the timing of policy options. These questions arise from the time lags that inhere in the policy process. A recognition lag is the time between the occurrence of an economic event and the realization by policymakers that government action is necessary; a policy lag is the interval between recognition of the need for action and agreement on appropriate measures; a financial lag is the period between enactment and effects on government receipts and outlays; an economic lag is the interim between changes in federal financial figures and the impact on decisions in the private sector. It is not only virtually impossible to time fiscal policy for maximum effectiveness, but the results may aggravate an economic deficiency or may remedy one weakness by creating another.

To overcome these obstacles at least partially, policy changes must be framed or launched in advance. Preventive measures are necessary before an economic slump or surge actually occurs. However, even when fiscal policy is considered suitable and farsighted, it remains only one of several factors that can affect the economic climate. The impact of unforeseen and uncontrollable developments can easily frustrate any budget plan. To prepare for economic aberrations might be an unwise investment if it triggers a chain of events that prove economically detrimental or if the anticipated contingencies do not materialize. In short, there are no ideal answers, only an assortment of more or less plausible alternatives.

Monetary policy is the responsibility of the Board of Governors of the Federal Reserve System, commonly known as the Federal Reserve Board (FRB). It is an independent agency of the federal government headed by a board of seven members nominated by the president and confirmed by the Senate. Members are appointed for fourteen-year terms and one term expires every two years. A member may not be reappointed after having served a full term. The chairman and vice-chairman are designated by the president and are subject to further Senate confirmation if they are sitting members. The two presiding officers may serve four-year terms and may be reappointed to such positions. However, the failure to be reappointed to a leadership post does not affect the fourteen-year term of a member.

The FRB is the central bank of the United States. It consists of the headquarters institution in Washington, D.C., twelve Federal Reserve Banks in districts throughout the country, and twenty-five branches of Reserve Banks. National banks, which are chartered by the federal government, are required by law to be members of the Federal Reserve System. Commercial banks chartered by any state may elect to become members if they meet the requirements established by the FRB. In addition to member commercial banks, the FRB exercises some supervision over all depository institutions, which includes nonmember commercial banks, savings banks, savings and loan associations, and credit unions. The FRB is financed by interest received on securities acquired through its regular operations and by fees for services provided to depository institutions.

The legally mandated goals of the FRB are to promote maximum employment, stable prices, and moderate long-term interest rates. Combined with its banking functions, this translates into a charge to provide adequate money and credit at interest rates calculated to foster full employment without inflation. The FRB was established on the general principle that government should not be permitted to directly exercise, through ordinary legislative and executive channels, the power to create money, which it may be tempted to do for mistaken premises or unsound purposes. It was considered imprudent to entrust such authority to entities directly responsible to the electorate. Such an arrangement would render it very difficult to implement politically unpopular, but economically appropriate, policies that resulted in relatively high interest rates.

The formal independence of the FRB stems from the tenure of board members, its statutory exemption from the appropriations process, and broad authorizing legislation. Its insulated administrative, budgetary, and legal status is reinforced by the conviction that the subject of money and practice of banking require specialized knowledge and professional expertise not traditionally possessed by executive- and legislative-branch officials. FRB independence means that as a U.S. government agency it must be guided by governmental objectives in discharging its responsibilities and may use its discretion to determine the manner in which to pursue them without being subject to the control of other federal entities. However, the inclination to exercise independent judgment that conflicts with current or proposed fiscal policy is circumscribed by an unarticulated aim, which is to protect the board's capacity to make an autonomous contribution to economic policymaking.

The FRB fashions monetary policy through the use of three instruments that regulate the amount of cash reserves held by depository institutions. The primary and most flexible instrument is open market operations, by which the FRB buys or sells government securities. Two other tools are the discount rate, which is the rate of interest charged by the FRB on loans to depository institutions, and reserve requirements, which set the ratio of reserves relative to potential liabilities that depository institutions must retain in their vaults. When the FRB purchases securities, lowers the discount rate, or reduces reserve requirements, it increases the volume of reserves, which expands the money supply. The result is to encourage a demand for loans since the release of more funds reduces interest rates. Should the FRB follow the opposite course, the money supply will decrease and interest rates rise. The board meets approximately eight times a year to reach decisions on these matters.

While the supply of money or its rate of growth can be effectively controlled by the FRB, the demand for money is determined by the level of economic activity. A change in interest rates has an inverse effect on the demand for cash and credit and on the aggregate demand for goods and services. An increase in the money supply generates economic expansion that produces lower interest rates and may cause inflation. A decrease in the money supply engenders economic contraction that usually boosts interest rates and may induce recession. The FRB is expected to formulate and implement monetary policy objectively and efficiently in a dynamic economy.

Much of the board's influence is due to the fact that it is able to act independently of partisan pressures. It tries to avoid embarrassing those who do act for political reasons and to refrain from major monetary decisions as elections approach. It is expected to act on the basis of objective data and scientific judgment in an environment that stresses political responsiveness. The FRB, in effect, is asked to be politically neutral while regulating an economic system that is not neutral in its results. Though charting monetary policy largely involves answers to professional questions and the use of economic equations, it cannot remain solely a technical matter. Even technically correct decisions are subject to economic uncertainty and political interpretation, while economic errors can create political problems.

Fiscal and monetary policy are based on an analysis of the same factors, directed at the same goals and subject to the same time lags. Both have direct and indirect, as well as long-term and short-term, effects. Monetary policy directly affects bank reserves, interest rates, and financial expectations. Fiscal policy directly affects disposable income, profit margins, and investment plans. Both ultimately affect employment, prices, and the growth rate. Numerous questions exist about the optimal mix of policies in regard to both their internal elements and external impact on each other. Excessive reliance on one policy instrument may produce undesirable side-effects too strong for others to overcome, while multiple policy initiatives may neutralize one another.

FRB decisions can significantly shape the conditions that prompt fiscal action and determine its effectiveness. In concrete terms, monetary policy governs the amount of interest paid and earned on government borrowing and lending and crucially affects certain programs that are heavily influenced by interest rates. Board members are constrained to judge, consciously or not, whether monetary policy should be subordinated to, supplement, or counteract fiscal policy or to use fiscal policy as one factor among others to be considered in forging monetary policy. Many different combinations of fiscal and monetary policies may be appropriate for achieving desirable economic goals. However, even when the courses pursued are consistent, the specific instruments influence the composition and consequences of economic activity. Thus, it is incumbent on the authorities responsible for each to try to coordinate their proposals and priorities.

Though the FRB is formally accountable to Congress, presidential obligations entail a greater degree of interaction with the board. While lacking any legal authority in the realm of monetary policy, legislation has conferred responsibility on the president for macroeconomic management. Since fiscal and monetary policy are functionally interdependent, presidents are motivated to ensure that they are compatible with each other. The president and FRB are both in a strong position to identify policy problems and prescribe proper remedies. The economists in the White House and the board tend to analyze options in similar terms and share the view that Congress is an obstacle to timely and effective economic policymaking. The president finds it desirable and feasible to work closely with the FRB on a continuing basis through unannounced personal communications and general public statements.

In its relations with the FRB, Congress tends to emphasize regular reporting and policy reaction. The board is required to report to Congress twice each year on its intended course, which provides an opportunity for legislators to schedule hearings. At these proceedings the FRB chairman responds to member questions and explains and defends board options. When Congress decides that monetary policy should be changed, its recommendations are embodied in a concurrent resolution. In case of persistent disagreement or intense dissatisfaction with the board, Congress may resort to legislation. It may either mandate structural reforms of the Federal Reserve System or enact laws to protect economic interests vulnerable to restrictive monetary policy. Board interaction with the legislature tends to be more public, episodic, and contentious than that with the executive.

Regardless of FRB action or inaction, its choices favor some societal interests over others. Because monetary policy can only effectively address one problem at a time, board members must decide which to attack and when to shift attention to another. Since all economic endeavor involves a certain degree of error, policymakers necessarily disclose a preference to err on the side of more or less monetary growth. Though the FRB is the government's chief mechanism for influencing the economy's short-run performance, it cannot prevent recession or guarantee expansion. It can only create a climate in which the former is less and the latter is more likely to occur.

In contrast with fiscal policy, monetary policy is more flexible with regard to its timing and substance. It can be modified or reoriented soon after it is determined that changes are necessary. Fiscal-policy authorities are more responsive to the needs of individuals and businesses harmed by the effects of recession. Monetary authorities are more responsive to the needs of the economic system when it confronts inflation. The prevention or suppression of inflation involves several unpalatable political choices. Thus, it is best left to an agency not subject to general public opinion or specific constituency pressure. Though the president and Congress may occasionally express their displeasure over FRB decisions, such comments may signify as much or more relief than they do regret.

BUDGET PROCESS

EXECUTIVE ESTIMATES

A proposed budget is submitted to Congress each January by the president for the fiscal year that begins the following October. The fiscal year is an accounting period that, for the federal government, extends from October 1 through September 30 and is designated by the calendar year in which it ends. The most active participant in the preparation of the executive budget is the OMB. Through its authority to supervise the administration of the federal budget for executive-branch agencies and evaluate the effectiveness of federal programs, it collects and digests most of the data used to formulate the executive budget.

The executive budget is formed by aggregating the thousands of programs administered, functions performed, and proposals originated by federal agencies into a coherent plan. This entails a thorough review of agency budget requests for future funding needs. In this undertaking OMB serves as a liaison between the president and all executive-branch agency heads. Its goal is to ensure that the final product reflects the policy choices endorsed and budget ceilings imposed by the chief executive. To coordinate this process involves more than merely framing guidelines and meeting deadlines. The need to incorporate and integrate diverse viewpoints and voluminous data into one comprehensive document inescapably entails decisions that have significant policy implications.

During the first phase of executive-branch budgeting the OMB notifies agencies about which questions should be addressed and materials prepared. Policy priorities are examined in light of economic conditions and outlined in terms of broad purposes. In the next phase, OMB provides technical assistance as formal estimates are framed. Agencies attempt to adapt legislatively mandated responsibilities with presidential priorities and must explain differences between proposed and current spending plans. The last phase comprises a review of all previous decisions, firm OMB recommendations to the president, and approval of final budget totals. Economic assumptions, fiscal policies, and program allocations are organized into a consolidated budget package.

The process of budget formation and review proceeds on three levels. The first is continual monitoring by budget examiners, who are specialists assigned to one or more agencies or to a given function. This covers specific activities and decisions in which agency budget requests are considered in relation to actual program needs. The second occurs periodically at the upper echelons of OMB when the director and subdivision chiefs, in conjunction with examiners, appraise agency proposals. Such action embraces the development of overall and long-range priorities against which agency objectives and preferences may be gauged. The third involves OMB interaction with the president and his chief advisers, which is usually scheduled once during each major phase. It is intended to assess political and legislative factors and to settle unresolved disputes or problems.

The executive budget process begins approximately nine months before the document is transmitted to Congress and eighteen months before the start of the fiscal year. The OMB, in cooperation with the Treasury Department and Council of Economic Advisors, prepares tentative economic assumptions, forecasts of national and international developments, and fiscal projections. After a presidential review, the OMB issues policy guidelines to agencies for their spring budget survey. The agencies draft reports on the resources consumed and results produced by existing programs and include a set of proposals that present their program goals and financial needs. These analyses focus on major issues and explore alternatives for addressing them.

Agency budget requests are based on their own objectives and priorities. Even when they seek the same funding level as the previous year, decisions must be made about the internal allocation of funds. Though last year's budget is used as the platform on which to construct this year's request, the prior total is composed of different elements. An uncontrollable component is fixed by legislative requirements. Another component reflects the need to remain abreast of inflation. A final component is discretionary, and though a relatively small proportion of an agency's budget, is the source of potential change in program functions.

General budget policies must be translated into detailed information on programs and finances. On the basis of policy and budgetary guidelines, economic assumptions, technical instructions, and spending ceilings provided by OMB, executive-branch agencies must prepare their budget estimates. Decisions are first made about allocations to various programs and then on the funding requirements of current and proposed programs. The estimates and program proposals represent an effort to correlate an agency's statutory obligations with the presidential agenda.

Budget offices within each agency supervise preparation of an internal review budget submitted to them by each administrative unit. This process may include hearings at which unit chiefs present and defend their requests as well as provide an opportunity to appeal budget-office decisions to the agency head. Upon the conclusion of these activities, the agency budget request for the next fiscal year is transmitted to OMB. It contains general policy analysis comparing total program benefits and costs as well as detailed program analysis comparing specific benefits and costs.

Upon compiling and evaluating this material, the OMB compares total estimated outlays with total estimated revenues and develops practical options for the president on fiscal policy, program issues, and budget levels. The emphasis here is on important program innovations or modifications, alternative long-range program plans, and budgetary projections. Following a second presidential review in June, general fiscal and social goals are established in regard to total budget size, program initiatives, and policy priorities. The OMB conveys these decisions to agencies, along with planning ceilings to govern the preparation of formal agency budget requests.

Despite the professional competence of OMB staff, the large volume of technical data collected, and extensive computer analysis, the budget is not a neutral document. It is an inclusive and elaborate presentation of political priorities that generates or indicates varying degrees of conflict between OMB and other federal agencies. OMB regularly reduces most agency budget requests because their combined total always exceeds acceptable levels set by the president and his advisers. Agency-OMB interaction is neither consistently antagonistic nor consistently cooperative. The general environment is conditioned by the availability of resources, while specific relationships depend on particular allocations. Practical restrictions on presidential participation permit or require OMB to exercise considerable discretion.

The shrewd use of information by agency officials can counteract OMB authority and inclination to pare budget figures. Some strategies include an over-statement of program costs in anticipation of budget cuts; an understatement of program costs to induce approval, followed by an appeal for supplemental funds to conserve the original investment; an agency response to OMB reductions that threatens to curtail or eliminate its most politically popular programs, with the expectation that public and congressional support will result in restoration of the cuts; or an agency may link its agenda to presidential policy commitments, which OMB would be reluctant to disapprove even if costs were more than desirable.

In September agencies submit their formal estimates and supporting documents to the OMB. This material is thoroughly analyzed, and agency representatives attend hearings held by budget examiners. After reexamining economic assumptions and fiscal policy from the standpoint of the economic outlook and presidential priorities, the OMB prepares detailed recommendations for presidential action. Final decisions are reached on agency budget figures and overall budget policy during this third presidential review in December. The OMB notifies agencies of these determinations, and unit heads revise their estimates to conform to presidential judgments.

The executive budget is shaped primarily by the OMB in consultation with the president, other officials with economic responsibilities, and agency managers. The OMB assesses agency budget estimates based upon its knowledge of agency performance to arrive at the resource needs of individual programs. Discussion with Treasury Department officials and members of the Council of Economic Advisers about economic conditions and trends results in figures for total outlays and receipts consistent with the fiscal diagnosis. The president provides political input through choices concerning policy commitments, the range of governmental activity, and public priorities. The OMB is expected to integrate the information and balance the objectives of all participants, a coordinating role that invests it with considerable influence.

The change in purpose of budget formulation from an almost exclusive concern with defraying the costs of government operations to a means for setting national priorities, managing the economy, and redistributing income, has fostered a more centralized approach to the process. It is now a system in which information continually flows up to OMB and OMB instructions flow down to the agencies. The result has been a consistent rather than a seasonal participation by OMB in the financial decisions of the executive branch.

The executive budget is a comprehensive statement through which the president expresses judgment about the relative merits of governmental activities in the context of a fiscal policy designed to stabilize the economy and meet social needs. It also provides Congress with an overall budget program that can be examined in parts, yet remain a general plan. Though it contains only estimates and recommendations, the executive budget offers an unusually favorable opportunity for the president to marshal support behind his programmatic preferences.

CONGRESS: AUTHORIZATIONS

The following paragraphs discuss authorizations in the narrower sense of financial measures rather than in terms of their broader meaning of substantive policy. Defined in its most technical form, an authorization is the legal approval to receive or commit public funds. This covers both the amount and method of spending that may be authorized. These decisions reflect the political standing of the policy in question or the relationship between the authorizing and appropriations committee. There are three types of authorizations, classified by duration, for programs whose funding level is subject to appropriations action.

Permanent authorizations are programs or agencies that, once established, continue in existence or operation until further legislative notice. The total that may be spent is left indefinite, to be determined through the appropriations process. This authorization category mainly covers recurrent expenses of a traditional or imperative nature. The lack of controversy about performance of the governmental activity does not preclude intense debate over budgetary implications. Routine expenditures include funds for agency operations, while a more vital function concerns the payment of interest on the public debt. While the former denotes established government priorities, the latter directly sustains governmental integrity. Appropriations committees may recommend a spending figure without waiting for substantive legislation from the authorizing committees.

Multiyear authorizations usually extend for from two to five years. They ordinarily specify the amount of money that may be appropriated for a given year and the amount authorized tends to be increased for each successive year. This type is generally applied to new programs for which the interval is considered a trial period or to others that would benefit from a measure of financial stability. In the former case, proponents had to forego a permanent existence to obtain sufficient support for its initiation, while the latter instance reflects a need for certain recipients of federal funds to make advance plans for efficient operations.

Annual authorizations normally stipulate definite funding levels and serve as a vehicle for maximizing authorizing committee influence over an agency or program. They enable legislators to write specific conditions into authorizing legislation to limit undesirable administrative discretion. Where political differences exist between the legislative and executive branches this approach affords the opportunity to control questionable agency budgetary practices. The regular renewal of legal authority also provides momentum for ample appropriations. A recent and emphatic congressional endorsement of program needs is a clear signal regarding its proper financial status.

It is to be expected that the level of funds appropriated for a particular agency or program will be less than the total authorized. To protect its priorities under these circumstances, an authorizing committee may earmark certain sums and include legislative language that mandates proportional reductions. Each authorized category of agency activity is assured of receiving an appropriation that reflects its proposed share of the full amount of funds as contained in the authorization. Appropriations committees are thus prevented from recommending that programs be eliminated by the denial or curtailed by the dearth of funds.

In contrast with measures that influence or limit the discretion of appropriations committees, authorizing panels may also establish programs that bypass or preempt the appropriations process. The more prominent of these funding methods fall into three categories based on their basic purpose. The first pair described below is designed to ensure that money will be distributed to designated recipients regardless of any contingency. The second pair serves to provide federal agencies with the flexibility needed to implement certain programs. The last pair is intended to encourage participation in or continuation of important communal activities or projects.

Permanent appropriations permit funds to become available each year under previously enacted legislation. They function automatically and allow agencies to spend without waiting for authority or appropriations to be granted by Congress. These are unrestricted legislative guarantees whose amount is determined by socioeconomic conditions over which government can exercise little control. The only way to avert or reduce expenditures would be to amend or repeal some existing law. Permanent appropriations eliminate uncertainty concerning the future availability of funds to meet the legal obligations of the United States. This type of legislation also protects programs against potentially adverse political developments. Major forms of such public business are social security, civil service retirement, and unemployment compensation.

Entitlement programs are open-ended commitments to defined classes of individuals or units of government where payment levels are guaranteed by law if stipulated eligibility requirements are met. Expenditures are limited only by the number of those who satisfy the legal criteria for receiving benefits, which usually depends on economic and demographic trends. Some entitlements are funded by permanent, while others are subject to annual, appropriations. In both cases the disbursement of funds is mandated by statutory formulas that effectively preclude the exercise of financial discretion to curtail benefits. The contractual nature of these programs means that many beneficiaries depend on them for their subsistence. Prominent examples of entitlements are Medicare, food stamps, and veterans' benefits.

The regular funding sequence for most spending measures, an appropriation followed by an obligation, is reversed for contract and borrowing authority. These types of funding are granted by authorizing legislation that exempts them from the appropriations process to facilitate forms of government activity connected with the unique needs of certain programs or projects. Contract authority permits a federal agency to make commitments in anticipation of an appropriation or of receipts to be credited to a Treasury account. If the use of receipts cannot cover these obligations, the appropriations committees must estimate cash needs for contracts coming due over the next fiscal year and provide sufficient money to make the required payments. Borrowing authority permits a federal agency to make expenditures for specified purposes from borrowed funds. An appropriation only becomes necessary when an agency is unable to cover its debts.

Contract authority enables agencies to commit funds based on agreements whose provisions or stipulations cannot be determined in advance or that require an indefinite period of time to fulfill. This approach has the advantage of providing the necessary lead time for construction and other long-term projects. The timing for the use of this device and the expenditures it involves remain at the discretion of executive-branch officials. Borrowing authority empowers agencies to obtain funds from the Treasury or the public. This method finances commercial-type transactions that generate earnings from which the Treasury can be refunded and owners of agency notes repaid. Such authority, which may be activated at any time, enables an agency to reborrow money as its outstanding debt is retired.

A contingent liability is established when legislation obligates the federal government to protect the financial interests of another party in the event of certain adverse developments. The two major forms through which this goal is pursued are guaranteed loans and insurance programs. Guaranteed loans constitute a federal pledge to repay a lender all or part of the principal and interest should a borrower default. Insurance programs provide coverage to indemnify individuals or entities against financial loss owing to specified events or hazards. Both denote that certain borrowers or insurees would contribute more productively to community welfare than others. Since neither defaults nor other contingencies can be anticipated, actual expenditures cannot be estimated.

Guaranteed loans enable borrowers to obtain funds at lower interest rates because default risk is eliminated. Federal loan guarantees do not reduce the actual risk involved in a project or activity, but only shift the burden of risk from the lender to the government. Their availability represents a decision that the social benefits to be derived outweigh the cost of manipulating credit allocation. Insurance programs are intended to protect individual contributions to bank accounts and pension funds, provide financial security against the possibility of personal misfortune or natural disaster, and alleviate the effects of industrial distress or local recession. They are long-term investments in services and activities whose psychological and material effects are given priority over their potential financial implications.

CONGRESS: REVENUE

To pay its bills and maintain its credit, government must be assured of a regular income through the power to impose and collect taxes. Congress may tax any right, duty, commodity, or transaction subject mainly to restrictions in the Bill of Rights. A tax may be primarily a revenue or regulatory measure or a combination of both. Which purpose predominates is often a question of degree since no tax can be exclusively confined to one or the other. As revenue provides the essential means by which national needs are met, the power to tax must be sufficiently flexible and forceful to achieve authorized federal objectives. Who should sacrifice how much to enable government to pursue specific goals is a question that engenders constant public debate.

Federal taxes may be broadly classified by their source, purpose, or effect. Source refers to the form of income or activity subject to taxation and includes the individual and corporate income taxes, social insurance levies, excises, and tariffs. Purpose covers policy objectives that affect the health and welfare of individuals or promote desired economic or social behavior. Effects pertain to the ultimate burdens borne by different population groups and the economic impact on various income categories. A common feature of all taxes, regardless of any other factors, is their intended and actual fiscal consequences. From a budgetary perspective, their role in the financial status of government outweighs all other considerations.

Most revenue is derived from permanent provisions in the tax code or social security law. The amount of annual receipts tends to rise steadily because of increases in the number of taxpayers and taxable transactions. Congress usually enacts some changes in the tax laws each year. Though such changes have only a slight effect on federal revenue, they can have a major impact on particular segments of the community. When tax reductions are proposed, legislators are less concerned with total figures than with specific provisions. Congress is inclined to treat revenue legislation as an opportunity to provide benefits to certain constituencies.

The basic elements of a tax code include a definition of income, criteria to determine the liability of taxpayers, rules that establish allowable deductions, and a schedule of tax rates. Most income is derived from wages and salaries, with other sources being business and property transactions and cash transfer payments; taxpayers are individuals, businesses, unions, cooperatives, or other legal entities; most deductions are expenses necessary to produce income. When all of these features are taken into account, the overall structure or a given levy may be described as progressive, proportional, or regressive. A tax is progressive if upper income categories are taxed at a higher rate than lower ones; it is proportional if all income categories are taxed at the same rate; it is regressive if upper income categories are taxed at a lower rate than lower ones.

Tax policy is a tool for both short-term fiscal adjustment and long-term economic management. In the former case, the temporary revisions of tax rates to expand or contract federal revenue can refine or enhance economic performance. This involves a recurrent need for tax changes to keep the economy on a desired course. Measures designed to have a more durable result are concerned with the capacity and propensity of taxpayers to invest in economically and socially profitable enterprises. The federal tax structure significantly influences the spending and saving habits of individuals and businesses. Tax incentives and penalties are key instruments for altering the fiscal condition of the federal government and financial plans of private citizens.

The House Ways and Means and Senate Finance Committees exercise jurisdiction over all tax measures in Congress. Their domain of authority also includes Medicare, Medicaid, social security, unemployment compensation, public assistance, and interest on the public debt. This means that in addition to having legislative custody of the tax code, these panels control programs that account for over 50 percent of federal spending. Within the confines of essential revenue needs and reasonable tax liability, the committees have ample discretion to frame financial proposals. Their extensive purview enables them to accommodate any revenue total to a wide variety of interests and purposes.

Another form of revenue legislation, which is considered as an exception to the key components of a normal tax structure, is known as a tax expenditure. Many provisions in the tax code grant preferential treatment to particular classes of taxpayers through cancelled, reduced, or deferred levies that result in revenue losses to the Treasury. Such losses are termed *tax expenditures* because they are equivalent to direct payments by the federal government to designated taxpayers. Tax expenditures are designed to encourage certain kinds of activities or to provide relief to individuals or corporations in specified circumstances by lowering their tax liability. In one respect such special provisions are similar to entitlement programs, where all those who meet stipulated requirements are eligible for them. In another respect they resemble direct spending programs since tax subsidies provide real economic benefits to those who receive them.

One of the advantages of tax expenditures is the simplicity of their administration. Taxpayers can apply for the benefit by merely making a few entries on a tax return that they normally file. Another advantage is the perception that tax expenditures do not involve the use of public funds. This enables a program that apparently minimizes governmental involvement to attract political support. Finally, by definition, a tax expenditure can only be granted to those who owe taxes or would owe them without the special provision. Thus, a taxpayer must earn enough income to qualify for the benefit. This requirement excludes those who fail to meet prescribed standards or make required efforts.

The disadvantages of tax expenditures are that each of the revenue losses incurred must be offset by higher taxes on everyone else. Thus, a program funded through the tax code tends to be viewed as an inequitable benefit. Tax rates are higher than would be necessary without tax expenditures. If there were fewer of them the tax base would be broader and the same amount of revenue could be raised with lower rates. In addition, because tax expenditures take the form of credits, deductions, exclusions, and exemptions, they complicate an already complex tax structure and increase the burden of those legislative and executive units responsible for tax policy and its administration.

Also within the jurisdiction of the Ways and Means and Finance Committees is the debt limit. This is the statutory limitation on the authority of the government to incur indebtedness or raise revenue through its borrowing power. It pertains to the total public debt outstanding rather than to the amount accrued in a fiscal year. The government is not permitted to borrow funds in excess of the limit, which is usually set at or below the level needed by the end of the fiscal year. Thus, Congress is obliged to raise the statutory debt limit at least once during each fiscal year. The annual growth of the public debt exceeds the figure for the annual budget deficit because the former includes certain intragovernmental borrowing that does not affect the latter.

Legislation to raise the debt limit is initiated by a letter from the Treasury Department to the chairman of the Ways and Means Committee stating that the government will be unable to borrow money if the authorized total is not boosted by a certain date. When Congress is called on to raise the limit more than once during a year it is because the initial estimate of the amount to be borrowed was too low or because the prior increase was less than the amount requested by the Treasury Department. The first reason is due to unforeseen economic developments and the second to definite political calculations. Increases in the debt ceiling are needed simply to allow the Treasury to finance budget deficits that Congress has previously approved.

Legislative action on this matter is necessitated by more than the demands created by earlier congressional decisions. Should the ceiling not be raised before the expiration of the existing limit, the government's ability to operate is jeopardized. The Treasury would be unable to borrow for the purpose of payments to meet legal commitments. After its cash reserves were depleted, it would be forced to default on its financial obligations. Even in the event of brief delays in the enactment of such legislation, the Treasury must resort to methods and measures that reduce financial efficiency and increase interest costs. In recognition of these imminent adverse effects, Congress deplores the necessity then passes the bill.

CONGRESS: APPROPRIATIONS

Appropriations are the main form of spending authority provided by Congress to each branch of the federal government. They authorize specified levels of funds to be committed by designated units for prescribed purposes. The constitutional provision that "No money shall be drawn from the Treasury, but in consequence of appropriations made by law" does not mean that there must be a specific appropriation for each itemized expenditure. It is construed as a requirement that there be an appropriation that is legally available before a financial obligation may be incurred. Legal availability refers to stipulations in an appropriation act that specify its purpose, time limits, and amount. Appropriations do not represent funds available in the Treasury, but are limitations on the amounts that agencies may obligate during the time period stated in the law.

In theory the authorizing committees are concerned with the substance of legislation, establish the purposes for which public funds may be used, and set a ceiling on appropriations for approved programs. The appropriations committees then determine what proportion of the funds authorized to finance enacted measures is actually needed, without assessing the worth or intent of statutory policies. In reality, appropriations decisions to allocate available funds among governmental functions and activities governs the scope and vigor of efforts to implement authorizing legislation. Since the level of appropriations may vary from no funds to the maximum authorized, the question of how much to spend for what purposes obviously has significant policy implications.

The appropriations committees are expected to furnish adequate financial support for authorized programs and to achieve the most economical expenditure of public funds. They endeavor to fulfill their frugality role through a detailed analysis of prior and projected agency transactions and their spending role by appropriating enough to accomplish program goals. The zone of discretion within which these panels operate is bounded by authorizing legislation, last year's appropriation, the coming year's estimates contained in the executive budget, and the most recent budget resolution approved by Congress.

In contrast with other standing committees, the appropriations panels do not have any discretion in regard to reporting bills — appropriations are necessary if the government is to continue to function. There are also many public services that are too politically or instrumentally vital to be curtailed despite the panels' prerogative to propose reduced spending for them. To neutralize or preclude the possibility of conflict with authorizing committees, members of appropriations committees try to convey the impression that their work is primarily an intra-governmental activity merely involving questions of financial management.

Though the appropriations committees might be reluctant to authorize a sum that can be interpreted as an attempt to annul substantive policy, they can, instead of provoking a direct challenge, control a program by a process of erosion. This is accomplished by appropriating sufficient funds for a program to survive in an attenuated form. Such action may involve an appropriation in installments as a means of encouraging or limiting certain policy decisions. To offset political discontent with some of the more unpopular spending cuts, the committees may recommend small appropriations for new or slight increases for existing projects of interest to particular legislators. This action enables the program to begin or continue and provides the opportunity for commitments and accomplishment that its advocates can use to generate political support for greater appropriations in the future.

Demands for budget increases tend to be specific, as legislators endeavor to enhance their reputations with certain constituencies. However, demands for budget reduction tend to be general, as legislators choose to leave the onus for making specific cuts on the appropriations committees. Among the more prominent reasons for reduced allocations are an economy drive precipitated by general economic conditions, suspicion or evidence of agency padding, disagreement with the substance or scope of a program, or reprisal for objectionable executive decisions. From an overall perspective, appropriations outcomes depend on several overlapping factors. These include the level of public and congressional popularity of a program, the legislative initiative and administrative performance of an agency, the degree of confidence that exists between committee members and executive officials, and the correspondence of committee and presidential preferences.

When the executive budget is submitted to Congress the members of each appropriations subcommittee receive detailed budget justifications from the agencies under their jurisdiction. This material explains, compares, summarizes, and supports in words and tables each agency's estimate of its appropriation. The subcommittee hearings generally do not probe deeply into established and stable programs with firm and substantial bases of support. Their focus is on administrative decisions as these affect the economy and efficiency of agency operations. The large majority of witnesses are administrative officials, who are prepared to discuss and defend their programs and budgets. These are examined from the standpoint of how an agency managed and consumed the increase it received last year and the purposes for which the current increase is needed. This means that questions and discussion concentrate mainly on new programs, increased costs, innovations in program administration, and internal reallocation of expenditures.

General appropriation bills are the primary vehicles for funding the annual activities of the federal government. These spending measures originate in committee and, in conjunction with revenue proposals, form the fiscal policy designed to implement the budget resolution. Both houses have rules that prohibit substantive legislation in general appropriation bills. This applies to the enactment of law where none exists and the amendment or repeal of existing law. Such a proscription reflects an effort to maintain a clear boundary between the jurisdiction of authorizing and appropriating committees. Another purpose is to prevent proposals whose merits have not been sufficiently scrutinized in committee from being attached to essential measures. Any legislative language that conflicts with, goes beyond, or qualifies authorizing legislation is deemed to violate the chamber rule. However, it is not unusual for such provisions to be incorporated into appropriations bills to remedy routine matters or meet the demands of urgent situations.

Some common types of legislative provisions that find their way into appropriations bills are those authorizing expenditures for activities not specifically mentioned in existing law, providing exemptions from statutory limitations, or permitting funds to be used for a period longer than stated in an authorization. Substantive provisions contained in annual appropriations acts are not construed as permanent legislation unless the language used therein or the nature of the text renders it clear that such is the intent of Congress. In general, legislation in an appropriations bill is more likely to be accepted if it is germane to the subject matter and reduces expenditures.

Appropriations committees may insert several types of provisions into their bills that are intended to control the spending decisions of federal agencies. Among the most common are limits on the purposes for or conditions under which funds may be spent, restrictions on the amounts that may be used for authorized purposes, and prohibitions on spending for objects not specifically mentioned in substantive legislation. An appropriations act may also designate the executive official who is to exercise discretion regarding the level of spending or the units to be assigned responsibility for expenditures. These constraints serve to narrow administrative discretion, set time limits if none are stated in authorizing legislation, or establish qualifications for recipients of federal funds.

Appropriations enacted by Congress without prior authorization can be obligated and spent except when the availability of funds is expressly made contingent upon the enactment of an authorization. One other way that the appropriations committees may parry authorizing legislation is through the use of line-item or lump-sum appropriations. The former applies to a single activity or purpose and limits the discretion of agency administrators. The latter covers several specific projects or items and provides the flexibility for meeting unforeseen or evolving conditions. Other statutory means that provide for flexible agency spending practices are contingency and emergency appropriations. A contingency appropriation is a separate grant for a specific purpose. It is additional obligational authority to be used when unanticipated needs arise, with the need to be determined by executives, consistent with the appropriations act. An emergency appropriation authorizes an agency to depart from prescribed purposes and applies to urgent conditions that arise during program operations. This does not increase the amount of funds available, but enables the unit to use budget authority granted elsewhere in the act when emergencies occur.

Though annual appropriations allow agencies to incur obligations for only one fiscal year, the funds to discharge such obligations remain indefinitely available until expended. This type of appropriation is mainly used for salaries and other operating expenses. Multiyear appropriations cover a specified period of time in excess of one year and are usually devoted to special activities of a one-time nature or programs subject to unique conditions. No-year appropriations provide for obligations and outlays until the purpose for which they are granted has been accomplished. These acts primarily finance benefit payments and construction projects where a time limit would not significantly contribute to the control of expenditures.

When funds are made available for a specified duration, the authority to obligate them will lapse when the period expires. To prevent the return of unused funds to the Treasury, Congress may reappropriate some or all of the unobligated balance. Legislative action to continue the obligational availability of previously appropriated money may authorize spending for the same or different purposes. The act of reappropriation applies only to annual or multiyear funds. Lapsing does not automatically occur with no-year money, which remains available until expended. However, no-year balances are returned to the Treasury when the purpose for which the appropriation was made has been accomplished for less than the amount originally granted.

Supplemental appropriations are acts that furnish funds in addition to those provided by general appropriation bills. Their purpose is to finance activities and projects that were not included or anticipated in the budget request for the current annual appropriation and that cannot be postponed until the next regular appropriations cycle. For certain activities that were not funded by regular appropriations or for others whose funding level was insufficient, urgent conditions may arise that render delay either politically or practically imprudent. The majority of supplemental requests are submitted to Congress with the president's budget in January. After being reviewed by the relevant sub-committees, they are usually packaged into an omnibus bill by the appropriations committees once or twice a year.

Supplementals may be grouped into three categories based on their relationship to authorizing legislation. An authorizing committee may be unable to complete its work in time for consideration in a regular appropriations bill. House and Senate rules that prohibit appropriations for agencies and programs that have not been authorized may also forestall funding. A supplemental becomes necessary to overcome the effects of delay when the authorization is finally enacted. New legislation that creates programs or amends existing ones and that goes into effect in the same fiscal year in which it is enacted requires a supplemental to provide funds. Finally, ongoing activities may compel a supplemental to meet emergency conditions that threaten life or property, economic conditions that generate a greater federal workload, financial conditions that make prompt payment a less expensive course than later ones, or legal conditions that mandate expenditures within the current fiscal year.

Continuing resolutions are temporary appropriations acts that enable existing federal programs to function after the expiration of prior spending authority. If Congress fails to complete action on one or more general appropriation bills before the start of the new fiscal year, it resorts to a continuing resolution that provides interim funding. In the absence of such action those agencies whose appropriations expire would be constrained to suspend operations. The lack of a regular appropriation may be due to delay in authorizing legislation, dilatory tactics by congressional opponents of certain spending programs, or the presidential veto of a general appropriation bill. Continuing resolutions are intended to furnish adequate resources for the orderly continuation of essential services during the interval required to enact regular appropriation bills.

The two basic elements of a continuing resolution are the limited period for which appropriations are made available and the maximum funding level for agencies covered by the law. Restricted duration is designed to give Congress sufficient time to finish work on the regular appropriation bills without eliminating the incentive to proceed expeditiously. The measure generally stipulates that the spending authority granted shall remain available until the enactment of a regular appropriation or a fixed cutoff date, whichever occurs first. Should Congress fail to pass a general appropriation bill before a cutoff date arrives, another continuing resolution becomes necessary.

The resolution usually provides only enough funds to keep existing programs operating at prevailing levels, though specific spending stipulations vary according to the status of the regular appropriation. To determine the sum of money appropriated for a given entity or activity by a continuing resolution often requires one to consult documents other than the law itself. The amount of funds provided may be the total stated in a pending appropriations act that has passed one or both houses of Congress; the amount requested in the most recent executive budget estimate; or limited to the current rate, which refers to the spending level for the present fiscal year. However, the resolution may contain the full text of regular appropriation bills that have not yet been passed or specify definite amounts in the same manner as is done in regular appropriation bills.

CONGRESS: BUDGET RESOLUTIONS

The congressional budget process begins with the transmittal of the executive budget to Congress in January. The House Appropriations Committee holds special hearings at which the director of the OMB, secretary of the Treasury, and chairman of the Council of Economic Advisers testify. These proceedings present an overview of budget policy through the discussion of economic conditions, fiscal options, and national priorities. The budget committees in each chamber commence more extended and detailed hearings that cover such matters as economic indicators and assumptions, the course and pace of economic trends, economic weaknesses and key issues, budgetary recommendations and alternatives, the fiscal impact of current and proposed policies, and allocation of funds among governmental functions. Witnesses at these hearings include administration officials, members of Congress, experts from the academic and business communities, representatives of national organizations, and other public and private parties.

The Congressional Budget Office (CBO) is required to submit its Annual Report to Congress by February 15. This document contains baseline projections that inform legislators of estimated revenues and expenditures under alternative inflation rates, economic conditions, and demographic trends. Since the whole can only be understood in relation to its parts, the CBO also computes baseline projections for all major programs and accounts that extrapolate spending trends over a five-year period. Though these figures are not published, they are used by the budget and other committees to reach decisions and prepare reports. This current policy data baseline provides a common set of numbers for the various participants in the congressional budget process. When a reduction or increase is proposed by some entity, it is calculated in terms of its deviation from this baseline.

All standing committees are required to transmit reports on their legislative plans for the coming fiscal year to the Senate and House Budget Committees by February 25. Officially known as Views and Estimates, these documents permit other committees to contribute to the formation of a budget resolution and provide the budget panels with some guidance on contemplated legislation and its fiscal impact for the coming fiscal year. These reports contain a concise discussion of the programs for which each committee is responsible and focus on the proposed levels of new budget authority that each anticipates it will approve. Authorizing and appropriating panels are obliged to organize their agenda early enough to give the budget committees a comprehensive picture of proposed congressional action for the year.

Both budget committees use the president's budget, information derived from their hearings, CBO reports, and the Views and Estimates of other panels to draft a budget resolution during March in a series of public mark-up sessions.

The Senate Budget Committee is instructed to report a resolution by April 1, while House Budget Committee action is not subject to a deadline. Congress is required to complete action on a budget resolution by April 15. Prior to its adoption neither house may consider any revenue, spending, entitlement, credit, or debt legislation. Budget resolutions are an exercise in legislative self-discipline intended to regulate the budgetary actions of Congress. They are not laws and neither appropriate funds nor raise revenues. Though unable to control expenditures in terms of amounts, rates, or types, they impose requirements on those congressional units responsible for public finance.

The intent of these prescribed dates is to encourage Congress to begin making its budget and spending decisions early enough to provide sufficient time for the consideration and passage of appropriations bills. However, the existence of a timetable does not ensure adherence to it and delays in the enactment of authorizations or on agreement to a budget resolution remain possible. In anticipation of this contingency, general appropriation bills may be brought to the floor of the House beginning on May 15, even if a budget resolution for the ensuing fiscal year has not been adopted. Whether or not Congress completes action on a budget resolution, the House Appropriations Committee must report all annual appropriations bills no later than June 10 so that the chamber can conclude all work on these measures by June 30.

The overall schedule and the exception to it for appropriations bills are designed to give the Senate adequate time to discharge its responsibilities in the appropriations process and resolve its differences with the House before the start of the new fiscal year. Otherwise a continuing resolution becomes imperative, which is an all too visible sign of legislative frustration or negligence. While the necessity for enactment of a continuing resolution may be reduced, so is the incentive to adopt a budget resolution. If appropriations may be enacted despite the status of a budget resolution, the urgency attached to the latter is attenuated. This signifies that strict compliance with a process devised to establish fiscal policy should not compel legislators to impair the ability of government to function smoothly.

In formulating a budget resolution Congress retains the discretion to decide on the appropriate combination of spending and taxation as long as the resulting levels of outlays and revenues are consistent with the maximum deficit amounts prescribed by law. The numbers in the budget resolution must be mathematically consistent. If legislators propose to reduce the deficit, they must approve either less total spending or more total revenue. If they choose to increase total spending, they must propose to increase either revenues or the deficit. This requirement applies to the budget resolution as reported by the budget committees and to any amendments offered from the floor.

Budget resolutions set aggregate fiscal policies and broad functional priorities for the next three fiscal years. They establish the framework within which Congress legislates on separate revenue, spending, and other budgetary measures. The resolution contains figures for total revenues and the amount by which they should be changed, total budget authority and outlays, the debt limit, the deficit or surplus, and total direct loan obligations and guaranteed loan commitments. It also allocates new budget authority, outlays, and direct and guaranteed loans among the various functional categories of the budget. The functional allocations must total to the corresponding budget aggregates.

During the spring and summer months, as Congress works on spending and revenue proposals for the upcoming fiscal year, the levels set in the budget resolution serve as constraints on legislative action. Any bill that would cause the spending ceilings or revenue floor to be breached or would cause the maximum deficit amount to be exceeded may be objected to by any member and automatically invalidated. If changing economic conditions or policy requirements erode the validity of the figures in the most recently adopted budget resolution, Congress may modify the measure at any time. In recent years, the practice has been to revise the budget for the current fiscal year through provisions incorporated into the budget resolution for the next fiscal year.

Major budget battles tend to center on the budget increment, or the amount by which the spending total for the coming fiscal year exceeds that of the current fiscal year. This is because the budget committees are able to exert more influence over new than continuing programs and over spending than revenue measures. Proposed programs cannot attract the solid political support that protects existing ones from being curtailed. The Ways and Means and Finance panels are subject to fewer constraints under the budget process than are the appropriations committees, whose actions are more comprehensible than decisions on the intricacies of the Internal Revenue Code.

Congress can strive to balance revenues and expenditures via one or more of the following means: curtail or abolish programs, increase taxes, authorize borrowing, or generate greater revenue through steady economic growth. The choice among these alternatives is affected by the legislative preference to distribute benefits as visibly as possible and costs as invisibly as possible. Thus, the first two routes are politically disagreeable and the latter two more desirable. The problem is that government can exercise relatively little control over borrowing and growth compared with its authority over services and taxes. When legislators must choose between potentially undesirable economic or electoral conditions, the former emerge as the lesser of two evils.

Budget resolutions are considered as vehicles for centralized, systematic, and coherent legislative action that can compete on a more equal basis with the president's budget. This is generally true, but not to a degree that would confer a status on the congressional budget equivalent to that of its executive counterpart. This is because procedure cannot completely overcome the competition between and among authorizing, appropriating, and budget committees. The attempt to coordinate duties and decisions has generated some redundancy in the system as each participant argues that its perspective is the most reasonable in terms of policy or most compelling in terms of politics.

Even though the budget has grown dramatically over the last two decades, budget choices are more difficult because that portion of the budget considered relatively controllable has significantly decreased. Furthermore, the congressional budget process, institutued in 1974, has expanded the number of participants, rendered the process more visible, produced more budget data, and added legislative requirements. Though this has given Congress the capability to deal more comprehensively and knowledgeably with the budget, it has introduced greater complexity into an already complicated undertaking.

The formulation of sound fiscal policy requires a systematic and periodic assessment of the objectives of the public sector, the balance between anticipated revenues and projected expenditures, and the relative tax burdens on individuals and businesses. The salience and efficacy of a budget resolution depend on the degree to which legislators politically accept and institutionally act in accordance with its provisions. Its informational dimension alone enables Congress to evaluate better the relative merits of fiscal measures in relation to general economic conditions and specific program commitments. By broadening and sharpening the legislative focus, the process enables each participant to see more clearly how each role fits into the overall endeavor.

To more firmly grasp the impact of the congressional budget process it is necessary to distinguish between the proposals to develop fiscal policy and the objectives that comprise any given budget resolution. Some legislators believe that a budget should primarily be an instrument to stimulate economic activity or accomplish national purposes. Other legislators regard it as a means through which Congress can establish and enforce its control over fiscal policy. Many members consider it simply as a vehicle to reduce spending. As budgetary matters moved into the forefront of political competition and economic argument, these viewpoints have become increasingly difficult to reconcile.

To ensure that the spending and revenue measures subsequently enacted by Congress conform to the figures prescribed by the budget resolution, the budget committees are authorized to initiate a reconciliation process. Its first stage consists of instructions in the budget resolution to designated committees. These directives specify the amounts by which existing laws or pending bills within the jurisdictions of each panel are to be changed so as to reconcile eventual spending, revenue, and debt totals with the provisions of the budget resolution. A deadline is usually set by which the committees are to submit their recommendations for achieving savings in one or more fiscal years. Since reconciliation language addresses only total figures, the panels are free to decide how and where to curtail the programs for which they are responsible.

The second stage covers the preparation of specific proposals by each committee and their transmittal to each budget panel, which consolidates them without substantive revision into an omnibus bill that it reports to the full chamber. The final stage is consideration and passage of the reconciliation bill on the floor of each house. The package approach renders it somewhat easier to pass program cuts in the interest of deficit reduction than it would be if each program was considered individually. It provides that a group of programs will simultaneously sustain their fair share of retrenchment. Congress is required to complete all reconciliation action by June 15, a date that enables legislators to apply all budgetary decisions to proposed authorization and appropriation bills.

Reconciliation represents consolidated budget cutting within a single measure, mandates the accountability of individual committees to Congress as a whole, and establishes a uniform time frame for prescribed action. Its general thrust is contrary to the normal mode of congressional decisionmaking. The process substitutes integrated for fragmented action, replaces bargaining and compromise with the enforcement of judgment, and imposes a hierarchical scheme on a decentralized institution and its autonomous units. The underlying rationale is that reconciliation enables Congress to reach all or any components of the budget to establish a comprehensive and consistent fiscal policy.

FINANCIAL TRANSACTIONS

The enactment of appropriations inaugurates the spending process for the new fiscal year. The expenditure of funds involves both routine administrative and nonroutine policy decisions. Agencies are monitored and regulated in regard to their funding levels, financial commitments, and expenditure rates. While most of this activity is guided by standard operating procedures, it is not always automatic or predictable. Unanticipated changes in economic conditions, political relationships, or statutory requirements can generate questions or quarrels about spending practices and priorities. From the congressional perspective, the key problem is how to reconcile a need for and limits on spending discretion.

Though Congress appropriates money, technically it grants budget authority. Budget authority is the legal authorization for an agency to spend money. When an agency decides to use some of its budget authority, it creates an obligation, which is a commitment to spend. To this point, however, no money has actually been drawn from the Treasury and spent. This occurs only when an agency pays its bills for the goods and services it has purchased. Then the budget authority that has been obligated becomes an outlay. An agency's outlays for each fiscal year consist largely of budget authority appropriated for that fiscal year. However, they also cover budget authority from previous fiscal years that has been obligated but not spent and some unobligated budget authority that has not expired.

After an appropriation bill is signed by the president, the secretary of the Treasury directs the treasurer of the United States to establish a credit equal to the aggregate amount of the appropriation. This is accomplished through the issuance of a warrant, which is an official document prescribed by law that specifies the amount of money authorized to be withdrawn from the Treasury. Each warrant creates an account in the Treasury from which an agency can make expenditures. Once accounts have been set up, agencies may incur obligations. As public creditors present bills for payment, checks are issued to liquidate the obligation.

The OMB is required by law to apportion appropriated funds to agencies for legally sanctioned activities and projects. Apportionment is the distribution of budget authority which then becomes available for obligation in an appropriation or fund account. OMB apportions funds to most agencies on a quarterly basis. Some apportionments cover other time periods or are based on unique program features. An agency is then limited to incurring obligations to the amounts specified for the time frame or activity. Under no circumstances are funds apportioned for periods longer than one fiscal year. The apportionment process is intended to promote an orderly and economical use of the amounts made available. It is also designed to prevent the obligation of funds in a manner that would lead to requests for supplemental appropriations.

Agencies may request changes in the level of or time periods for apportionments. OMB considers such appeals whenever their basis is compatible with program activities and are likely to increase efficiency or productivity. Reapportionments are approved when previous apportionments are no longer appropriate owing to changes in the amounts available for obligation, program requirements, cost factors, or the occurrence of unforeseen events. OMB may make apportionments or reapportionments in response to agency proposals or in accord with the results of its own analyses. Regardless of who exercises initiative, law prohibits obligations or expenditures from being in excess of apportionments or reapportionments.

Apportionments are cumulative, so that amounts not used in one period are available for obligation in a later period of the fiscal year. Allotments are under the control of each agency and are customarily undertaken by its budget office acting on authority of the agency head. It entails the extension of obligational authority to subunits on a monthly or quarterly basis. Apportionments and allotments provide administrative control and ensure that funds are managed in conformity with presidential priorities and agency procedures. Financial controls in the form of record-keeping requirements for appropriations, obligations, and disbursements ensure that funds are managed in accord with legal authority.

A certain degree of discretionary spending authority is necessary to meet contingencies and emergencies. The use of such discretion can trigger disagreement between the executive and legislative branches about the purpose and timing of expenditures. The central question is whether administrators exercise judgment so as to advance or frustrate goals established by law. Since OMB must review and approve agency spending plans, it is invariably drawn into such disputes if its own decisions do not cause them. How best to control the flow of funds and the amounts spent can become controversial matters because of the interpretation of statutory language or evaluation of social developments.

When the question is one of purposes, OMB must pass judgment on agency requests for a reprogramming or transfer. Reprogramming is the use of funds in an appropriation account for purposes other than those contemplated at the time of the appropriation. It is a reallocation from one program to another. Reprogramming may become necessary owing to changing program requirements, inaccurate cost estimates, or subsequent legislative enactments. As a legal matter, an agency is free to reprogram unobligated funds as long as the expenditures are within the general purpose of the appropriation and do not violate any other statutory restriction.

As a practical matter, reprogramming commonly involves some form of notification to or approval by the appropriations and/or authorizing committees. In a few cases the procedure is prescribed by statute. This approach covers situations in which the sums are in excess of a certain dollar figure, would entail significant program changes or commitment of funds, would increase resources for programs curtailed by Congress, or would create new programs. However, in most instances the committee review process is informal and stems from instructions or statements in committee reports, hearings, or interbranch correspondence.

A transfer is a transaction made pursuant to law that withdraws budget authority or balances from one appropriation account for credit to another. Transfers are made to carry out the purposes of either the account from which or to which funds are removed. Some agencies have limited transfer authority that sets a percentage limit on the amount that may be shifted from a given appropriation account and/or the amount by which the receiving account may be increased. This practice is justifiable when funds from one account are exhausted by unanticipated conditions and funds from some other accounts are likely to remain unused. It obviates the necessity for legislative action and can facilitate administrative and program efficiency.

Should an agency determine that conditions justify greater spending or saving than originally expected, the OMB has the final word on supplemental appropriations and impoundment proposals. When unanticipated developments combine with statutory obligations an agency may find that its budget is insufficient to meet legitimate program needs. If increased costs cannot be absorbed through reprogrammings or transfers, the agency submits a request for supplemental appropriations to the OMB. Supplementals are any amounts in excess of the total funds previously appropriated for the current fiscal year. Consideration of these appeals by the OMB does not guarantee that they will be approved for submission to Congress or, if approved, will reflect the full amount requested.

Available budgetary resources may be withheld from agencies through the apportionment process. The OMB possesses the authority to reserve funds from obligation to meet contingencies or effect savings made possible by changes in program requirements or more efficient operations. Any action or inaction by an administrative official to delay or revoke the obligation or expenditure of budget authority provided by law is an impoundment. Impoundments, which are intentional reductions rather than incidental practices that stop or slow expenditures, fall into two categories. A rescission is a presidential recommendation to repeal previously enacted budget authority, while a deferral is a presidential request to postpone the obligation of budget authority.

The president may seek to rescind budget authority whenever he determines that all or part of such authority will not be required to achieve the full objectives of a program, that a program is to be abolished, or that all or part of an annual appropriation should not be obligated. A rescission bill is legislation that cancels new budget authority or the availability of unobligated balances prior to the time when such authority would otherwise expire. Unless Congress passes the measure within forty-five days of continuous session from the day the message is received, the budget authority must be made available for obligation. Most rescissions spring from policy reasons and would reorient public priorities as established by earlier legislation. Congress may rescind all, part, or none of the amount proposed by the president.

Many deferrals are necessary because of the clear intention of Congress that funds not be used until some other specific actions are taken or certain conditions become evident. Deferrals must be submitted to Congress whenever executive judgment effectively precludes the obligation of budget authority for a limited period of time. They are intended to be a management tool and not a policy-making instrument. Thus, most are routinely approved by congressional inaction, but the authority to defer may not extend beyond the fiscal year in which the message requesting it is transmitted to Congress. Deferrals may only be overturned by an act of Congress and the common practice is to insert provisions in appropriations acts that disapprove them. Should it be determined that a deferred amount will not be necessary to fulfill the purposes of an appropriation, it can be resubmitted to Congress as a rescission.

The primary purpose of these procedures is to identify those areas or actions where major fiscal or programmatic differences exist between the legislative and executive branches. This is accomplished by comptroller general review at the second stage of the impoundment process, which follows presidential recommendations and precedes congressional decisions. A copy of each impoundment proposal must be sent to the comptroller general who, after examining it, informs Congress of its validity and probable effect. Should the executive either submit an invalid message or fail to proceed in accordance with congressional action on a valid one, the comptroller general is authorized to file suit to make the budget authority available for obligation. It is also the comptroller general's responsibility to report undisclosed rescissions and deferrals as well as notify

Congress when an impoundment has been misclassified. In the former case, such a communication is treated as if submitted by the executive, and in the latter, it nullifies the process initiated by the prior presidential message and triggers the appropriate congressional review mechanism. See figure 15 for key steps in the formation of a budget.

Executive Action
1. OMB issues guidance to agencies on the material to be developed for spring planning review (April)
2. Presidential advisers analyze general economic conditions and chart overall fiscal policy (May)
3. OMB transmits technical instructions to agencies for preparation of budget estimates and conformance with aggregate policy (June)
4. OMB reviews agency budget requests and prepares recommendations for the president (Sept.-Nov.)
5. President finalizes budget estimates and policies (Dec.)
6. OMB informs agencies of presidential decisions and prepares budget documents (Dec.)
7. Executive budget is submitted to Congress the first Monday after January 3

Congressional Action
8. Budget committees review the executive budget in hearings and deliberations (Jan.-Feb.)
9. CBO submits its Annual Report to the budget committees by February 15
10. Standing committees submit their Views and Estimates to the budget committees by February 25
11. Senate Budget Committee reports a budget resolution by April 1*
12. Congress completes action on the budget resolution by April 15*
13. Annual appropriation bills may be considered in the House as of May 15
14. House Appropriations Committee reports last annual appropriations bill by June 10
15. Congress completes action on reconciliation legislation by June 15*
16. House completes action on annual appropriation bills by June 30*
17. Fiscal year begins on October 1 and a continuing resolution is enacted if action on appropriation bills is incomplete*

Subsequent Action
18. Apportionments and allotments
19. Reprogrammings and transfers
20. Supplementals and impoundments*
21. Obligations and outlays

---

*Indicates steps that may or usually involve roll-call votes.

Fig. 15. Key steps and decision points in the formation of a budget.

DOCUMENTATION

OVERVIEW

The federal budget is neither established by a single act of government nor contained in a single government document. It is the outcome of a continuous process and is comprised of several series of publications. Budget materials are not merely compilations and descriptions of statistical data, though they are replete with tables and graphs. This form of information serves to translate the text into figures that can illustrate or substantiate, emphasize or summarize, the narrative portions of the presentation. The budget is a combination of past, present, and planned transactions within a framework shaped by the economic climate, financial resources, and policy options.

The budget consists of two major types of funds. Federal funds are derived mainly from taxation and borrowing and are used as needed for the general purposes and daily expenses of government. Trust funds are accumulated principally from compulsory social insurance programs and must be used for stipulated purposes. This legal restriction or preference means that trust-fund programs need not compete with other governmental functions for public funds and ensures beneficiaries that financial assistance will be available as prescribed by law.

Perhaps the most informative approach to a discussion of the issues and choices that pervade budget documents is through the concept of controllability. The size, composition, and trend of the federal budget can all be explained to a greater or lesser degree in terms of this concept. Controllability is the capacity of Congress and the president to prescribe the proportion of budget authority or outlays that is subject to definite limits for a given fiscal year. A relatively uncontrollable amount refers to spending levels mandated by existing law or prior obligations and which can only be altered by new authorizing legislation. A relatively controllable figure denotes potential expenditures whose magnitude can be determined by current appropriations legislation.

An expenditure will tend to be less controllable if it is not subject to annual action by Congress, if the amount to be spent is open-ended and not set by law, if it has its own source of revenue that can be used without recourse to an authorization, and if it is subject to only one rather than all three of the authorization, appropriations, and budget processes. It is not necessarily more difficult to reduce an uncontrollable than a controllable amount. These terms do not describe what Congress can or may do, but merely distinguish between what has already been done by law and what remains to be done in pending budget authority for a fiscal year.

Uncontrollable outlays constitute approximately three-quarters of the budget, with the largest category composed of entitlement programs and the fastest growing category being interest payments on the public debt. A common feature of entitlements and interest is the need for a stable and long-term commitment by the government to people who voluntarily and involuntarily participate in federal programs versus the need for Congress to exert budget control in both the short and long run. Nearly 50 percent of the budget is composed of programs that are indexed to inflation. The indexing of federal expenditures has maintained the real value of benefits provided, but has also mandated continually increased outlays.

Another aspect of controllability relates to the timing of obligations and outlays. The level of budget authority enacted by Congress limits the amount of money that can be obligated in a particular year. However, funds appropriated one year might not be obligated until the next, with expenditures occurring a year or two later. Obligated balances can be carried forward indefinitely until the obligation is paid, even when the appropriation is made for a single year. The results in carryover balances, or the amount of budget authority not used during a fiscal year and which remains available for conversion into outlays at some time in the future. Since outlays may not occur until after a fiscal year has ended, the lack of congressional control over the timing of expenditures precludes control over the spending totals for any given year.

The difference between budget authority and outlays is one reason that the total amount of annual federal spending is not the same as the total amount that Congress appropriates each year. The annual federal balance sheet is the difference between the amount of money the government receives from taxes and other sources and the amount of money the government actually spends. In addition, the relationship between the budget authority appropriated and the outlays of all government entities depends on the spend-out rates for each appropriation. The amount of funds spent in a fiscal year depends on congressional and agency decisions made for the current year as well as prior years. A significant consequence is that a reduction in appropriations does not necessarily produce an equivalent decrease in outlays. Statements of outlays in a current budget document are only estimates of cash flow.

Though the accrual of carryover balances mainly accounts for this lack of control over outlays, the reasons for their existence may be either inadvertent or intentional. Inaccurate budget estimates for program needs, or the inability to spend funds as rapidly as anticipated owing to unforeseen conditions, result in unplanned carryover balances. Some funding methods enacted by Congress, especially the use of trust funds, where reserves are necessary to meet payments, require such balances. Another deliberate reason involves the practice of appropriating funds on a multiyear or indefinite basis, which provides for necessary executive flexibility and reduces the congressional workload.

While about three-fourths of the annual budget is legally uncontrollable, most of the remainder is politically uncontrollable. In addition, the budget increment, or the amount by which outlays increase each year, is also uncontrollable. Thus, by the time the budget process for a given fiscal year is begun, most of the options have been foreclosed by earlier decisions. Though uncontrollable expenditures are mandatory under prior action and controllable ones discretionary through current choices, this distinction does not imply that the latter are always more desirable than the former.

Congress has consciously created funding arrangements that limit its ability to control all budget items because of the undesirable effects such control would entail. Complete control of all budget funds would vastly increase the workload of Congress, deny discretion to administrative agencies, and negate commitments represented by prior decisions. It would preclude countless public and private entities from making long-range plans, increase costs because of stop-and-go financing, and contribute to social instability. Congress has willingly accepted a loss of budget control to pursue other values, such as efficiency, stability, and financial certainty. Perfect budget control is inconsistent with other goals that are as important, if not more so, from the standpoint of effective government.

The question of controllability is one of degree and the activities to which control is most appropriately applicable. Investments in ongoing programs and projects are sunken costs that can neither be recovered nor discontinued without wasting resources. They also represent moral commitments and generate political momentum which increase their immunity to reduction or dismantling. For reasons of both sound economics and policy effectiveness, expenditures should remain fairly stable in the short run. Fiscal discretion, though limited in any given year, can be applied to less controllable as well as more controllable policy areas if political and economic conditions foster cooperation between the executive and legislative branches.

Though the budget as a whole does not change substantially from year to year, significant variations can and do occur within categories where flexibility exists. While all decisions are made in the context of the annual budget cycle, many important choices which introduce gradual changes in priorities will affect the budget for several or an indefinite number of years. Examples of these multiyear budget decisions include changes in tax laws, program authorizations, entitlement programs, and capital projects.

An ideal budget document should enable a reader to differentiate between those economic conditions or factors over which government can exercise some control and those beyond its ability to regulate; to identify matters that policies can affect immediately and those that can vary only gradually over time; to ascertain the major policy options available to government, the implications of each, and their relationship to existing programs; to distinguish among proposed actions, the goals to be achieved by such actions, the reasons and justification for them, and the factual data related to each; and to assess the possible indirect effects of proposals. However, the lack of time and tools precludes an integrated review of all budget items and the formulation of an explicit value and expenditure hierarchy each year.

Different participants in the budget process have different information needs. This is the reason for the inclusion of crosswalks in budget documents. A crosswalk is any method for converting budgetary data from one classification scheme to another. Budgetary information may be presented in several ways: by program goal, expenditure type, organizational unit, or object purchased. Federal budget structure is organized by function for fiscal purposes and by agency for appropriations purposes. Functional categories cover program goals and expenditure types, while agency schemes delineate units and objects. The multitude of budget documents is intended to enhance the quality of debate, disclose political commitments, facilitate policy control, and promote financial accountability. For the major publications, the key questions are what information to include, which points to emphasize, the validity of assumptions, and the credibility of projections. See figures 16 and 17 for categories of the federal budget.

The following discussion of budget publications is organized into three parts: the presidential budget, the congressional budget, and budget implementation. This entails a basically, but not strictly, chronological approach. Deviations from strict chronology are due to the fact that some documents are issued within a given time period rather than on a specific date, while others may appear at any time. A survey of budget texts is also affected by three overlapping phases of activity: that of budget formulation for the coming fiscal year and budget implementation for the current fiscal year; that of presidential and

Budget Functions	Agencies
National Defense	Defense Department
International Affairs	Defense, State and Treasury Departments
General Science, Space, and Technology	Energy Department, National Aeronautics and Space Administration
Energy	Energy Department, Tennessee Valley Authority
Natural Resources and Environment	Agriculture and Interior Departments, Environmental Protection Agency
Agriculture	Agriculture Department
Commerce and Housing Credit	Commerce Department, Postal Service, Federal Trade Commission
Transportation	Transportation Department, Interstate Commerce Commission
Community and Regional Development	Housing and Urban Development Department, Small Business Administration
Education, Training, Employment, and Social Services	Education, Health and Human Services, Labor Departments
Health	Health and Human Services and Labor Departments
Medicare	Health and Human Services Department
Income Security	Health and Human Services and Labor Departments
Social Security	Health and Human Services Department
Veterans Benefits and Services	Veterans Administration
Administration of Justice	Justice Department, Court System
General Government	Congress, General Services Administration, Office of Personnel Management
General Purpose Fiscal Assistance	Treasury Department
Interest	Treasury Department
Allowances (contingency funds)	
Undistributed Offsetting Receipts (miscellaneous transactions)	

Fig. 16. Functional categories of the federal budget correlated with major federal agencies.

National Defense. Outlays for military and civilian personnel, operating costs, weapons procurement, research and development, and military construction.

Entitlements and Other Mandatory Spending. Programs in which spending is governed by a law making all who meet their requirements eligible to receive payments. Subcategories are:

> **Health Care.** Includes outlays for Medicare and for the federal share of Medicaid expenditures.
>
> **Social Security and Other Retirement and Disability Programs.** Includes old-age, survivors, and disability benefits under Social Security, as well as other federally financed retirement and disability programs, including federal civil service and military retirement and disability programs, veterans' pensions and compensation, and Supplemental Security Income.
>
> **Other Entitlements and Mandatory Spending.** - Entitlements and other mandatory spending not included above. Major examples are: non-means-tested or partially means-tested benefits such as Unemployment Insurance and child nutrition; means-tested benefits such as Food Stamps and Aid to Families with Dependent Children; certain state and local grants such as the Social Services Block Grant; and agricultural price supports.

Nondefense Discretionary Spending. All nondefense programs for which spending is determined by annual appropriations, or by loan or obligation limits imposed in appropriation acts. The basic governmental legislative, judicial, and tax-collecting functions are included. A large part of this category represents the salary and expense accounts that finance the ongoing operations of the civilian agencies of government. Most grants to state and local governments (other than for benefit payments) and nondefense research and development are also in this category.

Net Interest. Interest payments on the federal debt, less interest received by trust funds and other interest payments to the federal government.

Offsetting Receipts. Proprietary receipts from the public and the employer share of employee retirement. Other receipts (for example, foreign military sales, trust fund receipts, and payments to trust funds) appropriately netted against outlays are included in the relevant categories above.

Fig. 17. Federal spending categories.

congressional actions concerning budget formulation or implementation; and that of the authorization, appropriations, and budget processes within Congress. The entire process for a single fiscal year actually extends over three years from the time agencies formulate their initial requests until final audits are completed.

PRESIDENTIAL BUDGET

1. *Budget of the United States Government* and *Supplement*. These two documents contain the president's budget message and an exposition of the proposals that form his budget policy. The budget message offers an overview of purposes and programs in the context of existing constraints and commitments. The executive budget proper presents aggregate estimates for appropriate levels of budget authority, outlays, revenues, surplus or deficit, and public debt. These figures are accompanied by detailed explanations and supporting data. Information on revenues and debt also includes recommendations for changes in existing law. It is this account that is of primary interest to the House and Senate Budget Committees as they formulate a budget resolution.

The heart of the budget is composed of twenty-one functional categories covering almost all programs and activities of the federal government. Functional categories array budgetary information according to major governmental purpose. Each federal activity is classified only under the function that corresponds to its paramount objective, though it may apply to others. Functional totals, which aggregate authorized expenditures by principal policy area irrespective of agency jurisdiction, provide officials with a useful survey of federal programs as a means of assessing current priorities. Information on the legislative and judicial branches, though included in the presidential budget, is simply incorporated to present a complete statement of budget policy and is not subject to executive discretion.

The figures for requested budget authority and estimated outlays for each function are presented in terms of national needs, agency missions, and major programs. National needs are the ultimate purposes for which funds are expended regardless of the means used. Agency missions are those responsibilities for meeting national needs assigned to particular units. Major programs are the legislative and executive means for accomplishing agency missions. Expenditures for each function may be broadly divided into those financing the delivery of public goods and services, the distribution of subsidies, and the disbursement of transfer payments. The first is intended to acquire the labor and materials directly used in the production of such goods; the second is intended to promote some public objective by reducing prevailing market costs for certain private entities; and the last is intended to provide recipients with a level of income they otherwise could not attain.

The totals for each function reflect budget estimates for each federal agency as approved by the president and his advisers. This is the spending authority the executive considers necessary to administer the programs already authorized plus any additions or reductions recommended for legislative approval. Also included are final budget figures for the last completed fiscal year and a discussion of the differences between the actual and estimated uncontrollable outlays by major program and revenues by major sources. In addition to the review of an earlier budget, there is a preview of future budgets. The economic assumptions and demographic trends that affect the long-range budget outlook are described and analyzed. Five-year projections of budget authority and outlays covering the coming fiscal year and the four following years are part of this forecast. A complete list of programs by agency complements the functional classification, to which it is cross-referenced, and serves as an introduction to the next volume of the presidential budget.

2. *Budget of the United States Government—Appendix.* This document presents detailed budget estimates arranged by agency and appropriation account, which is a designated fund established in the Treasury for authorized financial transactions. Included for each agency are budget data for each account, the proposed text of appropriations language, explanations of the work to be performed and the funds needed, and descriptions of new legislative proposals. The authorizing legislation for each program is cited and the last three digits of the OMB identification code for each program refer to its functional category. This information provides the most elaborate survey of governmental activities that exists in a single volume. The organization of data in the *Appendix* facilitates the preparation of appropriations bills and the exercise of funding control.

The basic building blocks of data in this document are the Program and Financing Schedules and the Object Classification Schedules. The former consists of a program section that lists obligations classified by activities or projects, and a financing section that cites the sources of funds available to meet obligations. Object classification identifies financial transactions by the nature of the goods or services purchased, regardless of the purpose of the program for which they are used. This format subdivides the budget into more manageable units that enable political participants and other interested parties to focus more clearly on particular areas of responsibility or concern.

An inventory of supplemental appropriations, budget rescissions, and budget amendments transmitted to Congress for the current fiscal year also appears. These presidential proposals are organized and presented as are the detailed budget estimates. They are also identified by House and Senate document number for those who wish to consult their complete text. These messages cover unanticipated developments that affect the budget and matters on which there may be a divergence between executive and legislative priorities. This mass of data, when used selectively, can clarify or supplement narrative or numerical statements in other budget documents. Both the *Budget* and *Appendix* have an extensive subject index.

3. *Special Analyses—Budget of the United States Government.* This document focuses on matters that cannot be adequately covered under either the functional or agency scheme. A separate volume that consolidates such information is of much value because many topics that are important for understanding budget policy apply to matters that embrace several agencies or programs.

Two alternative views of the federal budget are included. The Current Services Budget presents budget authority and outlays for the coming fiscal year based on the assumption that all programs and activities will continue at the same level as for the fiscal year in progress. These estimates do not reflect increases or decreases that are due to policy changes and provide a basis for identifying and analyzing such changes as recommended in the *Budget of the United States Government*. Budget policy changes include proposed legislation and appropriations for uncontrollable expenditures and augmented or reduced outlays for controllable programs. The National Income and Product Accounts (NIA) of the United States is an attempt to fashion a purely economic document that reflects the impact of federal sector transactions on aggregate economic activity. The NIA, in contrast with the *Budget of the United States Government*, uses gross rather than net figures and covers matters excluded by law from the federal budget.

Other parts of this volume present analyses of certain financial activities of the federal government that affect the economy. Among the more important of these are borrowing, credit programs, tax expenditures, and aid to state and local governments. The perspectives on the federal budget in this publication highlight the numerous ways in which public finance interacts with private enterprise and underscores the complexity of the relationship.

4. *United States Budget in Brief.* This is an abridged version of the *Budget of the United States Government*. Its concise format and nontechnical explanations are designed to inform members of the general public about the financial performance of the federal government.

5. *Historical Tables, Budget of the United States Government.* This volume provides data on budget receipts, outlays, surpluses or deficits, and federal debt that covers extended periods of time. The tables include various combinations of budget components and relate them to each other, to numerous economic factors, and to the gross national product. Figures for earlier years have been revised to be consistent with the current year presentation so that the data series are comparable over time.

6. *Management of the United States Government.* This volume contains the president's management message and discusses the goals and strategies of the president's Management Improvement Program. Its focus is on the efficiency of agency operations in terms of financial management and staff productivity. Also included is a discussion of the role that Congress plays in this area and of specific legislative actions that affect administrative performance.

7. *Supplemental Summary.* This is an update of the *Budget of the United States Government* and is submitted to Congress in July. It incorporates all revisions recommended by the president since January and provides an opportunity to explain and justify changes to his original proposals in view of evolving economic or other conditions. The figures in this document supersede earlier estimates and are discussed in terms of the overall budget outlook and each functional category.

8. Budget Amendments. These proposals may be submitted to Congress by the president at any time prior to the completion of legislative action on the budget for the coming fiscal year. They may either raise or reduce the original estimates, and those which are pending are incorporated into the *Supplemental Summary*. When budget amendments are transmitted or identified separately, they are cross-referenced to the pertinent page of the *Appendix*. The reasons for an amendment and its amount are always included.

9. *Economic Report of the President*. This document, also forwarded to Congress each January, complements the *Budget of the United States Government*. It discusses economic factors from a perspective that transcends the annual budget cycle and examines matters that the budget can influence only marginally, if at all. The *Report* describes the current state of the economy more comprehensively than does the executive budget and more closely relates the implications of proposed fiscal policies to economic conditions and trends. It also contains recommendations for the Federal Reserve Board on the monetary policy that would reinforce the administration's fiscal initiatives. The focus is on economic growth as measured by the annual rate of increase in the gross national product.

Numbers 1, 2, 7, 8, and 9 are issued as both executive branch publications and House documents. All of them are noted in the *Weekly Compilation of Presidential Documents* and are indexed in the *Monthly Catalog*.

CONGRESSIONAL BUDGET

The large number of congressional budget publications can be more conveniently discussed by dividing the congressional budget process into three stages.

INFORMATION GATHERING AND ANALYSIS

1. Budget Committee Hearings. These volumes contain testimony presented by key presidential advisers, members of Congress, the director of the Congressional Budget Office, and economists from the labor and business communities, as well as representatives of public interest groups. This information alerts the panels to some of the major issues as seen by other interested parties and serves to convey views that may have received little attention in the executive branch.

2. *Annual Report* of the Congressional Budget Office. This document is usually issued in two parts. The first presents a general discussion of the economic and budget outlook and provides an overview of the relationship between fiscal policy and economic conditions. The second focuses directly on major budget issues and available policy options for addressing them.

3. *An Analysis of the President's Budgetary Proposals.* This volume, also prepared by the CBO, examines the economic implications of the president's fiscal policy and explicitly contrasts executive assumptions and projections with those of the CBO. It also assesses the administration's policy proposals in light of any legislative action on similar or related measures.

4. Committee Views and Estimates. Though the format of these reports is not uniform, the information conveyed corresponds to the discussion of major programs in the *Budget of the United States Government.* In the House these accounts are compiled and issued as a budget committee print, while in the Senate they appear as part of the budget committee's report on the budget resolution.

5. Federal Reserve Board Reports to Congress. These reports, delivered in February and July, contain a discussion of the economic factors that shape monetary policy and influence the course of economic activity. This covers a recapitulation of the board's previously announced objectives as well as a review of their attainment and appropriateness. Their content also contributes to an evaluation of the interaction and coordination of monetary and fiscal policies. Both reports are issued as nonlegislative committee reports of either the Senate or House Banking Committee.

6. *Joint Economic Report.* Prepared and issued by the Joint Economic Committee, this document serves as an explicit reply to the *Economic Report of the President.* This report, in conjunction with 3 above, provides a comparison of executive and legislative perspectives and priorities in regard to the economic and political basis of the budget resolution. It appears approximately two months after the presidential budget is submitted to Congress and takes the form of a committee report.

These six publications are indexed in both the *Monthly Catalog* and *CIS/Index.*

CONCURRENT RESOLUTION ON THE BUDGET

1. Committee Reports. The reports of the House and Senate budget panels are the congressional response and counterparts to the *Budget of the United States Government.* Each report presents the text of its proposed resolution; compares the committee's revenue, budget authority, and outlay estimates with those of the presidential budget; contains three-year budget projections; proposes an allocation of the recommended level of revenues by major source and includes tax expenditure estimates by budget function; explains the economic assumptions and objectives that underlie the resolution; and discusses the information on which the amounts in the resolution were based and the relationship of such figures to other budget components. If the provisions of the most recently adopted budget resolution have been rendered impractical by

economic developments, the reports serve as a means to submit revised versions for approval.

Both budget committee reports also include an analysis of figures for each functional category. These presentations begin with the CBO baseline and proceed with an explanation of the economic and financial assumptions that underpin panel recommendations. Information about the amount of credit approved for each function is also included. A discussion of enforcement procedures, which primarily covers reconciliation instructions, completes the substantive aspects of each report. The House committee document contains a concise account of each budget function that includes a narrative description, notes all subfunctions, and identifies major programs and agencies. The Senate committee report contains a record of all roll-call votes taken by the panel, including the motion voted on, by whom proposed, and the names of those for and against.

2. The Resolution. This measure is composed of several parts. First come aggregate figures for revenues and the amount by which they should be increased or decreased, total new budget authority, budget outlays, direct loan obligations, primary loan guarantee commitments, the budget surplus or deficit, and the level of public debt. Next are functional totals for new budget authority, budget outlays, direct loan obligations, and primary loan guarantee commitments. Following the budget figures are mandates covering reconciliation and other procedural requirements. Finally, there are miscellaneous provisions regarding certain budgetary transactions that are singled out for special, but not necessarily favorable, treatment.

3. Floor Debate. Some special rules govern the chamber consideration of budget resolutions. These relate to the length of time allotted for action and the nature of amendments. Their purpose is to prevent unwarranted delay and ensure fiscal responsibility.

4. Conference Report. This document, which reconciles the differences between the House and Senate versions of the budget resolution, contains the full text of the measure. It also allocates expenditure totals among the authorizing and appropriations panels in each house because the functional categories of the budget overlap the jurisdictions of the standing committees.

5. Reconciliation Bill. When reconciliation involves more than a single committee in either chamber, the proposal and its accompanying report are issued by the Budget Committee. As with the budget resolution, some special rules apply to floor proceedings on this measure.

6. Congressional Budget Office Update. This report, formally entitled *The Economic and Budget Outlook: An Update*, is usually issued in August. It includes updated economic data and revisions of budget baseline figures affected by congressional action. Also presented are reestimates of federal receipts and outlays to reflect changing economic conditions.

It can be usefully compared with the *Supplemental Summary*, or presidential update, that appears in July.

Numbers 1, 4, 6, and the reports under 5 are indexed in the *Monthly Catalog* and *CIS/Index*. Numbers 2 and 3 appear in the *Congressional Record*. Since the reconciliation bill becomes a public law, it can be traced as described in chapter 8.

SPENDING AND REVENUE LEGISLATION

1. Hearings, Bills, and Reports. The actions and documents of the Appropriations, House Ways and Means, and Senate Finance Committees are covered by the description and analysis of chapters 4 through 8. Transfers are identified separately in all bills and reports issued by the appropriations committees. That part of printed appropriations hearings which contains each agency's budget request includes a schedule of appropriation accounts for that agency. The Joint Committee on Taxation, which serves as a research arm of the Ways and Means and Finance Committees, regularly issues analyses of proposed revenue measures that appear as committee prints.

2. Scorekeeping Reports. Following passage of the budget resolution, the CBO periodically issues these surveys, which tabulate congressional budget actions for a given fiscal year. They inform Congress of the status of its budget and of the estimated effects of enacted and pending legislation on the budget authority and outlay levels set in the most recent budget resolution. The two major parts of these reports array data by functional category and congressional committee. The final issue for a fiscal year includes a list of major changes in the presidential budget, by program, affected by legislative action.

3. *Appropriations, Budget Estimates, Etc.* This is a massive volume issued at the end of each session of Congress and printed as a Senate document. Most of it is devoted to the text of legislation passed during the session that granted budget authority. One section contains a detailed comparison of executive budget estimates, as presented in the *Appendix*, with the appropriations enacted by Congress. It also includes status reports on all rescissions and deferrals, though this information relates to the next stage of the budget process.

Number 2 is indexed in the *Monthly Catalog* and *CIS/Index*, while 3 can only be identified through the former.

BUDGET IMPLEMENTATION

1. Supplemental Appropriations. These proposals originate in the executive branch and legislative action is initiated by a presidential message submitted to Congress and referred to the appropriations committees. Each message includes the reason for the request, the amount requested for each agency, proposed appropriations language, and a cross-reference to the appropriate page of the *Appendix*.

2. Rescission Bills. These measures originate in the same manner as supplementals. Each message contains the amount of budget authority involved, the agency affected, a discussion of factors that justify each action, the estimated budgetary and programmatic effects, and a statement of whether it was proposed as an earlier deferral. The OMB identification code enables this information to be correlated with its relevant functional category and appropriation account.

3. Deferrals. These are transmitted to Congress as are proposed rescissions and both are frequently combined in a single document and contain the same information for each. When rescission or deferral messages identify the amount of funds appropriated in excess of executive requests, this indicates that the president is attempting to revive fiscal policy that Congress, through the appropriations process, has rejected.

4. Cumulative Reports. The OMB compiles and consolidates all information on rescissions and deferrals for the current fiscal year and transmits this data to Congress by the tenth day of each month. This communication notes the status of all proposed impoundments, including the date and description of legislative actions.

5. Comptroller General Reports. These reports to Congress review the accuracy of presidential impoundment messages and executive compliance with legislative action on such proposals. The cover page of these publications identifies the House or Senate document number assigned to the message being reviewed. Except where executive action is deemed improper or statements incomplete, the document merely describes the proposed impoundment and verifies the validity of the message without commenting on its substance.

6. *Decisions of the Comptroller General of the United States.* Numerous questions about the legality of government expenditures arise during the daily performance of agency responsibilities. Conclusive answers are needed to certify the validity of individual payments to program beneficiaries or verify the propriety of program outlays for goods and services. Such matters apply to the scope of authority granted to agencies by legislation and the conditions under which agencies may obligate and spend appropriated funds. When a problem is referred to the comptroller general for an opinion, the ruling is binding on the agency, but not on Congress or the courts. *Decisions* are published in monthly pamphlets and cumulated in annual volumes.

7. General Accounting Office Reports. The GAO is continually engaged in reviewing the financial performance of federal agencies. These audits cover all practices that affect the flow of public funds, including their receipt, management, and disbursement. Specific questions addressed are the reasonableness of obligations incurred or expenditures made and the cost, quality, or need for the goods or services provided or procured.

8. Presidential Vetoes. The president may veto appropriation and revenue bills on either fiscal or programmatic grounds. If Congress is still in session a message stating his reasons for disapproval is sent to the body of origin. Should the veto not be overridden, another bill modified to meet presidential objections may be passed at the same or a subsequent session. See chapters 2 and 8 for information on vetoed bills and accompanying messages.

9. *United States Government Annual Report* and *Appendix*. These two documents, prepared by the Financial Management Service of the Treasury Department are the official publications of receipts and outlays of the federal government. All other reports issued by any federal entity that contain similar data must be in agreement with the figures stated in the *Annual Report* and *Appendix*. They are used by the Congressional Budget Office to serve the needs of Congress, by the Office of Management and Budget to review the president's proposed budget, by the General Accounting Office to perform its audit activities, by the various agencies of government to reconcile their accounts, and by the general public to judge the performance of its government.

    The *Annual Report* proper summarizes the government's cash-basis financial position and results of operations. It presents selected data maintained in the central accounts based on information provided by federal agencies and Federal Reserve Banks. The *Appendix* contains the data that support the information in the *Annual Report*. Its most informative subdivision for budget purposes is part 3: Details of Appropriations, Outlays, and Balances. Arranged by organizational unit, it tabulates the budgetary elements of outlay accounts, which indicate the transactions that affect the budget surplus or deficit. Its index enables one to quickly ascertain the financial status of any agency or program.

Numbers 1 to 5 are printed as House or Senate documents; 1 to 4 and 8 also appear in the *Weekly Compilation of Presidential Documents*, while the information in 2 to 4 is also provided in the *Federal Register*. Number 4 identifies those issues of the *Federal Register* in which the information conveyed by 2 and 3 is included. Congressional action on numbers 1, 2, and 8 involve the entire legislative process. Numbers 1 to 5 are referred to the Senate or House Appropriations Committee for information or action. Appropriations committee reports on numbers 1 to 3 identify the Senate or House document number assigned to the message that prompted legislative action. See chapter 3 for further information on number 7. All budget implementation publications are indexed in the *Monthly Catalog*.

BACKGROUND MATERIAL

1. Joint Economic Committee. This panel, which has no legislative jurisdiction, was created to conduct continuing studies of national economic conditions and policies. Its analyses and inquiries cover all aspects of the performance of the economy and the economic role of government. The bulk of information collected and conveyed by the committee appears in its printed hearings.

2. Congressional Budget Office. Studies by this unit may focus on the budget under consideration, the impact of earlier budgetary decisions, the prospects for certain budget options, or the analysis of budgetary practices. This research may appear as committee prints of the Senate or House Budget Committee or as separate CBO reports designated as background papers or staff working papers.

3. Federal Reserve Board. The *Annual Report* of the Board of Governors mainly consists of a condensed, though complete, version of the discussions held during its regularly scheduled policy meetings. This information provides a concise overview of economic conditions and reveals the rationale for policy decisions.

Numbers 1 and 2 are indexed in both the *Monthly Catalog* and *CIS/Index*, while 3 can only be located through the former.

REFERENCES

Bach, G. L. *Making Monetary and Fiscal Policy.* Washington, D.C.: The Brookings Institution, 1971.

Fisher, Louis. *Presidential Spending Power.* Princeton, N.J.: Princeton University Press, 1975.

Ippolito, Dennis S. *The Budget and National Politics.* San Francisco: W. H. Freeman, 1978.

LeLoup, Lance T. *Budgetary Politics.* Brunswick, Ohio: King's Court Communications, 1977.

Lynch, Thomas D. *Public Budgeting in America.* 2nd ed. Englewood Cliffs, N.J.: Prentice-Hall, 1985.

Ott, David J., and Attiat F. Ott. *Federal Budget Policy.* 3rd ed. Washington, D.C.: The Brookings Institution, 1977.

Pierce, Lawrence C. *The Politics of Fiscal Policy Formation.* Pacific Palisades, Calif.: Goodyear, 1971.

Schick, Allen. *Congress and Money.* Washington, D.C.: The Urban Institute, 1980.

U.S. Board of Governors of the Federal Reserve System. *The Federal Reserve System: Purposes & Functions.* 7th ed. Washington, D.C.: Federal Reserve Board, 1984.

U.S. Congress. House. Committee of Conference. *Increasing the Statutory Limit on the Public Debt.* House Report No. 99-433, 99th Congress, 1st Session. Washington, D.C.: U.S. Government Printing Office, 1985.

U.S. Congress. House. Committee on the Budget. *The Congressional Budget Process: A General Explanation.* Committee Print, 99th Congress, 2nd Session. Washington, D.C.: U.S. Government Printing Office, 1986.

U.S. Congress. House. Committee on the Budget. *Congressional Control of Expenditures.* Committee Print, 95th Congress, 1st Session. Washington, D.C.: U.S. Government Printing Office, 1977.

U.S. Congress. Senate. Committee on the Budget. *Gramm-Rudman-Hollings and the Congressional Budget Process: An Explanation.* Committee Print, 99th Congress, 1st Session. Washington, D.C.: U.S. Government Printing Office, 1985.

U.S. Congressional Research Service. *Manual on the Federal Budget Process.* Report No. 87-286 GOV. Washington, D.C.: Congressional Research Service, 1987.

U.S. General Accounting Office. *A Glossary of Terms Used in the Federal Budget Process.* 3rd ed. Washington, D.C.: General Accounting Office, 1981.

U.S. General Accounting Office. *Principles of Federal Appropriations Law.* Washington, D.C.: General Accounting Office, 1982.

U.S. Office of Management and Budget. *Instructions on Budget Execution.* Circular No. A-34. Washington, D.C.: Office of Management and Budget, 1985.

U.S. Office of Management and Budget. *Preparation and Submission of Budget Estimates.* Circular No. A-11. Washington, D.C.: Office of Management and Budget, 1987.

Wildavsky, Aaron. *The Politics of the Budgetary Process.* 4th ed. Boston: Little, Brown, 1984.

Woolley, John T. *Monetary Politics.* Cambridge, England: Cambridge University Press, 1984.

Wrightsman, Dwayne. *An Introduction to Monetary Theory and Policy.* 3rd ed. New York: The Free Press, 1983.

11

United States Treaties

In general terms, a treaty is a formal agreement between or among nations to establish, modify, or terminate mutual privileges or reciprocal obligtions. It entails an external commitment to a foreign signatory and an internal responsibility for its enforcement. Though treaties are a form of domestic law, their international dimension affords greater latitude for official discretion than does the legislative process. The absence of prescribed time limits and unsettled standing of governmental precedents significantly affect treaty publications. The impact of these factors is noted at various points throughout the discussion and is more thoroughly treated in reference to sources that can be consulted to determine the status of treaties.

In the sphere of international relations, the term *treaty* applies to binding international agreements. The term *executive agreement* is one of domestic United States law only. However, because executive agreements are binding international compacts, they are considered treaties in international terminology. The major criteria for a binding international agreement are that the parties must intend it to be legally mandatory under international law; it should address significant matters, such as political commitments, a substantial amount of funds, or some form of continuing cooperation; it should clearly and specifically describe the obligations to be assumed. Though form is also a relevant factor, content and context are more decisive.

Under international norms, a treaty is an international agreement concluded between nations in written form and governed by certain standards of international law. This definition excludes agreements that are regulated exclusively by domestic law or that are not intended to create legal relations. For the United States, any international compact submitted by the president to the Senate for its approval, whether designated a treaty, convention, agreement, accord, articles, protocol, or otherwise, is a treaty. Other parties to such covenants do not necessarily recognize the difference between those formally considered as treaties under the U.S. Constitution and those that are not. This is because they assume that the international obligation, regardless of the form, will be fulfilled.

The Senate's constitutional authority to advise and consent refers to its action on a treaty submitted to it by the president after it has been negotiated but before it has been ratified. Though this is probably a more limited responsibility than originally intended, the basic functions of the Senate remain intact. They are to protect the rights of the states and prevent imprudent ventures by the president. These obligations complement presidential participation, which provides for national unity and governmental efficiency. In the international sphere, the legislative branch was expected to monitor the plans and course of the executive branch.

The first part of this chapter describes the general environment of American foreign policymaking. A combination of policy components, public duties, and procedural options shapes the political framework of treaty proceedings. The second part presents a detailed account of the treatymaking process as reflected in the roles of the president and the Senate. Emphasis is given to legal and political powers and limits at each stage of action. The final part surveys the textual trail formed by the numerous factors that produce a treaty. It covers the issuance, flow, and availability of documents that affect content and interpretation and publications that facilitate identification and location.

FOREIGN POLICY CONTEXT

ELEMENTS

Foreign policy may be defined in terms of principles, purposes, or practices. The first version consists of moral premises that serve as standards against which the decisions of policymakers may be judged. The second is comprised of those external objectives for which the United States is prepared to commit its resources. The third refers to relationships that have evolved between this country and the international community in general and other nations in particular. A definition that synthesizes these perspectives is the formal and authoritative expression of the national interest through diplomatic methods and constitutional procedures.

The national interest is a concept that nations apply as they try to influence the global arena to their advantage. It entails an effort to arrange an external environment for the nation that will enable the domestic society to preserve its basic values and achieve its primary goals. The essential features of any national interest are physical security, political autonomy, and economic viability. The conception of national welfare that prevails at any given time profoundly affects the design of foreign policy. Its content must be realistically based on a country's international power as measured by its capacity to mobilize resources, determination to pursue goals, and a comparison with other nations to do the same.

Diplomacy denotes the instruments and procedures used by nations to transact official business among themselves while at peace. It is the management of external affairs through the process of political negotiation. The key aims of diplomacy are the prevention or settlement of international disputes and maintenance of harmonious relations. Proficient diplomatic performance ensures that daily decisions conform as nearly as possible to the goals and priorities of a nation's global agenda. The continuous exchange of information that characterizes this endeavor represents an attempt to accommodate and integrate a nation's foreign policy with that of other nations.

Each nation simultaneously pursues several foreign policies depending on historical developments that have molded patterns of interaction between it and other international entities. From one standpoint a nation may seek to maximize its power for the purpose of national security. This approach stresses military and economic resources and applies to actual and potential adversaries. Another type of policy involves increased cooperation to enhance collective security. The essence of this course is international coordination and organization and pertains to allies and patrons. One other option is to offer or deny assistance as a means of exerting influence. Such conduct manifests conciliation or condemnation and is usually aimed at nonaligned nations.

The substantive areas of foreign policy include military affairs, alliance and assistance, trade and taxation, international arbitration and organizations, environmental and population problems, immigration and naturalization, transportation and travel, diplomatic and consular questions, and international law. This last category covers a body of rules considered legally binding by parties who pledge to comply with them. To advance their interests nations often agree to observe specified procedures or incur certain obligations. Increased international endeavor is an inescapable consequence of the impact of foreign developments on national issues and the effect of domestic policy on global matters.

Foreign policy may address major international issues, the role of international organizations, regions of the world, or individual nations. In regard to any given country or organization, it may be cooperative, competitive, or conflicting. Its underlying motivation may be traced to industrial development, nationalism, resource constraints, or ideology. It may be pursued through political, economic, military, or cultural means. Its conduct must be sufficiently flexible to modify strategies and devise innovations in response to changing conditions and in reaction to existing policies. Effective foreign policy requires comprehensive planning and continuous adaptation as well as continuity in the consistent pursuit of stable goals.

The U.S. stance in world affairs is most conspicuously revealed by the major alliances it has formed or joined. An alliance is an agreement between two or more nations to promote their common interests by collaborating to improve their power position. These relationships constitute the nucleus of foreign policy and chiefly account for its continuity and stability. Though such arrangements are established through treaties, formal documents can only outline types of cooperation and state general objectives. Actual means and specific ends must be educed from the observation and analysis of international conduct.

Unilateral commitments or declarations of intent may become binding international agreements when two or more nations pursue parallel courses. Though such action is technically unilateral in form, in effect it constitutes a bilateral or multilateral agreement. Nations may also conclude nonbinding agreements to maintain their political flexibility. They can be used to express broad policy guidelines that are subject to change without notice. This conduct may also represent a propaganda ploy that enables a party to declare support for a policy that it has no intention of following. Such a course also permits heads of state to make commitments intended to be honored, but without the need to observe cumbersome constitutional requirements or numerous procedural formalities.

National action in the international arena may be unilateral, bilateral, or multilateral. The first course offers the greatest latitude, but also risks the most opposition. The last option assures wider support, but generally entails a diluted product. A series of bilateral compacts enables obligations to be clearly defined and well tailored to meet mutual needs. This route also avoids the potential antagonism or ostracism generated by unilateral tactics and the attentuated or ambiguous results necessitated by multilateral agreement. Though most treaties are bilateral, many of the more important ones are multilateral.

INTERESTS

Any question that may become the subject of international negotiation must be within the power of the federal government to address. The needs of national security and strains on international stability warrant wide discretion in the conduct of foreign affairs. Thus, in the sphere of external relations the United States asserts plenary powers derived from the imperative of self-preservation rather than from the Constitution. Issues of global concern demand a unified national voice and uniform governmental response. Information about foreign developments should be promptly collected and analyzed at some central office. These conditions and factors invite, if not compel, the president to assume a leadership position in foreign affairs, while the appropriate role for Congress remains uncertain. It is of little avail to invoke the Constitution because it is concerned with the distribution rather than the exercise of power.

The presidential role combines legal authority derived from the Constitution and political responsibility based on practice. His formal powers in foreign affairs stem from several constitutional provisions. The president's duty to execute the laws faithfully includes those that concern foreign policy and also covers the need to interpret and apply international law. As commander-in-chief, he may deploy the armed forces to protect U.S. security, citizens, or property. His power to receive foreign diplomats has been construed to include the prerogative to recognize foreign governments. The appointment of diplomatic officials and personal envoys enables him to manage the foreign affairs establishment and control communication with foreign governments. He possesses the authority to negotiate treaties, submit foreign policy proposals to Congress, and conclude other international agreements.

The political status of the presidency also confers a formidable array of powers on the incumbent. U.S. hegemony of the free world necessarily means the president is a world leader whose words are always accorded much weight. The office provides a forum from which to articulate national purposes regarding our participation in international activities. The incumbent has the capability to assert the existence of a crisis and the need to meet challenges to our national interest. That the office is always *in session* enables the president to act swiftly when circumstances demand an immediate response. The unitary structure of the office permits the president, acting within his sphere of authority, to seize the initiative and virtually compel the Congress to acquiesce.

Congress also possesses significant constitutional powers in the field of foreign affairs. These are its power of the purse, to regulate international commerce, to authorize and maintain the armed forces, to create agencies and prescribe functions, and to advise and consent to treaties and nominations. Its growing political influence is due to the erosion of clear boundaries between domestic and foreign matters. However, its decentralized structure, local constituencies, collegial decisionmaking, and political diversity combine to limit its foreign policy role. Despite these handicaps, Congress can assert its power regardless of presidential protest or resistance. Though not well equipped to articulate national interests or formulate foreign policy, it can propose alternatives and encourage debate.

In the realm of foreign affairs the president possesses final decisionmaking authority since his opposition virtually precludes action. In conjunction with his affirmative powers it is generally conceded that the president is in the best strategic position to design foreign policy. However, competing views of its expedience generate different conclusions as to the role Congress should fulfill. Legislative attitudes about relations with the executive branch regarding international affairs revolve around the question of consultation. Effective consultation requires meaningful and timely involvement of an appropriate group of legislators in the framing of significant foreign-policy decisions by the executive branch. The key questions are what constitutes consultation, which matters warrant consultation, whom and when to consult.

Congressional opinion on this subject generally falls into three categories. Some members believe that the executive branch should control foreign policy and do not expect much consultation. The acceptance of a passive role for Congress means that it should provide the necessary legislative support for presidential decisions. Other members prefer to closely monitor executive-branch action and favor later consultation for the purpose of evaluation. The independent and critical review entailed by this adversarial role is considered more consistent with the separation of powers and serves to minimize potentially arbitrary or imprudent action by the executive branch. There are those members who view foreign affairs as a joint responsibility of both branches and advocate consultation in the early stages of policymaking. This partnership role involves active cooperation in setting goals and priorities to overcome obstacles connected with the separation of powers. These views are not associated with stable groups of legislators, but depend on the degree of satisfaction with current policies.

Recourse to legislation as a means to compel executive consultation with members of Congress poses a thorny problem. Laws that shape foreign policy when global events are sudden and severe can create rather than abate difficulties. Yet in the absence of legislation Congress can exercise little control over the conduct of foreign affairs. The need is to exert congressional leverage without impeding necessary executive flexibility. The key issue is not whether to delegate authority, but how much discretion the president needs or should be granted in the field of foreign policy.

The need for coherence in foreign policy confers an advantage on the president regarding its formulation. Coherence is the adaptation of appropriate means to articulated ends. Its presence is essential to avoid international misjudgment or misgiving as well as to garner domestic support and assure sound application. As the producer and director in most foreign policy ventures, the president can argue that the failure of Congress to agree with him will hinder his ability to pursue American interests on the international scene. But this fact is also the source of congressional opportunity, since the president must tailor his initiatives to satisfy legislative preferences to deter a reaction that would impair his effectiveness. Congress must also weigh the consequences of contention, since legislative action alone often has little impact on foreign entities. Thus, coherence is a concern of both branches and demands compromise between them.

Increased consultation can foster improved interbranch relations and generate more advantageous policy options. It can help to focus attention on the substance of issues rather than the prerogatives of each branch. Such a course also requires more time and reduces prospects for maintaining confidentiality. Furthermore, it does not guarantee legislative support or assure that congressional advice will be heeded. Much foreign policy does not involve treaties or legislation and thus provides no incentive for the executive branch to consult with the legislative branch. Combined perceptions of global affairs and domestic politics ultimately determine the nature of consultation. Though international developments and political imperatives promote presidential dominance, congressional influence may range from minimal to substantial depending on executive-branch priorities, performance, and persuasiveness.

AVENUES

Foreign policy may be established or enunciated in oral form. This occurs when the president declares the attitudes and intentions of the United States in matters that concern other nations. With rare exceptions, international agreements negotiated to implement policy are promulgated in formal documents. Major compacts may be concluded as treaties, statutes, or executive agreements. The choice of methods is at the discretion of the president, who may seek or shun congressional advice. These options exist because the questions that may be addressed by each approach tend to overlap. Such factors as the type of commitment, substance of provisions, actual or likely effects, and the context of negotiation and implementation do not provide clear criteria for distinguishing among the types of international agreements or for determining when which should be preferred. The different forms have been used interchangeably, though they are not interchangeable on all occasions.

Treaties may be preliminary or procedural documents that contain principles or guidelines upon which substantive treaties are to be based. They are usually considered necessary or desirable when the subject matter has been traditionally embodied in a treaty or is not entirely within the constitutional powers of either Congress or the president, the force of law without legislation is desired or implementing legislation will be needed, major commitments affecting national security or international stability are involved, or maximum formality is preferred to emphasize the enduring and binding nature of the compact. A survey of international precedent and U.S. practice indicates that procedure is the only consistent and definite difference between treaties and other international agreements. They require Senate approval; otherwise their content and effect do not offer concrete grounds for legally differentiating them from other international compacts.

Senatorial advice and consent refers to action on a treaty transmitted by the president after it has been negotiated and signed. However, the Constitution does not partition the treatymaking process into two separate stages of presidential negotiation and senatorial approval. Senate consent authorizes the president to ratify it, though the Constitution makes no mention of ratification. Since the authority to make treaties is shared by the Senate and the president, such compacts can only be ratified by the last party to act. Thus, it is the president's signature concurring in the Senate's action that constitutes formal ratification. Though the act of ratification is a presidential prerogative, it cannot be executed unless the Senate approves by a two-thirds majority.

International agreements may also be incorporated in legislation. If the enactment should not embody a complete compact, it may authorize the president to negotiate and conclude agreements on particular subjects or to conclude particular agreements already negotiated. A statute that grants the president authority to proceed with such arrangements may prescribe the goals to be pursued, describe the terms considered acceptable, and specify the form. In some cases Congress may approve presidential agreements by subsequent legislation to meet our international obligations. The legislative route grants an equal role to the House of Representatives and simplifies the parliamentary process. A proposal can be submitted simultaneously to both houses, with approval and implementation combined in a single measure. International agreements embodied in legislation also eliminate questions about whether a compact is self-executing, which does not require implementing legislation, or not self-executing, which does require such action.

As a member of the family of nations, the United States is presumed to possess all the powers claimed by other nations, including the prerogative to enter into compacts that are neither treaties nor statutes. Unless expressly limited by the Constitution, treaty or statute, the president may act under his general diplomatic authority to conclude executive agreements. Most international compacts are forged by the president independently exercising the inherent constitutional power of his office. Executive agreements may be subsequently approved by treaty or legislation or Congress may prevent their implementation by enactment of or failure to enact legislation. These compacts may also be negotiated in accordance with a prior treaty or law. Such authorization may cover an individual agreement or a broad category of pacts. When the president proceeds under his sole constitutional authority, the results may be protocols that constitute a stage in the development of a treaty or a *modus vivendi*, which is intended to serve as a temporary substitute for one.

Among the many reasons for the use of executive agreements are to avoid legislative delay or disapproval, to assure secrecy or speed, to settle routine matters that do not involve issues of foreign policy or versions of the national interest, to make arrangements that do not obligate the nation or Congress, to form commitments which the president has complete power to fulfill, and to address conditions that are soon expected to change. Executive agreements can create a political commitment, but not necessarily a legal obligation in the absence of congressional action. The exception is an agreement, whether or not authorized by treaty or statute, to implement a treaty. In all other cases the question is how far the president may militarily or financially commit the United States through his unilateral action.

Legislation requires the executive branch to submit all international agreements other than treaties, to which the United States is a party, to Congress no later than sixty days after they have gone into effect. If such agreements are classified, they are delivered to the Senate Foreign Relations Committee and House Foreign Affairs Committee under an appropriate injunction of secrecy. Though Congress still lacks control over the making of executive agreements, transmittal provides information that was not readily available before and on which it can base further action.

Though the amount of time that may elapse between the signature and ratification of a treaty can be lengthy, it allows public opinion to crystallize on matters that may have been negotiated in cloistered meetings. A prominent role for the Senate and Congress in foreign policy may be justified as a necessary compensation for the fact that the executive branch strives to shelter international endeavors from domestic pressures. Many citizens and members expect the legislature to serve as a bridge between executive proposals and public opinion. Thus, the Senate, through its authority to approve treaties, and the Congress, through its prerogative to enact implementing legislation, have an important qualitative impact on international agreements even if their quantitative impact seems slight.

The decision regarding which form of agreement is most appropriate is less a constitutional or legal than a political and practical matter. U.S. requirements for approving treaties make both the duration and outcome of the process uncertain. Potential detours and delays may convince some participants that it would be a cumbrous and futile undertaking. Democratic constitutional procedures sometimes seem incompatible with a sustained and stable foreign policy. While some secrecy may be necessary for successful negotiations, it is less justifiable regarding the agreements reached. However, it is unrealistic to expect the United States to handicap itself in the process of discussion or assign priority to means over ends. The question is one of concealing information not from the American public or Congress, but from those nations that may take advantage of such knowledge at the expense of the United States and its allies.

The inability to command a two-thirds Senate majority may lead to the use of legislation, while lack of majority support in either house of Congress may prompt the negotiation of an executive agreement. Another factor is whether substance is accorded a higher priority than procedure, since treatymaking restraints for the United States are procedural rather than substantive. The choice of means may be based on which form is easier to terminate or less subject to legitimate objections concerning a decision to terminate. Treaties and legislation supersede inconsistent provisions in earlier compacts and statutes. All three methods may shape the course of foreign policies, modify international law, or otherwise influence global events. However, a treaty is the only means by which the United States may sanction the domestic validity of laws at least partially framed by another nation or an international body. The following discussion, except when otherwise noted, pertains to bilateral treaties.

TREATY PROCESS

EXECUTIVE INITIATIVE

A proposal that the United States enter negotiations for a treaty usually originates in the executive branch in the course of its diplomatic activities with other nations or in its administration of foreign policy. However, public statements or executive communications by the president, secretary of state, or their subordinates may serve to initiate the process. On occasion Congress, its committees, or individual members may formally or informally propose that the president undertake negotiations. Though the executive branch officially inaugurates action, the reason or impetus to proceed may spring from Congress. Such recommendations may be embodied in legislation or resolution and may authorize, instruct, encourage, or suggest that negotiations be commenced.

An action memorandum prepared by the Department of State and approved by the secretary of state formally authorizes U.S. officials to negotiate a treaty. This document may request authority to negotiate or sign or to negotiate and sign an international agreement. It should describe the arrangements for congressional consultation that have been planned and should be accompanied by a draft of the proposed agreement and a memorandum of law that discusses and justifies the choice of either a treaty or executive agreement. Legislators insist that the more important international agreements be concluded as treaties or be authorized by Congress. Procedures have been developed to satisfy most congressional demands in this regard.

The Department of State periodically transmits a list of significant international agreements that have been cleared for negotiation to the House Foreign Affairs and Senate Foreign Relations Committees. Each panel then has the opportunity to consult with appropriate executive-branch officials as to the proposed form of the agreement. Under current practice, such consultation occurs at the time the action memorandum is prepared. The key factors whose consideration determines the form of an international agreement are the degree of commitment or risk for the nation, whether it is intended to affect state laws, whether it will require implementing legislation, past United States or present international practice as to similar agreements, the preference of Congress, the degree of formality desired, the proposed duration of the agreement, and the need for prompt action.

Most treaties are negotiated by ambassadors or foreign-service officers already assigned to particular countries or functions. The president designates the negotiators, who are usually serving in a relevant post and have been confirmed by the Senate. Should the president nominate someone who requires Senate confirmation, the Foreign Relations Committee uses the opportunity to discuss and influence prospective negotiations. Following designation or confirmation, the president furnishes the negotiators with full-power documents, which formally authorize them to represent the United States. Instructions that delineate positions and objectives are also issued to U.S. diplomats. Negotiation is the process by which the delegates of each government agree on the substance, terms, and text of an agreement.

The customary method of negotiating a bilateral treaty begins when the government proposing the compact presents a complete draft to the other. The Department of State has not established definite guidelines that address the necessity or desirability of consultation with senators at this stage. The nature and extent of consultation may take several forms, including the appointment of legislators as members of a delegation or as observers of international negotiations, or informal discussion with Senate leaders and members of the Foreign Relations Committee. Neither these nor any other mode of communication or collaboration is required. Though the negotiation of treaties may be pursued without consulting legislators, the interdependence of domestic and foreign affairs creates the need to obtain informal senatorial advice to cultivate legislative understanding and support. An executive-branch decision to solicit congressional counsel is one that depends on political factors, with key legislators usually kept apprised of negotiation developments.

Once negotiations are successfully completed, the treaty is signed by an official of the Department of State and approved or signed by the secretary. Though signing marks the conclusion of the negotiating process, it does not bring the agreement into force. Between signing and entry into force there is an interim period during which the parties are not legally bound though they have agreed to cooperate or pursue common goals. During this interval the governments are morally obligated to refrain from any action that would be inconsistent with the purposes of the treaty. The president may decide to apply the treaty provisionally, pending Senate consent, through the use of an executive agreement. However, this action can only be valid for matters completely within the president's legal authority.

The secretary of state formally submits treaties to the president for transmittal to the Senate. Since this may involve an independent review of the compact by the White House staff, the interval between signing and its actual delivery to the Senate can be lengthy, for either political or procedural reasons. The president may decide not to submit a treaty to the Senate if its consent seems unlikely or might require a struggle that he is not prepared to undertake. If not entirely satisfied with the product, he may transmit it to the Senate along with recommendations that it incorporate certain qualifications or stipulations as conditions to its approval of his ratification (see figure 18).

SENATE ACTION

Once received by the Senate, a treaty is referred to the Foreign Relations Committee and placed on the panel's calendar. There is no further progress in its journey until it is reported to the Senate. The decision to hold hearings or initiate other action on particular treaties is a prerogative of the chairman, who consults with the ranking minority member. Such decisions are significantly influenced by executive-branch preferences. At the beginning of each Congress the committee routinely requests a written statement of treaty priorities from the Department of State. Though this communication has no formal status, it is always a key factor in planning the panel's agenda. Some treaties may languish because of a lack of interest or time, while others may be expedited owing to their gravity or urgency. Unless the president clearly favors ratification, which is not necessarily true of treaties submitted by a predecessor, Senate action could be senseless, since the incumbent may decline to ratify despite Senate approval.

Though Senate rules do not require the Foreign Relations Committee to schedule hearings or issue a report, such action is customary. The panel holds each treaty for a reasonable period of time to permit public scrutiny and comment. Testimony at hearings is given by those familiar with the subject matter of the treaty and the manner in which it was concluded. These individuals are primarily, if not exclusively, Department of State officials. The views of those who will be affected by its terms, mainly representatives of other federal agencies and private organizations, are also presented.

The Foreign Relations Committee has several options regarding any given treaty. It may abstain from action or choose not to proceed beyond hearings. In either case, its reasons are conveyed to the Department of State and can be traced to criticism leveled at the compact before, during, or after hearings. Should the executive branch anticipate incomplete action, extensive modification, or outright

100TH CONGRESS *1st Session*	SENATE	TREATY DOC. 100–6

SUPPLEMENTARY EXTRADITION TREATY WITH THE FEDERAL REPUBLIC OF GERMANY

MESSAGE

FROM

THE PRESIDENT OF THE UNITED STATES

TRANSMITTING

THE SUPPLEMENTARY TREATY TO THE TREATY BETWEEN THE UNITED STATES OF AMERICA AND THE FEDERAL REPUBLIC OF GERMANY CONCERNING EXTRADITION SIGNED AT WASHINGTON ON OCTOBER 21, 1986

JUNE 25, 1987.—Treaty was read the first time, and together with the accompanying papers, referred to the Committee on Foreign Relations and ordered to be printed for the use of the Senate.

U.S. GOVERNMENT PRINTING OFFICE

91-118   WASHINGTON : 1987

Fig. 18. A bilateral treaty submitted to the Senate.

rejection by the Senate based on the hearings, the president or secretary of state may request the committee to suspend consideration pending the negotiation of a supplementary protocol to render the treaty acceptable. Such an agreement would be submitted to the Senate as a separate compact, considered simultaneously with and treated in the same manner as the original treaty.

When the committee acts affirmatively on a treaty, it reports a resolution of ratification to its parent body. Its executive report contains the panel's recommendations and reasons therefor (see figure 19). The alternatives are to propose that the treaty be approved without change, that it be approved with conditions that do not alter its text, that it be approved only if its text is amended, or a combination of the last two possibilities. Most treaties neither breed controversy nor sow uncertainty and are favorably reported without qualifications. In this case the committee will advise and consent to ratification while communicating its views through its executive report. This has the same effect on a treaty as statements of legislative intent that apply to public laws. These sentiments will be taken into account by the executive branch but will not necessarily be followed in implementing a treaty. The president need not take further action in response to report language.

Should substantive and/or political questions or objections arise, the committee may choose among various vehicles to express its views on or qualify its consent to ratification. The conditions attached to a resolution of ratification include amendments, reservations, understandings, declarations, and provisos. An amendment is a proposed change to the actual text of a treaty. Technically, the Senate cannot amend a treaty, but merely recommend revisions that it requires to be incorporated by the parties before it will grant its consent to ratification. A Senate amendment is a major substantive modification that compels renegotiation by both parties to the compact. The result may be acceptance by the other party, a revised version of the treaty that would then have to be submitted to the Senate, or an inability to reach agreement. An amendment that is ultimately incorporated into a treaty alters the obligations of each government.

Reservations are specific qualifications or stipulations that modify U.S. obligations without changing treaty language. They alter or limit the legal meaning or substantive scope of one or more treaty provisions and constitute an adjustment of the contractual relationship. A reservation gives notice that the treaty will not be accepted or implemented except under specified conditions. The most common type is a brief statement that the United States does not agree to a particular article or clause. Its effect is to annul the obligation stated in the provision as it applies to the United States.

A reservation may also modify rather than nullify a stipulation contained in a specific article or clause. It may construe one or more treaty provisions in a manner that is inconsistent with the intent agreed upon by the parties when the compact was signed. If the president accepts a reservation, he communicates its terms to the other party prior to his ratification. The other signatory may accept it, in which case the original provision is not binding on either party or is given a revised meaning, file its own reservation, request renegotiation, or reject it and refuse to proceed with ratification. A reservation must be explicitly accepted by the other party and becomes an integral part of the treaty.

99TH CONGRESS *2d Session*	SENATE	EXEC. REPT. 99-25

HAGUE CONVENTION ON THE CIVIL ASPECTS OF INTERNATIONAL CHILD ABDUCTION

SEPTEMBER 19 (legislative day, SEPTEMBER 15), 1986.—Ordered to be printed

Mr. LUGAR, from the Committee on Foreign Relations, submitted the following

REPORT

[To accompany Treaty Doc. 99-11]

The Committee on Foreign Relations, to which was referred the Hague Convention on the Civil Aspects of International Child Abduction, adopted on October 24, 1980, at the 14th Session of the Hague Conference on Private International Law and signed on behalf of the United States on December 23, 1981, having considered the same, reports favorably thereon with two reservations and recommends that the Senate give its advice and consent to ratification thereof.

PURPOSE

The purpose of the Convention is to establish uniform rules to be applied in cases of international child abduction.

COMMITTEE COMMENTS

This Convention addresses the problems created when children are wrongfully removed or retained abroad in connection with parental custody disputes. It requires that these children be promptly returned to the country of their habitual residence upon application of the left-behind parent, subject only to express conditions and narrow exceptions. It also provides for the establishment of a Central Authority in every party state to receive and facilitate the processing of return requests. The Convention could result in the return to the United States of numerous children who may be abducted to, or retained in, other states party to the Convention. It would, in turn, also provide for the return from the United States of children wrongfully abducted or retained in the United States.

71-119 O

Fig. 19. A Senate Executive Report on a multilateral treaty.

Understandings are not intended to affect the substantive terms or international obligations of a treaty. They are interpretive statements designed to clarify, but not alter, certain provisions or their legal effect. Under existing practice, the president formally communicates these qualifications to the other party as an official statement of U.S. policy. However, they need not be formally accepted for a treaty to be ratified. If agreed to by the president and the other signatory, they are considered a valid component of the treaty relationship.

Declarations are statements of the Senate's position, opinion, or intentions on policy issues raised by a treaty, but do not address specific provisions. They may be used to reassure certain constituencies or countries or serve to remind others of U.S. commitments or expectations. Provisos address matters incidental to the operation of a treaty or relate solely to domestic action. They focus on the eventual or probable impact that certain provisions might have on U.S. law or procedure. Neither declarations nor provisos entail formal notice to or agreement by the other party.

When a treaty is called from the Executive Calendar and brought to the Senate floor, it is considered in executive session. This means that the Senate meets to transact business that originates with the president, not that such meetings are closed to the public. Senators first debate and vote upon amendments proposed by the Foreign Relations Committee and then upon amendments offered by other members. The distinctive feature of these proceedings is that the treaty is read and open to amendment article-by-article. Once the amending process has been completed, the treaty itself is no longer before the Senate. The chamber next acts on conditions reported by the Foreign Relations Committee, followed by action on conditions proposed from the floor. These proposals are treated as amendments to the resolution of ratification.

The Senate neither votes on the treaty as a whole nor on its component articles. Rather it votes on amendments offered to the treaty, on amendments to the resolution of ratification, and on the resolution as a whole. It may amend the resolution, but may only propose amendments to the treaty. If amendments to the latter are approved, they are incorporated into the resolution, which states that the Senate gives its consent to ratification on condition that the parties accept the proposed amendments contained therein. Any procedural aspect of floor consideration may be altered, hastened, or omitted by unanimous consent.

Under the constitutional clause that provides for its advice and consent, the Senate may adopt a separate resolution to advise the president in the course of considering a treaty. It is transmitted to the White House for appropriate action and for a report on such action to the Senate within a specified time period. These sense-of-the-Senate resolutions constitute recommendations or requests and are not legally binding. However, their political significance can influence or elicit executive action when aimed at a treaty that is under negotiation, in committee, pending on the Executive Calendar, or on the chamber floor.

Because the large majority of treaties are unexceptional in nature, their consideration is accelerated and approval is a formality. When a number of similar and routine ones are pending, action is brief and swift as Senate consent is granted by a single vote to expedite chamber business. Since normal procedure prescribes a separate vote on each resolution of ratification and because other governments expect their agreements to receive special attention, the *Congressional Record* will show that they were voted upon individually. For those treaties that generate controversy, amendments and conditions are adopted by a majority vote, while the final ballot on a resolution of ratification requires a two-thirds margin for approval.

In its action on a treaty and resolution of ratification the Senate may consent without conditions, consent with qualifications, or disapprove. Disapproval may be expressed through inaction, incomplete action, or rejection by anything less than a two-thirds majority vote on the resolution. All treaties that reach the floor but that are not formally disposed of by the Senate are returned to the Executive Calendar. They are automatically referred to the Foreign Relations Committee calendar at the final adjournment of Congress. Though a treaty may remain pending in the Senate indefinitely, all proceedings lapse upon the expiration of a Congress. Future consideration of treaties that were neither approved nor disapproved requires that they be reported anew by the Foreign Relations Committee during the next or a subsequent Congress. Treaties rejected by the failure to secure a two-thirds majority also pass back to the committee unless the Senate acts affirmatively by resolution to return them to the White House.

An unperfected treaty is one that has been signed by representatives of the United States but has, for whatever reasons, failed to go into effect within a prescribed or practicable period of time. This is to distinguish such agreements from pending treaties on which further action is anticipated. Unperfected compacts include those never submitted to the Senate, withdrawn by the president, modified by the Senate or the other party in a manner that precluded ratification, or disapproved by the Senate through rejection or inaction. This last development is the usual senatorial method for withholding consent to controversial treaties without unnecessarily consuming legislative resources. Since treaties may remain before the Senate for an indefinite interval, a question may arise as to whether one is unperfected or pending. If its text or international conditions do not provide a clear answer, one would need to consult sources discussed in the last section of this chapter.

PRESIDENTIAL ACTION

The president is not obligated to ratify a treaty to which the Senate has given its consent. Upon Senate approval, the president may ratify it, resubmit it for further consideration at a later date, or decline to ratify it. Ratification is most likely in cases of unconditional Senate approval. When the Senate makes its consent conditional upon certain amendments, reservations, or understandings, the president must renegotiate the treaty based upon the amendments, approve the reservations, or accept the understandings before he can proceed to ratify. Such changes may have been made at the request of the president. He retains the authority to judge what international effect is intended by Senate action.

The designation of a qualification by the Senate is not conclusive. Irrespective of which term is used, its content or effect is of prime importance. The legal significance of a Senate statement depends entirely on its substance. One that alters or restricts the meaning or purpose of a treaty is an actual reservation, while one that addresses an incidental or procedural matter is not. Should Senate conditions be unacceptable to the president, he may refuse to ratify despite the fact that such conditions may be acceptable to the other government. If he decides to discontinue the process, he may issue a formal announcement to that effect or quietly remove the matter from his agenda. Refusal of the president to ratify has the same legal results as if the treaty has never existed, though the United States might be unable to avoid political consequences.

The president may resubmit a treaty to the Senate for reconsideration at any time prior to its ratification. If this course is followed, the treaty may be transmitted in its original form or in a form modified by further negotiations. The former option enables the president to delay ratification when an imminent change, advantageous to the United States or administration policy, is expected in the fundamental circumstances that produced the agreement. It also permits him, in cases where the Senate has attached unacceptable conditions, to wait for a more favorable legislative climate or a more receptive attitude by the other government.

When the president has qualms about Senate reservations but is still convinced that ratification is desirable, the question arises as to whether renegotiation is necessary. This becomes a political decision based on presidential objectives and the perceived significance of Senate action. The other party also retains the right to determine if a Senate statement modifies or interprets the treaty relationship in an unacceptable manner. The president may resubmit a treaty in a renegotiated form when Senate conditions render it unpalatable to him or the other party. However, the usual practice is to submit a protocol or supplemental agreement that serves, from the Senate's vantage point, to eliminate disagreeable language or clarify questionable provisions. Any such proposal is then submitted to the Senate for its consideration along with the original treaty.

Should the president concur with reservations or understandings adopted by the Senate, he communicates them to the other party. Ratification is normally deferred until the views of the other government on Senate action have been ascertained. Informally, such views are exchanged while Senate consideration is in progress. In response to Senate statements with which the president agrees, the other party has several options. It may accept or reject the qualifications, request further negotiations, or attach conditions of its own which the United States may, in turn, accept or reject. If the other signatory should propose a reservation after Senate approval, the president is obligated to submit it to the Senate for its consent prior to his ratification. However, it is at the discretion of the executive branch to determine whether a condition stated by a foreign government is a modification that requires Senate action. Though some or even most senators may disagree with such a decision, they have no formal recourse to influence or challenge it.

Presidential acceptance of Senate pronouncements is followed by the signing of the formal instrument of ratification, which contains the full text of all Senate conditions or qualifications. The other government may choose to remain silent rather than issue a formal reply regarding reservations or understandings. If it exchanges instruments of ratification, its silence is interpreted as official consent to statements incorporated into the document. Another government's understandings may be rejected without affected ratification. One party may proceed to exchange instruments while protesting or resisting an understanding. In this case, a treaty relationship is established with the parties in disagreement as to the application or intent of certain provisions.

If, despite the terminology, the president is persuaded that a Senate statement is a valid reservation or understanding, he must include it in the instrument of ratification or it must otherwise be made known that U.S. approval is subject to the terms added by the Senate. The president may find that the

Senate has advised him to be reasonably certain, without linking the matter with the formalities of ratification, that the treaty be given a definite interpretation. This may entail additional correspondence or a supplementary agreement with the other party. Whether induced by senatorial language or the result of executive judgment, a *statement of understanding, agreed minute*, or *exchange of notes* between chiefs of state serves to construe the precise meaning of treaty provisions. Such clarifications are legally binding in the absence of any further or inconsistent Senate statements. Where a clarification is the only obstacle to Senate approval, the executive branch may be able to convince legislators that specified provisions will be implemented in a certain manner. This may sufficiently satisfy senators so that renegotiation or additional transactions become unnecessary.

A treaty may be withdrawn from the Senate any time after it is submitted and prior to approval of a resolution of ratification. Withdrawal may be the result of executive or legislative initiative or collaboration. This procedure begins with the receipt of a presidential message requesting that a treaty be returned to the executive. The message is referred to the Foreign Relations Committee, which reports an executive resolution directing the secretary of the Senate to comply with the request. Upon Senate approval the resolution and all original treaty papers are delivered to the White House. Requests for withdrawal are invariably accorded favorable consideration.

Among the reasons for withdrawal are changed international conditions, a later international agreement, altered domestic political circumstances, or objections by members of the Senate. The president prefers to withdraw a treaty when it encounters serious opposition in the Foreign Relations Committee or on the floor rather than risk major amendments or formal rejection, which would jeopardize the possibility of concluding any agreement. Withdrawal, as an indirect method of disposing of unacceptable treaties, offers the president a diplomatic means to engage in further negotiations, which may result in the submission of a revised compact. A treaty withdrawn and resubmitted will be assigned a new designation. Even treaties disapproved by less than a two-thirds floor vote remain in the Senate until withdrawn.

RATIFICATION

Ratification is an international confirmation of a treaty embodied in a public document that is communicated to other nations in a manner prescribed by the agreement or governed by custom. It is a formal procedure that declares the intention of a nation to be bound by a treaty. Ratification is a national act that does not, of itself, bind a party to meet international obligations. To be bound internationally requires international action in the form of the exchange or deposit of instruments of ratification. It is this formality that ordinarily marks the entry into force of a treaty.

Under the terms of a treaty, instruments of ratification are exchanged at a specified time and place and it becomes effective upon the date of such action. A "Protocol of Exchange of Instruments of Ratification," sometimes referred to as a *procès-verbal*, attesting the exchange is signed by an official of each party at this time. While the instrument contains the text of the treaty and all qualifications, the protocol confirms the intentions of the parties to abide by the terms contained in the instrument. Declarations and provisos are not included in the instrument because they do not apply to the other party.

The effective date of a treaty can almost always be derived from its text. It may provide for entry into force on a fixed date or after a specified interval following the last ratification. However, there may be more than one date depending on whether international or domestic law is involved and whether the entry into force of different articles is explicitly staggered. The treaty may contain provisions or either party may have added stipulations that make its effectiveness contingent upon certain developments. Any Senate qualification to its consent, included in the instrument of ratification, takes effect as domestic law at the same time that the treaty becomes binding under international law. While the president may support the compact, he may defer ratification simply to allow time for Congress to enact implementing legislation, or the treaty itself may stipulate delay to allow the parties to adapt themselves to its requirements.

Although the exchange of ratifications is customarily the final step needed to bring a treaty into force, it is always proclaimed by the president. Receipt of a protocol of exchange by the Department of State is the prerequisite to the promulgation of a treaty through a presidential proclamation. This document announces that a treaty has entered into force and serves as legal notice for domestic purposes. It is normally issued as soon as practicable after a treaty has become effective. Since promulgation is a national act, its timing or absence does not affect the international obligation incurred.

At every stage of the treatymaking process (except for senatorial advice and consent to ratification)—initiation, negotiation, signature, ratification, exchange or deposit of ratification, and promulgation—the judgment of the president predominates. He may decide to terminate negotiations; if negotiated, he may prevent a treaty from being signed on behalf of the United States; if signed, he may decline to submit it to the Senate; if submitted, he may request it be withdrawn; if approved by the Senate, he may refuse to ratify it; if ratified, he may choose not to exchange ratifications. Though the president and the Senate may each exercise an unqualified veto in the making of treaties, the president has greater discretion and more opportunities to use it. While treaties cannot be concluded without presidential approval, they can be terminated despite the president's disapproval by the passage of legislation that is subject to his veto, but which may be overridden.

MULTILATERAL TREATIES

Some practices related to multilateral treaties differ from those that apply to bilateral compacts. Most multilateral agreements are negotiated and publicly discussed by many nations at international conferences that may span months or years. Nations often make concessions in one area to obtain concessions from other parties in other areas. The result is a complex package of interdependent and balanced elements that the Senate is called upon to accept or reject in its entirety. The possibility of amendments or other qualifications is virtually eliminated. This is because renegotiation is not feasible considering the number of parties involved and the intricate political and substantive relationships formed by the treaty.

The text of an agreement is usually made available to the press at or before signature. The Final Act of the conference is a publication that summarizes its proceedings, recounts its origins, lists the participants, describes its organization, cites the steps leading to each compact approved, and contains all resolutions and recommendations adopted. The draft treaty prepared for consideration by interested governments is issued as a separate document. The original copy of a multilateral treaty is deposited with an international organization or one of the signatories, and certified copies are furnished each party.

Any conditions added by the Senate in the process of approving a multilateral compact are communicated to the depository, which corresponds with other governments regarding the matter. An instrument of ratification is deposited with the original treaty; the depository notifies each party when one is received. Multilateral agreements become effective after a certain number or all parties, as stipulated in the treaty, have deposited their instruments. If it has gone into force for some signatories, it becomes effective for others upon the deposit of their ratifications. Thus, its effectiveness for a given government may be years later than its ratification.

The United States may adhere to a multilateral treaty rather than participate in its negotiation and ratification. Adherence refers to a nonsignatory that becomes a party to a treaty under terms that provide for such a contingency or if all parties to the original compact agree to permit other nations to enter the relationship. Adherence has the same effects as signature and ratification combined. U.S. adherence to a multilateral agreement requires Senate consent in the form of a resolution of adherence, and it would go into force for the United States upon the deposit of an instrument of adherence.

IMPLEMENTATION

Implementation involves two key issues and covers two distinctive spheres of action. The issues concern whether a treaty is self-executing or not and the responsibility of Congress in the passage of implementing legislation. A self-executing treaty is one that may be applied and enforced by the executive and judicial branches without prior domestic legislation. Executive-branch regulations are issued that assign and define administrative responsibilities. The realms of operation are the domestic and the international. The manner in which the issues are addressed and resolved have different implications and consequences for a treaty's domestic and international legal status.

Determining whether or not a treaty is self-executing is relatively easy when its text expressly recognizes the need for implementing legislation or when the subject matter falls within an area traditionally regarded as requiring congressional concurrence through legislation. The most certain way to ensure an instrumental role for Congress in the treaty process is through the exercise of its power to appropriate funds. When a compact requires such action Congress is in a strong position to influence executive-branch plans and action. When doubt exists as to whether a treaty is or is not self-executing, it becomes a matter of interpretation, initially for the executive and ultimately for the judiciary.

If a treaty is not self-executing, it is not the treaty but the implementing legislation that becomes domestic law unless the statute confers legal effect on the treaty itself. It is only through implementing legislation that non-self-executing treaties can become legally enforceable within the United States (see figure 20). Thus, the international obligation may exist for some time prior to internal validity. The entry into force of a treaty prior to the passage of implementing legislation places Congress in the difficult and awkward position of feeling compelled to acquiesce to prevent the United States from defaulting on its international obligations.

The need for implementing legislation provides the Senate and Congress with a second check on treaties. In enacting implementing legislation, Congress does not always pass laws in the precise form recommended by the president. Nor does it always appropriate the sum of money he considers necessary to properly implement a treaty. Passage of implementing legislation may be accomplished through a single measure or may be subject to annual or periodical congressional authorization. Sometimes treaties approved by the Senate and ratified by the president remain unfulfilled because implementing legislation is not enacted. Under the Constitution Congress possesses the power to proceed in accordance with presidential recommendations, to enact laws that deviate from executive proposals, or to decline to act. The weight to be given political and moral obligations is a question to be settled among the participants in the process.

If a nation with which a treaty is concluded should be dissatisfied with the legislative action of the United States, it must present a formal protest to the chief executive or pursue such other measures as it may deem necessary to protect its interests. Whether another nation has just cause for complaint is not a question amenable to domestic judicial determination. Once a treaty has entered into force, nations may differ about the interpretation of their obligations under certain of its provisions. If such a dispute arises, the parties may consult and negotiate a mutually satisfactory settlement. When this approach fails to resolve the matter, the parties may resort to more formal methods.

Conciliation is a nonbinding process in which the parties to a dispute agree to submit their differences to an international body. The object is to promote an acceptable solution without recourse to mandatory procedures or binding commitments. Arbitration differs from conciliation in that the parties agree to accept and implement the decision of a diplomatic panel in good faith. Treaties frequently contain an arbitration clause that commits the parties to submit disputes to special commissions whose members are selected by themselves. Adjudication differs from arbitration in that the parties refer their disagreement to an existing and independent tribunal of international jurists whose judgment they are bound to accept. This course may also be pursued in accordance with treaty provisions.

ALTERING OBLIGATIONS

The Constitution is silent on procedures for modifying, renewing, suspending, and terminating treaties, and agreement between the executive and legislative branches has not been reached on either the appropriate circumstances or proper mode. Those situations that require Senate or congressional participation and those subject to independent action by the president cannot always be clearly distinguished. Thus, some procedures and conditions that relate to practices in this realm of action lack the validity or certainty of those that lead to ratification.

I

99TH CONGRESS
2D SESSION

S. 1828

IN THE HOUSE OF REPRESENTATIVES

OCTOBER 18, 1986
Referred to the Committee on the Judiciary

AN ACT

To implement the Inter-American Convention on International
Commercial Arbitration.

1   *Be it enacted by the Senate and House of Representa-*

2   *tives of the United States of America in Congress assembled,*

3   That title 9, United States Code, is amended by adding:

4   **"CHAPTER 3. INTER-AMERICAN CONVENTION ON**

5   **INTERNATIONAL COMMERCIAL ARBITRATION**

"Sec.
"301. Enforcement of Convention.
"302. Incorporation by reference.
"303. Order to compel arbitration; appointment of arbitrators; locale.
"304. Recognition and enforcement of foreign arbitral decisions and awards;
       reciprocity.
"305. Relationship between the Inter-American Convention and the Convention on
       the Recognition and Enforcement of Foreign Arbitral Awards of
       June 10, 1958.
"306. Applicable rules of Inter-American Commercial Arbitration Commission.
"307. Chapter 1; residual application.

Fig. 20. Proposed legislation to implement a treaty.

Treaties may be modified by formal amendment, legislation, or executive agreement. A proposed amendment covers the revision, addition, or deletion of specific provisions. Amendments to a treaty require the same procedure as the original agreement unless otherwise stipulated in the compact. When the treaty itself or a subsequent treaty provides otherwise, or an act of Congress substantively affects a treaty, modification may not require Senate approval. It is for the executive branch to decide whether a proposed modification is an amendment that must be submitted to the Senate, a revision to be tacitly accepted without seeking Senate consent, or an adjustment that can be implemented through an exchange of notes between chief executives.

When a statute conflicts with an existing treaty provision or vice versa, the later action supersedes the earlier. In the former instance the treaty text or implementing legislation is repealed as domestic law. However, the international obligation remains valid and, if not otherwise honored, may produce political repercussions. Legislation may expressly modify a treaty or authorize the president to take such action through an executive agreement or upon the determination that certain conditions exist. The president may modify a treaty without legislative action if domestic law is not affected or congressional prerogatives are not infringed by a decision to clarify or interpret a debatable provision.

An agreement to extend or suspend an existing treaty is, in effect, a new compact and can be sanctioned only by the same procedure that authorized the original agreement. Treaties about to expire would have to be extended through another if it was agreed that all provisions remained desirable. If only some of its terms were considered as worth renewing, then the president would decide whether to negotiate a treaty or other form of agreement. The conclusion of a new treaty may expressly suspend the operation of an earlier one and may also provide that upon the expiration or termination of the later compact the provisions of the suspended agreement will resume their binding status. Through his power to recognize or not recognize foreign governments, the president can continue or suspend treaty relationships. An act of Congress may also grant the president authority to suspend a treaty provision or the entire compact.

A discussion of treaty termination entails an analytical distinction between reasons and procedures. However, in actual practice the differences between them are often blurred and there may be disagreement about the credibility of reasons or legitimacy of procedures. It cannot be convincingly argued that the power to sever a treaty relationship is limited by the power to create one. Key questions that do remain in doubt and subject to dispute include motives, timing, prerogatives, and strategy.

Treaties may be terminated by their expiration, which covers a variety of developments. The terms of a compact may provide for its own expiration at any time upon consent of the parties, at a certain date, or stipulate that upon the passage of a set period of time one party, after giving notice of its intention to do so, may discontinue the relationship. A treaty made for a specific purpose or intended to endure until a certain event occurs expires when the purpose is fulfilled or the event is acknowledged.

The parties to a treaty may decide to terminate it through the negotiation of a new agreement. The subsequent compact may supersede the earlier one either expressly or by necessary implication. A treaty relationship established without a specific provision for its expiration may also be dissolved by mutual consent. An agreement may lapse through desuetude, which denotes a situation where it is consistently ignored by one party or disregarded by both with the acquiescence of the other.

Since expiration is a form of termination that springs directly from the treaty itself, it rarely generates a quarrel though it may produce displeasure or disappointment. Collaboration by the parties to terminate a treaty, whether or not in pursuance of its terms, is even less likely to foment disagreement. It is the unilateral termination of treaty obligations in contravention of its terms or without consulting the other party that breeds the most controversy. Some reasons for the abrogation of a treaty are recognized as having more justification than others.

The violation of its terms by one party entitles the other to terminate a treaty relationship. Such action may be invoked as grounds for canceling or suspending the treaty in whole or in part. For the aggrieved party to declare the compact void it must be deprived of essential benefits under the agreement. This may occur when the violation concerns a major provision, reveals a willful refusal to comply, or involves an arbitrary interpretation. A significant or flagrant breach, as gauged by the aggrieved party, does not result in automatic termination. It does provide the offended government with the option to renounce obligations or demand compensation.

Congress may annul a treaty in one of three ways. It may refuse to pass implementing legislation, it may enact a conflicting law, or it may author a statute that expressly terminates a treaty. In these cases the agreement either fails to become or ceases to be internally binding within the United States, though the international commitment remains valid. In effect the United States is put into the position of defaulting on its obligations. The same results may ensue when the president and Senate approve a treaty whose provisions may constitute a breach of the terms of a prior compact concluded with a different party. Any of the developments described above may prompt the other party to denounce a treaty by giving notice of its intent to terminate the relationship or simply repudiate the pledge to observe it.

Another reason for unilateral action on treaty matters is based on a judgment that the conditions essential to the existence of an international obligation have ceased to exist. A fundamental change in political, economic, military, or physical status may serve as grounds on which to nullify a treaty. In addition, armed hostilities between the parties, between one party and an ally of the other, or between allies of each, may result in termination or suspension. Under his authority to conduct foreign affairs, the president determines whether another party remains capable of fulfilling its treaty obligations or has violated the agreement to an extent that warrants termination or suspension by the United States.

The authority to dissolve an international commitment seems to rest with the president since he alone is able to formally communicate with foreign governments. As the sole and official spokesman with other nations, the president is the person who transmits notice of imminent termination. Since the president acts for the United States on the international scene, he has the discretion to determine when treaty provisions have lapsed or were breached and to waive privileges or ignore obligations. Thus, he can effectively violate or terminate treaties and neither the Senate, Congress, nor the other party can prevent such action. When a foreign government wishes to terminate a treaty, it may notify the president, who may agree to the request with or without congressional approval.

Treaty termination practices of the United States can be summarized in terms of executive action pursuant to legislation or Senate authorization; executive action without prior legislative sanction, but with subsequent congressional or Senate approval; executive action without earlier legislative assent or later congressional endorsement. The choice of method usually depends on either the importance of the international question or the preference of the executive branch. It is clear that the government possesses the constitutional authority to terminate treaties on behalf of the United States. The general lack of uniform standards for interpreting governmental actions in this matter contributes to the difficulty of ascertaining execution or effects. See figure 21 for key steps in the life of a treaty.

Executive Action
1. Secretary of state authorizes negotiations
2. Diplomats undertake and complete negotiations
3. U.S. representative signs the treaty
4. Department of State prepares treaty papers
5. Treaty is submitted to the president
6. President transmits treaty to the Senate

Senate Action
7. Foreign Relations Committee hearings
8. Foreign Relations Committee deliberations and qualifications*
9. Foreign Relations Committee issues executive report with proposed resolution of ratification*
10. Chamber debate and adoption of qualifications*
11. Chamber approves resolution of ratification*
12. Chamber transmits resolution and treaty papers to the president

Presidential Action
13. Withdrawal* (may occur at any time during steps 7-10)
14. Renegotiation (if necessary)
15. Resubmission (equivalent to step 6)
16. Signs instrument of ratification
17. Exchange of ratifications
18. Promulgation

Subsequent Action
19. Implementation: executive directives, domestic law,* international arrangements
20. Modification: formal amendment,* legislation,* executive agreement
21. Termination: expiration, collaboration, abrogation*

---

*Indicates steps that may or usually involve roll-call votes.

Fig. 21. Key steps and decision points in the life of a treaty.

DOCUMENTATION

OVERVIEW

Though a treaty is not always denominated as such by the parties involved, certain standard features reveal its actual nature. The typical parts of a treaty are (1) preamble—includes the names and styles of the high contracting parties, an outline of their general objectives, the names and titles of the individuals designated as negotiators, and a statement that their full powers have been verified; (2) body—those articles containing the substantive stipulations of the agreement; (3) duration article—if for a definite period or until a specified event occurs, a date is entered or the contingency serves to dissolve it; (4) procedure article—provides for ratification, for the exchange of ratifications, and for entry into force; (5) attestation clause—formal statement of certification that includes the signatures and seals of the plenipotentiaries; (6) additional substantive articles—commonly termed *annexes* or *protocols*, these are often appended and signed by the parties with a declaration that they have the same force and effect as if they had been included in the body.

Treaties may be categorized in any one of several ways. These include classification by the number of parties, names of the parties, major purpose, subject matter, life span, or legal status. For the purposes of this study, the last characteristic is the most significant. Treaty status may be further subdivided into categories based on U.S. action to date. These possibilities cover treaties not submitted to the Senate; those still pending in the Senate; those approved by the Senate; those rejected by the Senate; those withdrawn by the president; and those approved by the Senate, but not ratified by the president. There is no definite duration for each stage of or for the entire treatymaking process. It is possible for a treaty to be in part executed, in part expired, and in part effective. A single source that provides all pertinent information about the status of a treaty—whether unperfected, pending, deferred, renegotiated, modified, suspended, or terminated—does not exist.

There are three ways to ascertain treaty status. Which route is best depends on how much information is needed and how soon. The most expeditious approach yields the least information. This involves communication with an office responsible for keeping track of such matters. Another method is to determine when and in what form the treaty was last issued as a U.S. government publication. Success in this effort, however, does not always provide a definitive answer. Finally, one might consult official documents that record and disclose such information in the course of a treaty's progress. Research on this scale merits an extended discussion that will be undertaken following a brief survey of some general and retrospective sources that furnish useful treaty information.

Treaties are ordinarily neither printed by the United States in any quantity nor are their texts generally available before they become effective. They usually appear first as Department of State press releases after being signed. They are next printed as Senate Treaty Documents upon transmittal by the president. Treaties are usually included in hearings issued by the Foreign Relations Committee and in the panel's executive report. They are printed in the *Congressional Record* under the date that their consideration commences on the Senate floor. Upon ratification, treaties appear in the *Weekly Compilation of Presidential*

Documents as part of the presidential proclamation that promulgates them. Since the *Statutes at Large* contains all proclamations, this is another source for their text.

Approximately six months to a year after a treaty has gone into force, it is issued by the Department of State as an unbound pamphlet in the official *Treaties and Other International Acts Series (TIAS)*. This series combined and succeeded the *Treaty Series (TS)* and *Executive Agreement Series (EAS)* in 1946. The agreements are numbered consecutively, though the order in which they are printed corresponds to their effective date rather than their chronological sequence. The *TIAS* print includes the English and foreign-language versions of the text, all important dates concerning its development and approval, the president's proclamation, and any correspondence or supplemental agreements affecting its content. The Final Acts of international conferences in which the United States participates also appear in this series. The *United States Treaties and Other International Agreements (UST)*, which was inaugurated in 1950, is the official treaty series published by the Department of State and is issued annually in a multivolume set that cumulates and replaces *TIAS*. Each volume of *UST* has an index arranged by subject and country that covers that volume only.

Treaties and Other International Agreements of the United States of America 1776-1949, compiled by Charles I. Bevans and published in thirteen volumes by the Department of State, including a comprehensive subject index, contains the text of all pre-1950 compacts. A commercial publication entitled *United States Treaties and Other International Agreements Cumulative Index 1776-1949*, edited by Igor I. Kavass and Mark A. Michael, and issued in 1975 as a four-volume set, provides superior access to treaties. An earlier four-volume set entitled *UST Cumulative Index*, edited by Igor I. Kavass and Adolf Sprudzs and published in 1973, covers the period 1950-1970. Volume 1 lists agreements in their *TIAS* order; volume 2 is a chronological index, volume 3 a country index, and volume 4 a subject index. The first three volumes include citations to *TIAS* and *UST*, while the last cites *UST* only. A one-volume supplement for the years 1971-1975 appeared in 1977. In 1976 this project became a loose-leaf updating service and its title was changed to *UST Cumulative Indexing Service*. *Unperfected Treaties of the United States of America 1776-1976* is a multivolume work still in progress and edited by Christian L. Wiktor. It is arranged chronologically with a cumulative index in the final volume and contains the texts of all international agreements that have failed to go into effect.

The most complete official source on the status of treaties is the annual *Treaties in Force (TIF)*, first issued by the Department of State in 1955. It covers all international agreements regardless of their nature or nomenclature to which the United States is a party and whose terms are still in effect. This includes treaties that amend, extend, or supplement prior ones and those that have become partially null and void. Compacts that have not expired by their own terms, been denounced by the parties, superseded, or otherwise terminated are listed. Included are those that have not been clearly or formally terminated although opertions under them may have ceased. Treaties that have been officially and completely terminated are not entered. The first part of *TIF* lists bilateral compacts arranged by country and by subject thereunder, and the second part lists multilateral agreements arranged by subject and by country thereunder.

The usefulness of *TIF* is limited by the fact that there is little correlation between the bilateral and multilateral subject headings, and all agreements are neither organized under nor identified by subject category or other signatory. The purpose of *A Guide to the United States Treaties in Force*, edited by Igor I. Kavass and Adolf Sprudzs, is to provide better access to particular treaties and agreements. It is planned for this publication, first issued in 1982, to be updated annually. To simplify and expedite the retrieval of information the *Guide* is divided into two volumes. Part 1 consists of numerical lists and a subject index for both bilateral and multilateral agreements. Part 2 consists of a numerical guide and chronological index for multilateral compacts only. Both parts provide the following information, when available, for each agreement: (1) official Department of State file number (*TS, EAS, TIAS*); (2) subject category under which it appears in *TIF*; (3) relevant signature, entry into force, and other key dates; (4) citation to where the official text is published; (5) notations on subsequent action, such as what agreements amend or are amended by it.

Part 1 of the *Guide* also contains an appendix that provides information on changes that have been made from the previous edition of *TIF* to the current one, including changes in classification categories, deletions, additions, and *TIAS* numbers that have been assigned to previously unnumbered agreements. It is arranged alphabetically by country for bilateral compacts and alphabetically by subject for multilateral ones. Part 2 includes two separate lists of countries and international organizations. Under each entry is a table of multilateral agreements to which each country or organization and the United States are both parties.

To facilitate efforts to ascertain the progress, status, and intent of treaties, those documents that are generated at each stage of their existence, from conception through termination, are discussed below.

EXECUTIVE ACTION

1. Initiation: Public statements by the president or secretary of state about the decision to negotiate a treaty appear in the *Weekly Compilation of Presidential Documents (WCPD)* or the *Department of State Bulletin*, respectively. The former is indexed cumulatively and cumulated and indexed annually in the *Public Papers of the Presidents of the United States*. Both the *WCPD* and *Public Papers* are issued by the National Archives and Records Administration. The *Bulletin* is issued monthly and is indexed annually. Since it normally contains some facts that apply to all subsequent stages as well, it will only be mentioned when it is the only or best source available.

2. Negotiation: Information about this stage relates to both positions and progress. If an existing international agreement or earlier legislation authorized negotiations, either might contain stipulations or guidelines to be followed. Citations to such sources usually appear in the *WCPD* or *Bulletin*. Neither the action memorandum nor negotiation instructions are published by the U.S. government. It is understandable that these documents would be kept confidential since their text or tenor may cover a discussion of substantive and political options, as well as other

sensitive matters. The course of proceedings may be monitored through the sources noted in 1 or Department of State press releases.

3. Signature: The *Bulletin* or a Department of State press release confirms that this stage has been reached. Initial U.S. printing of a treaty is in the form of a Department of State press release following its signing. Its text is preceded by a concise account of its history. The *Bulletin* also contains a brief statement of its purpose. The practice of postponing publication of treaties until the Senate removes its injunction of secrecy has been discontinued.

4. Treaty Papers: After signature, a report on the treaty, tracing its background and explaining its provisions, is prepared for transmittal by the secretary of state to the president. This report is accompanied by a covering letter, the original copy of the treaty, pertinent diplomatic correspondence, any supplementary agreements or additional legal analysis, and a draft message from the president to the Senate. If the president approves, he signs the message and forwards the papers to the Senate.

SENATE ACTION

1. Receipt of Presidential Message: Through the 96th Congress (1980), upon receipt of a treaty by the Senate, the papers were assigned a letter designation by the executive clerk. The official designation of the first set of such papers received during each session was Executive A, Congress and Session, while subsequent treaties were assigned letters in alphabetical order. If more than twenty-six treaties were submitted during a session, double lettering was used to identify them. Beginning with the 97th Congress (1981), these Executive Documents have been superseded by Treaty Documents, which are numbered in the same manner as Senate documents. A treaty retains its designation for as long as it remains in the Senate.

   Receipt by the Senate is noted in the *Congressional Record* and Senate *Executive Journal* as of the date it arrives, and in the *WCPD*. All three sources include the president's message, and the last two cite the appropriate Executive or Treaty Document number. Both types of documents are indexed in *CIS/Index* and the latter appears in the Serial Set as of the 97th Congress (1981). The Senate next adopts an order removing its injunction of secrecy; the papers are ordered to be printed as a Treaty Document; and they are referred to the Foreign Relations Committee.

2. Foreign Relations Committee action: The bound volume of the *Daily Digest* section of the *Congressional Record* indicates whether hearings have been held. Printed hearings can be located through the *Monthly Catalog* or *CIS/Index*. Executive reports issued by the committee are identified in the *Daily Digest, Executive Journal,* and *CIS/Index* and also appear in the Serial Set as of the 97th Congress (1981). These

reports may contain the president's message of transmittal, the secretary of state's report, treaty text, and an article-by-article analysis. If hearings were not held or held but not printed, the report will usually include statements delivered to the committee in lieu of or during such proceedings.

The committee report, along with the president's letter of transmittal, becomes the basic documents of legislative history for treaties. This is because the action memorandum, diplomatic instructions and negotiating records of the executive branch are seldom available to Congress and less accessible to the public. When the committee reports a resolution of ratification, its executive report is numbered in a sequence that applies to all such reports issued throughout a Congress. As an item of business, the resolution is placed on the Executive Calendar and assigned a calendar number based on its chronological order. Though the resolutions themselves are not assigned a number, they are identified by their Treaty Document number or Executive Calendar number.

3. Chamber action: Senate debate, which appears in the *Congressional Record*, can provide additional legislative history or interpretive guidance in the case of amendments and qualifications that are proposed and approved. All Senate amendments and qualifications, as well as the resolution of ratification, appear in the *Congressional Record* and *Executive Journal*. The *Executive Journal* also lists all treaties received from the president during prior sessions and that are still pending and contains a separate list of those submitted during the immediate session.

4. Final adjournment: The Foreign Relations Committee calendar provides a concise legislative history of all treaties either pending or on which action has been taken during the Congress for which it is issued. However, neither the *Executive Journal* nor the committee calendar are necessarily definitive sources on pending treaties because some are submitted only as an international gesture or for informational purposes rather than as a step toward ratification. The Legislative Activity Report issued by the Foreign Relations Committee following the final adjournment of each Congress and that appears in the Serial Set is a more available document than the committee calendar. It contains a complete account of the most recent congressional action on all treaties submitted to the Senate, including information about implementing legislation, and summarizes pending treaties. It also presents a legislative history of each treaty and lists all congressional publications on specific treaties and the subject of treaties.

PRESIDENTIAL ACTION

1. Withdrawal: The president's message requesting that a treaty be returned to the White House is printed in the *Congressional Record* and *Executive Journal*. Notice of this action also appears in the *Daily Digest* and *WCPD*.

2. Renegotiation: This development may occur prior or subsequent to final Senate action. Information regarding progress and results may be obtained from the *WCPD, Department of State Bulletin* or department press releases. Should renegotiation involve a substantive revision, the protocol or supplementary agreement in which it is embodied, though inextricably related to the prior compact, is processed as an original and distinct treaty. If renegotiation merely produces correspondence intended to clarify certain provisions, the papers need not be submitted to the Senate for its consent, but are usually transmitted for its information.

3. Ratification: A treaty approved by the Senate is delivered to the White House along with the resolution of ratification. These documents are then transmitted to the secretary of state, under whose direction department officials prepare an instrument of ratification for the president's signature. After being signed, the original and a copy are returned to the secretary, who also signs them and affixes the official seal of the United States. At this point, ratification is complete at the national level and the instrument is ready for international exchange. The *Bulletin* and *WCPD* record the facts on this action.

    An instrument of ratification includes the title of the treaty; its date of signature; the countries involved; the languages in which it is signed; its text; a statement regarding Senate action and the text of any amendments, reservations, or understandings; the text of any correspondence or other documents, such as lists, tables, charts, and maps, that affect its content; the text of all foreign pronouncements and stipulations; and a declaration by the president that he has reviewed the compact and ratifies it. The exchange or deposit of an instrument is noted in the *Bulletin* and the protocol of exchange is printed in *TIAS/UST*. The date of entry into force is given by *TIAS/UST* and *TIF*.

4. Promulgation: After it is drafted by Department of State officials, a proclamation is forwarded to the president for his approval and signature. It is then returned to the department for whatever further action may be necessary, including publication in *TIAS/UST*. The issuance of a proclamation is noted in the *Bulletin*, while its text first appears in *WCPD* and then in the *Statutes at Large*. This document includes the title and dates of the treaty; the names of the signatories; a list of all significant dates in its history; its text; the text of all Senate amendments, reservations, and understandings; all particulars concerning its effectiveness; and a statement that it is being made public so that its terms may be observed by all citizens. The similarity in content of the proclamation and instrument of ratification largely compensates for the fact that the latter is not published by the government.

SUBSEQUENT ACTION

1. Implementation: Information on executive-branch regulations and operations relating to this stage is provided by the *Bulletin, WCPD,* or

the *Federal Register*. Congressional action, in the form of implementing legislation, can be traced through the *House Calendar, Congressional Record*, and *CIS/Index* and is summarized in the Senate Foreign Relations Committee Legislative Activity Report. International transactions are cited in the *Bulletin*.

2. Modification: Treaties whose status or terms have been altered are listed in *Shepard's United States Citations—Statutes Edition*. Amended, revised, and extended compacts are identified by their *TIAS/UST* number and each entry cites the action that embodied the change. This publication is periodically updated by unbound cumulative supplements that are superseded by bound volumes. *TIF* and the *Bulletin* also provide information on this matter.

3. Termination: *Shepard's*, the *Bulletin* and *A Guide to United States Treaties in Force* provide the best coverage of this development. When the president gives notice to another government about U.S. action under the terms of a treaty, it is usually conveyed by a proclamation.

GENERAL COMMENTS

The *Current Treaty Index*, compiled by Igor I. Kavass and Adolf Sprudzs, is a cumulative index to *TIAS* that was first issued in 1982 and is planned to appear at least annually. It is arranged numerically, chronologically, by country, and by subject. The information provided is incorporated into the *UST Cumulative Indexing Service* as the treaties are issued in the bound *UST* volumes. *Current Treaty index, Shepard's* and the *Bulletin* are the main sources of information on recent treaty developments.

Additional sources of information may be cited in a treaty, which may refer to earlier treaties between the same or other parties, to treaties that did not go into effect, or to other official acts of the parties involved. It is always possible for the print media to supplement or supplant official sources in any given situation. The Treaty Office of the Department of State, the White House executive clerk, the Senate executive clerk, or the Senate Foreign Relations Committee may be contacted when all efforts to ascertain the status of a treaty prove unavailing or further information is needed on this or some other aspect of U.S. treaties. The most comprehensive bibliographic coverage of contemporary treaty publications is provided by the *Monthly Catalog* or the combination of *CIS/Index* and *WCPD*.

REFERENCES

Byrd, Elbert M., Jr. *Treaties and Executive Agreements in the United States.* The Hague: Martinus Nijhoff, 1960.

Dull, James. *The Politics of American Foreign Policy.* Englewood Cliffs, N.J.: Prentice-Hall, 1985.

Henkin, Louis. *Foreign Affairs and the Constitution*. Mineola, N.Y.: The Foundation Press, 1972.

Plischke, Elmer. *Conduct of American Diplomacy*. 3rd ed. Princeton, N.J.: D. Van Nostrand, 1967.

U.S. Congress. House. Committee on Foreign Affairs. *Executive-Legislative Consultation on Foreign Policy*. Committee Print, 97th Congress, 2nd Session. Washington, D.C.: U.S. Government Printing Office, 1982.

U.S. Congress. House. Committee on Foreign Affairs. *Strengthening Executive-Legislative Consultation on Foreign Policy*. Committee Print, 98th Congress, 1st Session. Washington, D.C.: U.S. Government Printing Office, 1983.

U.S. Congress. Senate. *The Constitution of the United States of America: Analysis and Interpretation*. Senate Document No. 92-82, 92nd Congress, 2nd Session. Washington, D.C.: U.S. Government Printing Office, 1973.

U.S. Congress. Senate. *Senate Legislative Procedural Flow*. 95th Congress, 2nd Session. Washington, D.C.: U.S. Government Printing Office, 1978.

U.S. Congress. Senate. *Senate Procedure*. Senate Document No. 97-2, 97th Congress, 1st Session. Washington, D.C.: U.S. Government Printing Office, 1981.

U.S. Congress. Senate. Committee on Foreign Relations. *International Agreements: An Analysis of Executive Regulations and Practices*. Committee Print, 95th Congress, 1st Session. Washington, D.C.: U.S. Government Printing Office, 1977.

U.S. Congress. Senate. Committee on Foreign Relations. *The Role of the Senate in Treaty Ratification*. Committee Print, 95th Congress, 1st Session. Washington, D.C.: U.S. Government Printing Office, 1977.

U.S. Congress. Senate. Committee on Foreign Relations. *Treaties and Other International Agreements: The Role of the United States Senate*. Committee Print, 98th Congress, 2nd Session. Washington, D.C.: U.S. Government Printing Office, 1984.

U.S. Congress. Senate. Committee on Foreign Relations. *Treaty Termination Resolution*. Senate Report No. 96-119, 96th Congress, 1st Session. Washington, D.C.: U.S. Government Printing Office, 1979.

U.S. Department of State. *List of Treaties Submitted to the Senate 1789-1934*. Washington, D.C.: U.S. Government Printing Office, 1935.

U.S. Department of State. *List of Treaties Submitted to the Senate 1789-1931, Which Have Not Gone into Force*. Washington, D.C.: U.S. Government Printing Office, 1932.

U.S. Department of State. *The Making of Treaties and International Agreements and the Work of the Treaty Division of the Department of State.* Washington, D.C.: U.S. Government Printing Office, 1938.

U.S. Department of State. *Treaties and Other International Acts of the United States of America.* Volume 1 (Short Print). Washington, D.C.: U.S. Government Printing Office, 1931.

U.S. Department of State. "Treaties and Other International Agreements." *Foreign Affairs Manual.* Volume 11, Chapter 700 (October 25, 1974).

U.S. Department of State. "Treaties and Other International Agreements: Procedure, Formalities, and the Information Facilities of the Department of State." *Bulletin.* Volume X, No. 255 (May 13, 1944). Washington, D.C.: U.S. Government Printing Office, 1944.

A

Standing Committee Jurisdiction
Classified by Major Subject or Policy Area

Three distinct factors account for the assignment of jurisdictional authority to the standing committees of Congress. The political factor is based on the acknowledgment or assertion of existing prerogatives supported by the nature of panel experience and number of its achievements. Also of importance are claims by organized private groups that their traditional working relationships with particular committees should not be disrupted. The practical factor involves efforts to distribute the legislative workload in an equitable manner, to accord each panel a share of some major functional area of government or prominent social issue, to avert incessant competition between committees, and to avoid unnecessary duplication of effort.

From the standpoint of this volume, the key factor is that of substance. The complexity of policy issues precludes either the political alignment or conceptual agreement necessary to design strictly logical jurisdictional arrangements. Although each chamber adopts official jurisdictional guidelines for the referral of legislation to committees, such rules cannot serve as precise or rigid standards. Committee jurisdictions expand and contract over time as substantive issues and political conditions evolve and affect public perceptions and institutional capabilities.

The segmented or mutual consideration of major policy areas by different legislative panels reflects the fact that issues are not isolated phenomena but constitute a complex web of interrelated elements. The existence of jurisdictional overlap among committees is inherent in the interdependence of public problems and programs and, therefore, cannot be eliminated. The evolution of contemporary issues and emergence of new questions demand ongoing changes in panel jurisdiction. However, no single procedure has been devised or entity authorized to adjust jurisdictional boundaries or settle disputes.

The following charts are intended to facilitate access to information issued by congressional committees. Their purpose is to counteract the difficulties posed by the assignment of different authority to corresponding panels in each house and by overlapping or ambiguous authority exercised by units within each chamber. The first chart is a listing of specific subjects correlated with those committees that exercise jurisdiction. The second organizes the spectrum of governmental activity into ten general categories, lists specific subjects that fall within the scope of each, and shows which committees play a leading role in each realm. The organic nature of politics and policies, among other things, precludes any claim that such a tool is definitive in its utility or exhaustive in its coverage. At best it can serve as a convenient guide and, perhaps, suggest other approaches that may meet particular needs better.

Though some general categories encompass twice as many specific ones as others, this is not a sign of their greater importance or scope. All comprehend vast areas of national endeavor that profoundly affect millions of people. Each specific category is listed only once under that general heading with which it primarily or most closely corresponds. Though this scheme does less than full justice to the interdependence and overlap of policy spheres, the focus is on committee jurisdiction rather than subject tabulation.

The list of House and Senate committees that follows is for the purpose of assigning a two-letter code to each panel that is used in both charts. The budget, small business and veterans' affairs committees for both houses are omitted owing to their limited, though still significant, jurisdiction. The House District of Columbia and Standards of Official Conduct Committees are also omitted for the same reason. The appropriations committees for each house have been omitted for two reasons. One is that their jurisdiction embraces the full range of public functions and the other is that their authority is exercised on the basis of agency funding rather than subject area. A select committee on intelligence in each chamber exercises primary jurisdiction in its field.

KEY TO STANDING COMMITTEES

House

Agriculture	(AG)
Armed Services	(AR)
Banking, Finance, and Urban Affairs	(BA)
Education and Labor	(ED)
Energy and Commerce	(EN)
Foreign Affairs	(FA)
Government Operations	(GO)
House Administration	(HA)
Interior and Insular Affairs	(IN)
Judiciary	(JU)
Merchant Marine and Fisheries	(MM)
Post Office and Civil Service	(PO)
Public Works and Transportation	(PW)
Rules	(RU)
Science, Space, and Technology	(SC)
Ways and Means	(WM)

Senate

Agriculture, Nutrition, and Forestry	(AG)
Armed Services	(AR)
Banking, Housing, and Urban Affairs	(BA)
Commerce, Science, and Transportation	(CO)
Energy and Natural Resources	(EN)
Environment and Public Works	(EP)
Finance	(FI)
Foreign Relations	(FR)
Governmental Affairs	(GA)
Judiciary	(JU)
Labor and Human Resources	(LA)
Rules and Administration	(RU)

SPECIFIC CATEGORIES

Category	House Committees	Senate Committees
Administrative Law	JU	JU
Advertising	EN	CO
Aged	ED	LA
Air Force	AR	AR
Air Pollution	EN	EP
Alcoholism	ED	LA
Aliens	ED	LA
Animals	AG	EP
Armed Forces	AR	AR
Arms Control	AR, FA	AR, FR
Arms Exports	AR, FA	AR, FR
Army	AR	AR
Arts	ED, HA	LA, RU
Aviation	PW, SC	CO
Bankruptcy	JU	JU
Banks	BA	BA
Biotechnology	SC	CO
Bridges	PW	EP
Broadcasting	EN	CO
Building and Construction	BA	BA
Business Regulation	EN	CO
Business Subsidies	BA	BA
Campaign Contributions	HA	RU
Census	PO	GA
Charitable Trusts	WM	BA
Children	ED	LA
Citizens Abroad	FA	FR
Citizenship	JU	JU
Civil Defense	AR	AR
Civil Law	JU	JU
Civil Liberties	JU	JU
Civil Service	PO	GA
Coal	IN	EN
Coast Guard	MM	CO
Coastal Zone Management	MM	CO
Coinage	BA	BA

Category	House Committees	Senate Committees
Commercial Law	JU	JU
Community Assistance	PW	EP
Computer Technology	EN, SC	CO
Congressional Operations	HA, RU	RU
Congressional Organization	GO, RU	GA, RU
Constitutional Amendments	JU	JU
Consumer Protection	AG, EN	AG, CO, LA
Copyrights	JU	JU
Corporations	BA, EN, WM	BA, CO, FI
Corrupt Practices	HA	RU
Credit	BA	BA
Criminal Law	JU	JU
Crops	AG	AG
Currency	BA	BA
Customs	WM	FI
Dairy	AG	AG
Diplomatic Service	FA	FR
Disaster Relief	PW	EP
Discrimination	ED, JU	JU, LA
Domestic Loans	BA	BA
Draft	AR	AR
Drug Abuse	EN, JU	JU, LA
Drug Safety	EN	LA
Economic Controls	BA	BA
Education	ED	LA
Elections	HA	RU
Electric Power	EN, IN	EN
Elementary Education	ED	LA
Emergency Mobilization	AR	AR
Employment	ED	LA
Energy Regulation	EN	EN
Energy Research	SC	EN
Energy Resources	EN, IN	EN
Entomology	AG	AG
Environmental Conservation	EN, IN, MM	CO, EN, EP
Environmental Research	SC	EP
Espionage	JU	JU
Executive Branch Operations	GO	GA

Category	House Committees	Senate Committees
Executive Branch Organization	GO	GA
Executive Power	GO, JU	GA, JU
Exports	BA, FA	BA, FR
Family Services	ED	LA
Farming	AG	AG
Federal Charters	JU	JU
Federal Courts	JU	JU
Federal Judges	JU	JU
Federal Paperwork	GO	GA
Federal Property	GO	GA
Federal Records	GO	GA
Fiber	AG	AG
Financial Institutions	BA	BA
Financial Investments	BA, WM	BA, FI
Fish	MM	CO
Flood Control	PW	EP
Food Distribution	AG, ED	AG
Food Inspection	AG, EN	AG, LA
Food Production	AG	AG
Foreign Aid	FA	FR
Foreign Loans	FA	FR
Forests	AG, IN	AG, EN
Foundations	BA, WM	FI
Government Contracts	AR, GO	AR, GA
Government Ethics	JU, PO	GA
Government Information	GO	GA, JU
Gun Control	JU	JU
Handicapped	ED, EN	LA
Harbors	PW	EP
Hazardous Materials	EN, PW	CO, EP
Health Care	EN	LA
Higher Education	ED	LA
Highway Construction	PW	EP
Highway Safety	EN	CO
Historic Preservation	BA, IN	EN
Holidays	JU, PO	JU
Hospitals	EN	LA

Category	House Committees	Senate Committees
Housing	BA	BA
Human Rights	FA	FR
Humanities	ED	LA
Hunger	AG, ED	AG, LA
Hydroelectric Power	IN	EN
Immigration	JU	JU
Imports	BA, FA, WM	BA, FI, FR
Indians	IN	Select Committee on Indian Affairs
Inland Waterways	EN, PW	CO, EP
Insurance	BA, EN	BA, JU
Intelligence	AR, FA	AR
Interest Rates	BA	BA
Intergovernmental Relations	GO	GA
International Arbitration	FA	FR
International Boundaries	FA	FR
International Finance	BA, FA, WM	BA, FI, FR
International Law	JU	FR
International Organizations	FA	FR
International Trade	BA, EN, FA, WM	BA, FI, FR
Interstate Commerce	EN	CO
Interstate Compacts	JU	JU
Intervention Abroad	FA	FR
Irrigation	AG	AG
Labor Relations	ED	LA
Law Enforcement	JU	JU
Libraries	ED	LA
Lobbying	JU	GA
Maritime Affairs	MM	CO
Mass Transit	PW	BA
Medical Insurance	EN, WM	FI, LA
Medical Research	EN	LA
Mental Health	EN	LA
Merchant Marine	MM	CO
Military Assistance	FA	FR
Minerals and Mining	IN	EN

Category	House Committees	Senate Committees
Monetary Policy	BA	BA
Monopolies	JU	JU
Motor Vehicles	EN	CO
Multinational Corporations	WM	FI
Museums	ED, HA	LA, RU
National Defense	AR	AR
Natural Gas	EN	EN
Natural Resources	IN, MM, SC	AG, EN
Naturalization	JU	JU
Navy	AR	AR
Neutrality Law	FA	FR
Noise Pollution	EN	EP
Nuclear Energy	AR, EN, IN, SC	AR, EN, EP, GA
Nuclear Exports	FA	FR, GA
Nuclear Waste	IN	EP
Nutrition	AG	AG
Occupational Safety	ED	LA
Oceans	FA, MM, SC	CO, FR
Organized Crime	JU	GA, JU
Outer Continental Shelf	IN, MM	CO, EN
Parks	IN	EN
Patents	JU	JU
Pensions	ED, WM	FI, LA
Pesticides	AG	AG
Petroleum	EN, IN	EN
Pipelines	EN, PW	CO, EN
Plants	AG	AG
Ports	MM, PW	CO, EN, EP
Postal Service	PO	GA
Poverty Programs	ED	LA
Precious Metals	BA	BA
Presidency	GO, JU	GA, JU
Price Controls	BA	BA
Privacy	GO, JU	GA, JU
Product Safety	EN	CO
Public Administration	GO	GA
Public Buildings and Grounds	PW	EP

Category	House Committees	Senate Committees
Public Debt	WM	FI
Public Health	EN	LA
Public Lands	IN	EN
Public Utilities	EN	EN
Railroads	EN	CO
Reclamation	IN	EN
Recreation	IN	EN
Refugees	JU	JU
Regulatory Practices	EN, JU	CO, JU
Rehabilitation	ED	LA
Retirement	ED, WM	FI, LA
Rivers	PW	EP
Rural Development	AG	AG
Schools	ED	LA
Scientific Research	SC	CO
Secondary Education	ED	LA
Securities	BA, EN	BA
Shipping	MM	CO
Social Security	WM	FI
Soil Conservation	AG	AG
Solid Waste	EN, PW	EP
Space Commercialization	SC	CO
Space Communication	SC	CO
Space Exploration	SC	CO
Sports	EN	CO
State and Local Government	GO	GA
State Boundaries	JU	JU
Strategic Stockpiles	AR	AR
Student Loans	ED	LA
Subversive Activities	JU	JU
Surface Transportation	EN, PW, SC	CO, EP
Tariffs	WM	FI
Taxation	WM	FI
Telecommunications	EN, JU	CO, JU
Territories	IN	EN
Terrorism	FA	FR, JU
Tourism	EN	CO

Category	House Committees	Senate Committees
Toxic Substances	EN, PW	EN, EP
Trademarks	JU	JU
Treaties	FA	FR
Unemployment	WM	FI
Unions	ED, JU, WM	FI, JU, LA
Urban Renewal	BA	BA
Vessels	MM	CO
Vocational Education	ED	LA
Voting	HA, JU	JU, RU
Wages	ED	LA
Warfare	AR	AR
Water Pollution	MM, PW	EN, EP
Water Power	PW	EP
Water Resources	IN, PW	EN, EP
Water Transportation	PW, SC	CO
Weapons	AR	AR
Weights and Measures	SC	CO
Welfare	WM	FI
Wilderness Areas	IN	EN
Wildlife	IN, MM	EP

GENERAL CATEGORIES

Business and Finance	House Committees	Senate Committees
Advertising	EN	CO
Banks	BA	BA
Biotechnology	SC	CO
Broadcasting	EN	CO
Business Regulation	EN	CO
Business Subsidies	BA	BA
Coinage	BA	BA
Computer Technology	EN, SC	CO
Copyrights	JU	JU
Corporations	BA, EN, WM	BA, CO, FI
Credit	BA	BA

Business and Finance	**House Committees**	**Senate Committees**
Currency	BA	BA
Domestic Loans	BA	BA
Economic Controls	BA	BA
Financial Institutions	BA	BA
Financial Investments	BA, WM	BA, FI
Food Production	AG	AG
Insurance	BA, EN	BA, JU
Interest Rates	BA	BA
Interstate Commerce	EN	CO
Merchant Marine	MM	CO
Monetary Policy	BA	BA
Patents	JU	JU
Precious Metals	BA	BA
Price Controls	BA	BA
Securities	BA, EN	BA
Shipping	MM	CO
Space Commercialization	SC	CO
Space Communication	SC	CO
Sports	EN	CO
Taxation	WM	FI
Telecommunications	EN, JU	CO, JU
Tourism	EN	CO
Trademarks	JU	JU
Weights and Measures	SC	CO

Education and Employment	**House Committees**	**Senate Committees**
Aliens	ED	LA
Arts	ED, HA	LA, RU
Education	ED	LA
Elementary Education	ED	LA
Employment	ED	LA
Foundations	BA, WM	FI
Higher Education	ED	LA
Humanities	ED	LA
Labor Relations	ED	LA
Libraries	ED	LA
Museums	ED, HA	LA, RU
Occupational Safety	ED	LA

Education and Employment	House Committees	Senate Committees
Pensions	ED, WM	FI, LA
Retirement	ED, WM	FI, LA
Schools	ED	LA
Scientific Research	SC	CO
Secondary Education	ED	LA
Student Loans	ED	LA
Unemployment	WM	FI
Unions	ED, JU, WM	FI, JU, LA
Vocational Education	ED	LA
Wages	ED	LA

Energy and Transportation	House Committees	Senate Committees
Aviation	PW, SC	CO
Coal	IN	EN
Electric Power	EN, IN	EN
Energy Regulation	EN	EN
Energy Research	SC	EN
Energy Resources	EN, IN	EN
Hydroelectric Power	IN	EN
Maritime Affairs	MM	CO
Motor Vehicles	EN	CO
Natural Gas	EN	EN
Nuclear Energy	AR, EN, IN, SC	AR, EN, EP, GA
Petroleum	EN, IN	EN
Pipelines	EN, PW	CO, EN
Public Utilities	EN	EN
Railroads	EN	CO
Surface Transportation	EN, PW, SC	CO, EP
Vessels	MM	CO
Water Transportation	PW, SC	CO

Environment and Natural Resources	House Committees	Senate Committees
Air Pollution	EN	EP
Animals	AG	EP
Coastal Zone Management	MM	CO
Crops	AG	AG

Environment and Natural Resources	House Committees	Senate Committees
Dairy	AG	AG
Entomology	AG	AG
Environmental Conservation	EN, IN, MM	CO, EN, EP
Environmental Research	SC	EP
Farming	AG	AG
Fiber	AG	AG
Fish	MM	CO
Forests	AG, IN	AG, EN
Historic Preservation	BA, IN	EN
Irrigation	AG	AG
Minerals and Mining	IN	EN
Natural Resources	IN, MM, SC	AG, EN
Noise Pollution	EN	EP
Nuclear Waste	IN	EP
Outer Continental Shelf	IN, MM	CO, EN
Parks	IN	EN
Plants	AG	AG
Public Lands	IN	EN
Reclamation	IN	EN
Recreation	IN	EN
Soil Conservation	AG	AG
Solid Waste	EN, PW	EP
Water Pollution	MM, PW	EN, EP
Water Resources	IN, PW	EN, EP
Wilderness Areas	IN	EN
Wildlife	IN, MM	EP

Governmental Affairs	House Committees	Senate Committees
Census	PO	GA
Citizenship	JU	JU
Civil Service	PO	GA
Congressional Operations	HA, RU	RU
Congressional Organization	GO, RU	GA, RU
Elections	HA	RU
Executive Branch Operations	GO	GA
Executive Branch Organization	GO	GA
Executive Power	GO, JU	GA, JU
Federal Paperwork	GO	GA

Governmental Affairs	House Committees	Senate Committees
Federal Property	GO	GA
Federal Records	GO	GA
Government Contracts	AR, GO	AR, GA
Government Ethics	JU, PO	GA
Government Information	GO	GA, JU
Holidays	JU, PO	JU
Intergovernmental Relations	GO	GA
Interstate Compacts	JU	JU
Lobbying	JU	GA
Naturalization	JU	JU
Postal Service	PO	GA
Presidency	GO, JU	GA, JU
Public Administration	GO	GA
Public Debt	WM	FI
Space Exploration	SC	CO
State and Local Government	GO	GA
State Boundaries	JU	JU
Territories	IN	EN
Voting	HA, JU	JU, RU

Health and Social Services	House Committees	Senate Committees
Aged	ED	LA
Alcoholism	ED	LA
Charitable Trusts	WM	BA
Children	ED	LA
Consumer Protection	AG, EN	AG, CO, LA
Drug Abuse	EN, JU	JU, LA
Drug Safety	EN	LA
Family Services	ED	LA
Food Distribution	AG, ED	AG
Food Inspection	AG, EN	AG, LA
Handicapped	ED, EN	LA
Hazardous Materials	EN, PW	CO, EP
Health Care	EN	LA
Highway Safety	EN	CO
Hospitals	EN	LA
Hunger	AG, ED	AG, LA

Health and Social Services	House Committees	Senate Committees
Indians	IN	Select Committee on Indian Affairs
Medical Insurance	EN, WM	FI, LA
Medical Research	EN	LA
Mental Health	EN	LA
Nutrition	AG	AG
Pesticides	AG	AG
Poverty Programs	ED	LA
Product Safety	EN	CO
Public Health	EN	LA
Rehabilitation	ED	LA
Social Security	WM	FI
Toxic Substances	EN, PW	EN, EP
Welfare	WM	FI

International Affairs	House Committees	Senate Committees
Citizens Abroad	FA	FR
Coast Guard	MM	CO
Customs	WM	FI
Diplomatic Service	FA	FR
Espionage	JU	JU
Exports	BA, FA	BA, FR
Foreign Aid	FA	FR
Foreign Loans	FA	FR
Human Rights	FA	FR
Immigration	JU	JU
Imports	BA, FA, WM	BA, FI, FR
International Arbitration	FA	FR
International Boundaries	FA	FR
International Finance	BA, FA, WM	BA, FI, FR
International Law	JU	JU
International Organizations	FA	FR
International Trade	BA, EN, FA, WM	BA, FI, FR
Multinational Corporations	WM	FI
Neutrality Law	FA	FR
Nuclear Exports	FA	FR, GA
Oceans	FA, MM, SC	CO, FR

International Affairs	House Committees	Senate Committees
Refugees	JU	JU
Tariffs	WM	FI
Terrorism	FA	FR, JU
Treaties	FA	FR

Legal Affairs	House Committees	Senate Committees
Administrative Law	JU	JU
Bankruptcy	JU	JU
Campaign Contributions	HA	RU
Civil Law	JU	JU
Civil Liberties	JU	JU
Commercial Law	JU	JU
Constitutional Amendments	JU	JU
Corrupt Practices	HA	RU
Criminal Law	JU	JU
Discrimination	ED, JU	JU, LA
Federal Charters	JU	JU
Federal Courts	JU	JU
Federal Judges	JU	JU
Gun Control	JU	JU
Law Enforcement	JU	JU
Monopolies	JU	JU
Organized Crime	JU	GA, JU
Privacy	GO, JU	GA, JU
Regulatory Practices	EN, JU	CO, JU
Subversive Activities	JU	JU

Military Affairs	House Committees	Senate Committees
Air Force	AR	AR
Armed Forces	AR	AR
Arms Control	AR, FA	AR, FR
Arms Exports	AR, FA	AR, FR
Army	AR	AR
Civil Defense	AR	AR
Draft	AR	AR
Emergency Mobilization	AR	AR

Military Affairs	House Committees	Senate Committees
Intelligence	AR, FA	AR
Intervention Abroad	FA	FR
Military Assistance	FA	FR
National Defense	AR	AR
Navy	AR	AR
Strategic Stockpiles	AR	AR
Warfare	AR	AR
Weapons	AR	AR

Urban and Community Development	House Committees	Senate Committees
Bridges	PW	EP
Building and Construction	BA	BA
Community Assistance	PW	EP
Disaster Relief	PW	EP
Flood Control	PW	EP
Harbors	PW	EP
Highway Construction	PW	EP
Housing	BA	BA
Inland Waterways	EN, PW	CO, EP
Mass Transit	PW	BA
Ports	MM, PW	CO, EN, EP
Public Buildings and Grounds	PW	EP
Rivers	PW	EP
Rural Development	AG	AG
Urban Renewal	BA	BA
Water Power	PW	EP

REFERENCES

Congressional Yellow Book. Washington, D.C.: The Washington Monitor, Inc., 1986.

U.S. Congress. House. *Constitution, Jefferson's Manual and Rules of the House of Representatives.* House Document No. 98-277, 98th Congress, 2nd Session. Washington, D.C.: U.S. Government Printing Office, 1985.

U.S. Congress. House. Commission on Information and Facilities. *Inventory of Information Resources for the U.S. House of Representatives: Part I— Internal Resources.* House Document No. 94-537, 94th Congress, 2nd Session. Washington, D.C.: U.S. Government Printing Office, 1976.

U.S. Congress. House. Select Committee on Committees. *Committee Reform Amendments of 1974.* House Report No. 93-916, Part II, 93rd Congress, 2nd Session. Washington, D.C.: U.S. Government Printing Office, 1974.

U.S. Congress. House. Select Committee on Committees. *Final Report.* House Report No. 96-866, 96th Congress, 2nd Session. Washington, D.C.: U.S. Government Printing Office, 1980.

U.S. Congress. Senate. *Standing Rules of the Senate.* Senate Document No. 99-22, 99th Congress, 2nd Session. Washington, D.C.: U.S. Government Printing Office, 1986.

U.S. Congress. Senate. Temporary Select Committee to Study the Senate Committee System. *First Report, With Recommendations.* Senate Report No. 94-1395, 94th Congress, 2nd Session. Washington, D.C.: U.S. Government Printing Office, 1976.

U.S. Congress. Senate. Temporary Select Committee to Study the Senate Committee System. *The Senate Committee System.* Committee Print, 94th Congress, 2nd Session. Washington, D.C.: U.S. Government Printing Office, 1976.

Washington Information Directory 1986-87. Washington, D.C.: Congressional Quarterly, Inc., 1986.

APPENDIX

B

Legislative Information Resources

This annotated inventory has a dual function. One is to provide a more detailed description of certain works cited in the chapter bibliographies. The other is to supplement the textual discussion and chapter bibliographies by noting sources and services not previously mentioned. This book endeavors to array the relevant information and outline some research techniques necessary to make the best use of congressional publications. This appendix is aimed at those who desire to explore congressional affairs, including the policy agenda, in greater depth or scope.

The entries below are intended to serve as a quick reference tool for some of the more accessible information packages and research aids. They include types that may be used by either or both participants in and observers of legislative activity. This is a select sample rather than a sweeping survey of useful titles and issuing offices that provide pertinent information. Though some furnish similar or the same information, it cannot always be anticipated which may be more readily available in a given situation.

The criteria for inclusion are one or more of the following: incisive or comprehensive treatment of the subject, unique or instructive format, thorough bibliographic coverage, compilation of otherwise scattered data or material, only or most convenient source for certain information, and ready access to current developments. Under the six headings of Background Material, Legislative Process, Legislative History/Status, Federal Budget, U.S. Treaties, and National Issues, the entries are subdivided into Congressional, Other Federal, and Nonfederal Sources. With a single exception, the items in this appendix are omitted from the Document Index.

The three reports cited immediately below, taken together, offer a particularly illuminating introduction to the information needs and routes that characterize the congressional environment.

U.S. Congressional Research Service. *Basic Reference Sources for Use by Congressional Offices.* Report No. 84-218 C. Washington, D.C.: Congressional Research Service, 1984.

A guide to materials and services prepared to assist members of Congress and staffs in organizing and operating a congressional office. The subjects covered are: congressional office management, congressional structure and practice, legislative responsibilities, executive-branch relations, constituent services, and general reference sources.

U.S. Congressional Research Service. *Conducting Legislative Research in a Congressional Office.* Report No. 85-002 GOV. Washington, D.C.: Congressional Research Service, 1985.

A guide designed to assist the new legislative assistant who is undertaking a research assignment. Its main purposes are to identify the basic elements of legislative research and to describe means for locating sources of information relevant for legislative issues.

U.S. Congressional Research Service. *Parliamentary Reference Sources: An Introductory Guide.* Report No. 86-175 GOV. Washington, D.C.: Congressional Research Service, 1986.

This report defines the concepts and practices that form the foundation of parliamentary procedure in Congress. It discusses the relationship of rules and customs to one another and describes the official sources from which they are derived in each chamber.

BACKGROUND MATERIAL

CONGRESSIONAL SOURCES

U.S. Congress. House. Office of the Law Revision Counsel. "The Congress," Title 2 of the *United States Code.* 10th ed. Washington, D.C.: U.S. Government Printing Office, 1983.

A codification of the general and permanent laws that pertain to the legislative branch. It covers organization, operations, members, and employees.

U.S. Congress. Joint Committee on Printing. *Congressional Directory.* Washington, D.C.: U.S. Government Printing Office. Published biennially for each Congress.

This volume contains information on the organization and personnel of all three branches of government. It includes biographical data on and committee assignments of members of Congress, floor plans of the Capitol, and maps of congressional districts.

U.S. Congress. Joint Committee on Printing. *Government Depository Libraries.* Washington, D.C.: U.S. Government Printing Office. Published biennially as a committee print.

A directory of federal depository libraries and an overview of the depository library program.

U.S. House and Senate Document Rooms.

These offices provide information on the availability of and distribute bills, resolutions, committee reports, public laws, chamber documents, and chamber calendars.

Superintendent of Documents	Superintendent of Documents
U.S. House of Representatives	U.S. Senate
The Capitol, Room H-226	Hart Office Building, Room B-4
Washington, D.C. 20515	Washington, D.C. 20510
(202) 225-3456	(202) 224-7860

NONFEDERAL SOURCES

Barone, Michael, and Grant Ujifusa. *The Almanac of American Politics.* Published biennially by the National Journal in Washington, D.C.

This volume contains analytical, descriptive, and statistical information on members of Congress and their constituencies. It includes data on and discussion of individual voting records and recent election campaigns.

CIS U.S. Congressional Committee Hearings Index 1833-1969
CIS U.S. Congressional Committee Prints Index
CIS U.S. Serial Set Index 1789-1969

These three multivolume sets published by the Congressional Information Service in Bethesda, Md., are comprehensive finding aids that identify each publication individually. The user guide for each set discusses the history and nature of the class and furnishes useful information on printing practices and document availability.

Congressional Staff Directory. Published annually by Congressional Staff Directory, Ltd., in Mt. Vernon, Va.

This volume contains background information on members of Congress and their constituencies, but mainly covers the organizational elements of the legislative branch. It includes biographical data on those who serve on member, committee, party, chamber, and support agency staffs.

D'Aleo, Richard J. *FEDfind.* 2nd ed. Springfield, Va.: ICUC Press, 1986.

This is a catalog of finding aids to information by and about the federal government. It also describes government offices and computerized services that specialize in legislative coverage and documentation.

Garner, Diane L., and Diane H. Smith. *The Complete Guide to Citing Government Documents.* Bethesda, Md.: Congressional Information Service, 1984.

A manual for writers and librarians that addresses questions that relate to the identification of government documents, including congressional publications, and the elements involved in their bibliographic citation.

Goehlert, Robert U., and John R. Sayre. *The United States Congress: A Bibliography.* New York: The Free Press, 1982.

A listing of over 5,500 books, articles, essays, and dissertations on the history, powers, structure, procedure, and members of Congress. It is arranged under fourteen topical headings and contains subject and author indexes.

Guide to Congress. 3rd ed. Washington, D.C.: Congressional Quarterly Press, 1982.

A comprehensive narrative on the history, powers, organization, and operations of Congress. It includes a discussion of legislative interaction with the electorate and the executive branch. The conduct and privileges of as well as the support and services available to members are also covered.

Kile, Barbara, and Audrey Taylor, eds. *Directory of Government Document Collections and Libraries.* 4th ed. Bethesda, Md.: Congressional Information Service, 1984.

A factual description of government document collections and the organizations and agencies that maintain them. It covers all libraries in the United States that have a significant amount of U.S. government publications.

Morehead, Joe. *Introduction to United States Public Documents.* 3rd ed. Littleton, Colo.: Libraries Unlimited, 1983.

The relevant chapters are a concise guide to current congressional materials and on publications that furnish information about them. It includes extensive bibliographic information on both primary and secondary sources.

Ornstein, Norman J., et al. *Vital Statistics on Congress, 1986-87 Edition.* Washington, D.C.: American Enterprise Institute, 1986.

A presentation of historical and contemporary statistical data on all aspects of Congress as an institution and the activities of its members. It covers legislative, political, financial, and administrative matters.

Politics in America. Published biennially by Congressional Quarterly in Washington, D.C.

This volume contains personal profiles of members of Congress and political profiles of their states and districts. It includes an evaluation of each member's legislative and electoral performance.

Schmeckebier, Lawrence F., and Roy B. Eastin. *Government Publications and Their Use.* 2nd rev. ed. Washington, D.C.: The Brookings Institution, 1969.

A chapter on congressional publications is an indispensable historical survey. It describes and explains the evolution of each type and provides information on search and retrieval. Further information is contained in a chapter on federal laws.

The Washington Lobby. 5th ed. Washington, D.C.: Congressional Quarterly Press, 1987.

A thorough examination of the role of lobbying in American national politics that covers the activities of private citizens and the president as they relate to Congress. A historical survey and several recent case studies are included.

LEGISLATIVE PROCESS

CONGRESSIONAL SOURCES

U.S. Congress. House. *Constitution, Jefferson's Manual and Rules of the House of Representatives.* (House Manual). Published biennially as a House document.

This is the official guide to parliamentary procedure in the House. It contains the chamber rules with annotations of current practice written by the House parliamentarian. Through use of an extensive index one can find all the citations to a given rule, practice, or precedent.

U.S. Congress. House. *How Our Laws Are Made.* Published periodically as a House document.

A concise but thorough account of the legislative process intended for the general public. It traces a proposed law from its origin as an idea through its publication as a statute.

U.S. Congress. House. *Procedure in the U.S. House of Representatives.* Latest edition issued in 1982, with annual cumulative supplements.

This volume describes the more important modern precedents of the House as selected by the House parliamentarian. Each precedent is summarized in a paragraph within chapters arranged by topic. The opening paragraph(s) usually give a brief introduction to the relevant written rule or general principle that governs the procedure. It contains an extensive index.

U.S. Congress. House. Committee on Science and Technology. *Legislative Manual.* 4th ed., 1985. Published periodically as a committee print.

This publication provides a detailed description of the requirements and alternatives that confront a floor manager at each stage of the legislative process. It is an insider's guide to legislative procedure and contains examples of certain documents, such as forms, letters, and notices, that are unfamiliar to the uninitiated.

U.S. Congress. Senate. *Enactment of a Law.* Published periodically as a Senate document.

A primer on the legislative process aimed at the general public. It emphasizes the organization and procedure of the Senate and complements *How Our Laws Are Made.*

U.S. Congress. Senate. *Senate Legislative Procedural Flow.* 1978. Prepared by the Senate Legislative Clerk.

The contents of this booklet were originally intended to explain the use of a computerized legislative tracking system. It covers the legislative and administrative steps and procedures that comprise the lawmaking process. A detailed format and comprehensive approach provide information and facts not readily available elsewhere.

U.S. Congress. Senate. *Senate Manual.* Published biennially as a Senate document.

This volume contains the standing rules and orders of the Senate, rules for the regulation of the Senate wing of the Capitol, extracts from the *United States Code* that pertain to the Senate, and a list of all individuals who have served in the Senate.

U.S. Congress. Senate. *Senate Procedure.* Published every few years as a Senate document.

This annotated compilation describes the significant precedents and practices of the Senate since the recodification of its rules in 1884. It is organized by topic into chapters that are arranged alphabetically. Each chapter begins with a presentation of the general principles that govern the procedure. It contains an extensive index.

U.S. Congressional Research Service. *Guiding a Bill through the Legislative Process: Considerations for Legislative Staff.* Report No. 86-48 G. Washington, D.C.: Congressional Research Service, 1986.

A discussion of the major choices and demands that confront those responsible for assisting in the progress of a legislative proposal. It focuses on the key questions to be addressed and tasks to be performed at each stage of the legislative process.

U.S. Congressional Research Service. *House and Senate Rules of Procedure: A Brief Comparison.* Report No. 86-822 G. Washington, D.C.: Congressional Research Service, 1986.

A contrast of the formal rules and informal practices in both chambers. It highlights the role of individual members and the impact on proposed legislation.

U.S. Congressional Research Service. *An Introduction to Conference Committee and Related Procedures.* Report No. 84-215 G. Washington, D.C.: Congressional Research Service, 1984.

A discussion of the more common procedures used by the two houses to reach agreement on legislation passed by each. This brief survey outlines the routes followed by the House and Senate to resolve their differences on related measures.

U.S. Congressional Research Service. *An Introduction to the Legislative Process on the House Floor.* Report No. 86-96 G. Washington, D.C.: Congressional Research Service, 1986.

An explanation of the rules and practices that govern the consideration of public measures in the chamber. It offers a concise discussion of the usual procedures and decisionmaking patterns that characterize the manner in which the House transacts business.

U.S. Congressional Research Service. *An Introduction to the Legislative Process on the Senate Floor.* Report No. 87-176 G. Washington, D.C.: Congressional Research Service, 1987.

A companion report to the previous entry.

OTHER FEDERAL SOURCES

U.S. Office of Management and Budget. *Legislative Coordination and Clearance.* Circular No. A-19. Washington, D.C.: Office of Management and Budget, 1979.

This publication contains the instructions and guidelines that govern the OMB disposition of executive-branch agency recommendations on proposed, pending, and enrolled legislation. It also includes a discussion of procedures for the timing and preparation of agency legislative proposals.

NONFEDERAL SOURCES

Oleszek, Walter J. *Congressional Procedures and the Policy Process.* 2nd ed. Washington, D.C.: Congressional Quarterly Press, 1984.

This book describes the interaction of rules, precedents, pressures, and strategies as they affect a bill from its introduction to final passage. This involves an analysis of how procedural requirements influence both the political environment and substantive policy.

LEGISLATIVE HISTORY/STATUS

CONGRESSIONAL SOURCES

Legislative Status Office of the House of Representatives (202) 225-1772.

This unit provides information on the status of any legislation introduced in either chamber, including whether hearings have been held, the names of sponsors, and committee report numbers.

Senate and House Democratic and Republican cloakrooms.

These offices provide a daily recorded announcement on the latest legislative developments. Senate Democrats: (202) 224-8541; House Democrats: (202) 225-7400; Senate Republicans: (202) 224-8601; House Republicans: (202) 225-7430.

NONFEDERAL SOURCES .

Congressional Index. A weekly loose-leaf service of the Commerce Clearing House in Chicago.

This service provides information on the status of all pending legislation. It indexes proposals by subject, sponsor, companion and identical bill number. Enacted bills are indexed by subject, sponsor, bill number, and public law number.

Electronic Legislative Search System from Commerce Clearing House in Chicago
LEGI-SLATE, a subsidiary of the Washington Post Company in Washington, D.C.
Washington Alert Service from Congressional Quarterly in Washington, D.C.

These three commercial computer services provide bill status and related information on congressional activities.

Johnson, Nancy P. *Sources of Compiled Legislative Histories.* Littleton, Colo.: Fred B. Rothman, 1981.

This is an annotated bibliography of documents, books, and articles covering the 1st through the 96th Congress. Its first part is arranged by publisher and its second part is organized chronologically. There are author, title, and act indexes.

United States Code Congressional and Administrative News. Published by West Publishing Company in St. Paul.

This contains full text of all public laws and committee reports, with a superior legislative history table. It is issued bimonthly when Congress is in session and monthly when it is not, with annual bound cumulations.

FEDERAL BUDGET

CONGRESSIONAL SOURCES

U.S. Congress. House. Committee on the Budget. *The Congressional Budget Process: A General Explanation.* Committee Print, 99th Congress, 2nd Session. Washington, D.C.: U.S. Government Printing Office, 1986.

This publication provides background information on and an overview of the congressional budget process. It also contains several valuable attachments, including the text of the Congressional Budget and Impoundment Control Act of 1974, as amended; a summary and explanation of the Balanced Budget and Emergency Deficit Control Act of 1985 (Gramm-Rudman-Hollings); and House precedents interpreting the former.

U.S. Congress. House. Committee on the Budget. *Congressional Control of Expenditures.* Committee Print, 95th Congress, 1st Session. Washington, D.C.: U.S. Government Printing Office, 1977.

A thorough discussion of the concepts, issues, practices, and proposals that relate to the power of Congress to control federal spending. The subject is analyzed from the vantage point of legislative procedure and coordination as well as that of policy issues and alternatives.

U.S. Congress. House. Office of the Law Revision Counsel. "Money and Finance," Title 31 of the *United States Code.* 10th ed. Washington, D.C.: U.S. Government Printing Office, 1983.

A codification of the general and permanent laws that pertain to the budgetary and financial affairs of administrative agencies. Its key topics are the executive budget process, the role and responsibilities of the Treasury Department, and financial management requirements.

U.S. Congress. Joint Economic Committee. *Economic Indicators.* Published monthly as a committee print.

This report is prepared by the President's Council of Economic Advisers and issued through the Joint Economic Committee. It contains statistical information on total output, income, and spending; employment, unemployment, and wages; production and business activity; prices; money, credit, and securities; and federal finance.

U.S. Congress. Senate. Committee on the Budget. *Gramm-Rudman-Hollings and the Congressional Budget Process: An Explanation.* Committee Print, 99th Congress, 1st Session. Washington, D.C.: U.S. Government Printing Office, 1985.

A brief survey of the purposes and features of the congressional budget process. It emphasizes the revised budget timetable as mandated by the amended budget act.

U.S. Congressional Research Service. *An Introduction to the Spending and Budget Process in Congress.* Report No. 86-20 GOV. Washington, D.C.: Congressional Research Service, 1986.

A discussion of the basic elements that comprise the congressional budget process. This covers the coordination of various roles and the control of different types of decisions. It addresses the major factors and questions that shape and pervade legislative action.

U.S. Congressional Research Service. *Manual on the Federal Budget Process.* Report No. 87-286 GOV. Washington, D.C.: Congressional Research Service, 1987.

This handbook is intended to help congressional users of federal-budget information to understand the process and interpret the data. Each chapter explains the status of a given stage of action and the procedures and documents associated with it. The major rules, roles, and requirements are discussed in terms of their general purposes and specific functions.

U.S. Congressional Research Service. *Selected Economic Statistics: Definitions, Sources of Current Information, and Historical Tables.* Report No. 85-108 C. Washington, D.C.: Congressional Research Service, 1985.

A nontechnical guide to economic statistics that generate the most reference questions. The subjects covered are economic growth, banking and finance, business and labor, prices and wages, federal finance, and international trade.

Congressional Budget Office. To obtain any CBO publication one may contact:

Office of Intergovernmental Relations
Congressional Budget Office
House Office Building Annex #2
Second and D Streets, S.W.
Washington, D.C. 20515
(202) 226-2809

OTHER FEDERAL SOURCES

U.S. Board of Governors of the Federal Reserve System. *The Federal Reserve System: Purposes and Functions*. 7th ed. Washington, D.C.: Federal Reserve Board, 1984.

A handbook on the structure and operations of the Federal Reserve Board. It describes the board's role in the formulation and implementation of monetary policy.

U.S. General Accounting Office. *A Glossary of Terms Used in the Federal Budget Process*. 3rd ed. Washington, D.C.: General Accounting Office, 1981.

This is a basic reference source of standardized definitions for use and used by participants in and observers of the federal budget process. It introduces and clarifies the most common and important concepts and elements that structure practices and objectives.

U.S. General Accounting Office. *Principles of Federal Appropriations Law*. Washington, D.C.: General Accounting Office, 1982.

This manual discusses the general guidelines and requirements as well as the specific statutes, regulations, comptroller general decisions, and court rulings that govern the obligation and expenditure of appropriated funds. It is intended for use by staff members of GAO, Congress, and federal agencies, and for the information of the general public.

U.S. Joint Financial Management Improvement Program. *Financial Management Functions in the Federal Government*. Washington, D.C.: Joint Financial Management Improvement Program, 1979.

This booklet describes the functions of the central financial agencies of the federal government. It explains their roles and responsibilities for providing financial guidance to operating agencies. The key entities covered are the Office of Management and Budget, Treasury Department, General Accounting Office, and Congressional Budget Office.

U.S. Office of Management and Budget. *Instructions on Budget Execution*. Circular No. A-34. Washington, D.C.: Office of Management and Budget, 1985.

This document contains the regulations that govern the management and disbursement of appropriated funds by executive-branch agencies. It covers the control mechanisms and reporting procedures that exist to ensure efficiency of and accountability for financial transactions.

U.S. Office of Management and Budget. *Preparation and Submission of Budget Estimates*. Circular No. A-11. Revised and issued annually by the OMB.

This document contains official guidance in the form of general policies and technical instructions that govern the formulation and publication of the presidential budget. It is particularly instructive regarding the derivation and types of information presented and the data required to support and justify requests.

U.S. Office of Management and Budget. To inquire about the availability of any OMB publication one may contact:

Publications Office
Office of Management and Budget
New Executive Office Building
Washington, D.C. 20503
(202) 395-7332

NONFEDERAL SOURCES

Collender, Stanley E. *Guide to the Federal Budget*. Washington, D.C.: The Urban Institute, 1987.

An annual publication that provides a thorough explanation of how to read and use the budget documents submitted by the president to Congress. It also describes the steps in the executive budget process and the role of key participants.

Schick, Allen. *Congress and Money*. Washington, D.C.: The Urban Institute, 1980.

An extensive and intensive examination of the creation and operation of the congressional budget process. It describes and analyzes the role of legislative participants and the impact of their activities on institutional decisions that concern federal finance.

U.S. TREATIES

CONGRESSIONAL SOURCES

U.S. Congress. House. Committee on Foreign Affairs. *Congress and Foreign Policy*.

An annual committee print that reviews the role of Congress in foreign policy during the previous year. It may focus on the constitutional and political duties of Congress, interaction between the legislative and executive branches, or the nature of specific international issues.

U.S. Congress. House. Committee on Foreign Affairs. *Strengthening Executive-Legislative Consultation on Foreign Policy.* Committee Print, 98th Congress, 1st Session. Washington, D.C.: U.S. Government Printing Office, 1983.

A study of relations between the executive and legislative branches in the foreign-affairs field. It discusses the background and nature of consultation as well as the problems that impede it and proposals to improve interbranch cooperation. An extensive annotated bibliography is included.

U.S. Congress. House Committee on Foreign Affairs and Senate Committee on Foreign Relations. *Legislation on Foreign Relations through 1986.* Joint Committee Print, 100th Congress, 1st Session. Washington, D.C.: U.S. Government Printing Office, 1987.

An annual publication that compiles foreign relations legislation, treaties, and related material. It includes executive orders of the president and regulations issued by the Department of State. All such documents are in force as of January 1, 1987. It is arranged by major topic and has a subject index.

U.S. Congress. House. Office of the Law Revision Counsel. "Foreign Relations and Intercourse," Title 22 of the *United States Code.* 10th ed. Washington, D.C.: U.S. Government Printing Office, 1983.

A codification of the general and permanent laws that pertain to international activities and affairs. It covers U.S. government agencies and officials, cultural and military programs, international cooperation and organizations, American citizens abroad, and foreign nationals in the United States.

U.S. Congress. Senate. Committee on Foreign Relations. *International Agreements: An Analysis of Executive Regulations and Practices.* Committee Print, 95th Congress, 1st Session. Washington, D.C.: U.S. Government Printing Office, 1977.

A study of executive-branch procedures and practices by which international agreements are formulated and entered into by the United States. It also assesses these arrangements and requirements in terms of congressional participation and oversight.

U.S. Congress. Senate. Committee on Foreign Relations. *The Role of the Senate in Treaty Ratification.* Committee Print, 95th Congress, 1st Session. Washington, D.C.: U.S. Government Printing Office, 1977.

A collection of materials that highlights selected aspects of the Senate's role in the treaty process. Its major topics are chamber action and options, a historical analysis of the meaning of *advice and consent*, and a discussion of U.S. abrogation of treaties.

U.S. Congress. Senate. Committee on Foreign Relations. *Treaties and Other International Agreements: The Role of the United States Senate.* Committee Print, 98th Congress, 2nd Session. Washington, D.C.: U.S. Government Printing Office, 1984.

This study summarizes international and domestic law on the making, interpretation, and termination of treaties and other international agreements. It is a manual for the use of those in the Senate who participate in this undertaking and a guide to the general public on issues involved in the process. An extensive annotated bibliography is included.

U.S. Foreign Relations Committee and Executive Clerk. To inquire about the status of treaties one may contact:

Committee on Foeign Relations	Office of the Executive Clerk
U.S. Senate	U.S. Senate
419 Dirksen Office Building	The Capitol, Room S-134
Washington, D.C. 20510	Washington, D.C. 20510
(202) 224-4651	(202) 224-4341

OTHER FEDERAL SOURCES

U.S. Department of State. *American Foreign Policy: Current Documents.*

An annual publication that compiles the principal public foreign policy messages, addresses, statements, interviews, reports, press conferences, and congressional testimony of executive-branch officials. First issued in 1956, it provides information on the scope, goals, and implementation of U.S. foreign policy.

U.S. Department of State. *Digest of United States Practice in International Law.*

An annual volume that describes and analyzes official and unofficial materials and methods relating to recent developments in the field. The key chapter is entitled "Law of Treaties and Other International Agreements."

Treaty Affairs Office and White House Executive Clerk. To inquire about the status of treaties one may contact:

Office of Treaty Affairs	Office of the Executive Clerk
Department of State	The White House
2201 C Street, N.W.	1600 Pennsylvania Avenue
Washington, D.C. 20520	Washington, D.C. 20500
(202) 647-1345	(202) 456-2226

NONFEDERAL SOURCES

American Journal of International Law. Published quarterly by the American Society of International Law in Washington, D.C.

This periodical contains articles on concepts and issues that concern as well as policies and procedures that guide U.S. conduct in regard to international agreements. It includes a section entitled "Contemporary Practice of the United States Relating to International Law" that notes the latest developments.

Miller, Gordon W. "Researching Treaty Information: An Annotated Guide to Key Reference Sources." *RQ* 25 (Winter 1985), 204-12.

Arranged by type of publication, this article offers a comprehensive introduction to treaty research through brief descriptions of the more important and accessible sources.

Plischke, Elmer. *United States Foreign Relations: A Guide to Information Sources.* Detroit, Mich.: Gale Research, 1980.

A chapter on treaties and agreements identifies the principal documents and compilations published by Congress and the Department of State. It also includes information about indexes useful for research purposes and selected unofficial collections of and commentaries on treaties and agreements.

Schmeckebier, Lawrence F., and Roy B. Eastin. *Government Publications and Their Use.* 2nd rev. ed. Washington, D.C.: The Brookings Institution, 1969.

A chapter on foreign affairs provides a historical survey of U.S. government publications on the subject. Additional information is contained in the chapter on congressional publications.

NATIONAL ISSUES

CONGRESSIONAL SOURCES

U.S. Congressional Research Service. *Congressional Research Service Review.* Published ten times a year and available through the U.S. Government Printing Office.

A professional journal primarily for members of the congressional community. It contains analytical articles on substantive policy issues that are also of interest to other government officials and the general public.

U.S. Congressional Research Service. *Major Legislation of the Congress.* Published monthly while Congress is in session and available through the U.S. Government Printing Office.

This periodical provides summaries of topical issues and of major legislation introduced to address them. It is arranged by subject and includes a background discussion of an issue and information on the content and status of major bills that relate to it.

OTHER FEDERAL SOURCES

General Accounting Office. To obtain information on the availability of GAO reports and other of its publications one may contact:

U.S. General Accounting Office
P.O. Box 6015
Gaithersburg, MD 20877
(202) 275-6241

NONFEDERAL SOURCES

Brookings Review. Quarterly journal of the Brookings Institution in Washington, D.C.

The institution is a private, nonprofit organization devoted to research and education on public affairs. Its aim is to apply growing knowledge to emerging and current issues that confront American makers of public policy.

Congressional Digest. Published ten times a year by the Congressional Digest Corporation in Washington, D.C.

Each issue features a pro/con discussion by members of Congress of a current legislative question. An overview of each topic precedes the discussion and notes recent congressional action on relevant proposals.

CQ *Weekly Report.* Published by Congressional Quarterly in Washington, D.C.

Each issue describes and analyzes all major legislative progress, presidential policy proposals, and political activities that affect the consideration of key measures. It covers the roles and goals of individual members of Congress as well as the political and procedural aspects of congressional action.

National Journal. Published weekly by National Journal in Washington, D.C.

It contains commentary on the major issues and topics that influence the formation and adoption of national policies. Articles on pending and proposed legislation include information on the views and plans of key members of Congress. A regular feature is a checklist of vital issues.

PAIS Bulletin. Published bimonthly by the Public Affairs Information Service in New York City.

A subject index to current literature on political issues and public policy. It covers government and nongovernment books, articles, pamphlets, and reports on economic and social conditions.

Policy Review. Quarterly journal of the American Enterprise Institute in Washington, D.C.

The institute is a nonprofit, nonpartisan public policy research and education organization. Its purpose is to provide objective analysis of national and international issues for the information and use of those who influence and approve governmental decisions.

Document Index

An asterisk (*) identifies those items abstracted in *CIS/Abstracts*.

Subject Index